# Not Yet a Placeless Land

## Tracking an Evolving American Geography

### Wilbur Zelinsky

University of Massachusetts Press • AMHERST AND BOSTON

LC 2011010042
ISBN 978-1-55849-871-6 (paper); 870-9 (library cloth)

Designed by Dennis Anderson
Set in Janson Text with Berthold Walbaum Book display
by Westchester Book
Printed and bound by Thomson-Shore, Inc.

Library of Congress Cataloging-in-Publication Data

Zelinsky, Wilbur, 1921–
Not yet a placeless land : tracking an evolving American geography / Wilbur Zelinsky.
    p. cm.
Includes bibliographical references and index
ISBN 978-1-55849-871-6 (pbk. : alk. paper)—
ISBN 978-1-55849-870-9 (library cloth : alk. paper)
1. Human geography—United States.   2. Cultural geography—United States.
3. National characteristics, American.   4. United States—Civilization.
5. United States—Historical geography.   I. Title.
GF503.Z45 2011
304.20973—dc22

2011010042

British Library Cataloguing in Publication data are available.

To all those departed ones whom I sorely miss and who helped make my life joyful and meaningful, namely:

Ab and Minna Abernethy
Angharad of Derring-Do
Homer Aschmann
Augie Doggie Mighty Manfred
Calvin Beale
Catherine Bell
Ann Benson
The original Bob Bialek
John Black
Jim Blaut
John Borchert
Bernard Brindel
John Brush
Helen Cary
Fred Cassidy
J. N. Copland
Lou and Chloe Davenport
Floyd Dell
Ida Epstein
Wilma Fairchild
Rose Falstein
Allen Fonoroff
Barbara Hughes Fowler
Sam Furash
Hans Gerth
Marshall Glasier
Harvey Goldberg
Rhoda Gould
Alan Gowans
Henry Greene
David Grene
Casey and Helen Gurewitz
Kurt Hanslowe
Chauncy Harris
Rikki Harrison
Donald Q. Innis
J. B. Jackson
Bob Johnsrud
Terry Jordan
Jim Lahey
Harry Lassen

Glenda Laws
Joan Lee
Bernie Levin
Lowell Livezey
Tony Malone
Charles Mann
Barbara Mastoon
Irving Mastoon
Harold Mayer
Bob McNee
Scudder Mekeel
Hans Neuberger
Clarence Newman
David and Mary Niddrie
Nikki
Jim Parsons
Clifford Pilz
Arthur Robinson
David Rubinfien
Carl Sauer
Junius Scales
Lou Seig
Lawrence Shapiro
Paul Simkins
J. McA. Smiley
Frank Smith
David Sopher
Joe Spencer
George R. Stewart
Thais Lilith Jezebel Skittercat
Glenn Trewartha
Ed Ullman
Nick and Helen Vergette
Anatole Volkov
Leo Waibel
Inez "Snooky" Williams
Ralph and Zena Winstead
John K. Wright

*and, most of all,*
Gladys Zelinsky

Whither you will: all places are alike.

CHRISTOPHER MARLOWE, *Edward II* (1594)

"Placelessness," then, may simply be place ignored, unseen, or unknown.

LUCY R. LIPPARD, *The Lure of the Local*

# Contents

# Tables

# Preface

STILL ANOTHER plunge into terra incognita. Or is it a labyrinth this time?

This book is the latest, possibly final, chapter in a lifelong quest to grasp the realities of American cultural and social geography. It has involved countless miles, days, and hours of observation, reading, discussion, day-dreaming, and brooding. *Not Yet a Placeless Land* supersedes, and substantially corrects or modifies, *The Cultural Geography of the United States*, initially published in 1973 and reissued in revised form in 1992. Its most direct antecedent, however, is *Nation into State* (Zelinsky 1988a), while it feeds on all the articles assembled in *Exploring in the Beloved Country* (Zelinsky 1994b) and various subsequent publications of mine.

As I discuss in more detail in Chapter 1, this is the very first systematic inquiry into the validity of the widespread belief or assumption that our nation-state has become so thoroughly rationalized and homogenized by means of modern technology and by centralized governance and business enterprise that all but faint vestiges of genuine places have vanished. Be forewarned that the quest for a sensible assessment of the actual situation is long, complex, and beset with perplexities. Before we are done we shall have wandered deep within the realm of paradox.

Along the way it has been necessary to touch on a multitude of topics, so many indeed that what follows is something of a preparatory sketch for the much more ambitious tome I can never hope to realize. Other authors have dealt with some of these issues in detail, sometimes definitively (and it has been necessary to exploit their findings much too briefly); but for all too many others we have only partial or superficial coverage, and for still others none at all. If this opus succeeds in nudging other investigators into filling some of the gaps, I shall be overjoyed. And, given the obvious fact that this is a fallible, pioneering effort, one of my fondest hopes is that eventually some intrepid scholar will do the job properly and render this volume obsolete.

The question so single-mindedly pursued in the following pages is entwined with much vaster issues. I resist the temptation to veer off into them for a single compelling reason. It is my lack of competence to add much of value to the work of others who have expertly explored some of those grander questions. Perhaps the grandest of them all—and one I cannot avoid mentioning here—is the angst that afflicts so much of contemporary humanity, the sense of being adrift, homeless in a universe of doubtful meaning (literal placelessness is just one of the symptoms). It is a malaise effectively expressed in many recent works of fiction, verse, the visual arts, film, and theater but also falls within the purview of the social scientist. Thus we live today in a world in which many of us are fascinated by genealogy and antiques or are involved in resurrecting and celebrating the past—or seek variety and some sort of emotional redemption in distant places. Still more indicative of a profound rootlessness of human beings flailing about in the flood of time is the rather sudden latter-day craze for science fiction, a medium whereby we can find sanctuary in both other worlds and other eras. Once again, my presentation only brushes along the fringes of such overarching concerns.

As the reader will soon realize, I do not confront the immensely fashionable theme of globalization head-on, thrusting it instead to the sidelines with only the occasional fleeting mention. But a deeper interpretation of what follows will recognize this inquiry as comprising, in large part, a case study of the recent operation of globalizing processes—in addition to several others—in making the United States a special or not-so-special place and also of how such processes enhance or crush the individuality of the nation's component parts.

I maintain that, if globalization has recently become such an increasingly unavoidable issue in the American story, it has been an active, steadily growing force in worldwide human behavior throughout the past five hundred years or so. Indeed it is an inseparable element of the overall modernization project. (In pre-modern times, there may have been intermittent, relatively feeble episodes of globalistic phenomena, but that is another topic and irrelevant to the matters at hand.) In any event, as time went on, globalization gathered strength and accelerated so that, finally, after the twentieth century was well under way, a few scholars accorded it some notice and gave it a name. Then, within the past thirty or forty years, the notion has saturated the general public consciousness. (For entrées into the relevant literature, see Pieterse 1995; R. Robertson 1995; Beck, Sznaider, and Winter 2003). Furthermore, as it happens, in the case of the United States, we have a playing field of exceptional transparency, a land with far fewer of the residual complexities that cloud the scene in other portions of the world, so that globalization—that interactive web of vital transnational economic, social, and cultural dealings and their consequences—is arguably more nakedly manifest here than anywhere else. We have, then, an elephant in the room, so to speak—the looming, growing relevance of globalization—something it would be tedious to acknowledge repeatedly. But it is worth noting in passing that the United States is much more often the author of the forces and influences in question which shape a globalized world than it is the recipient.

The intellectually curious reader may well wonder how the plot plays out at the planetary level. Are we approaching a placeless world, whether a denouement of contracted cultural and social diversity or else a set of hybridized novelties, or perhaps some combination of sociocultural flatness and a pandemic of local mutations? If the planetary interconnectedness of finance, manufacturing, commerce, and news media has become so pervasive of late, as exemplified in the doings of the jet set, what of the lives of all those still multitudinous homebodies and the territorially distinctive landscapes they have fashioned over so many generations? To date no one has been brave or rash enough to initiate the necessary research, and I shudder to think of the monumental drudgery it would entail. I have merely nibbled at the challenge with a study of ethnic restaurant cuisines in North America (Zelinsky 1985) and another of the worldwide historical geography of modern western male attire, the "Standard Suit" (Zelinsky 2004). But what is wrong in daydreaming about such a colossal effort?

Then, in a work that takes minimal heed of the rest of the world, I have avoided head-on collision with the troublesome question of American exceptionalism (Shafer 1991; Lipset 1996; Madsen 1998). Of course, one could simply dismiss the subject with the truism that all places are exceptional and the observation that to dwell on the American case would be an unnecessary distraction from the main business at hand. But I must confess that the empirical evidence here provides useful fodder for those who would argue the exceptional character of American exceptionalism.

Here it is most necessary to point out that an inquiry of this kind would not be appropriate for any other nation-state of the twenty-first century. It is only in the United States, within scholarly discourse and casual conversation among laypersons, that we encounter repeated, taken-for-granted comments on an apparent growing sameness in the geographic scene from border to border. To the best of my knowledge—and for reasons too particularistic to get into here—no such laments are heard in the other large settler countries—Canada, Australia, South Africa, or Brazil. Similarly, has anyone been complaining about erasure of interregional distinctions within France, Italy, Germany, Spain, India, or Indonesia? If Shanghai has become a world city, as indeed it has, such a development has not washed away the sharp, age-old sociocultural differences among China's various sections. Likewise, the entry of Johannesburg, Moscow, and Bangkok into a global network of supercities has done little to cancel out the regional particularities of their hinterlands. The United States is singularly susceptible to the charge of territorial homogenization by virtue of the relative shallowness and spatial coarseness of its identifiable sociocultural entities, as contrasted to the Eurasian situation, in addition to the exceptional vigor of the centripetal forces I deal with later in this volume. Thus our case is the last place left standing, there being nothing comparable in the Old World or indeed in the rest of the New World.

Apart from a general avoidance of other parts of the world, there is a further narrowing of focus in the strictly territorial, horizontal grounding of this work. The concern throughout is with the history, geography, nature, and fate of places from the most miniature up through the most expansive of regions. Although I am well aware of the importance of "communities without propinquity" (Webber 1970) and indeed have done some scouting of the phenomenon myself (Zelinsky 1974), the modus operandi here is to consider only those things that are visible, tangible, or somehow countable and mappable and thus, incidentally, largely avoiding all those many interesting developments in social space. It follows, then, that this inquiry is thoroughly empirical and inductive in character. It is also bereft of any theoretical or ideological agenda or baggage, of any technological advocacy, of any preconceived notion or hope as to what the answer would turn out to be. This book, then, is simply the product of a curiosity too urgent to be throttled.

To the probable dismay of many a reader, there are no photos to be seen in these pages. This is not an oversight or a simple cost-saving tactic but rather part of a carefully considered strategy on the part of the author, who has lavishly illustrated other books and articles. Such earlier efforts, along with those by many other toilers in the vineyard, fall mostly within a more primitive phase of scholarship, one of fact-gathering and preliminary hypotheses. Now we operate in an era when a substantial band of investigators are generating a goodly number of monographs at a sophisticated level that pry loose and unwind the complexities of the American story, often without including a single picture. Thus the intention here is to ascend above the simplicities of description and initial exploration, to assume that our knowledge of the material and nonmaterial aspects of the phenomena making up the American scene, as embodied in text, drawings, and photographs, has been approaching completion, that the mission of the camera has been largely realized. Instead of reinforcing the argument, the inclusion of photos could be redundant and might distract from an analysis that seeks to distill inner meanings from our assemblage of evidence. Those who crave the pictorial can consult an abundance of accessible sources, which, I trust, are adequately flagged throughout this opus.

Although, operationally, this has been a solo enterprise, I owe a debt, one much too large to repay, to several particular colleagues. First there is Donald Meinig. There may be no occasion here to cite particular passages of his, but, nonetheless, in the deepest of ways my perception of the American scene has been inspired and guided by his astonishing four-volume *Shaping of America* (1986–2004) and various earlier publications. Then Don, Joseph S. Wood, Stanley Brunn, an anonymous reader, and Michael Zuckerman, that remarkable historian at the University of Pennsylvania, have critically reviewed earlier drafts of this opus, and their cogent comments and suggestions have been enormously beneficial, especially Michael's incisive sixteen-page single-spaced critique. I am also grateful for the aid and comfort bestowed during the infancy of this project by Joel Garreau, Denis Wood, and Joan Houston Hall. I would have been lost in preparing the manuscript without the technical assistance of Stephen Matthews, Dan Meehan, Melissa Morrow, Sarah Rundle, and Hollis Zelinsky. Finally, at the publishing end of this enterprise, I stand in awe of Carol Betsch, my exceptionally adroit copy editor. Thanks to all!

# Not Yet a Placeless Land

# 1    The Argument

## Approaching the Question

Is THE United States becoming a placeless land? Have all those place-to-place differences in our humanized landscapes and the communities that inhabit them, has all this geographic particularity become a thing of the past? Although our pollsters may never have posed this intensely geographic question to a sample of the public, such a judgment would seem to be virtually universal nowadays among our rank-and-file citizenry. Furthermore, the great majority of men and women in the knowledge industry who have commented on the topic have endorsed the notion of nationwide homogenization in terms of economy, landscape, lifestyle, and all manner of consumption, offering publications with such titles as *The Geography of Nowhere*, *No Sense of Place*, *Country of Exiles: The Destruction of Place in American Life*, and *Television and the Erosion of Regional Diversity*. Indeed "a rising chorus of modern-day Jeremiahs proclaims the death of place in American life" (Halttunen 2006, 1).

In any event, how could we not believe in the dissolution of American places awash as we are in mass-produced commodities, bombarded ceaselessly by nationally uniform news, entertainment, and advertising in our print and electronic media? We are a population, after all, that spends much of its time outside the home (all too often a cookie-cutter structure devoid of regional resonance, where television mesmerizes us several hours a day) shopping or eating in lookalike chain or franchise operations, driving along featureless highways built to governmental specifications, sitting in anonymous airports, and sleeping in forgettable motels.

It is essential to note that, whenever I speak of "place," the reference is solely to mappable tracts of humanized land or objects, that is, place as a personal or social construct. However much Americans may have been modifying terrain, biota, soils, hydrology, atmosphere, and even climate, it

1

would be ludicrous to speculate about a convergence of the various physical regions of the land.

What is the true picture if we look at the country closely and dispassionately? Although there are lesser revelations along the way, the central argument, or finding, of this volume is a counterintuitive, indeed paradoxical, one: that, since its inception, the United States has experienced constant homogenization spatially in terms of society, culture, economy, and, most visibly, the built landscape, *but*, at the same time, it has also retained the identity of many of its multitudinous places and, in fact, increased their number and variety while also preserving the integrity of some regionally defined cultural items. Such a claim will initially strike many, probably most, readers as dubiously contrarian, even outlandish. I believe, however, that after we have sifted the large and varied mass of evidence in the following pages, we may become reconciled to a convoluted reality, the fact that we live in a land where simple generalities seldom hold up against critical inspection.

What, then, do we mean when speaking of our humanized places? In the most general sense, a place is a specific humanly created and humanly perceived, real or imagined segment of terrestrial space-time. "Place stands in contrast to space. Space is an empty theater in which something may or may not happen. When something does happen, we say it 'takes place,' and the space becomes a place" (Griswold 2008, 5).

Given the innumerable modes of genesis, past and present, it is fair to say that our universe of places is virtually infinite. In terms of size, they can range all the way from a single chamber or cave upward to the entirety of a nation-state. Temporally, a place's duration can stretch from a matter of hours or even minutes to entities persisting for millennia. The most fully realized places are usually the objects of a certain degree of cogitation or emotion, whether affection, curiosity, coveting, dread, or loathing. Every individual can generate places in abundance—dwellings, workplace, play area, hideaway, or something emerging from dreams, reading fiction, or listening to music—or else places can be the product of collective cognition by a social group. Thus a major category of place is the localized variety, those patches of territory that may be meaningful to the immediate community but are less obvious to the stranger, for example, neighborhoods, plazas, parks, playgrounds, lovers' lanes, hangouts, and the like.

For the purposes of this study, I limit attention to a single category of places (but one that is more than huge enough): such fractions of the American territory as are recognized as distinct places by the general public or a significant portion thereof. And, once again, such entities can vary in magnitude from the single structure or meadow to a major culture area or to the national borders and can also be ephemeral or enduring for centuries.

Given such contracted scrutiny—the field of widely acknowledged places—we are still left with more than one possible strategy for assessing placefulness or placelessness in the United States past or present. The approach I have chosen is to imagine what a curious, observant, tireless traveler, one utterly free of tunnel vision, would have encountered in crisscrossing the land at a leisurely pace at the present moment or in earlier times. Comparison of two or more such circuitous journeys could go a long way toward resolving the central question that drives this inquiry: How placeless is the United States now or was it in times past? But rather than offering a simple diary or travelogue of our traveler's findings, it is more useful to arrange the observations systematically by category of phenomenon and, where appropriate, in historical sequence.

In the chapters that follow I begin by setting forth, over a period of 220-plus years, the evolving artifactual world, the ever more elaborate physical apparatus, along with the centripetal social and political arrangements which formed the stage on which these imaginary expeditions could come about. Thus in Chapter 2 we witness the knitting together, mentally and corporeally, of the vast American expanses and their varied societies, an apparent homogenization of the republic that seems unstoppable, at least until recently, when various types of diversity seem to be on the rise. The most palpable and visible results of such "massification" of the country appear in the built landscape, especially as glimpsed through a wide-angle lens in Chapter 3.[1] But such simplicities are compromised in Chapter 4 when our indefatigable voyeur, venturing frequently along less-frequented paths, sets aside the generalized approach and focuses instead on innumerable unpredictably located man-made places. Thus a countercurrent of ever more varied and complex diversity comes into view.

The next two chapters oblige our traveler to take a more leisurely approach, to dawdle for extended periods in various localities so as to gauge the territorial integrity of such place-making cultural features as language, religion, political behavior, foodways, music, and dress, inter alia, in Chapter 5 and coherent general cultural regions and subregions and regionalism in general in Chapter 6, with results that cannot be reduced to simple headlines. A final chapter attempts to make sense of an exceedingly complex reality, one where yes and no are flawed responses to our seemingly simple question.

Let me settle a final prefatory question before getting down to business. Why the choice of the United States as a case study in what amounts to a rehearsal for an attack on a much vaster topic? Over the past few centuries what effects has the enormous process of modernization—and globalization in particular—had on the character, life, and durability of all places and regions? If we seek answers to such questions and hope for eventual theoretical generalizations, we must bypass older, relatively stable societies where cultural inertia and the heavy hand of the past inhibit sudden or rapid change in their social and cultural geography. It makes good sense, then, to turn to a set of a dozen or so settler countries, lands overseas (or far overland) conquered and occupied by Europeans over the past five hundred years or so. They should provide far more transparent laboratories in which to track the workings of modernization.

But there are important qualifications. In three instances—Canada, Australia, and Chile—the countries are seriously segmented by the nature of their physical geography, so that large uninhabited tracts fracture the field of play. In the cases of Israel and Uruguay, they are so relatively minute in area that questions of regions or other extended places are moot. Then the ideal situation is one in which the country has enjoyed full sovereignty after shedding external control. The United States was the first of the group to attain this critical condition, followed a few crucial decades later by Argentina, Brazil, and Chile, while it was only well into the twentieth century before South Africa enjoyed complete autonomy. As of today, Siberia is still subservient to Moscow, and Canada, Australia, and New Zealand have not fully severed an umbilical cord stretching back to London.

We are left, then, with the United States among all the settler countries as the least flawed candidate for an exercise such as the present one. While it is a choice rising above convenience and accessibility of evidence for an author who happens to be one of its citizens and has an emotional investment in the territory, it is also a choice beset by possible complications. There is no way to gauge the degree to which I can attribute the findings to the exceptional characteristics of American culture (exceptionalism rears its troublesome head) rather than to whatever universal principles inhere in the process of modernization. How would things have turned out if the American Revolution had floundered and all of British North America remained British? Or if the real estate in question had fallen into firm and lasting Spanish, French, or Dutch control? Then we must be alert to the actual pervasive Americanization of so much of the world over the past hundred years or so. Given the sheer heft of American influence—in economic, military, and cultural terms—almost everywhere around the planet, how can one be sure that whatever change in placefulness has been going on elsewhere does not deviate from the dictates of abstract theory? But we must leave such speculations for another day.

## What Do the Wiseacres Have to Say?

It is easy enough to confirm a scholarly near-consensus regarding the demise of American placefulness by quoting an abundance of sources. The earliest author to have dealt with the question methodically may have been Lord Bryce in his magisterial work, *The American Commonwealth*. In a remarkable chapter titled "The Uniformity of American Life," one based mainly on observations made in the 1870s and 1880s (1995 [1914], 1475–85), he reports the monotony of the humanized landscape and ways of life in general—but Bryce also took note of some "joyful exceptions." Then, much more recently, possibly the most strident of place-deniers has been Alvin Toffler in his influential *Future Shock* (1970). "We are witnessing a historic decline in the significance of place to human life" (75). Then, in a passage bearing the unequivocal title of "The Demise of Geography," he declared that "place, it is now recognized, is no longer a primary source of identity. Differences between people no longer correlate closely with geographical background . . . Mobility has stirred the pot so thoroughly that the important differences between people are no longer place-related" (92). However, Alexis de Tocqueville had upstaged Toffler a good deal earlier with the statement that "variety is disappearing from the human race; the same ways of acting, thinking, and feeling are to be met with all over the world" (1945 [1835], 240).[2]

In one of the earlier modern pronouncements on the erosion of American regional identity, in a volume covering the practice of geography, Derwent Whittlesey noted that "certain trends in contemporary life tend to undermine regional consciousness . . . The current tendency to substitute the mobile individual for the earthbound social group as the unit of society loosens or breaks the hold of group-solidarity and weakens regional cohesion" (1954, 54). Subsequently, many other scholars have joined the chorus, for example, Tunnard and Pushkarev (1963, 10), F. Davis (1979, 131–32), Claval (1998, 134), Zukin (2004, 258). Many further valedictions to a fading territorial diversity could be documented, but only at the risk of exhausting the reader's patience.[3]

One must interject an important qualification to any discussion of American placelessness. Those who champion the notion do not envision a literal eradication of point-to-point differences. Instead they claim to see a preponderant repetition over space of the same suite of man-made features, a predictability of pattern rather than the absence of any pattern. One must also add the observation that such anxiety, indeed something nearing panic at times, seems to be a peculiarly American phenomenon. To the best of my knowledge, nothing like it has appeared in any other first world country, at least with respect to its internal human geography. I have had much greater difficulty in ferreting out dissident points of view. Indeed the items cited below represent the near-totality of my haul.

Frederick Jackson Turner may have been the earliest scholar to worry about the leveling of differences within the nation, specifically in terms of political behavior. In an essay titled "Is Sectionalism in America Dying Away?" initially published in 1907, he asserted, "I, for one, am not ready to believe that it is clear that sectionalism is to die out . . . It will be many years before the sectional distribution of the [ethnic] stocks, with inherited customs, institutions and ways of looking at the world will cease to be reflected in the sectional manifestations of public opinion and in the sectional distribution of votes in Congress" (1932, 312). But note that Turner did not foresee eventual stabilization of diversity or a possible reversal of convergent trends.

Another early observer of the American scene—and someone who actually used her eyes to look beyond conventional wisdom—was novelist Ruth Suckow, who arrived at a maverick opinion "at the end of such a journey [by train across the United States], the much talked-of standardization of gasoline stations and chain stores seems nothing but a hasty superstructure erected of necessity coupled with energy to bridge the gaps of an overwhelming variety" (1930, 2146). If other iconoclasts part company with the majority view of the contemporary world, they do so in brief statements unaccompanied, alas, by any empirical support, such as Abler (1973, 191), Agnew and Duncan (1989, 3), D. Harvey (1996, 318), Steiner and Wrobel (1997, 6), Tomlinson (1999, 88), Kotkin (2000, 6), Cowen (2003, 66–88). But perhaps the most pregnant of observations comes from Doreen Massey and Pat Jess. "Globalization has not resulted in places all becoming the same but rather in greater permeability, openness and hybridity in terms of place and culture" (1995a, 217). Subsequent chapters will add some flesh to this bare-boned claim.

What may be the most forceful of contrarian endorsements, however—and certainly one that warms the cockles of my disciplinary heart—comes from conservative political commentator David Brooks.

> Let's say you are a [*sic*] 18-year-old kid with a really big brain. You're trying to figure out which field of study you should devote your life to, so you can understand the forces that will be shaping history for decades to come. Go into the field that barely exists: cultural geography . . . Not long ago, people said that globalization and the revolution of communications technology would bring us all together. But the opposite is true. People are taking advantage of freedom and technology to create new groups and culture zones . . . far from converging into some homogeneous culture, we are actually diverging into

lifestyle segments . . . Not long ago, many people worked on farms or in factories, so they had similar lifestyles. But now the economy rewards specialization, so workplaces and lifestyles diverge . . . If you are 18 and you've got that big brain, the whole field of cultural geography is waiting for you. (2005, A23)[4]

But shortly after composing an earlier draft of this chapter, I came across two remarkable volumes (Bishop 2008; Florida 2008) then fresh off the press which contravene the conventional wisdom by arguing that, during the past few decades, American cities have been becoming more unlike and that indeed many Americans "are taking advantage of freedom and technology to create new groups and culture zones." I discuss this argument further in the following chapter.

## The Empirical Evidence

Unfortunately, this will have to be one of the briefer passages in this book: "For the encounter with the messiness and particularity of actual cultural practice is of course dangerous for theories—like the homogenization thesis—established at the distance of broad abstraction" (Tomlinson 1999, 6).

Although scholars have documented the undoubted convergence over time of various demographic and economic attributes within the United States—a topic taken up in Chapter 2—there have been remarkably few efforts to gauge diachronic trends in the spatial distribution of cultural items or of placefulness in general. The most serious attack on such questions dates back more than four decades, a study titled "Are Regional Cultural Differences Diminishing?" (Glenn and Simmons 1967; also see Glenn 1967). It is an analysis, by age of respondents, of answers to some forty-four questions from nine Gallup polls taken from the 1930s onward and one National Opinion Research Center survey, using four census regions. The conclusion? "The data fail to support the belief that regional differences have declined appreciably; instead they suggest that many kinds of differences have increased" (180).

After a diligent search, I have tracked down only one other study that confronts the temporal dynamics of American "massification" (aside from my research on personal names [Zelinsky 1970] discussed in Chapter 5) and the Bishop and Florida publications: an analysis of the regionalization of country music (Peterson and Di Maggio 1975). Their general finding is that the pattern of indulgence in this form of entertainment has been shifting from a regional to a class framework.

In subsequent chapters I shall introduce and scrutinize whatever scattered facts may be at hand that bear on our central question: has the United

States been becoming less diversified territorially and less placeful in sociocultural terms? The reader who cannot abide any but simple yes or no answers may bid me farewell at this point. Anticipating the outcome of a long and twisting journey, I can hint that the verdict will be complex and nuanced—and ever so much more interesting than a simple yea or nay.

### On Placelessness and Non-Places: The Contributions of Relph and Augé

If there is so little published material directly addressing the single broad question that has driven my research, I have benefited greatly from some remarkable monographs that illuminate tangential issues and offer precedents of sorts for the present work. In his *Place and Placelessness* (1976) and later in *The Modern Urban Landscape* (1987)—works that have yet to be superseded—Edward Relph has given us a masterful treatment of both the nature of place and the various dimensions of placelessness—its origins, manifestations, and implications. His presentation of what is correctly regarded as a product of modernization and is focused on North America is too intricate and many-sided for any sort of adequate summary here. But although Relph refrains from heavy-handed editorializing, it is clear that he is distressed by "an environment without significant places and the underlying attitude which does not acknowledge significance in places" (1976, 143), and longs for corrective action.

The only notable deficiency in these pathbreaking publications is that, with their uninterrupted emphasis on landscape and matters territorial, Relph manages to overlook another important aspect of placelessness: the deracinated individual. If placelessness, as expressed in landscape terms, is decidedly a latter-day phenomenon rendered inevitable by modern technologies and the demands of advanced capitalism and its "invisible hand," placeless individuals have been with us for many centuries as a small, but significant, minority of the human species. Thus itinerant merchants, mariners, privateers, Gypsies, mercenaries, mendicants, scholars, clergy, missionaries, and entertainers have roamed the earth year after year without settling into any permanent abode.

What is exceptional about the current era is the much greater incidence of rootless persons who, by choice or necessity, can shift from place to place during much or all of their adult existence.[5] "Throughout most of human history, individuals lived in life-worlds that were more or less unified . . . rarely, if ever, would [one] have the feeling that a particular social situation took him out of this common life-world. The typical situation of individuals in a modern society is very different" (Berger, Berger, and Kellner 1974, 65).

Thus still another facet of placelessness that has flourished in recent times, if much more rarely in the past, is "community without propinquity," a notion quite effectively expounded initially by Melvin Webber (1964a, 1964b, 1970). As Claude Fischer and Ann Stueve (1977) concluded: "Combined with the findings . . . that attachment to place is multidimensional and that people are attached in various specific ways, these results severely challenge theories about local social life that consider local roots as natural or psychologically necessary . . . Notions that modern life can provide community without propinquity come closer to describing the actual role of place today than do ideas of natural or authentic community" (186).

Ancillary to our understanding of modern placelessness is another recently recognized concept: the non-place. Thanks to Marc Augé's brilliant exploration of the "anthropology of supermodernity," we can now appreciate the importance and singularity of these entities. Like other types of place, the non-place is a social construct occupying a specific site. But non-places are different by existing as they do in socially vacuous spaces: limited-access highways, truckstops, airports, supermarkets, shopping malls, motels, railway stations, public lavatories—necessary facilities assuredly, but uninhabited and seldom loved.[6]

> The hypothesis advanced here is that supermodernity produces non-places . . .
> The distinction between places and non-places derives from the opposition
> between place and space . . . As anthropological places create the organically
> social, non-places create solitary contractuality . . . "Anthropological place" is
> formed by individual identities, through complicities of language, local refer-
> ences, the unformulated rules of living know-how; non-place creates the
> shared identity of passengers, customers, or Sunday drivers. (Augé 1995, 78,
> 79, 94, 101; also see Tomlinson 1999, 54)[7]

But the term "non-place" may be something of a misnomer because these entities, unloved, disregarded, or tangential to more vibrant sorts of places though they be, may comprise a valid subspecies, an intermediate class of entities on a continuum between intensely placeful sites and those adrift in a total emotional vacuum. Thus, for example, an airport or bus station may be a genuine place for its long-term employees if only a boring non-place for the clientele, and the vacant overgrown city lot totally ignored by the passing motorist may be a wonderland, a rich, meaningful play space for the "underprivileged" kids of the neighborhood. But, having acknowledged the existence, multiplicity, and fuzzy definition of non-places, I shall do my best to ignore them in the following pages. After all, the subject happens to be the fate of more conventional places.

## Probing the Conventional Wisdom

My perusal of the documents noted above, along with passing comments and insinuations in other publications both scholarly and popular, combined with absorption of information from all manner of informal sources, has led me to a series of generalizations about the prevailing perception of placelessness issues among Americans. One that we have already encountered—that the homogenization of American places has been, or is being, consummated—calls for no further comment. But such a belief logically implies the geographic diversity of the past. It is noteworthy that such an impression, one so strongly embedded in the popular as well as academic mind, has never received the critical scrutiny it merits. I trust that the following chapters will cast some light on the matter. But, to anticipate the findings, the picture that emerges is a complicated one, registering both increasing and lessening diversity. In fact, in some important respects early America was a more homogeneous land than the country we occupy today.

There is no lack of unanimity on another issue: that placelessness is deplorable. If there is any observer who revels in the perceived situation, I have yet to identify him or her. Neither has anyone come forward with a plausible formula to remedy our geographic distress. Far from exhaustive is the following list of those uttering woeful lamentations: Tunnard and Pushkarev 1963; Meyrowitz 1985; Kunstler 1993; W. Leach 1999; K. A. Myers 2001. Ian Nairn is unequivocal: "[The American scene] is probably the most characterless and least differentiated mess that man has ever made for himself" (1965, 146). But few jeremiads are more heart-wrenching than the complaint of Michelle Goldberg as she sought out megachurches in metropolitan peripheries.

> With their endless procession of warehouselike chain stores and garish profusion of primary-colored logos, the exurbs are the purest of ecosystems for consumer capitalism . . . the banality is aggressive and disorienting. Driving through many of these places in states from Pennsylvania to Colorado, I've experienced more than a few moments of vertiginous panic where I literally could not remember where I was. (2006, 58)

Many recent authors have unfailingly associated what they regard as the contemporary placelessness of the United States with the much grander phenomenon of globalization. The ongoing torrent of literature dealing with this topic seems to grow larger with each passing year and shows no sign of ever tapering off; but studies of its cultural dimensions are limited in number, with the most commendable being Appadurai 1996, Tomlinson 1999, Cowen 2003, Kraidy 2005, and Goodman 2007. Clearly much still remains to be researched and written, but, to anticipate later discussions, Douglas Goodman provides a commonsensical interim judgment: "The question as to whether globalization increases cultural homogeneity by establishing common codes and practices or whether it increases a heterogeneity of newly emerging differences seems now, to many analysts, to have been answered. Globalization does both" (2007, 340).

If everyone agrees that the United States is a prominent participant in—and, arguably, even the drum major leading—the globalization spectacle, there also appears to be a general consensus that its effects (though still muted, I maintain) are more outwardly visible here than anywhere else.[8] The reason is simple. Throughout nearly all the Old World and most of Latin America, culture areas and all manner of cultural practice have had many centuries or even millennia to sprout, take form, vary, and entrench themselves deeply into the land. In such places the stigmata of globalization may appear and superimpose themselves on a venerable scene, but the physical and sociocultural heritage of the past will endure after a fashion. The American case, by contrast, is one of shallower, recent culture areas and phenomenal mobility and transience. We can speculate that globalized practices may become more conspicuous in the days to come, if they are not already decisive components of the American scene. But it is significant that virtually all discussions of placelessness seem to focus on the United States. That sort of tunnel vision is likely to persist.

## What Makes Places Different—or the Same?

If we examine the world with care, we soon learn that there are several forces, or processes, that create and mold those socially constructed entities we call places—certain territories containing distinctive human communities—making them similar or unlike in varying degree. Providing a full understanding of all the processes and dynamics involved in creating place-to-place differences or similarities is a scholarly challenge no one has yet seriously attempted. But for the purposes of this book, keeping in mind the limitations of our explanatory apparatus, it is essential to identify such processes as we can and see whether, when, and how they have been operating in the case of the United States. As I list and discuss each of them singly below, however, it is also important to realize that none of these individual processes exists or works in total isolation from the others. On the contrary, they may overlap, frequently two or more at a time, in extremely complicated ways. It would become tiresome to emphasize such a truism repeatedly in the chapters that follow, so I trust that the thoughtful reader will keep this axiom in mind.

I have arranged the processes in extremely rough chronological order, that is, according to the period when the given process began to assert itself in a meaningful way. The following list is not necessarily exhaustive. For example, other scholars might consider including topophilia or technological change as autonomous agents.

### Organic Evolution

Like all organisms, human beings have been evolving biologically, slowly but surely, over hundreds of thousands of years as random genetic mutations occur and can be passed on to offspring if they enhance success in bodily survival and reproduction, in social relations, or encounters with a physical environment that varies from one locality to another—or are neutral in effect. For groups that remain relatively isolated for millennia, the eventual result will be palpable, visibly unique somatic, or "racial," communities, as has happened, for example, among the Australian aborigines and Inuit.

This process thus contributes to the making of recognizably different places or perceptions thereof. However, a mere five centuries of Euro/African occupation of the Americas is far too brief a period for this process to have had appreciable effect. Thus, if there are interregional differences today within the United States in body size, configuration, physiology, or other physical traits (a tempting topic yet to receive adequate attention), the cause may be lifestyle rather than genetic. There will be no further need to mention this process.

### Cultural Drift and Local Invention

In a manner precisely analogous to organic evolution, human beings, as bearers of culture, frequently experience random or deliberate mutations in their thinking and behavior (as may some of our brighter anthropoid kin). Although most of such change is usually so slight as to be undetectable at first, if there is further evolution in the same general direction or if the effect is immediately beneficial in terms of community welfare, economic benefit, or simple pleasure, or, at worst, neutral in impact (as, for example, shifts in speech patterns or artistic motifs), the innovations are likely to survive and be passed on to later generations. In many instances, cultural drift may take the form of conscious invention by individuals—for example, a new song, dance step, or curse, an improved version of a tool, or a cleverly designed ornament—and be adopted by the entire group. But, in other cases, changes in various departments of cultural behavior may occur quite automatically, if slowly, while not being immediately detected as they follow certain inherent rules or laws, such as those we have partially deciphered in shifts over time in pronunciation of vowels and consonants. In any event, if the community undergoing such changes remains relatively isolated for a long enough period, it can acquire thereby a distinctive individuality. *Cultural drift and local invention* manifests itself much more rapidly than organic evolution, and, in fact, can be observed in the course of a single lifetime. Since it does operate quite perceptibly in the United States, we shall have occasion to acknowledge it in subsequent discussions.

### Interaction with the Environment

Human beings can respond to, and interact with, their physical surroundings and events, whether consciously or otherwise, in a manner much more immediate than the slow operation of organic evolution. The resulting set of cultural and social changes—and thus differentiation from other places— is especially noticeable when a migrating group encounters unfamiliar environmental circumstances. Consequently, *interaction with the environment* is decidedly in play when we consider the American story.

### Cultural Diffusion and Other Modes of Interaction over Space

The transmission of cultural traits and innovations from distant or neighboring communities to other places has been going on from time immemorial, initially in casual fashion through trade, capture of war prisoners, circulation of brides, or other intermittent contacts. Such leisurely movement of cultural items would, of course, tend to reduce place-to-place differences. In contrast, in historic times the diffusion of part of one place's set of uniquenesses to other localities has become more rapid, even instantaneous, given the availability of modern technologies, first writing, then printing, and recently modern modes of transport, commerce, and electronic communications, and, in many instances, it is something done deliberately and methodically. Thus what we might call a latter phase of *cultural diffusion* is now a major factor in engendering the so-called placelessness of the United States.

### Demographic Change

The character of places—and the differences between them—can alter, gradually or, occasionally, abruptly, as fertility, mortality, and migration exert their effects. Simple growth or decline in population size is obviously significant, and never more so than in cases of genocide or ethnic cleansing. If the gradual or sudden arrival of alien immigrants can profoundly change the personality of place, shifts in age structure, sex ratio, and class can also have a major impact on the degree of place-to-place difference or similarity. Clearly *demographic change*, and most especially migration, has been much in evidence within the American scene throughout the history of the nation.

### *Ethnic/Racial/Religious/Class Tropism and Repulsion*

We have here a process that is closely akin to demographic change, but differs qualitatively in the intentionality of its place-making. During much of recorded history, various social communities, defined in ethnic, racial, religious, or class terms, have tended to cluster together or, conversely, to shun or actively cordon off alien groups. Examples are all too numerous, including our contemporary Hutterites, nineteenth-century Mormon communities, the medieval Jewish ghetto, South African apartheid, and the Japanese American relocation camps during World War II. On a rather less pernicious level, we have our gated communities as well as the de facto ethnic/racial enclaves that have been so common in American metropolises.

### *The Pursuit of Pleasure*

For most of human existence, the problems involved in physical survival, in providing sufficient food, water, and shelter and protection from disease, enemies, and other disasters, have absorbed most or all of the time and energy of ordinary folks. But, over the past several centuries, then taking a quantum leap in the final third of the twentieth century, a larger and larger fraction of the world's population has climbed past a critical threshold of affluence, so that the *pursuit of pleasure* in all its many forms has become a major preoccupation of the masses as well as the elite. Of course, many of the pleasantries in question can be enjoyed in situ, but, increasingly, the pursuit of pleasure means travel to, or temporary or long-term sojourns in, appealing localities and hence, a reordering of places and greater distinctions among them. Such developments are conspicuous in the United States and becoming ever more so.

### *The Modern Market System in Alliance with the State*

Here we have, arguably, the most potent of all the forces reshaping the republic since its birth. Consequently, it will engage much of our attention in the chapters that follow. In particular, as will be recounted in detail in Chapter 2, the modern capitalist system, operating in intimate collusion with its alter ego, the national (and subnational) governmental apparatus (the revolving door never seems to come to rest) and following basic economic laws, has methodically worked toward the rationalization, standardization, consolidation, and leveling of American territory and its population, driving single-mindedly toward maximum power and profit. One cannot stress strongly enough that economic and geographic rationality is the supreme principle at work here.

At various points in the inquiry, it makes sense to separate the two components of the process—the market and the state—since, despite their incestuous coupling, the interests of the business firm and the political establishment do not always mesh. Such a bifurcation brings up a phenomenon or problem that many commentators have noted recently: that in many ways the transnational corporation has become so powerful, indeed quasi-sovereign, as to transcend the shackles of the individual nation-state, while the latter may be approaching irrelevance regarding some of the larger issues of global existence. Exploration of this important matter is far beyond the range of this inquiry (or the competence of the author) and is best left to other, more fearless, investigators.

### Arbitrary Governmental/Corporate/Individual Locational Decisions

For reasons having to do with the foibles or whims of governmental and business decision makers (and sometimes their spouses) or their biographies, local lobbying and accidents of history, or because of the initiative of exceptional private individuals, the American landscape is strewn with various features that, in terms of grand economic or political logic, have no business being where they are. (How else to explain Hearst Castle, Watts Tower, Hershey, Pennsylvania, St. Louis's monumental arch, Mount Rushmore, or those sets of three crosses sporadically encountered along our highways?) Chapter 4 examines such unpredictable phenomena in detail. This is a process probably more in evidence in the United States than elsewhere because of the powerful strain of individualism that pulses through the national character and the general affluence that makes its expression feasible.

### Self-Conscious Place-Making

The practice of designing and occasionally creating entire agglomerated settlements according to some meaningful plan dates back at least as far as Thomas More's sixteenth-century Utopia, and indeed much further back to the towns founded by Phoenicians, Greeks (including Alexander the Great), and the Romans. The distinction here is between the premeditated settlement and the much more frequent case of the town or city that grew spontaneously at a propitious site more or less in accordance with market forces. This process has some similarity with the preceding one but with the important difference that the former usually involves single isolated features, whereas the latter aspires to fabricating entire communities.

Fanciful depictions of ideal towns or cities have appeared in print over the past few centuries, often with detailed maps. Among the earlier material realizations of such fantasies, after such idealistic efforts as Philadelphia,

Savannah, and Washington, have been the many utopian colonies of nineteenth-century America, usually destined for early failure, but with the spectacular exception of Mormon Zion. One might add to the list the more crassly motivated projects of railroad companies and land speculators, along with the series of mini-worlds calling themselves world fairs that began with the Chicago extravaganza in 1893. This process never really flourished in all its exuberant variety until the twentieth century, when we begin witnessing garden suburbs, the New Deal's model towns and TVA settlements, such freestanding projects as Disney's Celebration or Mendocino County's Sea Ranch, and a constellation of grandiose theme parks, the more elaborate shopping malls, retirement communities, museum villages, and the like.

IT IS worth noting, by way of summary, that these ten processes are not unidirectional in effect. As it happens, a majority of them function so as to make places distinctive and the country more diversified. But although only two (cultural diffusion and the modern market system in alliance with the state) work in the opposite direction—toward territorial uniformity—they can be especially potent, rivaling or overcoming the others in their stifling of diversity. Only a single process (demographic change) eludes simple categorization.

As a postscript to the foregoing presentation, it is important to stress the strength of an abiding principle, but not a process: *cultural inertia*. Whenever a cultural trait or practice or culture area becomes firmly established, however arbitrarily, it can take on a life of its own. Thus none of my readers are likely to live long enough to witness the end of the American aversion toward eating horseflesh or worms or males wearing skirts, our acceptance of black as the color of mourning, or April Fools pranks. Such conservatism is hardly a negligible factor as we reflect on the life of American places.

Now on to the telling of a multilayered epic!

# 2 E Pluribus Unum? The Mashing vs. the Sorting of America

## The Challenge

As of 1783, after overcoming truly fearsome military odds, the unlikely infant American republic had just wrested its independence from the grip of the Western world's richest and mightiest nation only to face an equally daunting task: how to create a viable polity and economy. Unfortunately, there were no precedents to fall back on. During this period, the Western world had just begun the process of crafting something utterly new, the modern nation-state, with the most notable progress registered in France, Great Britain, the Netherlands, and Prussia.[1] In those countries, forging the new entity was a top-down affair, with a strong central governmental apparatus imposing its will on a set of heterogeneous regions and localities, thereby creating at least a nascent sense of nationhood and a certain uniformity in the ways life and work were conducted from border to border.[2]

But the American situation was quite different. The thirteen quasi-sovereign former British colonies were bound together only loosely within a weak, fragile confederacy, the national borders remained quite insecure and unmarked, and all the states were suffering economic distress. Moreover, the new regime with scarcely more than three million inhabitants, and a fifth of them slaves, had fallen heir to a vast amount of largely uncharted real estate—with incalculably rich economic potential—but lacked the means to travel or communicate quickly, safely, or cheaply across most of its wide expanses or the mechanisms for effective governance of the unsettled territory. "Many Europeans believed that a society without a unifying church, a vigilant bureaucracy, and a habit of obedience could not survive" (Leonard 1995, 29). There was not much immediate improvement until after another close call in 1787 when, by the narrowest of margins, the new Constitution was adopted and a presumably sturdier central government took office shortly thereafter.

17

That the improbable United States did, in fact, survive and eventually become a full-fledged nation-state, indeed as valid an example of the species as is on display in today's world, offers us a reality verging on the miraculous. It was not the only settler country to initiate the process, of course, but perhaps the solitary total success story in its transition from a motley string of colonies to a tightly organized, centralized nation-state with a decided degree of sociocultural conformity. Canada, South Africa, and Australia—all of them facing a similar challenge of vast territory and small scattered European populations—have never quite attained the American level of cohesion and cultural uniformity.[3]

Given its precarious parturition and that initial floundering about, the salvation of the republic may well have been its emergent nationhood (without discounting a certain element of economic self-interest) and a singular sense of providential mission, something fortified by the travails of the Revolution and the expulsion of a considerable minority of Loyalists. But a trans-colonial sense among the various colonists of being American, of belonging to a special brotherhood, one distinct from merely being aggrieved, far-flung Britons, had begun to be detectable by the mid-eighteenth century as recruits from widely separated locals fought side by side in various campaigns against the French or their aboriginal allies and as the first Great Awakening (ca. 1725–50) engulfed the spiritually famished from New England to Georgia (Zelinsky 1988a, 225–30). In addition, a sluggish, but effective, intercolonial postal system had been functioning since 1753.

Whatever its origins, it was and is a nationhood quite unprecedented and unique. In contrast to other nations that eventually achieved statehood, this was decidedly not a matter of blood and soil. Given that many of the newly minted Americans were not of English, or even British, origin, we do not behold here any assertion of ethnic identity. Moreover, not enough time had elapsed to generate strong bonds with the land on the part of congenitally restless settlers. There was no foundation myth and, before 1776, no heroes to venerate. No single Christian denomination, then or later, claimed dominion over all or most of the citizenry, and theirs was not yet a recognizably distinctive language or dialect–or diet, dress, or architecture. Neither can we find any homebred literature, art, music, or theater of consequence.

What did bind the masses together was indeed something revolutionary: the democratic ideal, the sovereignty of the freedom-loving individual (presumably male and of the proper skin pigmentation) in pursuit of wealth and happiness. Implied thereby was the election of temporary rulers and total rejection of the trappings of feudalism and the monarchical and, in fateful addition, the belief that America had been divinely ordained to set forth a redemptive model, a light unto the world. Some other countries have subsequently borrowed and shared some of these principles, but in none of the later instances was the American Idea crucial to the formation of nationhood. The emergence of the American ideology, inchoate or hesitant though it may have been at first, was crucial. The fact that there already existed in the United States, as in other lands on the verge of modernization, a deep, invisible homogeneity in the livelihood patterns and social relationships was of little practical consequence in lieu of a novel cohesive ideology. The primeval type of sameness was cellular and unorganized, hardly the raw material for a well-oiled market economy or a muscular national state.

As we shall see, in confronting the manifold difficulties threatening its well-being or even survival, the American community sooner or later rose to the challenge at various levels from the most local to the national. If, in so doing, the net result has been a certain degree of territorial homogenization, this outcome was a by-product of various programs, not the doing of a cabal meeting periodically in secret conclave. During the early years of statehood, no individual or group promulgated the goal of a placeless land, hardly an ideal to stir men's souls. But if such was the product of our political and business machinations and if power and profit continued to accrue to the worthy, so be it.

But before recounting the remarkable tale of the building of a powerful, unified nation-state, it is essential to examine the initial situation. How diverse or uniform did the infant republic happen to be?

## A Diversified Young America?

Given a virtually universal belief today of a homogenizing United States and also the assumption that this is a recent development, it follows logically that all the believers in question envision a past for the country in which decided place-to-place diversity was the norm. How much truth is there in such a vision? As it happens, we have no simple response to the question. At one level of cultural, social, and economic reality we do find considerable uniformity, while, at another, emphatic regionalization of the geographic scene happens to have prevailed.

Let us appraise the situation as of 1783, the year in which the newborn state won international recognition, and its general persistence over the next several decades before the powerful forces of industrialization, urbanization, and ideological conformity began the radical reshaping of the landscape. According to the first census in 1790, some 3,929,000 persons (not counting Native Americans) inhabited the thirteen former colonies and

their unorganized territories, and a varied lot they were. There were unevenly distributed batches of the English (of quite varied original identity)
and of Scottish, Cornish, Irish, Welsh, German, Swiss, Dutch, Huguenot,
Swedish, Finnish, Jewish, and sprinklings of other European immigrants,
in addition to the substantial African American population. Over the course
of just a few generations, varied mixes of these transplanted settlers, each
boatload bearing with it particular religious, linguistic, and dietary preferences as well as inherited customs, music, folklore, and sets of skills, all these
former neighbors and strangers came together in unfamiliar physical settings
which they were obliged to react to, consciously or otherwise. Simultaneously, they learned a fair amount from their new neighbors, whether European, African, or aboriginal.

The result was the creation of a set of novel culture areas on the seaward
side of the Appalachians, a development noted in greater detail in Chapter
6. These regions–New England, the Dutch-Flemish tract along the lower
Hudson and portions of Long Island, the Pennsylvania Culture Area, and
the various patches within the South Atlantic states that later coalesced
into the South–certainly did not become as deep-rooted or internally var-
iegated as their Old World antecedents. Not for them the localized patois,
legend, unique cheese or wine, pattern of dress, local saint or hero.

Nevertheless one may argue that in this era of wretched, costly overland
transport and only an embryonic national political apparatus (until canals,
railroads, and the telegraph came to the rescue) the juvenile United States,
for the most part still hugging the seaboard, attained its greatest ever internal
cultural diversity. These initial cultural areas, except for the largely extinct
Hudson River valley area, survive today after a fashion, although diluted or
altered in interesting ways. Moreover, within this overwhelmingly agrarian
national community, some specialized zones of business enterprise had already materialized: the tobacco culture that so dominated much of Virginia
and Maryland; the Sea Islands cotton, indigo, and rice plantations along
the coast of South Carolina and Georgia; various localities specializing in
harvesting and exporting lumber and other forest products; places adjoining salt licks that were sources for this essential commodity; and a wide scat-
tering of iron forges, or furnaces, at points enjoying a local abundance of the
necessary raw materials.

Then it would not be fair to ignore the pockets of alien folk (apart from
the highly diversified First Nations, to borrow Canadian parlance) residing as of 1783 and the following several decades often outside the reach of
official federal power but within the political borders of the United States.
These would include the French, or temporarily Spanish, zone of southern
Louisiana and spots along the Gulf Coast, the French outposts in southeast-

ern Missouri and points in Michigan and Indiana, the feeble, fitful Spanish presence in Florida, the well-entrenched Spanish in California and New Mexico and subsequently in Texas, the Russians in Alaska and northern California, and, of course, much later, the Hawaiians. Not entirely outside the picture was French Quebec or the Maritime Provinces on which Yankees frequently cast a covetous eye.

If the evidence for place-to-place diversity in the early republic is substantial, the case for a pervasive sameness in the social and personal realm may be even more compelling (Labovitz 1965, 71). It may be difficult nowadays to visualize the United States as of 1790 when census enumerators recorded less than 5 percent of the total population as residents of urban places, that is, agglomerated settlements with 2,500 or more inhabitants. And most of these urban centers were pitifully small by current standards.

What do we find in turning our attention to the rural spaces of early America, the territory accounting for the vast majority of the citizenry? By any measure, it was an extraordinary panorama. The European newcomers had acquired a vast expanse of "undeveloped" real estate of incomparable richness (the only possible parallels being the Slavic incursion into Siberia or the Canadian, Australian, Argentinean, and Brazilian land rushes). As beneficiaries of a novel political system, they were freeholders possessing in fee simple, or perhaps leasing, tracts of land of a magnitude far beyond the wildest dreams of their Old World kinfolk. They had thus divested themselves of any traces of feudalism or other ancient forms of land tenure. Furthermore, there was no European precedent for their feverish level of spatial mobility, involving roughly 20 percent of the population annually, and, incidentally, a rate persisting to this day without major fluctuation (Thernstrom 1973, 220–41). Nonetheless this was still an agrarian society at an early stage of modernization that shared much of the social and cultural mind-set of European and Asian peasantry, most notably perhaps in regard to the status of women.

As already suggested, the inquisitive foreign visitor—and their numbers were notable from the eighteenth century onward—would have been struck by a fair amount of variety in the visible scene. In addition to differences in crops and livestock—for example, maize vs. wheat, horses vs. oxen or mules, swine vs. sheep, as mandated by environmental constraints and the development of local varieties of livestock, fruits, and vegetables—there were broad regional and often highly localized peculiarities to be seen in house and barn types and church buildings, in fencing, in food and drink, speech patterns, denominational membership, political attitudes, and social manners. But he or she would probably not have commented on dress, or music, for not enough time had yet elapsed for any noticeable local evolution.

When we turn to the life-patterns of the two sexes, we find that the world of the early and the many millions of not-so-early rural American males, who outnumbered their city cousins until well into the twentieth century, was rather less circumscribed than that of their mothers, wives, and daughters, but not by a great deal. The great majority were full- or part-time farmers or ranchers whose careers were lived out within a decisively narrow space. If the local community depended on the services of a gristmill, sawmill, or tannery, the operator might divide his time between such sites and his farm. Teachers and preachers, both often itinerant, gravediggers, blacksmiths, shoemakers, and other artisans usually devoted only some of their working hours to their craft. If physicians or attorneys were called for, one found their homes or offices only in the county seat or the nearest substantial town.

What foreign visitors certainly would *not* have noted or commented on, since it simply replicated the situation back home, was the pervasive pattern of life and labor shared by able-bodied adult women and older girls through-out rural America. Most of our evidence comes from the northeastern states for the obvious reason that there is where the documentary materials are most abundant and where the concerned scholars were born or have come to reside, but there is no reason to doubt that their findings would apply elsewhere. Aside from a minute fraction of all females, those few who enjoyed a privileged existence in major cities or on southern plantations (think Abigail Adams, Fanny Kemble, Martha Washington, Mercy Warren), "the main tasks of women everywhere were domestic service and the production of goods for household consumption or sale in the marketplace" (Perkins 1988, 141). "The letters and diaries written by eighteenth-century women reveal that most women shared a surprising uniformity in the events of their lives" (Ogden 1986, 7).

Jeanne Boydston has depicted the universal drudgery vividly.

> In 1750, as in 1650 . . . country women washed, cleaned, kept chickens for eggs, meat and feathers, tended small barn-yard animals, foraged for berries, fished, clammed, and kept kitchen gardens. They helped slaughter animals and preserve meat, milked cows, made cheese, butter, cider, wine, and beer. They sewed and knitted, quilted and spun, and prepared all of the food for family consumption, collecting and chopping kindling and spending long and dangerous hours coaxing cooking fires to just the right temperature. (1990, 12)

Then, writing about the early nineteenth century, she continues,

> [William] Alcott was quite familiar with the types of work performed by women in their own families . . . cooking, baking, washing clothes, mending and darning, serving meals, building fires, attending to lamps . . . Missing from this picture is the making of the soap, that the wash might be done, the

lugging and heating of water, the tiresome process of heating and lifting cast-irons, the dusting and sweeping of rooms, the cleaning of the stove, and the mending of the stocking and the coat now in need of repair. (1990, 148; also see Cowan 1983, 16–39; Ulrich 1983; Matthews 1987; Babbitts 1993; 1421; Cott 1997; Cross and Szostak 2005, 38–52)

But omitted from this catalog of endless chores was nursing and the tending and rearing of young children.

Moreover, the daily grind for women did not change substantially as the nineteenth century wore on since the great majority of Americans still inhabited the countryside (Berger 1979). Even a century ago, it would have been rather pointless to execute an *Atlas of American Women* as Barbara Shortridge did in 1987. Nowadays cartographic depiction of the lives and attributes of twenty-first-century American females would call for a good number of rather complicated plates.

After this tour of the countryside, it may be instructive to weigh such evidence as we have concerning the internal zonation, the more intimate spatial arrangements, of what were then metropolises, places like Charleston, Boston, New York, and Philadelphia. What Sam Bass Warner (1968) has written concerning Pennsylvania's leading city may well apply elsewhere: "The rummage of classes and occupations found in many Philadelphia blocks continued the old tradition of mixed work and residence characteristic of American and English country towns . . . Social and economic heterogeneity was the hallmark of the age. Most areas of the new big city were a jumble of occupations, classes, shops, homes, immigrants, and native Americans" (11, 50; also see Hershberg et al. 1981, 460–91).

In her analysis of late eighteenth-century Reading, Pennsylvania, Laura Becker reinforces Warner's observations.[4] And, drawing on personal experience, I can recall the impoverished alley dwellings of Washington, D.C., in the early 1940s, literally a stone's throw from some of the more desirable addresses of the city or the situation in Athens, Georgia, in the 1950s, where one could find black servants living in closest proximity to their white employers, as was also the case in nineteenth-century Charleston (Radford 1976). Then, during fieldwork on the Pennsylvania town—places of eighteenth- and early nineteenth-century origin—I was impressed by the degree of intermixture among different types of land use and among social groups (Zelinsky 1977).

Adopting a broader perspective on the evolution of the urban environment, Eugene Victor Walter perceptively notes that

modern changes associated with the industrial revolution of the eighteenth century caused great dislocation and relocations, rearranging the structure of places in the city. In the nineteenth century, these changes generated a new topistic ideal—to segregate good and bad experience, locating wealth and filth in separate places. The new ideal denied the old nature of a town—formally a common place of shared experiences, including com-passion (meaning shared feelings), shared expressive space, and a common diet of symbols. Instead the town became a system of differentiated places separating the extremes of experience. Slums and suburbs today are historic products of this topistic differentiation . . .

. . . The spatial zoning of poverty is not a universal characteristic of urban life. The slum—meaning a district of the city occupied exclusively by the poor—came into the world at the end of the eighteenth century, a topomorphic product of the industrial revolution. (1988, 23–24, 37)

Yi-Fu Tuan concurs: "The pure neighborhood that deliberately excludes poor people and enterprises of low status is a relatively modern phenomenon. In England, even in the seventeenth century social and economic areas within the city were not yet clearly demarcated and labeled" (1978, 96).

One wonders what Benjamin Franklin, or Frederick Engels, would have made of the gated communities that have become such conspicuous features of virtually every prospering American city during recent times (Low 2003).[5] In any event, one can accept the generalization that the limited number of early American cities, all of them small in size and population, were strikingly more scrambled functionally and socially in their internal socio-economic makeup than the situation we observe today, one in which compartmentalization, or balkanization, has become the universal rule.

The general point here is that from earliest settlement until well into the nineteenth century or even beyond, even as modernization was beginning to triumph, the American landscape—and especially its rural component—was one of precapitalist cellular communities with weak, intermittent connections to the larger world (M. Merrill 1977).[6] What was happening here was in accord with the Great Transformation occurring worldwide on a staggered schedule. In the words of Karl Polanyi, "in spite of the chorus of academic incantations so persistent in the nineteenth century, gain and profit made on exchange never before played an important part in human economy. Though the institution of the market was fairly common since the later Stone Age, its role was no more than incidental to economic life" (1944, 43).

American students of the matter have reached a general consensus, echoing Polanyi's statement. On the eve of the market revolution in America the market was, at best, only a secondary force. As Charles Sellers describes the situation,

The market fostered individualism and competitive pursuit of wealth by open-ended production of commodity values that could be accumulated as money.

But rural production of use values stopped once bodies were sheltered and clothed and bellies provided for. Surplus produce had no abstract or money value, and wealth could not be accumulated. Therefore the subsistence culture fostered family obligation, communal cooperation, and reproduction over generation of a modest comfort. (1991, 5)[7]

Christopher Clark tells us that "markets existed, of course, but their significance was often smaller than had been assumed. Rural societies, and the towns that handled commercial transactions, were essentially pre-capitalist. Production and exchange were usually household based, and used family, or other forms of dependent labor" (1996, 24).

As late as the 1870s, according to Robert Wiebe, small-town life was America's norm, and a certain uniformity prevailed then throughout small-town America. "Depending upon the lines of transportation, groups of these towns fell into a satellite pattern about a larger center, to which they looked for markets and supplies, credit and news. But however much they actually relied upon an outside world, they still managed to retain the sense of living largely to themselves" (1967, 2; also see W. E. Fuller 1964, 283, 287–314; Hilliard 1972, 2; Perkins 1988, 57–90; Wilentz 1997). Referring to an earlier period, Sellers reprises the findings of many other colleagues:

Except in the earliest period of settlement most farm folk lived within a day's ride of a store, around which there often developed a little village or county-seat town . . . [T]he farm household labored first and foremost to insure its subsistence and its reproduction in the next generation. Only after these requirements were met was additional labor expended to produce a small "marketable surplus" of such high-value farm products as whiskey, maple sugar, potash, and salted beef and pork, or livestock, which could be driven to market on the hoof. Modest sales provided enough money or store credits to pay taxes and procure such essential items as salt, powder and shot, cooking and eating utensils, and iron for tools. With a little additional labor the family could periodically enjoy tea, coffee, or refined sugar and gradually acquire such luxuries as crockery and window glass. (1991, 14–15)

And, speaking of country stores (Schlereth 1989a), any readers old enough to have encountered those formerly ubiquitous establishments may recall how similar they tended to be in form and contents. A similar observation also applies to our rapidly vanishing mom-and-pop stores, also independently owned and operated, once so prevalent in our larger cities. Both types of enterprise bear a striking resemblance to the national and regional chains of convenience stores that have been mushrooming everywhere in recent years.

There is still another approach to the question of territorial monotony, or lack thereof, in North America and elsewhere, and one that transcends the passage from a premodern to a capitalist world: Central Place Theory. It assumes that, given an agrarian society dwelling and working within a reasonably level and uniform plain, a hierarchical system of marketing and service centers will automatically develop, specifically a nested set of inter-locking hexagonal areas, ranging from the merest hamlet and its immedi-ate tributary area upwards to the large regional metropolis whose range embraces all the lesser layers of hexagons. It was the German geographer Walter Christaller (1933) who, in a splendid burst of creativity, initiated the theory after his investigations in southern Germany. It is worth empha-sizing that, whatever its regularities in terms of economic geography, the German area in question is quite diverse in terms of its built landscape, dia-lects, dress, customs, and other aspects of culture. Subsequently, another German, the economist August Lösch (1954), working in the 1930s and 1940s, further elaborated the theory. It languished in relative obscurity until En-glish translations of the two crucial volumes appeared in the midst of the so-called Quantitative Revolution in Anglophone geography, which peaked ca. 1950–63.

The result was a remarkable outpouring of literature, scores of articles and respectful coverage in textbooks, mostly by American geographers, work-ing out the potentialities of the theory (Berry and Pred 1965; Getis 2007). Empirical testing produced substantial confirmation of the validity of Cen-tral Place Theory in Iowa and South Dakota (Berry 1967, 5–23, 30–40) and Snohomish County, Washington (Berry and Garrison 1958). But perhaps the most convincing demonstration of the theory's worth is evidence yielded from southwestern Wisconsin (Brush 1953; Brush and Bracey 1955).[8]

Then, as of 1967, we confront one of the deepest mysteries in the history of American geographic thought and practice: an abrupt, almost total ces-sation of scholarly activity dealing with central places. Indeed the only seri-ous latter-day effort I can identify occurs in John Hudson's study of the network of towns founded by railroad companies in the northern Great Plains, an analysis which once again confirms the soundness of the central place idea as revealed in the thinking of shrewd business executives (1985, 16, 69). Its eclipse could be attributed to the rather sudden demise of the Quantitative Revolution as it was supplanted by those trendier modes of in-quiry that are still in vogue. In any event, the moral remains. Ceteris paribus, today, as in the past, we can still observe a repetitive, predictable pattern in the spatial array of most larger and lesser settlements.

Thus central place geometry is something that transcends historical epochs, being observable in modern or postmodern times as well as the premodern. However, not all the notable towns sat at their proper theoreti-cal sites, as would be the case with Des Moines, Springfield (Illinois), Indianapolis, Columbus (Ohio), and their like. Predestination, in the shape of physical geography and the imperatives of long-distance commerce, as set forth so masterfully by James Vance (1970), dictated the location of New York City, Boston, New Orleans, Chicago, Toledo, Pittsburgh, and a string of settlements of respectable size stretching southwestward from Baltimore along the fall line. And, foreshadowing things to come, Washington, D.C., arose where it did as a result of political finagling rather than geographic cleverness.

But, over and above such questions of geometric pattern, there has been a notable phenomenon relevant to the settlement network, something linking past to present: the psychological gulf between countryside and truly urban places. If, however, what was once real and strong, a dichotomy between city and countryside, has weakened considerably over time, our collective mind-set has not yet caught up with the reality. Even as the facts on the ground have altered so profoundly—from a land once overwhelmingly rural to one in which at least four-fifths of the national population is essentially urbanized (a powerful argument for the homogenization hypothesis) and much of the rural remainder lives in psychic or economic thrall to the metropolis—in mental terms we still inhabit an idyllic past. Indeed in our durable "social imaginary" (to use Charles Taylor's [2007] coinage) Americans are still wont to view cities, and especially the larger ones, with some suspicion as sinks of iniquity and to hanker after a Middle Landscape of virtuous small towns and the nearby smiling family farms with their stalwart yeomen.

In summary, then, the situation during the formative years of the republic would have appeared both familiar and unfamiliar to anyone from the Old World scanning its built landscape and socioeconomic fabric. On the one hand, the varied ethnic clumps had not yet become fully Americanized, but still a nation-building project was afoot in advance of anything observable elsewhere. And if cultural regions had formed, they were not nearly so sharply defined as their counterparts in the Old World. Neither had the individual rural localities acquired distinctive personalities such as one sees in Italy, Spain, Mexico, or India. Yet the multitude of farmsteads (whose residents all shared a decided family resemblance, their *genre de vie*, in terms of work and family attributes) had dealings with nearby post offices and an array of marketing and political centers at predictable distances away. But any such formulaic regularity was seldom perfect given the intervention of rugged terrain and major streams and marked differentials in the productivity of specific tracts of land. And such differences in economic pattern and thus in choice of crops, livestock, and labor force combined with the lingering legacies of European religious and ethnic antagonisms to generate place-to-place tensions over and above the fundamental commonalities in life-pattern and social axioms among an overwhelming agrarian community. (Although not many observers would have been so prescient as to anticipate the cataclysmic clash that was to bloody the land in 1861.)

So, in summarizing a complex, messy early American reality and trying to add up all the incommensurables, it would be highly simplistic to characterize our emergent nation, in the midst of transformation from a premodern past, as being more or less placeful than whatever we witness today. It is most important to note that the geometry of spatial diversity does not follow a single mathematical formula. The metric that one could apply to a country overwhelmingly composed of essentially self-sufficient cellular communities is useless in a nation where (as described in the following pages) all its components are bound together within a centralized, interdependent network of economic and social transactions. Thus a preliminary response to the assertion that the early United States was more geographically diverse than our latter-day republic must be a Scotch verdict.

## The Role of Symbols

As we resume our narrative, it is important to note that neither state nor nation can prosper if it fails to exploit a stockpile of nationalistic or statist symbols. And there is no better illustration of this truism than the American story, for it is inconceivable that the troubled young republic could have endured, then soared to greatness, without the emotional energy generated by a set of hallowed symbols. Since I have dealt elsewhere (Zelinsky 1988a) with this topic in considerable detail, the sketchiest of summaries must suffice here.

The central—and original—finding of my study was that the shifting character of the various symbols adopted and widely used from the days of the Revolution through the late twentieth century sensitively reflects the transition of the American community from a period when the idea of the nation—but the very special American nation with its commitment to superlative, universal ideals—reigned paramount, and the state was only a necessary nuisance, to a gradual usurpation of these incandescent principles as we progressed into the current period of statefulness when a transcendent, essentially amoral state apparatus commands the devotion and uncritical obedience of the multitude. Moreover, it can be argued that the current nation-state has as its essential raison d´être the perpetuation of the wealth and power of a controlling elite. I believe this to be an important finding, but irrelevant to the argument I develop in this study. Consequently, there will be little further occasion to refer to it again.

The advent of the Revolution called for the creation and widespread dissemination, almost overnight, of a set of fresh symbols in a land where previously they had been few and far between, only the occasional British flag or statue or portrait of the monarch and some other historical worthies. Thus the almost instantaneous canonization of George Washington and later other military and political leaders and their representation in paintings, cartoons, statuary, medals, ceramics, samplers and other textile items, all manner of decorative objects, and eventually on stamps, coins, and paper currency. Simultaneously, Miss Liberty and the Liberty Pole became inescapable in folk iconography. The United States has a claim to the invention of the national holiday with the prompt, boisterous celebration of July fourth from 1777 onward, along with Washington's birthday, other soul-stirring anniversaries, and the pomp and circumstance of the presidential inauguration. Patriotic oratory flourished as did nationalistic verse and rousing ditties, American heroes and nationalistic terms began to appear with increasing frequency in the names of cities, counties, townships, and natural features as well in names of persons and businesses (Zelinsky 1983). The grief occasioned by George Washington's demise in 1799 was deep and universal, inspiring many a sermon and other public demonstrations. The bald eagle, later to become *the* statist totem, made its quiet debut on the national seal. Another sign of things to come, despite its rather inauspicious early substance, was the founding of a national capital city, a place that initially inspired scarcely any emotional tremors.

Still another portent of transition in the inner essence of the Union was the concoction of Uncle Sam during the War of 1812, a figure destined to become the embodiment of the state (not the nation) as Miss Liberty became a ghostly remnant. The Stars and Stripes, a preeminent statist symbol that had remained rather inconspicuous during its early decades, gradually came to dominate the symbolic scene, especially during and after the Civil War; subsequently, the red-white-and-blue motif was to become ubiquitous in every conceivable venue (Marvin and Ingle 1999). Statist architecture, in appropriate classical styles, became widespread from the late nineteenth century onward, not just in Washington but in state capitols, courthouses, city halls, and other public buildings and banks as well (Craig 1984). In parallel fashion, nationalistic and statist monuments have become virtually universal in the ceremonial centers of settlements large and small. A late nineteenth-century development was the founding of jingoistic veterans organizations that eventually acquired and exercised much political clout in local and national affairs. The same period witnessed the invention of the Pledge of Allegiance to the flag and its rapid adoption by all the public schools. After Washington, D.C., had acquired its matchless abundance of sacred sites, of stately edifices, grand vistas, monuments and memorials, cemeteries, and other shrines of nationalist/statist import, we begin to witness great streams of pilgrims arriving there—and in lesser numbers at other sanctified places—to perform the rites of citizenship.

It only remains to be said that what may have originated as the agenda of inspired individuals and local groups later became the programs of large formal organizations operating hand in hand with government organizations. Such campaigns were vital to the operation of modern nation-states as they leveled off the bumps and hollows of the nation's mind-set. "Every central government worships uniformity; uniformity relieves it from inquiry into an infinity of details, which must be attended to if rules have to be adapted to different men, instead of indiscriminately subjecting all men to the same rule" (Tocqueville 1945 [1835], 240).

The cumulative effect of all the visible and verbal expressions of American nationhood has been to make them a normal, seldom-noticed part of our quotidian existence, but something deeply ingrained within our inner being. As Michael Billig has so successfully argued, "in the established nations, there is a continual 'flagging,' or reminding, of nationhood" (1995, 8). "These reminders, or 'flagging,' are so numerous and they are such a familiar part of the social environment, that they operate mindlessly, rather than mindfully" (1995, 38; also 93–127).

## Measuring Land and Other Crucial Things
### Dividing the Land

Among the most pressing of the many problems confronting the young republic was the question of how to dispose of the vast tracts of unclaimed land within the public domain. After much wrangling, New York, Connecticut, Massachusetts, Virginia, the Carolinas, and Georgia agreed to surrender their claims to trans-Appalachian territory to the federal regime in the 1780s. And perhaps none too soon since, after cessation of hostilities, many land companies and other parties had been casting greedy glances on much of the presumably empty and undeveloped (in Euro-American terms) real estate, and bands of squatters and speculators had already begun filtering into virgin territory.

The federal decision makers had no practical precedents to fall back on. From the outset of European settlement onward, the individual colonies, major landholders, townships, and other local entities had improvised a varied set of methods for dividing the land among individual proprietors, nearly all of them irregular or "metes and bounds," marking boundaries by means of streams, trees, boulders, and other natural features or some arbitrary geometry (Price 1995). Somewhat more methodical was the long lot division devised by the French and Spanish authorities and honored by subsequent American administrators.

The rush of events precluded the extensions of any such traditions into the vast new frontier zone. Thus among the most consequential of early congressional enactments was the Northwest Ordinance of 1787, which, inter alia, established rather arbitrary boundaries and territorial governments for five future states and, then, a system of rectangular survey for all the unsettled portions of the public domain. This system, as formulated by Thomas Jefferson and his associates, is the ultimate in simplicity, regularity, and economic efficiency (Pattison 1957; H. B. Johnson 1975, 1976; J. B. Jackson 1979; C. A. White 1982; Linklater 2002). After establishing a prime meridian and baseline for a given broad expanse of territory, surveyors proceeded to mark off a series of compass-oriented townships, six miles by six miles in extent, and, within each, thirty-six square-mile sections. Subsequent landowners often exercised the option of further slicing the section into rectangular chunks. Although not legislatively mandated, almost inevitably public roads followed along section, or half section, lines. Beginning in northeastern Ohio in the late 1780s, the surveyors set about their task at a frantic pace, usually barely in advance of the land-hungry, but sometimes not.

A rectilinear cast of mind soon took firm hold on the general imagination. Similar, but not identical, schemes of rectangular survey were adopted by several states for their unsettled areas: in northern Maine, western New York, northwestern Pennsylvania, western Georgia, and about half of Texas (Price 1995, 8). Then, within farmland, fields and fences paralleled section lines, and farmhouses squarely faced the section-line road. In addition, there was wholesale mimicking of rural rectangularity in the layout of streets in most nineteenth-century cities and villages (Linklater 2002, 193–201). But not to be overlooked was the powerful example of the widely admired Philadelphia city plan. All this regularity, all this exhibition of spatial boredom,[9] is abundantly clear to the transcontinental air passenger who deigns to peer out the window at the land below, and certainly contributes to the widespread impression that the United States is a placeless land as survey and property lines override the infinitely diversified natural contours of the land with its irregular heights and depths and wandering streams.

Another way of arriving at much the same sentiment—the perception of a cohesive, homogeneous slab of territory—was to take the cartographic route. Early on, American mapmakers flooded the market with representations of whatever the total extent of the United States happened to be at the moment, and such images imprinted themselves deeply on the viewers' minds. Indeed "it was common readers who inaugurated the nation by poring over geographic texts that produced and reproduced their cultural community as a geographic reality" (Brückner 2006, 113–141, quot. 141). Then, after the conterminous United States reached its current limits in 1853, that rudimentary emblem, the bare outline of the country filled in with some uniform tint or left blank, has served as a sacred icon and one that somehow stirs the soul of the citizen.

### Currency and Other Essential Metrics

Rationalizing the disposal of "empty" territory was only one of the predicaments bedeviling the founding fathers and their successors. There prevailed something approaching chaos in the currency and coins being circulated in the various states. "From 1834 to 1856 the silver money of this country consisted, to a large extent, of foreign coins, more or less worn, chiefly Spanish and Mexican, but with a considerable sprinkling of English, French, German, and Scandinavian pieces" (H. White 1914, 35). It required nearly a century before locally issued coins and banknotes were supplanted by a workable banking system and a thoroughly nationalized currency bedecked with all manner of nationalist symbols (Mihm 2007). Until then, the most pressing issue was the proliferation of thousands of locally issued bills in every imaginable denomination.

It took even longer to standardize ways for measuring weight, length, area, volume, temperature, time, and other urgent dimensions of the physical world. "While Congress had been considering the matter, most of the states had, independently of one another, secured and adopted standards. Most of the standards thus adopted were brought from England; nevertheless, standards of the same denomination differed widely among themselves, thus perpetuating confusion in the commerce between adjacent states" (L. A. Fischer 1925, 4–5). As early as the 1780s, the indefatigable Thomas Jefferson began agitating for regularization of all the many ways of measuring things being practiced across the land (P. C. Cohen 1982, 112–13, 127–30; Linklater 2002, 63–67), but progress was slow and hesitant. Thanks in large part to the efforts of Ferdinand Joseph Hassler, one of the unsung heroes of American history, the Treasury Department adopted standard measures in 1832 and Congress followed suit in 1836. But the process of legal enactment was not fully completed until 1857 (Linklater 2002, 212–22).

If the nation finally enjoyed total internal consistency in measuring all manner of things and conditions a century and a half ago, there still remains for consideration the vexatious question of the metric system. Soon after the first French Republic conceived and implemented this universal system, many other countries accepted it, while metric measurements replaced all competitors throughout the scientific community. But its triumph has not been quite global. Six nations, including the United States, remain holdouts officially, at best making only partial use of the system; and even in Western European countries, where it has held sway for two centuries, many merchants and craftsmen still resort to premodern modes of measurement.

More to the point, there may be a profound moral in the American story. Despite a vigorous governmental campaign in the 1970s and 1980s to replace all traditional measures with the ultra-rational metric (which has no relationship to the human body), apparently the only lasting result so far has to do with bottled beverages. Thus "in states like Iowa, Alabama, Missouri and Illinois, where speed limits had been designated in kilometers in the 1980s, the signs were removed in the 1990s" (Linklater 2002, 281). I suspect we are not dealing here with the quirks of our political system or personal whim but something much more deep-seated, aside from the likelihood that America had become so rich and powerful it could afford to dismiss the opinions and practices of the majority of humankind. As Linklater identifies it:

> Even in countries which had adopted the metric system for more than a century, where children grew up educated in it and thinking in terms of a single unit of length, weight and capacity, a residue of organic measures remained stubbornly in existence . . . People insist on using them in direct exchange because it is an unconscious sign of belonging to the community, of knowing the local dialect, as opposed to the stranger who would use the metric term. Here the metric system's strength, its invariable, universal uniformity, becomes its weakness. Like all forms of globalization, it saps the sense of local autonomy. (2002, 280–81)

## Space-Time Compression: The Railroad Revolution

When the United States was born, the modes and pace of locomotion as well as the technology of road building had not advanced a whit since the days of antiquity. On land, the pedestrian or runner could manage ten to forty miles a day, depending on road quality, weather, and terrain, while the figures were only marginally better for those riding horses or being hauled in horse-drawn carriages. At sea or on streams, the traveler was at the mercy of the strength and steadiness of wind and current. In the United States, conditions were inferior to the better sections of Western Europe. With the exception of a few short stretches of carefully engineered and maintained turnpikes that exacted tolls, overland travel was notoriously a wretched experience over questionable surfaces and dependent on unreliable roadside services, as attested by countless travelers' accounts.

The first significant advance (if we bypass the tentative potential of the hot-air balloon in the late eighteenth century) was the advent of the steamboat during the early nineteenth century, but its adoption came about hesitantly and slowly in the decades to follow. If we ignore the rather marginal cases of semaphores, smoke, light, and sound signals, and pigeon post, the transmission of information could not take place any swifter than a horse or ship could move, so that transportation and communication remained synonymous.

The truly revolutionary event was the invention, perfection, and rapid deployment of the steam railroad, initially in Great Britain in the 1820s and 1830s, then, soon after, in the United States. It is a tale told so often and so well by others (J. B. Vance 1986) we need not relate the details here, but the outcome was plain enough.[10] The new technology enabled the process I call the *modern market system in alliance with the state* to begin shifting into high gear. By the 1840s and, most emphatically, by the Civil War years, wherever it penetrated, the railroad had supplanted highway travel and had begun rendering redundant the series of new canals that had enjoyed so much favor and excitement a few years earlier. Moreover, the railroad had the potential, frequently realized, of reaching roadless areas and those far removed from navigable streams. But it is also important to point out that, initially at least, the national government played only a minimal role in fashioning the rail network. Instead we witness corporate business competition at its most ferocious and grasping. The incidental economic, political, and military fallout of these battles was huge as the northern states far outpaced the southern in laying track. Lines usually running east-west were hardly conducive to the flourishing of Dixie.

What occurred, then, was an exponential quickening and quantitative boosting in the circulation of passengers, commodities, information, and ideas. Quite obvious was the means for weaving together a mass market and setting the stage for an omnipotent central government. But there was one transformation the railroad could not effect: erasing the gap between countryside and town. Until well into the twentieth century, city dwellers and farm folk (the latter initially far more numerous) lived in two separate worlds. Travel between them was slow, costly, difficult, and hazardous on ill-maintained roads, and, for much of the year, simply impossible because of mud, snow, or ice (Moline 1971, 36–37).

As it happened, the 1840s may have been the most pivotal of decades in the human geography of the United States. In addition to the steam railroad, the electric telegraph entered the scene abruptly, the practice of photography was beginning to spread far and wide, and the modern business corporation was manifesting itself in a serious way.

The impact of the railroad has been much broader, much more profound than the simple quantitative acceleration of movement and space-compression in the hauling of passengers, commodities, and information. As ably argued in a remarkable study by Wolfgang Schivelbusch (1986), the most revolutionary changes wrought by the railroad were social, political, and psychological. No longer was the traveler in plodding, intimate, not always pleasant contact with his surroundings. Instead the voyeur's staccato glimpses of the railside world meant fraying any real connections with mundane reality (as so richly documented in Dickens's travel episodes), an alienation hugely intensified with the advent of air travel.[11]

> The alienation from immediate, living nature that was initiated by the mechanization of motive power was increased as the railroad was constructed straight across the terrain, as if drawn with a ruler . . . As the natural irregularities of the terrain that were perceptible on the old roads were replaced by the sharp linearity of the railroad, the traveler felt that he lost contact with the landscape . . .
>
> . . . As the space between points—the traditional traveling space—was destroyed, those points moved into each other's immediate vicinity . . . The isolation of localities, which was created by spatial distance, was the very essence of their identity, their self-assured and complacent individuality . . .
>
> . . . The regions, joined to each other and to the metropolis by the railways, and the goods that are torn out of their local relation by modern transportation, shared the fate of losing their inherited place, their traditional spatial-temporal presence, or, as Walter Benjamin sums it up in one word, their "aura." (Schivelbusch 1986, 23, 38, 41)

As psychologically, economically, and socially radical as the coming of the revolutionary steam railroad proved to be, we cannot ignore its immediate landscape impact. There was much reshaping of terrain in the countryside, while, in towns and cities, entire neighborhoods were transformed and the passenger and freight depot became the focus of a secondary downtown (Stilgoe 1983). When the transcontinental railroads penetrated the western half of the land barely ahead of pioneering settlers, they platted a series of towns at suitable intervals following much the same repetitive design (T. W. Harvey 1982, 1983; Hudson 1985). The degree to which the railroad contributed to whatever overall standardization of the general American landscape may have occurred and thus to placelessness is certainly a complicated question. The only certainty is that it is part of the equation. The question is further complicated by the fact that recent decades have seen the elimination of much trackage and a reduction in passenger and freight service.

## The Problem of Time

Although the railroad companies and their suppliers made steady progress, individually and collectively, in designing and manufacturing locomotives, cars, rails, ties, signal systems, and ancillary facilities and managed to reach general agreement as to rail gauges, there remained one major difficulty that was not readily overcome: how to schedule and operate their trains safely and efficiently when each of their stations necessarily had to observe local, that is, sun, time (essentially a non-problem in the relatively small countries of western Europe). "At mid-[nineteenth] century, there were 144 official times in North America . . . The majority of people in 1870s were still able to arrange time to suit their convenience, even arranging a noon-time stroll to watch the dropping of the local time-ball and to take out their watches and make a precise adjustment. How better maintain communal integrity? Every self-respecting town on the continent had a right to its own newspaper, its own baseball or cricket team and its own individual time" (Blaise 2000, 34, 83).

But such parochial temporal autonomy would simply not do for a railroad company—or for passengers and shippers—when the various stations along the line were communicating instantaneously via telegraph and were subject to much uncertainty about precise times of departure and arrival (M. O'Malley 1990, 64–67).[12] The solution was obvious enough: establishing a set of east-west time zones, one hour apart, each spanning approximately fifteen degrees of longitude. The actual implementation was beset by all manner of economic, political, and sociocultural obstacles, so that it was not until March 1881 that the Connecticut legislature became the first in the nation to accept standard time (O'Malley 1990, 96). Then, after much negotiation, the entire American railroad industry adopted standard time on November 18, 1883 (ibid., 99–143; also see W. F. Allen 1904; Schivelbusch 1986, 42–44; Bartky 1989). The following year, thanks in large part to the strenuous efforts of Sir Sandford Fleming, a worldwide system of standard time came into being and has never been successfully challenged over the years.

Jubilation over the new time regime has been far from universal; grudging acceptance is probably the best way to characterize the general mood. At a localized intimate scale, factory workers have perennially resisted the notion of time-clocks, but, of course, meaningful opposition to standard time has long since vanished.[13] Today any respectable adult American would feel naked if he or she were to appear in public without a watch, (or, more recently, a cell phone) and might be uneasy if the timepiece were off by more than a minute or two. Something fundamental has overtaken us. "Standard time amounted to a reconstruction of authority—the authority Americans used to govern themselves both in private and public life, at work and in play. But supplanting nature and God with clocks and watches, standard time replaced religious guidelines for dividing up the day, or 'natural law,' with secular authorities based on efficiency and convenience" (M. O'Malley 1990, ix; also see Blaise 2000, 105).

### Of Time and Light

Other technological innovations have transformed the meaning of time for Americans, most notably the invention of cheap electrical lighting in the late nineteenth century and its universal adoption. Such illumination has made it practical for factories and stores to operate around the clock and, in the extreme case of clockless, windowless casinos, to ignore time completely. In times past, city streets were almost totally devoid of pedestrians and vehicles after nightfall, but, after street lamps—initially using gas— and storefront lighting were installed, night effectively turned into day, so that there was little to inhibit nocturnal public activity (Bolton 1979; Jakle 2001). Thus, whatever reservations we may have concerning the homogenization of American places, there is no doubt that the irregularities of temporal behavior have been tamed and flattened away.

## Air-Conditioning Arrives

The acquisition of artificial lighting is not the only way to obliterate or outwit time. The challenge of doing away with, or modifying, seasons of the year has intrigued inventors for ages. And, in a sense, prehistoric peoples mastered the problem millennia ago in a limited fashion with the practice of heating buildings and shelters, thereby producing a sort of extended summer. But finding ways to reduce excessive warmth and humidity during the hot season proved to be a much more difficult proposition, and a rather urgent one for Americans, suffering as they do from violent temperature extremes over much of the land. The early expedients were far from ideal: designing dwellings so as to preserve coolness and/or maximize air currents or to circulate air over blocks of ice.

During the late 1880s, engineers began to tinker with devices for mechanical cooling, and early in the twentieth century they finally came up with marketable devices (O. E. Anderson 1972; Cooper 1998). At first, only a few factories, office buildings, and mansions of the wealthy were able to install the costly machinery and ducts. But gradually, as the technology improved, the devices became cheaper and less cumbersome, and, as levels of personal income rose, by midcentury a significant percentage of homes, workplaces, vehicles, hospitals, and other public buildings were being air-conditioned. Incidentally, the turning point for many individuals was the joy of cooling off in a movie theater during a heat wave (as I can attest from personal experience). The results have been dramatic.

> Air-conditioning . . . has in just a century transformed the United States. In-door weather "manufactured" by air-conditioning equipment has—whether we accept the claims of its promoters or the complaints of its detractors—tamed the nation's anarchic seasons and imposed uniformity on a climatically diverse continent. It has helped reshape cities, houses, farms, even our bodies, coming closer than any other technology to producing the "weatherlessness" long envisioned by American utopians who have typically confused techno-logical control with social perfection. (Ackermann 2002, 1)

For those industrial processes where ambient levels of humidity and temperature are critical, it now became feasible to locate facilities in any region of the country (Cooper 1998, 30–31). Air-conditioning has also made it possible for architects to ignore regional climate in designing their struc-tures and thus to reduce geographic contrasts within the built landscape (Arsenault 1984, 621). More generally, the technology, as Raymond Arsenault claims, may have contributed to a "radical decline in regional distinctive-ness" (1984, 616), and nowhere more so than in the American South, where it has meant a veritable revolution in patterns of work and general living. But one must keep the situation in perspective. As Arsenault observes, "not all southerners live in air-conditioned homes, ride in air-conditioned cars, or work in air-conditioned buildings. Among rural and working-class blacks, poor whites, migrant laborers, and mountaineers, air-conditioned living is not the norm" (1984, 189). Within metropolitan areas in and out of the South, the new technology has sharpened and deepened the spatial and social di-vide between haves and have-nots, as Robert Thompson (2007) has so amply demonstrated for Houston.

Air-conditioning has also had a decided impact on our population geog-raphy. Although it is only one of several relevant factors, there can be little doubt concerning the efficacy of the technology in helping reverse the for-mer heavy migration of southerners toward the North and West, and also to encourage the in-migration of northerners to the South and a general movement to Arizona and New Mexico (Arsenault 1990, 191). And, finally, we have the shift in American dietary patterns brought about by refrigera-tion (O. E. Anderson 1972, 273–86). Partially supplanting canning and other primitive methods of food preservation, seemingly fresh frozen food from afar in America or abroad made it possible to ignore the calendar in planning meals. As far as the supermarket is concerned, seasons of the year have become a distant memory.

## Further Transportation Developments

The arrival of the steam railroad (and the concurrent electric telegraph) was *the* decisive event in the transformation of the space economy and of personal and social sensibilities, a development central to the modernization project. Subsequent innovations in the technology of travel and movement of freight, important as they were to become in terms of speed and penetration of territory, are fundamentally just variations on a basic theme: a turn from the organic and local to the artificial and rootless.

Crucial as railroad and telegraph may have been to the material progress of the Union, at least one serious problem had been left unsolved by the end of the nineteenth century: the efficient circulation of persons and goods within major cities. The sheer magnitude of population growth and territorial extension of some scores of metropolises, the increasing distance between home and workplace, between factory and retail outlet, and the difficulties of other necessary trips had begun to place unbearable strains on older forms of transport. An ever smaller fraction of the population could walk to place of employment or pleasure. Horse-drawn, then electric, trolleys were only a partial stopgap, as were horse-drawn wagons, pneumatic tubes, telegraphy, or the new-fangled telephone. The bicycle was a pleasant but inadequate expedient. The answer arrived at the dawn of the twentieth century.

As much as any other invention, the automobile—along with the related truck, bus, motorcycle, scooter, tractor, motor home, motorboat, etc.—has revolutionized American life and landscape. Within a few years, what had been the rich man's toy became something all but the very poorest could afford or borrow, and by the many millions they rushed to acquire this new, unlimited form of personal mobility and the ability to reach any point in North America having a road leading to it.

But an initial problem was the availability and quality of roads. It took many years of political agitation and extraordinary expenditures before driving within and between cities, and between town and farm, became a comfortable reality (Berger 2001). In the beginning, the setting of physical standards and maintenance was the responsibility of the individual states and, to a lesser degree, that of counties, townships, and municipalities, so that certain mild variations in the roadscape prevailed from locality to locality.

But, after the federal government entered the picture in the 1920s and created a national system of numbered highways, the scene began to assume a decided regularity (J. E. Vance 1986, 507–26; Kaszynski 2000, 55–136).

The ultimate project, of course, was the heroic 44,000-mile Interstate system, announced in 1954 and essentially completed by the turn of the millennium (T. Lewis 1997). The result is a virtually uniform transcontinental artifact that, along with related limited-access expressways within major cities, perhaps more than any other landscape feature, proclaims the case for placelessness. The designers and engineers have rigidly adhered to a single set of specifications, making scant concession to terrain or other local peculiarities. Perhaps the only relief from uniformity, aside from state-mandated speed limits, may be found in special designs for rest stops that some states have instituted. It is noteworthy that the ostensible and clinching argument for federal funding and oversight of the Interstates was their military value, as a system for the efficient movement of troops and materiel during critical periods. The Civil War had amply confirmed the indispensability of the antecedent rail system. Here again military and economic factors intermeshed at the national scale: the *modern market system in alliance with the state* blooming away!

Taking into account the network of some 3.9 million miles of improved roads and multiple millions of highly standardized vehicles in use today, it is abundantly clear that the internal combustion engine has had an incalculably great effect in shaping the American economy, landscape, sociology, and psychology.[14] But, in terms of space-time compression, its impact may be most apparent in the shrinking, and often virtual elimination, of the rural/urban gap in life and behavior (Moline 1971, 94–121; Rae 1971, 155–69; Berger 1979). Thus, in a study dealing with Spartanburg, South Carolina, we learn that

> Spartans took advantage of this greater accessibility in many ways that were reflected in the daily newspaper. Obituary notices listed deaths in communities as far away as thirty miles; Spartanburg civic organizations and women's clubs included members from outlying towns and villages; churches in surrounding towns advertised their Sunday services as if they were as centrally located as the First Baptist Church on Main Street; and nearby communities held sporting events that brought together residents from the entire county and beyond. (H. L. Preston 1991a, 134)

But the impact of the personal auto went far beyond the erosion of rural isolation. "Family life simply became more complex. No longer did one choose friends, recreation, and religion on the basis of proximity. The new associations included people from geographically separate units, with differing social, political, and economic viewpoints. Time had ceased to be the barrier it once was" (Berger 1979, 75).

That the automobile and its siblings have affected and altered virtually every aspect of American life is a given. But, apart from its invigoration of the economic system and enhancement of the grip of the state, how have automotive vehicles changed the reality, or perception, of place-to-place differences? Here is a knotty question no one has ventured to explore methodically. One would expect the work and vacation trips of so many Americans to so many distant points to have some effect on the ways the outsiders envision them and how the places being visited could be modified or how, because of all the transient strangers, their residents might revise their self-images (Edensor 2002, 127). For the time being, we can only speculate.

The next, and presumably final, advance in transportation technology to affect the American scene has been aeronautical. As haulers of passengers, mail, and high-priced merchandise, aircraft have had only a rather limited, incremental impact on American life rather than the revolutionary consequences of auto and truck. Although the significance of air transport in sharing sociocultural items at the international scale is considerable—and a topic beyond the range of this study—and greater than that of the automotive, its domestic role in the possible homogenization of American life can best be regarded as simply a modest extension of that of land-based vehicles. Access to flights is confined to a limited number of airports with rigid schedules, except for the affluent few who own or lease their own aircraft.

Furthermore, these airports and their ancillary facilities comprise an archipelago of isolated pinpricks on the landscape when viewed from space, as contrasted to the dense network of highways, streets, clots of parking lots and service facilities, along with all the countless private garages and driveways for the road-based vehicle, or to the web of rail lines.[15] However, it is interesting to note that, with the helicopter, we finally have acquired a genuine magic carpet. It is now feasible to hover over, and usually land on, any spot within the national territory. If the friction of distance or inaccessibility has been abolished, at least in this special costly way, what can we say now about remoteness as being a deterrent to placelessness?

## Unity via Communication
### The Printed Word

One attribute of eighteenth-century America that made it a truly exceptional society was a literacy rate that apparently exceeded that of all other parts of the world (Leonard 1995, 29), with the possible exception of Iceland, for reasons that are not entirely clear. Furthermore, such primacy persisted throughout the next century as universal education became a reality rather than just an ideal. Although the ability to read—and, to a lesser extent, to write—varied by gender, social class, region, and race, the fact that an adequate number of Americans were literate was crucial in achieving political independence and, subsequently, in cobbling together a viable economy and polity. It was a unique convergence of religious, moral, political, and economic factors that generated an "American ideology of literacy" that "sought to hold in equilibrium a quest for a place in heaven and for material improvement and individual growth on earth" (Gilmore-Lehne 1993, 2419).

The pace of growth in colonial America's publishing industry was nothing short of phenomenal. "No less than twenty-nine newspapers circulated weekly throughout the colonies in the 1770s" (Gilmore-Lehne 1993, 2415), in addition to a flood of books, pamphlets, almanacs, and other printed items imported from overseas. "The early republic was the first society in history to test what would happen when the printed page carried news for all" (Leonard 1995, 28).

Government and publishers were complicit in the drive toward national unification (in an early manifestation of the *modern market system in alliance with the state*), and the postal system was one of the earliest, most deliberate and effective mechanisms for forging such unity (W. E. Fuller 1972, 79–108). "The generation that drafted the Constitution and the First Amendment adopted below-cost newspaper postage as a means of uniting a fragile nation" (Kielbowicz 1989, 179). In effect, then, the federal government "committed the nation's resources to forge, through a joint venture with private publishers, a system of mass communication indispensable for a growing nation" (Kielbowicz 1989, 31).[16] Although the subject of much squabbling and political in-fighting over the years, the policy of subsidizing the mailing of newspapers and, later, magazines at below-cost rates has remained intact to this day.[17]

The central regime was responsive to the universal clamor for local post offices, so that "by 1828, the American postal system had almost twice as many offices as the postal system in Great Britain and over five times as many offices as the postal system in France. This translated into 74 post offices for every 100,000 inhabitants in comparison with 17 for Great Britain and 4 for France" (John 1995, 5). This achievement is all the more impressive when one considers the sheer hugeness of the American territory. It must also be noted that, for the great majority of Americans then, these thousands of local post offices were the only, or certainly the most important, tangible evidence of the existence and vitality of a federal regime. They were also critical nuclei for the bonding of rural neighborhoods.

After much political agitation, the American postal system attained its ultimate territorial penetration with the inauguration of daily Rural Free Delivery in the 1890s. Previously, the farmer and his family had found it costly in terms of time and effort over usually execrable roads to reach the nearest town and its post office. With the eventual paving of highways and use of autos by mailmen, fast, frequent access to mail, publications, and parcels became a feature of daily rural existence. But by lessening the gap between town and country, RFD had unintended consequences (W. E. Fuller 1964, 287–314).

> Before the RFD was established, there were hundreds of little communities in rural America, most of them identifiable by their local post offices, and people who lived within their boundaries had a sense of belonging and a community spirit which showed itself in their occasional social meetings . . . but the rural delivery system had the effect of expanding the community, loosening up old, familiar relationships, and often wiping out long established neighborhoods altogether. For when rural routes came through an area, many of the little fourth-class post offices disappeared, and with them went the identity of the community and finally the community itself. In Reno County, Kansas, for example, rural delivery eliminated sixteen post offices in ten years. (Ibid., 283)

Thus, rather inadvertently, the craving for convenience contributed to nationalization of the countryside and erosion of local community.

In treating the print medium, we can hardly avoid the question of the autonomy of American language. Although some early observers began to notice Americanisms in colonial speech by the eighteenth century and regional dialects had begun to emerge, commonalities between language as spoken and written in the motherland and across the ocean (at least by the educated) remained supreme. Moreover, whatever regional distinctions could have been detected in America were less by at least an order of magnitude than what prevailed within Great Britain, a situation that persists to this moment.

In any event, political independence unavoidably gave rise to the notion of linguistic autonomy. In the ensuing discourse no figure was more pivotal than Noah Webster (1758–1843). During the early years of his long career, "Webster, a staunch Federalist and ardent proponent of the union, hoped to mitigate political tensions by erasing local linguistic differences" (Brückner 2006, 103; also see Shoemaker 1966, 248; Monaghan 1983, 13; Kramer 1992, 57, 60) and also standardizing a distinctively American version of the English language. "He envisioned the creation of what he later called 'a federal language,' which would be uniform throughout the United States and be distinctly different from the tongue of the mother country" (Monaghan 1983, 38).

Although it may be somewhat extreme to state that "it is probably due to Webster's efforts to reform the language that the English language in America is more uniform than it is in England or than is the language spoken by the people living in various sections of any other large country" (Shoemaker 1966, 305),[18] Webster's publications did contribute substantially to the solidification of national sentiment. And none more so than his enormously popular *Blue-Black Spelling Book*, which inculcated unabashed chauvinism in the minds of its young readers (ibid., 64–113, 182–92). Indeed "Webster regarded his earliest text, the speller, as a nationalist tool" (Monaghan 1983, 13). The 24 million copies sold between 1783 and 1847 may justify the claim that "he did more than any other man to unify America" (Warfel 1936, 94). But perhaps his most enduring achievement, and one that consumed most of his later years, the heroic Dictionary, was not a nationalistic tract (Rollins 1980, 124–27), for he had by then largely forsaken the crusade for linguistic particularity. What he did accomplish was the permanent standardization of American orthography, to the annoyance or amusement of our British brethren.

Noah Webster was not the only author to tap the schoolbook market with both commercial and ideological success (Zelinsky 1988a, 147–52). Among the more acclaimed was his contemporary, Jedidiah Morse (1761–1826), a pioneering student of the subject, with his influential and frankly propagandistic book, *The American Geography*. But no writer for the classroom was more celebrated or durable in effect than William Holmes McGuffey (1800–1873) with the numerous editions of his *Reader*. "In its many editions and millions of copies (it is still not entirely out of print), McGuffey's *Reader* was for many years standard fare for the majority of the elementary classrooms. In essence, it was a catechism of nationalism for 'McGuffey's' was more than a textbook or a literary collection of 'elegant extracts'; it was, in sum, a portable school for the new priests of the republic" (Lynn 1973, 23; also see Minnich 1936, Capenter 1963, and Zelinsky 1988a, 149–50).

As Joseph Moreau observed, "authors of the first widely used history texts attempted to create the kind of usable past Webster desired" (2003, 31). Then, with only modest modifications, the tradition initiated by Morse, McGuffey, and their competitors has continued until today in the production of texts for elementary, high school, and college students. At a loftier level, such early historians as George Bancroft churned out volume after volume celebrating nationalistic ideals and a glorious past, as had many an author of fiction and verse. But, training our sights on the schools, it is remarkable that, in a country, unlike most others, lacking a central bureaucracy for administering educational affairs, state and local school boards have devised curricula and selected textbooks with strikingly similar messages, a package of presumed facts, ideas, and attitudes comprising the American Credo (Elson 1964, 166–69; Curti 1968, 124–28). Thus in a comprehensive study of early twentieth-century texts, Bessie Louise Pierce found that "from the analysis of nearly four hundred textbooks representing different subjects taught in the schools the conclusion inevitably must come that the American is taught to respect and venerate his forebears and the institutions which they designed and developed" (1930, 254; also see Nietz 1961 and Noah, Prince, and Riggs 1962).

But, during the late twentieth century, there has been something of a seismic shift in underlying attitudes toward the American past and ideals cherished over the generations, a critical rethinking on the part of academics and some members of the general public—indeed a spirit of skepticism or outright debunking. "Now we find considerable diversity of outlook and approach among competing texts, much nervous shifting of direction, and even turnabouts, in the race to keep abreast of the times and to minimize the pressure of conflicting ethnic/religious/political constituencies. Although old-fashioned nationalism is by no means extinct in elementary and secondary school texts or some popular periodicals, the former consensus has been shattered" (Zelinsky 1988a, 152; also see FitzGerald 1979). I suspect that the ongoing dissension or confusion in the American textbook world is linked in part at some subliminal level to the recent turn toward the regional and local by so many Americans, a phenomenon treated in some detail in a later chapter.

While newspapers may have become cheap enough to be within reach of almost everyone, the fancier national and regional magazines and certainly most books were priced beyond the budgets of ordinary folks. What eventually led to the universality of an American readership cutting across space and class, a mass public able to absorb all manner of printed and pictorial inducements to nationalist, then statist, fervor, was the public library. Starting in a small way in the eighteenth century with collections of material accessible to members of various voluntary associations, local libraries gradually became more numerous and public throughout the nineteenth century, eventually receiving support by taxpayers (P. Williams 1988; Martin 1998, 1–7). As of 1900, some two thousand were in existence, and by 1918 they numbered close to six thousand (Martin 1998, 11).

The single person most responsible for this rapid upsurge was a generous Andrew Carnegie. "By 1917, Carnegie had promised 1,679 libraries to 1,412 towns at a cost of well over $41 million" (Van Slyck 1995, 22). And, incidentally, the well-built structures in question usually bear a strong family resemblance, being designed as they are in a neoclassical mode. Never was the library's nation-building agenda more openly in view, as "an Active Instrument for Propaganda," than during the country's involvement in World War I, a period when the Americanization of the large recent immigrant population had become a major public issue (Wiegand 1989).

### Words Spoken and Sung

The kneading together of a widely scattered population into a creature feeling, thinking, and believing as a single organism entailed more than the printed word, vital though that may have been to the project. Beginning in Massachusetts in 1826 (Canning 2005, 8), residents of a number of localities spontaneously founded institutions for popular instruction called lyceums, where lectures, discussions, concerts, and other entertainments for the improvement of minds were presented at regular intervals. Frequently these events featured important authors, clergymen, scholars, celebrities, and other notables enrolled in the lecture circuit. "The Lyceum not only had a civic role in creating a sense of 'Americanness' among disparate people spread over a large territory, but lyceum activity also provided a mechanism to affirm a specific New England culture as the national norm" (A. G. Ray 2005, 7). By 1840 at least four thousand lyceums were active in the eastern half of the country; then during the 1840s and 1850s the movement took root in the further reaches of America (Rieser 2001, 353–54; A. G. Ray 2005, 21).

Somewhat later, specifically 1872 in upstate New York, the lyceum morphed into a more elaborate institutionalized enterprise, the Chautauqua (Schlereth 1989b; Rieser 2001, 355, 357–58; Canning 2005). These were annual warm-weather affairs, initially idealistic and nonprofit but later commercialized, running for a week or two in appropriate or specially designed suburban or bucolic facilities reminiscent of camp meetings. The intent was to mingle uplift with entertainment, so that the programs included inspirational orators, scientific demonstrations, singers, playlets, orchestral numbers, and a certain amount of vaudeville for their middle-class audiences. When the movement was in full bloom, in the form of Circuit Chautauqua, a given troupe would circulate from one venue to another. "Within twenty-five years of Chautauqua's founding, over one hundred towns, mainly in the Midwest, held assemblies on grounds patterned after the original Chautauqua" (Rieser 2001, 355), and "by the end of World War I, Circuit Chautauqua could be found in every state of the Union" (Canning 2005, 10).[19]

The social and cultural impact of the Chautauquas was significant. "Despite ridicule from the urban avant-garde, the circuits . . . served as vital links to the outside world for some six thousand small towns" (Rieser 2001,

357). Charlotte Canning tells us that "the absence of a national media, until the arrival of radio in the 1920s, positioned Chautauqua as one of the few ubiquitous experiences that linked people across the United States" (2005, 39). More to the point, "by performing the America they wanted to exist, Chautauqua and its communities helped to make that America exist, even if only for the duration of the performance" (ibid., 5). After the heyday of the movement in the early 1900s competition from movies, radio, and other distractions proved to be too much for Circuit Chautauqua, which expired in 1932, although the original New York birthplace still carries on a sort of afterlife, and Chautauquas still operate in the western portions of the nation.

Although it is difficult to plot any direct role in a nation-building program, we cannot afford to ignore the probable contributions of other frankly commercial itinerant enterprises. As soon as transportation facilities made such businesses feasible, traveling menageries, theatrical troupes, minstrel shows, and vaudeville companies, as well as individual lecturers, crisscrossed the land (S. Thayer 1997; R. M. Lewis 2003). "By 1829 . . . the National Road was carrying several good-sized caravans of living animals and skilled performers, and the Mississippi and Allegheny rivers had flatboat theaters in operation before that date" (Buckley 1993, 1616). A certain diffusion of knowledge and attitudes from the greater world would have been inevitable.

But, out of the welter of competing attractions, can there be any doubt that the one most signally effective in capturing the attention and affection of the general public—and also working toward the forging of national oneness— was the railroad circus (S. Thayer 1997; J. M. Davis 2002)? Originating toward the close of the nineteenth century, this dazzling form of entertainment attained its peak of popularity during the early 1900s, in meaningful coincidence with the apogee of Chautauqua activity, and still lingers on today. As for the larger significance of the Circus Age, I can do no better than quote at length from Janet Davis's brilliant exploration of the topic.

> The gargantuan railroad circus helped catapult a "nation of loosely connected islands" into a modern nation-state with an increasingly shared national culture. Blanketing its far-flung markets months in advance of its coming, the circus abetted the rise of modern advertising with its totalizing tactics: thousands of colorful posters featuring lithe bodies beckoned audiences with images of eroticism and danger, while press releases personalized the upcoming show with tantalizing stories . . . about the lives and loves of various human and animal stars. The invasive railroad circus gave its scattered customers a shared knowledge base about the world creating a palimpsest for subsequent American media representations of the globe. The circus' itinerancy and its

three-ring scramble of time, space, and habitat imbued it with a kind of frenetic placelessness that prepared its audiences for the ascendancy of disem-
bodied modern media technologies: Hollywood movies, radio, television, and
the internet. In effect, the pervasive railroad circus—and its animal-bedecked
trains, flipping cars, aerial bicycles, glowing electric generators, costly spectacles, and exotic performers—helped hasten the nation's move toward a mass
consumer culture. (2002, 228)

## The Togetherness of Sport

In lieu of any more obvious point in our reasonably logical sequence of factors to insert the rather maverick topic of sport, let us agree to do so here as
we consider the role of another form of mass entertainment—and, more
specifically, baseball—in the formation of a unified national psyche (Edensor 2002, 78–81). That a certain sport may be identified with a given nation
and even cherished as its special heritage is something that occasionally
comes to pass, as in the case of Japan's sumo wrestling, Canada's ice hockey,
England's cricket, or Russia's chess. Does baseball qualify? It is certainly
indigenous to the United States, despite its obscure British forerunner, and,
unlike most other American inventions, its exportability to other lands has
proved to be rather limited. Originating rather haphazardly and locally in
the 1850s, by the end of the century baseball had become wildly popular
throughout the land in its softball and other informal versions, as well as in
a highly formalized professional form.

Coincidentally or otherwise, "baseball's acceptance as America's game
paralleled the spread of the railroad to every corner of the pioneering nation. By the 1880s baseball was known or played throughout the country
just when the railway network bound the nation together." Moreover, during the trying days of Reconstruction, "baseball provided a ritual and sport
around which the country could rally" (Rossi 2000, 10, 12). In a quite curious way, this sport with no regional connotations combined nostalgia for a
romanticized agrarian past and the clockless leisure of that vanished era
with a set of distinctly modernizing trends, with rigid rules and uniforms,
precisely demarcated areas, and, most significantly, the way in which it lends
itself to all manner of statistical formulations.[20] During its long season, but
especially during playoffs and the World Series, baseball can commandeer
much of our collective attention, thrusting the many millions of fans, in all
our endless variety, into a single set of vicarious bleachers and providing
much of the small talk of casual conversations.

The other organized sports, amateur and professional, that have captured the loyalty of participants and fans throughout the nation do have

some bearing on our central question. Thus, to the extent that football, basketball, golf, tennis, bowling, ice hockey, and, to some degree, soccer are now universal American pastimes, that fact simply reinforces the notion of a placeless land. Any regionalization of their popularity is either problematic or ephemeral (Rooney and Pillsbury 1992).One may note, however, how the rapid spread of imported golf and locally invented baseball, both beginning in the late nineteenth century from initial footholds in the Northeast, nicely illustrates the workings of *cultural diffusion*. At another level of activity, there are tantalizing hints of possible past regionalizations of the varied informal games of an earlier America as documented in *DARE*, the multivolume *Dictionary of American Regional English* (Cassidy and Hall 1985–), and their possible survival up to the present.

## The Telegraph

As the first significant conduit for the process of *instantaneous cultural diffusion*, the arrival of the electric telegraph on the American scene in the 1840s was a momentous, indeed revolutionary, development in the realm of human communication.[21] Thus, in addition to the mutually profitable symbiosis between the new medium and the railroad industry, many other enterprises—manufacturers, wholesalers, banks, newspapers, grain and livestock dealers, road shows, speculators—and, not least, the federal government quickly realized the indispensability of wired information. In addition, it immediately became a priceless military weapon. Indeed it is impossible to envision an alternative scenario for the Civil War for armies lacking the technology. But "perhaps the greatest value of telegraphy to the country was the part it played in breaking down isolation throughout the length and breadth of the land, and in fostering the feeling of nationality. Upon the completion of the transcontinental telegraph in 1861, for example California was no longer a distant province only nominally associated with the government in Washington; it became an integral part of the nation" (R. L. Thompson 1947, 442–445, quot. 445).

There were, however, decided limitations in the spatial reach and social penetration of the telegraph (Cherry 1977, 115). Access was available only at a finite number of offices, frequently at rail depots, and only trained operators could transmit and interpret the code during fixed working hours. Moreover, the high cost per word precluded many a potential user and also shortened the message while altering its style. Although Western Union did eventually initiate home delivery of telegrams, their receipt was not always the occasion for joy. In fact, few experiences were more disconcerting for the householder than the messenger boy's rap on the door in the middle of the night.

The role of telegraphy in erasing spatial and other barriers was not to be limited to the domestic scene. In 1866, with the first successful operation of a submarine cable from North America to Europe and soon thereafter the availability of such transoceanic links along other routes, we have, for the first time ever, the piecing together of a system of *instantaneous* world-wide transmission of commercial and other forms of information (Hugill 1999, 29–34). This radical innovation, supplanting as it did the leisurely progress of intelligence by ship over periods of weeks or even months, meant the demolition of a major obstacle along the triumphal march of globalization.

## The Telephone

Just as had happened a generation earlier with the electric telegraph, the arrival of the telephone in the 1870s proved to be an enormous boon for the business community. We can surmise that, in aiding and abetting the operation of all kinds of enterprises, including the governmental, the telephone contributed materially to the centralization and standardization of economic life—and perhaps indirectly to the leveling of social and cultural characteristics—throughout the land, in addition to affecting the morphology of the metropolis. But teasing out the extent and nature of such an impact on the national scale is a challenge to which no scholar has yet fully responded.[22] When it comes to the social consequences of the telephone, our knowledge remains fragmentary. "For all the quotidian importance to people everywhere, the telephone has been little examined" (Katz 1999, 3).

The telephone is vastly superior to the telegraph as a medium of interpersonal communication since it is immediate, intimate, open-ended, and relatively inexpensive. However, until recently, long-distance calls were costly and cumbersome to arrange, so that nearly all telephone conversations were local. According to the solitary scholarly exploration of such conversations, the sociological effects were significant. In his exemplary and exhaustive study of the social role of the telephone in three California communities—Palo Alto, San Rafael, and Antioch—over the period 1890–1940 relying on contemporary documents, Claude Fischer generated some surprising results.

> The intensification of local contact [via telephone and automobile] may act to preserve and even enhance local patterns of habit, attitude, and behavior, and serve as an inhibitor of the process of cultural leveling which is so commonly assumed as an outstanding and unopposed tendency of contemporary life . . .

... In sum, we found but a few modest changes in localism. The net trend was in the direction of greater attention to the outside world. Yet, rather than indicating a *displacement* of local interest, these changes suggest a simultaneous *augmentation* of local and extralocal activities ...

... The evidence suggests that by using the telephone, people—especially women—more easily maintained and reinforced social relations; that the telephone was a device supporting parochialism. (1992, 195, 220–21, 267)

Another important finding of Fischer's was that "the telephone's social role was more evident for rural than for urban families" (1992, 99). Indeed the telephone, along with all the other blessings of rural electrification (D. C. Brown 1980, x), radically altered the character of farm life. And it was a fairly rapid change. Although in 1935 only 16 percent of farms were equipped with telephones, the number had risen to 96 percent by 1985 (U.S. Rural Electrification Administration 1986, 6; also see U.S. Rural Electrification Administration 1974). During the early phase of rural telephony, that of the party line, the new technology intensified and improved the social environment of conjoined households (Sola Pool 1977, 6). Later, as private lines became universal and the ramifications of instantaneous communication became manifest, the telephone largely ceased to serve as a sort of localistic social glue. Instead its long-term effect was to narrow urban-rural differentials of all sorts and to stimulate rural out-migration.

## Rural-Urban Convergence and the Galactic Metropolis

However elusive or qualified the evidence for other kinds of sociocultural homogenization over extended tracts of American territory, the reality of rural–urban, or metro–nonmetro, convergence is indisputable. The arrival of the telephone, RFD, mail-order merchandise, autos, trucks, improved roads, and computers drastically narrowed the gap between the lifestyles of persons in town and countryside. Concurrently, there was the demographic evisceration of most of rural America during much of the twentieth century, with steady out-migration and largely negative economic change, to the point where fewer than 2 percent of the national population is now engaged in full-time farming or ranching, and countless villages and hamlets are derelict or on the verge of expiring. Such a development might seem to render the convergence question moot.

But, by the 1970s, it had become clear that relationships between urban and rural areas were being transformed so as to produce a much more complex picture. During the final decades of the past century, we witnessed the so-called metro–nonmetro Turnaround with the result that, in some years, in toto, the non-metro counties have been gaining in residents and at other times have suffered only insignificant losses. One reason appears to be that many former farm folk are able to support themselves by commuting as far as fifty miles daily to part-time or full-time jobs in town or city. But an equally important factor in the ongoing transformation is what might be characterized as the urbanization of the countryside.

In the terminology of Peirce Lewis's (1983) seminal essay, a "galactic metropolis" has been materializing over the greater part of the land. Moving beyond the suburbs, a growing number of Americans now live in bucolic isolation or in a strip of new houses along the highway and with no involvement in the rural economy. Some are retired, others commute to distant work sites, and still others are able to work out of home offices. In addition, we have the transient multitudes: the proprietors or renters of second homes who are present seasonally, the hordes of other vacationers, and, further, the occasional new factory or warehouse and the wide variety of other features noted in Chapter 4 that can show up at unpredictable rural sites. It is apparent that our new technologies of travel and communication have loosened territorial bondage to a remarkable degree and, in the process, have greatly eroded the ancient contrast between walled town and open countryside that was once so stark and absolute. How or whether such spatial freedom has modified the larger patterns of sociocultural regionalization is a topic best left to another chapter.

## Recent Advances in Interpersonal Communication

During nearly all of the first century of its operation, the telephone system was place-based, anchored in specific sites, in homes, offices, and roadside booths. Eventually, however, such placefulness has eroded as mobile, wireless telephony arrived, initially in the form of citizens band radio. Much more consequential has been the enormous recent triumph of the cell phone, which seems to have become *the* universal business and personal device in this country and elsewhere. What have been, or are likely to be, the effects on the social and cultural geography of the United States? Apparently James Katz is the only scholar to have pondered the matter seriously. His assessment of the impact of wireless communication, which I must quote at some length, may also apply to e-mail, the Internet, and other such innovations still gestating.

> Because wireless by definition does not require expensive "fiber to the home," and may lead to uniform access pricing independent of location . . . it could have some remarkable impacts in terms of economic geography and population density. There are even some who expect that wireless communication will reduce the outflow of people from rural areas by making dispersion and

isolation less burdensome. And perhaps at the most extreme, some predict that wireless communication will herald a new age of "eagle nests," in which a lone expert can conduct business and live an engaged lifestyle based in a remote, idyllic location. In terms of the first expectation—that wireless communication will reverse out-migration, especially by young people, from farms and small towns—there seems to be little evidence to support it . . . In our opinion, wireless communication has little more likelihood of being able to do this than did its precursors. . . . The second area—allowing experts splendid solitude physically while maintaining personal influence and business presence remotely (via wireless communication)—is somewhat more plausible. (1999, 32–33)

Katz's second expectation seems borne out, after a fashion, by various journalistic accounts of how the rich, super-rich, and assorted celebrities have been buying up large tracts of the most scenic portions of Montana, Wyoming, and Idaho for their sumptuous second homes (with private airstrip and jet aircraft, of course) and perhaps initiating an unprecedented new cultural region in the West. But, in any case, in general terms telephony, whether wireless or based on land lines, has certainly facilitated economic transactions and thus furthered the interconnectivity of all corners of the country and presumably lessened their differences. Any encouragement of localism has turned out to be transient.

## The Electronic Mass Media

Pervasive, important, and massifying though they may have been, the initial American communication media—mail, newspapers, periodicals, books, telegraph, and telephone—have been overtaken and overshadowed by another series of electronic devices that threaten to hold the eyes and ears of the nation in thrall. A crucial distinction between this second group and their precursors is that the latter were to a certain degree interactive or else could be digested at whatever pace the user preferred. Except for the phonograph, the new mass media demand a completely passive audience, one in sync with the transmitters. The process of *instantaneous cultural diffusion* invades the scene and begins taking over the stage.

### The Phonograph

The first and least intrusive of these latter-day marvels was the phonograph. Electronically or mechanically recorded and reproduced speech and music has been on sale in American shops since about 1890, and, throughout a series of technological changes and improvements, the merchandise has enjoyed a reasonably healthy sales history among all strata of the population as it has progressed from wax cylinders to vinyl records, then tapes, compact discs, and beyond.

The social science literature concerning the phonograph is surprisingly sparse; indeed there is only a single full-length monograph to date (Kenney 1999). Although William Kenney tells all we need to know about the history, technology, economics, and social concomitants of recorded sound, he offers no enlightenment as to the phonograph's possible role in promoting sociocultural spatial convergence.[23] We can assume that the companies in question generally aimed their product toward the national, rather than any regional, market, although some niche outfits have catered to racial and ethnic publics. Did such mass marketing of popular and art music, as well as other entertainments, tend to eliminate or dampen regional practice and preference? What effect, if any, did phonograph records have on regional deviations in the American language? We can only speculate as to the answers.

### Cinema

In contrast to the phonograph situation, the outpouring of literature on motion pictures is so vast it would call for a weighty volume simply to catalog all the significant titles. With so many goodies to choose from, I shall refrain from citations and simply distill some generalities based on my eighty years of gaping at the silver screen.

Once it had outgrown its primitive nickelodeon stage, the movie industry aimed its output, with stunning success, at the national and international market. It is an industry which, as in the case of newspaper and telephone firms, is a highly centralized oligopoly and one that efficiently manages thousands of movie houses and schedules simultaneous openings and closings of features from coast to coast. The fact that millions of passive movie patrons—and, later, radio listeners and TV viewers—are conjoined at the same instant represents a momentous watershed development in the evolution of human society. It is reasonable to assume that, without any conscious program to do so, the great preponderance of films have projected a standardized, sanitized vision of American life and ideals, including celebration of national heroes, and hence have been conducive to the nation- or state-building enterprise.

There is also little doubt that movies have fostered conformity in slang, clothing styles, and more. As for the smoothing out of regional dialects, it is best to defer discussion to a later chapter. During periods of collective trauma—World War I, World War II, the Cold War, and perhaps the Great Depression—American films openly rallied to the flag. On the other hand, they have also perpetuated and intensified regional stereotypes, especially with respect to the South and a mythical West; and certain box-office hits have imprinted on our minds indelible notions as to the personalities of, say, small-town Minnesota or rural Iowa. Similarly, the particularized images and sounds of certain cities, such as San Francisco, Los Angeles, New York, New Orleans, Seattle, and Chicago, have been reinforced, if not created, by the magic of motion pictures.

### Radio

The story of American radio is less simple and straightforward than is the case for the phonograph or film. Once the technology had arrived on the scene in the early twentieth century, it was something the lone individual could play with. Although producing records or movies and marketing them calls for rather heavy capital investment, any mechanically adept person (almost always male) could spend a few dollars and jerry-build his own transmitter and receiver, then begin contacting fellow hobbyists all around the world. In the 1920s and 1930s many thousands of ham radio operators pursued this pastime of one-to-one communication, a superior and cost-free version of telephony. A number still do, and are especially useful during local emergencies. But once entrepreneurs began to realize the commercial and communal potential of the novel medium around 1920, radio stations began broadcasting to the public at large in town after town, while manufacturers made receiving sets widely available.

Although the American government was initially quite standoffish, as it had been during the infancy of railroads, telegraphy, and modern highways, many other nations were quick to realize the political potential of radio. Thus it became and remains a state monopoly in many countries as did the telephone system. (In the case of Canada, the wiseacres in Ottawa have assiduously exploited the airwaves, via both radio and television, in a campaign to unify a transcontinental population still suffering from an anemic sense of nationhood.) In the United States, it was only after the commercial success of pioneer stations had induced many competitors to leap into the fray, thus producing severe technical problems, that the federal establishment finally stepped in. Its function has been to license stations, assign appropriate frequencies on the electromagnetic spectrum, and generally ensure that the proprieties are observed. Only belatedly did Washington enter the scene rather indirectly with the creation of National Public Radio. Despite the high quality of its programming and generally elite character of its audience, NPR remains a bit player within the overall broadcasting game.

In her insightful study Susan Douglas (2004) found that "nearly every commentator in the 1920s who wrote about radio and speculated on its impact predicted that radio would foster national unity" (76). If its effectiveness in enhancing regional, local, and other subcultures is difficult to ascertain, the efficacy of radio in promoting American nationhood or statehood is unquestionable, as Douglas has demonstrated:

> Reading the newspaper may have been a crucial first step in cultivating this sense of national communion. But radio broadcasting did this on entirely new geographic, temporal, and cognitive levels, inflating people's desire to seek out, build on, and make more concrete the notion of the nation . . . this technology made imagined communities more tangible because people now listened to a common voice and a shared event at truly the exact moment as others around the region, or the country. (2004, 23–24; also see Lenthall 2007)

And indeed such transcendent togetherness occurred more than once, for weighty reasons or just the simply sensational, as, for example, during FDR's fireside chats and other presidential utterances during traumatic moments or the dribbling out of election returns or such transfixing episodes as the second Louis-Schmeling bout, the Hindenburg disaster, a mine rescue, the Lindbergh kidnapping trial, or the ninth inning of the seventh game of a World Series when the nation's collective heart almost stops beating.

Then, at a more mundane level, radio *may* have had some effect in standardizing American speech. "By the 1930s the fully established networks and the advertisers who controlled much of radio programming *did* impose a standard of radio pronunciation" (Douglas 2004, 103).[24] On the other hand, radio "allowed the listener to cultivate a love-hate relationship with both regionalism and nationalism, homogeneity and difference" (Douglas 2004, 76). With an immediacy more emotionally fulfilling than had been feasible with specialized journals, local and network programs could bind together imagined brotherhoods, pre-existing communities without propinquity, such as boxing fans, gardeners, pet owners, born-again Christians, mystery devotees, polka enthusiasts, blues aficionados, booklovers, followers of political gurus. Or they could develop new ones, such as the millions of housewives vicariously suffering the travails of soap opera heroines, or ring-carrying members (like your author) of the Orphan Annie Club.

Early on, many a local broadcaster sought to exploit radio's potential for celebrating and enriching local and regional life. Indeed that was the mission of the University of Wisconsin's WHA, one of the very earliest stations anywhere, with its zealous educational and regional agenda (R. Davidson 2006), and other statewide networks, such as those in Nebraska and Pennsylvania, have followed suit. Then there are the isolated efforts at creating genuine community stations.

Community radio forefronts diverse local musics and nurtures a sense of difference-within-place through an interweaving of musical genres and talk. Community programmers become conduits between listeners, performers, and local sites; they tie listeners to location by chatting about—and to—local clubs and performances, controversies and events, to which listeners are incited to attend . . . in community radio, in contrast to commercial and public radio, the boundary between programmers and listeners is fluid and dynamic. (Berland 1998, 140–41)

Unfortunately, as any long-distance driver can attest after trolling the local AM and FM stations on his or her car radio dial, such ideal community operations are a vanishing rarity. (For a detailed, anguished account, see Hilliard and Keith 2005.) What one usually hears is much the same standard potpourri of pop hits and syndicated talk shows fed to the local outlet from some central sources, plus a smattering of local news, traffic, and weather. Some observers claim that "satellites and the Internet are homogenizing all radio content and eliminating local services" (ibid., 170). Nonetheless, there are some significant and interesting regional and city-to-city differences in non-syndicated programming by local stations discoverable by the driver who keeps turned to the radio.[25] Unfortunately, although trade sources offer a plethora of raw data, American geographers have yet to exploit this promising topic in anything like the detail it merits. If there is a recent diversification of formats offered by satellite radio (Hilliard and Keith 2005, 172), only a relatively small number of subscribers have as yet availed themselves of this amenity. On balance, then, the effect of eighty-odd years of radio broadcasting has leaned more in the direction of smoothing out place-to-place differences rather than preserving or enhancing them.

### Television

Shortly after the end of World War II, black-and-white television technology had reached an acceptable level, so that manufacturers could risk marketing sets in quantity and local stations could initiate the broadcasting of programs to a nearby public voracious for entertainment and information in pictorial form. As we all know, the new medium was a quick and roaring success. Its history replicated, albeit at an accelerated pace, the experience of newspapers and radio: the mushrooming of enterprises almost everywhere, relying on revenue from advertisers, followed by national syndication of content and eventual oligopolization by a few larger corporations. By the 1960s, three networks had gained control of hundreds of stations, indeed all but a handful of municipal and university operations. The result was the "the provision of a centrally produced, standardized, and homogeneous common [television] culture" (Hirsch 1978, 400). The scholarly consensus reflected the obvious: "Television advertising quickly emerged as a new vocabulary all Americans could share, a common language that often crossed the social divisions of gender, race, class, and geography . . . Television advertising was thus part of the larger standardization of American consumer culture in the postwar era, when national brands, retailers, franchises, and chains flattened out regional differences and bridged demographic diversity" (Samuel 2001, ix–x).

Most such observations were speculative, however, lacking confirmation in empirical studies. But one speculation was tested, "that the political correlates of once distinctive local and regional cultural patterns will . . . decline in strength" (Hirsch 1978, 412). Michael Morgan analyzed data which indicated that "on a variety of political and social attitudes and opinions, the outlooks of heavy viewers from different geographic regions tended to be more homogeneous compared to those who watched less television" (1986, 123).

We would seem to have here an open-and-shut case. As a mass narcotic (see Postman 1985), television, to a degree surpassing that of any other communication medium, serves to generate a national population remarkably uniform in thought, taste, and actions. End of story? Not quite. Once more, new technologies enter to scramble the scenario. One of the few technical shortcomings of early television was the fact that transmission towers could seldom vault images farther than thirty or forty miles. Left in the dark, so to speak, were many millions of potential rural viewers. The solution—in a rare instance of innovation emanating from the hinterland (apparently nonmetropolitan Pennsylvania)—was cable television (Parsons and Frieden 1998). Thereby a rural entrepreneur, who was able somehow to hook into national television streams or who could initiate his own programming, could retail the product via underground cable to a goodly number of local subscribers. Not the least of its virtues is cable TV's ability to transmit along an almost unlimited number of channels. The new system has caught on rapidly and widely during the past few decades. Initially there was a certain enthusiasm over the potential of the medium for home-grown programs and the nurturing of local togetherness. But, as happened earlier with radio, such hopes have been realized only fitfully at best. Community channels are available in many localities, but attract only a minor slice of the viewership.

Another technological development has entered the picture, one whose social and cultural impact we have not yet begun to understand: satellite-based television. It is now possible for the subscriber or the householder who has properly installed a dish on the roof to receive upward of four hundred channels bounced off a small satellite poised in stationary orbit far above the earth's surface. The majority of the channels in question cater to special-interest clienteles, much as have many periodicals over the years, and to a limited extent, radio stations. The outcome is a profound splintering of a viewing public along lines of personal proclivities rather than location, class, or other traditional markers of identity, communities (if we can call them that) without propinquity. Until some serious empirical inquiry is forthcoming, we remain unenlightened as to the ultimate implications for a society that spends much of its time viewing "slivercast" images directed at placeless bands of brothers and sisters. Patrick Parsons and Robert Frieden have stated the quandary effectively:

> The fragmentation of the broadband audience has implications beyond the competitive arenas of the news and entertainment industry. Social observers have expressed concern about the potential decline or even disintegration of a common social language and ideology. As early as 1969, media scholar James Carey commented on the centripetal and centrifugal functions of mass media. The former acted as a social glue that helped bind the culture in a common rhetoric. That is, no matter what one's ethnic or political background, every-one watched pretty much the same kind of television . . . Television consti-tuted a relatively unified vision of the American landscape, one which few people could, or chose to, escape. Cable and satellite services today program to micro-levels of taste and interest. As audiences and sub-audiences gravitate to these slivercast channels, goes the argument, the centripetal force that brings people together is not just lost but replaced by a centrifugal, expansive force that pushes people apart . . . and to the extent that those specialized channels offer a different vision of and language about the outside world, viewers' col-lective perceptions are concurrently divided and, perhaps, isolated . . . Heavy empirical support of the substantive existence of a centrifugal force is as yet undeveloped. (1998, 325–26)

Generating such empirical evidence to confirm or negate the centrifugal hypothesis is a project that should rank high on the social science agenda.

Given today's transportation options and the latest fads in electronic communication—and the promise of even more to come—it is plain enough that we have recently crossed a fateful threshold in the historical geography of work and residence. More and more of us are unshackled from the con-straints of specific sites for the production of goods, services, and informa-tion and enjoy a wide array of choices as to where to live and recreate. Hy-pothetically, then, a placeless society might be hatching. In actuality, as Joel Kotkin (2000, 7–11) has cogently argued, the outcome is quite to the con-trary: a reordering of place-to-place differences rather than their abolition. If we can pick and choose where to live and work, the selection may be for localities that are pleasant or exciting (the *pursuit of pleasure*) or where we can hobnob with soulmates and the shunning of places that fail to satisfy such criteria.

At an equally fundamental level, the communication scene today suggests that, during the late twentieth century, we may have slipped across another of the more crucial watersheds of modern history. Previously Business and the monolithic State had been the most congenial of bedfellows, each unconditionally loyal to the other within each country. Nowadays, as I note further on, the two entities may have had something of a parting of the ways, or perhaps a trial separation. Governed as always by a bottom-line mentality, many a firm has learned that there is much profit to be sought by bypassing nation-state boxes, by no longer marketing exclusively to the masses of a given country but rather cultivating consumers with special appetites, thus going global. Homogeneity pays—up to a point; but, with the most modern of communications, heterogeneity and the casting of the widest net may pay even more.

## Advertising

After our treatment of the various modes of modern communication, the notion of devoting a section to the topic of advertising may seem a trifle redundant. But we have here a peculiar industry and a truly massive entity in terms of dollars spent, one arguably more central than any other to the hypothesis of a placeless land, and one that operates as a loose cannon, so to speak, above and beyond the capabilities of any specific type of communication.[26] It merits special notice.

The vast, sophisticated advertising industry we know today is a twentieth-century creation. "The change in advertising between about 1900 and what had come before was sharp, definite, and transforming" (Smulyan 2001, 527). In earlier times, advertising was a local, haphazard affair, largely confined to newspaper publicity for products and services within a limited area, and spreading information in rather crude fashion.

Around the turn of the century, two problems confronted the republic: how to Americanize the enormous influx of unassimilated immigrants and how to market the flood of standardized goods pouring out of all those grand new factories. The fledgling advertising industry rose to the challenge.[27] Fully flexing their powers of persuasion by the 1920s, it was the ad men who tackled head-on the task of molding a new homogenized national mind-set, one essential for the smooth, profitable operation of the economy. And "it was in the 1950s that the proffered dreams of the captains of consciousness, worked out in the twenties, really began to take concrete form.

It was a period of monumental change. The commodity market parodied the patterns of 'conspicuous consumption' that Thorstein Veblen had noted among rich capitalists and middle-class imitators at the turn of the century, this time 'democratized' on a mass scale" (Ewen 2001, 206; also see Turow 1997, 23).

Although local advertising remains necessary and persistent, it is the major ad agencies operating nationally (and now internationally) that have become veritably the captains of consciousness. And they have exploited every conceivable device for bulking up their clients' sales and services while downplaying regional differences: newspapers, magazines, radio, television, billboards, skywriting, jingles, logos, messages on clothing, mass mailings, automated phone calls, the Internet, product placement in films, and TV.[28]

As the advertising industry grew lustily during the early twentieth century, it both nourished and fed on a parallel development: national polls and surveys. Especially from the 1930s onward, "modern survey methods helped to forge a mass public. They also shaped the selves who would inhabit it, influencing everything from beliefs about morality and individuality to visions of democracy and the nation" (Igo 2007, 282).

In any event, exploiting all the many new and old devices at their disposal, the advertising agencies scored a mighty triumph. We can credit the advertising enterprise with a substantial role in fashioning the United States of the 1950s and early 1960s, when the children and grandchildren of all those motley alien immigrants had become 100 percent Americans, a period when the country had achieved its all-time peak of sociocultural conformity (see Oakley 1986; J. L. Wilson 2005, 67–87) and when its citizens were obediently spending and consuming at a profligate rate. But this edenic climax could not last. Ethnic, racial, religious, political, psychological fissures were working toward the surface.

Even the cleverest of marketing campaigns cannot stem the tidal swings of social change. The ad agencies are learning to adjust as the television audience has begun to splinter, novel social groups are becoming visible, and as a certain undertow toward the regional and localistic, which we will explore at a later point, has become noticeable. The moral may be that there are finite limits to the powers of persuasion that even unlimited advertising budgets and the most virtuosic of media beguilements cannot overcome.

The word in the ad industry was that the increase in media fragmentation was a direct response to . . . social fractionalization. Advertising practitioners did not see this as bad. As U.S. society becomes more divided, it needed more outlets to reflect those divisions. People no longer wanted to be treated in "batches," as mass markets. As early as the 1960s, specialized periodicals had begun to replace mass-circulation magazines. Now the three-network universe was beginning to erode in favor of a multichannel world. To many ad executives such changes reflected a society with increasingly divided interests, "a public moving to its own drumbeat." (Turow 1997, 41)

## Big Business as Juggernaut

Most of the commodities consumed in the young United States were produced locally, in the household, on the farm or by nearby artisans. The exceptions, such as salt, spices, rum, tobacco, guns, ammunition, various metal utensils and implements, and much reading matter arrived by way of the independent local merchant or itinerant peddler operating via a rudimentary wholesaling system. "Most goods were sold as unbranded commodities, and the wholesalers wielded the power in the system" (Strasser 1989, 10; also see Tedlow 1993). But, as the technology of manufacturing advanced, as did means of transportation, and more capital became available, large mills and factories materialized. Incidentally, it is rather remarkable that such a lively capitalist economy could somehow flourish during the early nineteenth century in a country struggling with a rather chaotic, unstable banking system (H. White 1914, 31–40; Friedlander 1996; Mihm 2007).

The goods gushing from the new manufactories found a receptive market by virtue of being cheaper (in terms of time and labor) than the traditional locally generated items and presumably more consistent and superior in quality. But a troublesome issue still beset the entrepreneurs: that many of their products were indistinguishable from those of their competitors. The solution was simple and effective: labeling the product with a brand name (Hart and Murphy 1998; Lury 2004). Such specifications of packages of flour, cans of peas, patent medicines, shirts, or cigars, in addition to announcing false claims of diversity, might be said to contribute to an erasure of placefulness.[29] A related strategy has been the suppression of local variety, as in the mass marketing of fruits and vegetables. Thus our supermarkets present us with only a handful of highly processed, branded types of apples, pears, and tomatoes, while the scores of old treasured local varieties— some quite delectable—are threatened with extinction.

Another winning ploy, one initiated as early as the 1840s with McCormick Harvesters (Dicke 1992, 15–16), was for the manufacturer or his marketing department to set up a national or regional network of franchised distributors. Although the nineteenth century witnessed several of such endeavors, including the notable Singer Sewing Machine system (Ritzer 1993, 31) and the auto dealerships managed by the major manufacturers in the early twentieth century, franchising did not fully come into its own until the late twentieth century, and as a business strategy it is still on the ascendant. In the form of motels, eating places, and filling stations, inter alia, it has become an increasingly familiar component of the American landscape. As part of this general development, many an enterprise, once invincibly local, such as hardware stores, funeral homes, and real estate offices, was scooped up and embedded within a national firm. In the majority of cases, the parent company exercises close control over the franchisee's business practices and often the conformity of the premises to a standard, readily recognizable physical model.

In a parallel and contemporaneous development, we have the chain store phenomenon, something which first appeared in 1859 (Lebhar 1952, 20–55; also see Strasser 1989, 221–33). "The institutions of today's culture of consumption were put in place as early as the 1870s, with the establishment of the first department stores, mail-order catalogs, and five-and-dimes" (Zukin 2004, 257). And the highly successful pioneer in the realm of five-and-dimes was F. W. Woolworth, whose shops, initially confined to the Northeast, eventually spread to all corners of the nation, a program soon to be emulated by other chains of variety stores (Winkler 1970 [1940]). By 1929, according to the Bureau of Census's Retail Census, the 159,638 chain stores accounted for 10.8 percent of all retail shops and 60.6 percent of all department stores (Lebhar 1952, 63).

Although the chain of Harvey railroad-related restaurants began in 1876 (Langdon 1986, 5–8), the serious advent of franchised or chain eating places awaited the arrival of the personal auto. The White Castle chain of small hamburger emporia was established in 1921, "the first extensive restaurant organization to have a completely uniform architectural image" (Langdon 1986, 30). Howard Johnson's roadside restaurants proved to be another early success. "Originated in New England, and spread southward through Virginia before World War II (with two outlying restaurants in Florida), Johnson adopted a pseudo-colonial design for his buildings, structures intended as reminiscent of New England town halls/churches" (Jakle and Sculle 1999, 51). In another gesture of faux regionalism, the early Dairy Queens sported a Pennsylvania Dutch motif (ibid., 187).

In any event, automotive travel inevitably produced standardized nonlocal roadside architecture and bills of fare (Dicke 1992, 122). The central offices of such chains as McDonald's (Boas and Chain 1976; Langdon 1986) and national networks of motels (Jakle, Sculle, and Rogers 1996) and service stations (Lohof 1974; Vieyra 1979) have gone to great pains to devise and install a single invariable design for all their facilities, although revising them periodically as popular taste evolves. In the process, concessions to local or regional tradition were usually minimal. The moral of William Wrigley's experience in marketing chewing gum applies to the full range of franchised and chain businesses as well as to manufactured commodities. "In 1906, William Wrigley had been in the chewing-gum business for fifteen years, producing several successful brands, each regionally popular: Juicy Fruit in Texas and the Southwest, Sweet 16 in the South. Rather than choosing to confront regional prejudice by making one of them into a national brand, he created a new flavor—Spearmint—that did not correspond to any of the existing types" (Strasser 1989, 142).

It is easy enough for the onlooker to be dazzled by the bright lights, garish signs, and architectural predictability of the businesses lining the commercial strips on the outskirts of any of our cities and to assume that all those nationally franchised service stations, motels, eating places, drug stores, clothing shops, and so on are incontrovertible evidence for the reality of a placeless land. But the actuality is more complicated. If we take eating places, for example, franchises and chain establishments are far outnumbered in most localities by independent locally owned and operated coffee shops, restaurants, greasy spoons, sandwich shops, caterers, and the like. The reader has only to check listings in his or her city telephone directory to verify the claim. And, then despite the fearsome ingenuity of the folks involved in becoming rich through broadening the scope of franchising, there are still quite a few lines of business that remain impregnable—for the time being. In table 2.1, I offer a partial list of such enterprises, to

Table 2.1. A Partial List of Types of Enterprises Not Yet Subject to Franchising

| | | |
|---|---|---|
| antique shops | drive-in movies | music schools |
| architectural offices | dry cleaners | musical instruments |
| army and navy stores | East Indian restaurants | painting contractors |
| art galleries | excavating contractors | pawn shops |
| art supplies | farmers markets | photographic studios |
| bail bonds | firework stands | plant nurseries |
| barber shops | fortunetellers | plumbers |
| beauty parlors | gift shops | pool halls |
| bicycle dealers | gun dealers | race tracks |
| body shops | horse farms, riding stables | shoe repair |
| bridal shops | Jewish delis | sign painting |
| cabinet makers | junkyards | tailors |
| carpet shops | landscaping services | tattoo parlors |
| Chinese restaurants | laundromats | taxidermists |
| costume shops | lighting supplies | tree surgeons |
| country clubs | locksmiths | used car lots |
| detective agencies | massage parlors | veterinarians |
| diners | monument dealers | wineries |

which I must append the thought that some of these unique, localized businesses *may* offer their own special landscape signatures.

Much less visible than the entities noted above is another industry—the mail-order business—that has probably done more to scrape off the social, cultural, and material irregularities of the American scene than any other. This is one of those innovations that was inevitable, awaiting only the arrival of proper postal and rail systems, the technology for cheaply printing massive amounts of text and detailed illustrations, and a few intrepid, tireless promoters to become a reality. It arrived simultaneously and developed along roughly parallel lines in the United States and Great Britain in the 1870s (Coopey, O'Connell, and Porter (2005, 14–15). "Montgomery Ward may be said to have started the mail order business in 1872 in Chicago. He was followed by Richard Sears, who put out his first catalog in Minneapolis in 1886 . . . The mail order system of distribution was ideally adapted to the needs of a large rural population scattered over a country of vast distances" (R. E. Wood 1948, 8).

Both Sears, Roebuck and the late, lamented Montgomery Ward were immensely successful in catering primarily to a rural and small-town clientele throughout the land (Asher and Heal 1942; Latham 1972) and were emulated by several smaller, but still profitable, mail-order houses. Eventually this pair of retailing giants set up a series of department stores in major cities. Although Sears and Montgomery Ward initially offered a rather limited range of commodities, they rapidly broadened their inventory until they were able to deliver all imaginable, and some unimaginable, items a family of modest means might desire. Thus, for example, at one time they provided their customers with gravestones at bargain prices and an assortment of nicely designed, affordable cottages, many of which are still in use today. Their catalogs, which overflow with raw material for historians and geographers, made no concessions to regional likes or dislikes, but we might conjecture that one could ferret out regional preferences if access to sales records were available. Still it is not excessive to claim that, more than any other single industry, the mail-order houses had smoothed out many of the visible wrinkles in the material face of the nation by the early twentieth century.

But perhaps even more consequential in cultural and psychological effect than whatever contribution the mail-order firms made to leveling place-to-place differences in outward appearances was the impact of the many millions of catalogs issued annually or seasonally and, in particular, the massive Sears, Roebuck productions. "To the western homesteader, the mail-order catalogue (often nicknamed the 'homesteader's bible') became a department store between covers, a banking and credit source, an etiquette adviser, and a down-home vade mecum of modernity" (Schlereth 1989a, 373). By midcentury, one observer noted that it had "become the best-known book in the United States, a part of American folklore, and, passing strange for a tool of business, it has also become the object of widespread affection. Wherever the traveler goes in the United States, he will find the catalog" (Emmet and Jeuck 1950, 255 [quoting David L. Cohn]).

The preceding paragraphs have chronicled the modern market system operating at full blast. The result—the standardized goods and services dominating shops and households from coast to coast, the seemingly endless repetition of look-alike franchise and chain stores, and all those shopping malls with a strong family resemblance—would convince the casual observer of the leveling power of capitalism working its sorcery under the sheltering wing of a benign state.[30]

But the most persuasive argument for the unifying potency of the modern market system is to be seen in the functional and symbolic heart of our collective existence: the downtowns, or central business districts, of our hundreds of urban places. The repetitive pattern speaks volumes. " 'You can tell what's informing a society by what the tallest building is,' the late scholar Joseph Campbell said in a television interview with Bill Moyers. 'When you approach a medieval town, the cathedral is the tallest thing in the place. When you approach an eighteenth-century town, it is the political palace that's the tallest thing in the place. And when you approach a modern city, the tallest places are the office buildings, the centers of economic life' " (Nisbet 1990, 7). And since money is the lifeblood of economic life, it is only appropriate that banks enjoy pride of place with their premises more often than not at the busiest downtown corner (Gill 1990, 5).

### The Military Gambit

The maintenance of a large citizen army and navy composed of volunteers or conscripts is one of the signal innovations of the modern nation-state, and nothing serves the nation-building project more effectively than having the armed forces wage the right kind of war. As suggested earlier, the involvement of the various colonial militias in Great Britain's North American conflicts may well have been a key factor in the gestation of future American nationhood. Then, although we might classify the American Revolution as a sort of civil war, the euphoria of hard-won victory among the rebels, a collective pride that glowed on for decades, most certainly fueled the lusty growth of nationalism in the young republic. However, the place of the military in antebellum America was not a privileged one. Indeed both army and navy remained puny in terms of size and appropriations. In a peculiarly American manner it was the local militias that captured the devotion of the citizenry at first rather than the national armed forces.

Subsequent international conflicts had mixed results in terms of strengthening the state or wiping out provincial attitudes. The virtually forgotten (though vividly recalled by Canadians) War of 1812 resulted in a stalemate after generating much intersectional political bickering. Similarly, the Mexican War was politically divisive, although it was a smashing military success.

The Civil War was entirely different matter, of course. Indeed it may be argued that, aside from setting the country irreversibly on its current economic and political path, the War between the States also profoundly altered the mind-sets of both North and South. In addition to instilling a sense of national purpose transcending locality or region among Northerners, the exposure of hundreds of thousands of Union troops to unfamiliar places and distant populations and to comrades from remote homes must have had its nation-building effect. And, similarly, among the Confederate warriors the conflict may have been crucial in crystallizing a sense of Southernness that still shows no sign of vanishing, but one that may have been only embryonic previously. "Four years of fighting for the preservation of their world and their heritage, four years of measuring themselves against the Yankee in the intimate and searching contact of battle, had left these Southerners far more self-conscious than they had been before, far more aware of their difference and of the line which divided what was Southern from what was not" (Cash 1941, 104).

The scorecard for the solidifying effect of subsequent wars presents us with a decidedly mixed pattern. The brief and triumphant Spanish-American War yielded both a flush of jingoism and a flurry of political protest, the latter especially virulent during the subsequent Philippine Campaign. In the case of the Indian Wars of the 1870s and 1880s and of various American military adventures in the Caribbean and Central America and along the Mexican frontier throughout much of the twentieth century, the public remained either unaware or indifferent. Americans were certainly aware of the Korean War during the early 1950s, but its impact on the domestic scene is problematic, as is the case of the widely approved first Gulf War in 1991. In violent contrast, the Vietnam War and the engagements in Afghanistan (2001–) and Iraq (2003–) have proved to be profoundly divisive along partisan or ideological lines if not in territorial terms.

We can advance the strongest case for the efficacy of the military gambit in bolstering national unity with the American experience during and after the two world wars. The entrance of the United States into World War I in

April 1917, after much anti-British and isolationist agitation, finally resulted in a condition of virtual hysteria, an unprecedented patriotic fervor (to the discomfiture of the large German American minority) that, one might argue, completed the healing process between North and South that had been advanced by the Spanish-American War. Then American participation in World War II (the "Good War") generated an even more meaningful coming together of the citizenry (excepting the Japanese Americans and some German Americans and Italian Americans) along with a massive churning and spatial redistribution of millions of volunteers and draftees and workers in munition and armament plants and shipyards. I dare say that never, before or after, have the American multitudes been so tightly joined together in spirit than they were on December 8, 1941 (unless September 11, 2001, takes the prize).

In addition to the direct contribution of certain military episodes to the cause of the nation- or statehood, in the afterglow following every major war with a positive outcome from the American Revolution onward, veterans established their long-lasting associations, some of which have maintained many hundreds of chapters throughout the land. Such groups as the Grand Army of the Republic, American Legion, and Veterans of Foreign Wars have exercised a good deal of political clout at the national level as well as more locally. They have consistently pushed a statist agenda in preference to local or regional interests.

This excursion into the military realm leads us, quite logically, into a consideration of uniforms. As a corner within the seemingly infinite cosmos of dress and ornament, the rich galaxy of uniforms is packed with information about individual and group identity and larger social and cultural questions.[31] Nevertheless, the topic has enjoyed remarkably scant scholarly attention. I can identify only three book-length treatments: those by Nathan Joseph (1986) and Jennifer Craik (2005) and Paul Fussell's (2002) collection of brief, witty essays. But these publications, useful though they may be, are far from definitive and leave much unsaid.

Although our immediate concern here is with the role played by uniforms in sustaining affinity with national or statist goals, they do serve other functions. Perhaps the most general of purposes is to associate the wearer with his or her occupation and often to elevate self-esteem. It is a relationship that transcends location or citizenship. Thus we have the costumes worn by the clergy, judges, academics (on special occasions), doormen, railway conductors and porters, symphony musicians, choristers, members of marching bands, ushers, chimney sweeps, chefs, nurses, many school students, members of athletic teams, and, in a less positive light, convicts.[32] Perhaps the transnational Standard Suit worn by executives and white-collar workers around the world also qualifies as a uniform (Joseph 1986, 69; Zelinsky 2004).

The most direct involvement of uniforms with the nation- or state-building project is, of course, their latter-day universality within the armed forces.[33] Thus it is rather surprising to learn of the long delay in achieving uniformity of uniforms within the American army, navy, and marines. "The dress of the Continental Army, though specified from time to time under general orders by the Commander in Chief, was rarely worn" (Elting 1974, v). Although there were attempts to standardize what was being used by service personnel as early as 1788 (Emerson 1996), success was long in coming, in part because of the involvement of many branches of the military and problems of supply. Indeed the process was not consummated for Northern troops until the end of the Civil War (Windrow and Embleton 1970). "Granted that most of the Union troops were more or less in issue clothing, we now are only beginning to appreciate the actual variety of what they wore" (Elting and McAfee 1982, vi).[34] But uniformity has been maintained quite rigorously in later times, albeit with periodic revisions to keep abreast of the winds of fashion.

Inspired by the military example, other branches of the national bureaucracy have rather recently adopted standardized garb for all those of their staffs who engage the public. Thus, in the case of the National Park Service, the rangers initially improvised their uniforms, but "superintendent Horace M. Albright changed this at Yellowstone in 1922 by requiring the purchase of a regulation uniform as a condition of employment" (Workman 1991, 4; also see Fussell 2002, 170–73). There have been similar developments for customs inspectors (U.S. Customs Service 1997) and, most conspicuously, among the great throng of postal workers. We might note, parenthetically, the national uniformity in post office vehicles and mailboxes. And, further, with only a slight stretch of the imagination, standardized post office buildings and federal courthouses amount to a kind of uniform in brick or stone.

Faithfully mimicking the federal model, state and municipal jurisdictions have instituted standard uniforms for state troopers, policemen, and firefighters (Fussell 2002, 93–96). Even though there may be minor variations from place to place, at any site one readily recognizes the job description of the workers in question. Then there are the Boy Scouts, Girl Scouts, and Camp Fire Girls with uniforms that resonate to the statist project.

There has also been a significant recent development within the civilian work force: mandatory adoption of corporate uniforms. Thus "above all, airlines recognize the importance of having a striking corporate livery" (Craik 2005, 119; also see Fussell 2002, 85–92). On a daily basis, we encounter the men and women of United Parcel Service and Federal Express wearing their prescribed costumes (and driving their instantly recognizable vehicles) (Fussell 2002, 80–84). Then, among many other examples, there are the countless employees of chain restaurants and fast food places and other retail chains who are obligated to observe the company's dress code, or the desk-bound office workers sporting the corporate blazer. "As the journalist Carina Chocano noted, "Recent decades have seen an explosion in the number of people who wear uniforms to work. An estimated ten percent of the American workforce is required to wear them every day" (ibid., 84). Jennifer Craik poses a thought-provoking question: "At a time when our culture is saturated with concepts of individuality and a preoccupation with consumer choice, uniforms are more pervasive then ever—especially in the workplace. Why are we so fond of conformity despite our quest for individuality and difference?" (2005, 106). Whatever the answer, it should be obvious that the boundary zone between state and private enterprise is quite porous and ambiguous.

## Economic and Demographic Convergence?

Given the vigor and multiplicity of the centripetal forces that have flourished across the land for more than two centuries, we can hardly avoid posing a key question: what degree of territorial uniformity has the American population realized in terms of its economic and demographic attributes?[35] This is not the occasion for a definitive answer. Bringing the issue up to date would call for a hefty monograph on the order of the massive three-volume study for the period 1870–1950 that Everett Lee, Carol Brainerd, Richard Easterlin, Hope Eldridge, Ann Ratner Miller, Simon Kuznets, and Dorothy Swaine Thomas (redoubtable scholars all!) managed to complete from 1957 to 1964 (Kuznets, Miller, and Easterlin 1960; Eldridge and Thomas 1964). What must suffice for the moment is the sketchiest of overviews.

As any detailed review of census data and compendia of vital statistics would readily confirm, the persistent trend in all the standard demographic measures from 1790 through at least 1960 has been a narrowing of differences among regions and states and between urban and rural communities. Such convergence is most emphatic in the case of sex ratios, but is also notable when we consider age structure, life expectation, fertility, death rates, marital status, household size and composition, literacy, and educational attainment.[36] But one must also note that, whatever convergence may have occurred nationwide in terms of morbidity and mortality, we still have to contend with major territorial differences in patterns of disease and cause of death (Pickle et al. 1996).

A goodly number of scholars have attacked the question of the spatial career of the American economy and with generally consistent results. For example, after examining state-level data on personal income and gross state product for the years extending from 1840 to the 1980s, Barro and Sala i Martin concluded: "We find clear evidence of convergence" (1990, abstract). Eldridge and Thomas, in summarizing statistics running from 1880 to 1949–51, observe that "it is apparent . . . that there is a marked convergence of subregional income levels toward the national average over time" (1964, 349; also see Bradshaw 1988, 58; Kim 1997, 28, 30). Moreover, an accompanying graph by Eldridge and Thomas and a set of four maps (1964, fig. 5.6, 347) vividly confirm a steady decline in regional disparities in service income per worker.[37] We find the same sort of change in labor force structure, at least at the state level. "State labor force structures, in terms of both participation rates and industrial distribution of the labor force, generally display considerably more similarity in the middle of the twentieth century than they did in the last decades of the nineteenth" (Kuznets, Miller, and Easterlin 1960; also see Easterlin 1960; Kim 1997, 31–32).

Then, after their analysis of all manner of demographic and economic indicators for the period 1790–1960, Labovitz and Purdy (1970) reach the firm conclusion of decided convergence among nine census regions. But the conclusion is much less firm when we introduce the factor of scale. If long-term demographic and economic convergence among census regions or states has been obvious enough, the picture can appear quite different at a more localized scale. Evidence abounds that the twentieth-century spatial segregation of classes and ethnic/racial groups within American cities far exceeded their relatively random disposition in the eighteenth century. Then, to take the example of one fairly old state, Kentucky: in its entirety it may well have narrowed its socioeconomic differences with other states over a two-hundred-year period, while it is arguable that its intercounty gaps in well-being were greater in 2000 than in 1800.

When we turn to the historical geography of the ethnic/racial composition of the American population, the scenario is a good deal more complex and challenging, and certainly not reducible to a simple plus or minus on the convergence scale. Anyone discoursing on the topic in the 1950s would have had a much easier task than mine today. The foreign-born, initially overwhelmingly of European origin, have accounted for a significant fraction of total population throughout American history. This was especially the case from about 1840 to 1914, when the immigrant tide was massive, so much so as to strike fear and loathing into the hearts of many of the native-born.

But, with the flood reduced to a trickle by World War I and the highly restrictive legislation in effect in the early 1920s, an assimilation process, already in full swing, had worked its magic. The children, grandchildren, and great-grandchildren of Caucasian newcomers had largely shed their alien ways, and, through education in school, church, and workplace, intermarriage, migration, and general acculturation, had become nearly indistinguishable from old-stock Americans.[38] Moreover, in 1950, as a percentage of total population, the foreign-born were down to 6.7 (as compared to 14.4 in 1910), with most of those individuals relatively advanced in years. The substantial minorities—African American, Native American, Latino, Caribbean, and Asian—were still socially and spatially segregated, although much interregional reshuffling of blacks had taken place, along with local shifts, a phenomenon intensively studied by demographers and geographers then and since.

The solid consensus, as of 1950 and still today, according to too many studies to cite, is that there had been little significant lessening of the spatial apartheid within American metropolises between blacks and Hispanics on the one hand and whites on the other. But the majority population was not greatly concerned with the spatial inequities of lesser breeds. In short, if ever there was an era when the melting pot seemed to have performed as hoped and promised, the 1950s would qualify. It may be more than mere coincidence that the decade in question was also one of exceptional prosperity and optimism, social conformity, and general self-satisfaction.

But it was not to last. Responding, if only indirectly, to large-scale forces operating throughout the world, in 1965 the U.S. Congress enacted a fundamental liberalization of immigration law, one opening the nation's gates to a larger, more diverse influx of future citizens. In addition, other legislation, before and after 1965, admitted significant numbers of refugees and asylum-seekers from various foreign military and political conflicts and other disasters. Then, at a rate that seems to rise every year, the United States has received a much more substantial volume of undocumented aliens, principally from Latin America and the Caribbean but from other parts of the world as well. The actual number of foreign-born persons illegally residing, or temporarily working, in the country is the subject of ceaseless controversy, but one may safely assume it to be in the several millions. In any event, according to the 2000 census enumeration, the foreign-born accounted for 11.1 percent of the total population. If we were to factor in all the illegals, that value must now exceed the previous maximum recorded in 1910. An additional consideration to keep in mind is that, taken in their entirety, the foreign-born register higher fertility rates than the native-born, thus amplifying their overall demographic impact.

Demographers have been paying close attention to the movement and location of the newcomers, a pattern involving many nontraditional destinations and a rather general spatial dispersion, in addition to concentrations in such major ports of entry as New York City, Los Angeles, San Francisco, Chicago, and Miami (Frey and Liaw 1999; Millard et al. 2004; Durand, Massey, and Capoferro 2005; Goździak and Martin 2005; Kritz and Gurak 2006; Lichter and Johnson 2006; Suchan, Perry, and Fitzsimmons 2007, 94, 97, 100–103, 141–54). In an effort to gain further insight into what appears to be a decided recent geographic diversification of ethnic scene in the United States, I have computed for all the metropolitan areas extant in both 1980 and 2000, according to the Bureau of the Census, the combined total of Hispanics and Asians, both native-born and immigrant, as percentage of total population.

Presented in table 2.2 are the figures for a large representative sample. Considering all the data, including places not listed in the table, I found that in every single case but one—Memphis, which experienced a slight decline—a significant increase in the Hispanic/Asian component had occurred over the twenty-year period following 1980, when the effects of the 1965 legislation had begun to be felt in a major way. The changes would have been even more striking if I had included the substantial number of other recent immigrants and their offspring, persons such as Africans, Haitians, Poles, Russians, Hungarians, and other Europeans.

In any event, what is startling, beyond the anticipated surge in numbers in metropolises already home to hosts of the foreign-born, is their substantial representation in the twenty-first century in places where they had been rarities in earlier times. Among the more notable examples are Charlotte and Raleigh, North Carolina, Atlanta (Duncan 2004), Poughkeepsie, New York, Elkhart, Indiana, Nashville, Green Bay, and Manchester, New Hampshire. Immigrants were attracted, though in modest quantity, even to cities within the so-called Rust Belt such as Detroit, Buffalo, and Pittsburgh. And who could have anticipated that Hispanics and Asians as a percentage of Atlantic City's population would jump from 4.4 to 19.4 over just two decades?

As always, the dominant factor guiding immigrants to traditional and novel destinations has been the economic. Thus the attraction of Latinos to the poultry industry in the Southeast (Haverluk 2004; Kandel and Parrado 2004) or packing plants in the central states (Chapa et al. 2004; Millard et al. 2004) or the drawing power of college towns and high-tech centers for the professionally trained. But, in addition, we have the well-meaning efforts of resettlement agencies that have directed refugees to some rather arbitrary locations, such as Laotians to Minneapolis–St. Paul (Brown, Mott, and Malecki 2007).

Table 2.2. Hispanics and Asians in Selected Metropolitan Areas as Percentage of
Total Population, 1980 and 2000

| | 1980 (%) | 2000 (%) | Increase 1980–2000 (%) | | 1980 (%) | 2000 (%) | Increase 1980–2000 (%) |
|---|---|---|---|---|---|---|---|
| Los Angeles, Calif. | 19.4 | 57.1 | 37.7 | Providence, R.I. | 2.5 | 10.5 | 8.0 |
| Fresno, Calif. | 32.1 | 55.2 | 23.1 | Charlotte, N.C. | 1.5 | 9.2 | 7.7 |
| Phoenix, Ariz. | 8.8 | 31.1 | 22.3 | Oklahoma City, Ok. | 3.2 | 10.9 | 7.7 |
| Las Vegas, Nev. | 9.6 | 31.3 | 21.7 | Ann Arbor, Mich. | 3.6 | 11.2 | 7.6 |
| San Francisco / | | | | Hartford, Conn. | 5.4 | 12.9 | 7.5 |
| Oakland, Calif. | 20.5 | 42.1 | 21.6 | Minneapolis– | | | |
| Houston, Tex. | 15.5 | 36.9 | 21.4 | St. Paul, Minn. | 2.0 | 9.2 | 7.2 |
| San Diego, Calif. | 19.4 | 39.9 | 20.5 | Hickory, N.C. | 0.9 | 7.8 | 6.9 |
| Dallas– | | | | Champaign– | | | |
| Fort Worth, Tex. | 9.4 | 29.1 | 19.7 | Urbana, Ill. | 3.5 | 10.4 | 6.9 |
| Orlando, Fla. | 4.5 | 22.8 | 18.3 | Milwaukee, Wisc. | 3.0 | 9.8 | 6.8 |
| Reno, Nev. | 6.8 | 23.9 | 17.1 | Athens, Ga. | 1.5 | 8.1 | 6.6 |
| Poughkeepsie, N.Y. | 3.6 | 19.4 | 15.8 | Grand Rapids, Mich | 2.7 | 8.9 | 6.2 |
| Miami, Fla. | 24.1 | 39.2 | 15.1 | Ocala, Fla. | 2.2 | 8.0 | 5.8 |
| Atlantic City, N.J. | 4.4 | 19.4 | 15.0 | Madison, Wisc. | 2.1 | 7.8 | 5.7 |
| New York, N.Y. | 12.4 | 27.3 | 14.9 | Des Moines, Ia. | 2.1 | 7.6 | 5.5 |
| Sacramento, Calif. | 14.5 | 29.1 | 14.6 | Manchester, N.H. | 1.1 | 6.5 | 5.4 |
| Chicago, Ill. | 9.0 | 23.2 | 14.2 | Kankakee, Ill. | 1.6 | 6.9 | 5.3 |
| Washington, D.C. | 5.7 | 19.7 | 14.0 | Green Bay, Wisc. | 0.8 | 5.9 | 5.1 |
| Seattle, Wash. | 5.7 | 18.1 | 12.4 | Rochester, Minn. | 1.7 | 6.8 | 5.1 |
| Denver– | | | | Bloomington– | | | |
| Boulder, Colo. | 12.0 | 24.4 | 12.2 | Normal, Ill. | 1.5 | 6.3 | 4.8 |
| Portland, Ore. | 3.9 | 15.4 | 11.5 | Lansing, Mich. | 3.7 | 8.4 | 4.7 |
| Salt Lake City, Utah | 6.2 | 17.1 | 10.9 | Lexington, Ky. | 1.1 | 5.8 | 4.7 |
| Fayetteville, Ark. | 1.3 | 12.0 | 10.7 | Philadelphia, Pa. | 3.4 | 8.1 | 4.7 |
| Elkhart, Ind. | 1.6 | 12.0 | 10.4 | State College, Pa. | 1.9 | 6.4 | 4.5 |
| Tyler, Tex. | 3.5 | 13.9 | 10.4 | Indianapolis, Ind. | 1.2 | 5.3 | 4.1 |
| Atlanta, Ga. | 1.7 | 11.8 | 10.1 | Lawton, Okla. | 7.3 | 11.4 | 4.1 |
| Nashville, Tenn. | 1.0 | 10.8 | 9.8 | Columbus, Ohio | 1.4 | 5.5 | 4.1 |
| Burlington, N.C. | 0.8 | 10.2 | 9.4 | Asheville, N.C. | 0.7 | 4.7 | 4.0 |
| Boston, Mass. | 3.6 | 12.9 | 9.3 | Detroit, Mich. | 2.4 | 6.4 | 4.0 |
| Boise City, Idaho | 3.1 | 12.3 | 9.2 | Binghamton, N.Y. | 1.3 | 5.2 | 3.9 |
| Raleigh, N.C. | 1.6 | 10.8 | 9.2 | Buffalo, N.Y. | 1.7 | 5.3 | 3.6 |
| Bridgeport, Conn. | 8.3 | 17.1 | 8.8 | Fargo, N.D. | 1.0 | 3.6 | 2.6 |
| Worcester, Mass. | 2.5 | 11.0 | 8.5 | Pittsburgh, Pa. | 1.0 | 2.2 | 1.2 |
| Bellingham, Wash. | 1.8 | 9.8 | 8.0 | | | | |

Mexicans and other Latinos have been such a large, conspicuous component of the ongoing incursion that some observers have proclaimed the
Hispanicization of the country and the mainstreaming of Mexican American
culture (Haverluk 2003), but possibly in ways that do not replicate earlier
immigrant experiences. Thus Mike Davis claims that "as emergent Latino
pluralities and majorities outgrow the classic barrio, they are remaking urban
space in novel ways that cannot be assimilated to the earlier experiences of

either African-Americans or European immigrants" (2000, 39). But, whether it is Latinos or others, there is no doubt of the emergence of distinct new neighborhoods in a number of cities, places that show no sign of fading away soon, such as a Puerto Rican district of Cleveland (Benedict and Kent 2004), a Vietnamese enclave in suburban Washington, D.C. (J. S. Wood 1997b), and the transformation of formerly Jewish Devon Avenue in Chicago to a bustling East Indian hub (Rangaswamy 2006).

It is now abundantly clear that there has been a serious interruption in the mashing of America. Overall, then, since 1965 the nation has experienced a significant increase in ethnic diversity, but an increase shared quite unevenly from place to place. With no end in sight to further licit and illicit additions to the country's population from other lands, we can anticipate fresh and larger lumps in that immense melting pot we call the United States.

## Entering a New Epoch
### The Score So Far

By any objective standard, the American achievement, the fabrication of a seemingly monolithic nation-state, is quite astonishing. Could even the boldest soothsayers in 1783 have foreseen a country whose 300 million–plus loyal inhabitants had succeeded in occupying a vast transcontinental expanse within a tightly integrated political and economic system, one displaying a notable degree of sameness from coast to coast? Given a virtual tabula rasa in which to operate—an overwhelmingly rural society on the cusp of modernity characterized by a marked degree of premodern social and economic sameness—an omnipotent economic system in lockstep with an ever more potent centralizing political regime had worked its sorcery.

We have witnessed the efficacy of deploying a set of nationalistic symbols in creating a unified mind-set. In practical everyday terms, the federal government has operated in many ways so as to bring about a homogenized land: by instituting a postal system serving every home and business; by the methodical surveying of unoccupied portions of the national domain; by adopting a standard currency and ways of measuring every significant dimension of physical objects and encouraging standard time zones; and by waging at least one Good War and making uniforms part of daily existence.

On their own, ordinary citizens have enlisted in the nation-building project by patronizing lyceums, Chautauquas, and, yes, circuses, reading jingoistic publications and singing patriotic songs, engaging in baseball, the national pastime, and sending their children to public and private schools where national glory and love of country form important components of the curriculum. All the foregoing developments have resulted in a perception shared and cherished among nearly all of our third-of-a-billion citizens: that the United States is a transcendent, indivisible entity, a noble brotherhood providing us with the most meaningful of personal and collective identities. Whatever the objective reality, this perception matters mightily.

Then, in the form of game-changing innovations, most notably in the realms of transport and communication, but also by introducing air-conditioning, modern technology has been conspicuously successful in transforming the land and greatly lessening place-to-place differences. In addition, the business community has been hyperactive in shaping a uniform, placeless throng of consumers by means of mass-produced commodities and services, franchised and chain retail enterprises, mail-order firms, and, of course, advertising. But one must qualify this triumphalist tale by noting that major business corporations have not driven from the scene all those many local independent shops, although the attrition has been fearful, and that, as subsequent chapters will demonstrate, significant residual regional cultural patterns still persist and all manner of unpredictable features in the humanized landscape can surprise the American traveler. And if our eighteenth-century cities and towns were a reasonably egalitarian jumble of social groups, classes, and occupations, since sometime in the mid-nineteenth century urban places have been stubbornly balkanized in terms of class, income, and racial/ethnic identity. No abolition of placefulness here.

### The Big Sort

As I have already argued, after some two hundred years the convergent trends noted above appear to have attained their ultimate success in the 1950s, or perhaps the early 1960s. It was then that, despite the occasional temporary setback and the frustrations of the Korean War, the general trajectory of economic growth and personal flourishing from colonial times onward had moved the country up to a level beyond historical precedent. The age-old challenge of physical survival had been met and overcome, and material betterment for each succeeding generation was now something to be taken for granted. All regions and virtually all cities were being buoyed upward on a sea of rising prosperity. There had been a marked narrowing of the economic gap between regions and a reduction of differences among the various portions of the country in all the important demographic indexes and measures of social well-being. All this and something approaching obliteration of the venerable gulf between town and country and virtual amnesia concerning the plight of immigrant and racial minorities.

For many Americans, then and now, this extended/climactic decade (realistically a period lasting from the late 1940s through 1963)[39] may have seemed bland and boring, lacking the sizzle of the 1920s and its Jazz Age, the rich cultural and political ferment of the 1930s, or the social convulsions of the 1960s (the fabled decade that actually ended in the early 1970s), but "for most Americans in the midfifties, the United States was a very good place to live . . . With this atmosphere it was perhaps inevitable that the midfifties would be a time of consensus. Not for many decades had so many Americans agreed upon so many fundamental issues" (Oakley 1986, 314). But late in the decade and signaling the imminent arrival of new varieties of woe, there came a significant development in social space (and thus a topic tangential to this geographic enterprise): the Generation Gap (McCormack 1985, 11; Oakley 1986, 314). Subsequently, of course, we have experienced much finer temporal slicing of the population beyond the initial binary split between older and younger.

Then, following the quietude of the 1950s, something profoundly unsettling and largely unexpected came to pass, and quite abruptly, during the final third of the twentieth century.[40] We would do well to be wary of the Presentist Fallacy, the understandable human tendency to consider one's particular lifetime as the most important ever. However, there is now such a powerful understanding, one shared by much of the general public as well as virtually all the concerned scholarly community, that we have just passed a "hinge moment" in the human chronicle that there can be little doubt of our having suddenly entered an unprecedented era. What remains undecided is what label to attach to the current period. Postmodern, Post-Fordist, Postindustrial, Postmaterialist, the Age of Authenticity? In any case, a seminal study by Ronald Inglehart and Christian Welzel provides us with the grand historical panorama, the "human development sequence," within which we can begin making sense of recent evolutions.

> The core of the human development sequence is the expansion of human choice and autonomy . . . During the past half century, socioeconomic development has been changing people's formative conditions profoundly and with unprecedented speed. Economic growth, rising levels of education and information, and diversifying human interactions increase people's material, cognitive, and social resources, making them materially, intellectually, and socially more independent . . . In short, socioeconomic modernization brings the objective capabilities that enable people to base their lives on autonomous choices. (2005, 2–3)

The historical uniqueness of contemporary America manifests itself in several ways. One of the most fundamental changes has been in the realm of religion. Concurrent with serious declines in the fortunes of main-line denominations, including the Roman Catholic as well as Protestant—and thus in inter-generational fidelity—has been the rise of evangelical, Pentecostal, and other fundamentalist movements, along with explosive growth in megachurches in suburbia and exurbia and an equally significant boom in unconventional spiritual questing. Then, as we have seen, the ethnic complexion of the country has been acquiring novel forms and levels of complexity since 1965. Also symptomatic of the new order of things has been the slivercasting of radio, television, and cyberspace audiences, as we have also noted above.

The past few decades have seen a profound restructuring of the American family as more and more couples cohabit without benefit of a marriage license, gay and lesbian couples have begun to win social and legal acceptance (and some have begun to cohabit *with* the benefit of a marriage license), divorce becomes routine, aged parents and grandparents less often share the household, and both partners are so frequently wage earners. There has also been a dramatic improvement (but still far from complete) in the status of women and seismic shifts in sexual attitudes and practices. Then we have a recent, qualitatively deeper American engagement in transnational transactions, financially, touristically, culturally, and otherwise.

But the truly revolutionary development has been the utter latter-day centrality to the socioeconomic and geographic scene of the self-actualization of the individual, "doing one's thing," This is something due, in no small measure, to rises in both personal income and level of education. As the journalist Bill Bishop put it, "unsurpassed prosperity had set people free— free to think, speak, move, and drift. Unsurpassed prosperity had enriched Americans—and it had loosened long-established social moorings" (2008, 255).[41] One of the general results of this burst of self-fulfillment has been a greater emphasis on consumption of the good things of life, including optimum places for work and leisure.

The ongoing geographic consequences of the "Big Sort" (to quote the title of Bishop's groundbreaking report) are manifold. At the macro scale, as the hard-to-classify social scientist Richard Florida (2002, 2005, 2008) has painstakingly demonstrated, the economic fortunes of census regions and, more particularly, metropolitan areas have been diverging as relatively young, skilled, upwardly mobile participants in the creative industries have gravitated to locales offering diversity, tolerance, cultural excitement, and other amenities, but, perhaps most critically, a critical mass of like-minded folks. Consequently, over the past few decades there has been a radical departure from the earlier historical geography of metropolitan economies. We must wait patiently, possibly for decades, before scholars furnish us with definitive analyses of economic and demographic developments since the

1960s such as we have for the previous hundred years. But some provisional generalizations are at hand.

Whereas previously all American cities of a certain size shared a ride on an upward economic escalator, nowadays it is only the fortunate minority that enjoys growth in wealth, population, and appeal to talented and ambitious self-seeking migrants. Left in the dust are the metropolises that offer few or none of whatever qualities resonate with post-industrial sensibilities. And they are either stagnating or suffering loss of numbers, morale, and vitality (Florida 2008, 93–99).

At a more intimate scale and to a degree unparalleled in the past, Americans have been sorting themselves out in space in terms of class and income (whoever heard of gated communities two generations ago?), age, political ideology, religious orientation, leisure pastimes, and cultural appetites, in addition to whatever residual racial/ethnic segregation may still prevail. To take just political segmentation, there may be no emphatic spatial trends in the relative strength of the two major parties at the state level (as discussed in Chapter 5), but analysis at the county level reveals that "from 1980 to 2000 the segregation of Republicans and Democrats increased by about 26 percent" (Bishop 2008, 10); and the percentage could be even higher were we to examine ballots by precinct.

In an original and promising approach to finding geographic logic in such diversities within what had been an apparently homogenizing nation, Michael J. Weiss has come forward with the cluster concept (1988, 2000). Using zip code areas as spatial building blocks and exploiting the databases of the marketing firm Claritas, he identified some forty clusters in his initial volume and sixty-two twelve years later.

> The characteristic that defines and separates Americans more than any other is the cluster . . . Every household has been assigned to one of these clusters, and their tastes and attitudes have been predicted by census data, market research surveys, public opinion polls, and point-of-purchase receipts. According to cluster theory, people with similar demographics naturally gravitate to each other and share similar tastes in products, services, media, and homes—whether they live down the block or in another cluster community across the continent. (2000, 178)[42]

The picture that emerges from the numerous maps provided by Weiss is that of a flawed mosaic, one in which the befuddled artist has not gotten the pattern quite right. Thus there is a decided, somewhat predictable, but far from perfect, repetition of the tiles—clusters with such fanciful labels as Winner's Circle, Golden Ponds, Norma Rae-ville—in logically ordered arrays across the country.[43] This intriguing tessellation is in a state of constant flux, as Weiss is at pains to point out, and is something that surely merits further monitoring and analysis. Unfortunately, the social science fraternity has failed to rise to the challenge thus far. Aside from problems entailed in gaining access to proprietary data, other scholars may be dissuaded by Weiss's huckstering tone in publications that seem inspired more by the pot at the end of the rainbow than by disinterested enlightenment.

If there can be little doubt that what we are witnessing today in the United States—and, to a certain extent, in other first world nations and the more fortunate developing countries—is no longer simple geographic homogenization of people and places but rather an intensifying specialization of economic function at the regional and metropolitan level and the parceling, the sorting out, of distinctly different residential areas at the neighborhood scale. Although it is extremely foolish to try anticipating future developments in anything as complex as the social geography of the United States, how can one help wondering about the sustainability of the present situation?

And there is a supreme irony in that present situation, almost as though the gods have been perpetrating a cosmic jest. The current phase of the human geography of the United States and other privileged lands could not have been realized until most of the general population reached a critical, unprecedented level of affluence circa the 1960s. But, virtually simultaneous with this achievement, whether by chance or through some deep underlying mechanism, we have also begun to witness overall economic stagnation or, possibly, signs of an impending long-term downturn. Although a few thousand Americans may have become grotesquely wealthy and too many free-spending others have gone deeply into debt, for the vast majority of the wage-earning population real income has not gone up but, to the contrary, has been declining perceptibly since the early 1970s. Thus, inter alia, the great surge in female employment, two-earner families, moonlighting, delayed retirement, and so on. Moreover, at the time of writing, the economic (not to mention ecological) outlook for the nation and the world at large is at best problematic. What will be the consequences for our post-1965 geographic patterns? The only answer is to live long enough to find out.

IN SUMMARY, then, this chapter has chronicled the radical transformation of the human geography of what became the United States during four centuries of European occupation. In the simplest of terms, what we have witnessed has been the replacement of one form of social and geographic homogeneity throughout the land, an essentially premodern pattern, by an utterly distinct and novel modern variety. Thus, until the nineteenth century was well advanced, an overwhelmingly agrarian society (outside the few commercial centers of consequence) everywhere followed much the same ways of living and working within largely self-sufficient communities enjoying only weak, sporadic contact with the greater national or world economy.

Then, over the past century and a half, the constantly growing might of the modern market system, working in tandem with a centralizing state, has fashioned a totally different sort of place-to-place sameness. It is one in which people and places have become intensely integrated over space and interdependent economically, socially, culturally, and politically. But, unlike its predecessor, the contemporary spatial order is not one of simple replication from one patch of settlement to another. Instead the United States can be characterized as a collection of several dozen kinds of population cells or clusters, each distinct as to socioeconomic composition and each repeated, with modifications, from one location to another from border to border.

So have we already answered the central question that drives this inquiry? Not at all. As three of the later chapters will demonstrate, when we view the American scene at different angles and at a more intimate scale, some interesting complexities emerge and render problematic any straightforward answer to the question of placelessness.

# 3 Pondering the Built Landscape

In chronicling all the many mechanisms working over time toward the "mashing of America," the previous chapter does indeed present a strong case on behalf of the Homogenization Hypothesis. But we have not yet turned our gaze—or that of our imaginary traveler—on the actual scene. When we do so, scrutinizing the built landscape, despite some interesting qualifications, the case becomes even more persuasive—and the relevance of the Big Sort somewhat questionable or peripheral.

What is it that we are looking at? Paraphrasing the words of the late, great J. B. Jackson, the built landscape, as distinguished from whatever the "natural" or non-human landscape may happen to be, is a composition of man-made or man-modified spaces and things serving as infrastructure for our collective existence. It is so vast, complex, and time-dependent an assemblage of features, one that cries out for monographic treatment,[1] that what follows can be no more than a sketch, albeit one that demands far more verbiage than any single topic in our other chapters. I must also gratefully note that, in considering the built landscape, and in contrast to most of our other topics, we are generally blessed with an abundance of data. Although certain significant features still lack serious treatment, for others, such as houses, barns, and town morphology, we have almost too much detail, thanks to the labors of cultural and historical geographers, folklorists, architectural historians, historic preservationists, artists, photographers, and lay enthusiasts. I hasten to add that, like language, religion, and other items, the landscape artifacts we create also respond to central axioms of our cultural systems.

Contrary to popular mythology, when European explorers and settlers entered North America in the sixteenth century, they did not encounter a pristine wilderness. What they found instead was a profoundly humanized

82

continent inhabited by many millions of persons who had been present for quite a few millennia. These aboriginal societies had greatly modified fauna, flora, soils, and terrain. We can credit them, inter alia, with creating and maintaining large tracts of grassland and open forest, laying out a network of foot trails, inventing a variety of dwellings, and building substantial settlements, especially in the Mississippi Valley.

Although we can never piece together the totality of the pre-Columbian built landscape, it is clear that its character varied considerably from place to place. Today, despite the near-extinction of the First Nations, their physical traces are still quite visible, and not just in those corners of the Southwest, Pacific Northwest, and other regions where they manage to hang on. Thus we have those many hundreds of ceremonial or burial mounds, some of impressive size, most notably in the Ohio Valley, the cave dwellings and surviving Hopi pueblos in New Mexico, substantial kitchen middens along stretches of the South Atlantic and Gulf coasts, and various modern highways that faithfully follow the routes blazed by our predecessors, not to mention a rich legacy of place-names.

### The Era and Spaces of Local Initiative

All those settlers arriving from Europe, Russia (spottily in Alaska), Mexico, and the Antilles—and the slaves from Africa—brought with them their particular nonmaterial culture but also whatever technology, tools, plants and livestock, and notions as to what comprised a proper living and working habitat they had inherited. Given such diverse heritages and the varied degree of unfamiliarity of their new surroundings, the obvious outcome was a spatially contrasting set of built landscapes.

The initial chore of appropriating or purchasing land and bounding it did not involve any consistent set of practices in the future United States until the federal government intervened with its system of rectangular survey in the 1780s, as did a few of the states at various times. Until then, an irregular metes and bounds system prevailed within tracts occupied by Northwest Europeans (Price 1995) and has persisted ever since, causing endless vexation among proprietors and attorneys, while traditional patterns of land division were followed in the Southwest by Hispanic pioneers thrusting northward into a rather familiar environment. As in Quebec, the French long-lot pattern along river valleys dominated early Louisiana and portions of Texas (Jordan 1974). All these property lines seem destined to last in perpetuity. Roads—almost never hard-surfaced—footpaths, and farm lanes were improvised by early human occupants and their livestock. Many of these sinuous passageways remain on the scene in modernized form.

*House Types*

After the frontiersmen crept out of their tents or whatever crude shelter they managed to cobble together from tree boughs, hides, canvas, turf, or anything else that was at hand, the first order of business was to construct weatherproof dwellings or perhaps barns or stables for the livestock. In doing so, they honored the mental templates imported from overseas or, in the case of the Hispanic Southwest, from Mexico and, ultimately, Iberia.[2] The usual result was a stripped-down version of whatever had been popular in a quite specific corner of the previous homeland—be it in England, Scotland, Wales, Ulster, Flanders, the Netherlands, France, Scandinavia, Switzerland, or Germany—and thus much place-to-place diversity in the early American settlement scene. In the semiarid Southwest, adobe and stone had to suffice, but in the well-watered eastern half of the country, with its superabundance of timber, wood became the universal building medium. Clearly the process of *interaction with the environment* dominated the earlier phases of European settlement since pioneers could seldom avail themselves of materials shipped in from distant points.

If wood prevailed at first, it was in the form of thick-hewn planks, boards, poles, and shingles, but decidedly not logs. Despite the popular legend to the contrary, the first western European settlers along the Atlantic seaboard were unacquainted with log-building techniques. Only toward the end of the seventeenth century, with the advent of Swedish and Finnish settlers, and perhaps some Germans and Swiss from certain Alpine tracts, do we find knowledge of this simple, cheap, and superlatively effective mode of constructing houses, barns, and outbuildings diffusing to the population at large (Shurtleff 1939; Jordan 1985). But once it did, the technology spread like wildfire; and, as it diffused, considerable local and regional variety ensued in terms of log-notching and overall design of structures (Jordan 1978a; W. E. Roberts 1984).[3]

But what to do when the forest peters out, as happened to those homesteaders who ventured into the Great Plains? In the treeless environment of most of Kansas and Nebraska, where lumber and brick were not viable options for cash-strapped pioneers, they began resorting in the 1870s to building houses, barns, and even schools and churches from thick blocks of sod (Welsch 1968; Muilenburg and Swineford 1975, 25). Later, of course, such structures were replaced by wooden ones after highways, railroads, and a degree of prosperity made such acquisitions feasible.[4] Trying another expedient, a number of ordinary settlers in north-central Kansas built homes, shops, and other structures from a local bed of singularly workable limestone, a mode of construction otherwise quite rare in America except among the well-to-do (Muilenburg and Swineford 1975, 58–88). Still other possibilities were the use of baled hay for wall construction, a practice carried on in the Nebraska Sand Hills from 1910 to 1940 (Welsch 1968, 109) or building in clay or adobe during the pioneering phase of settlement in the Great Plains (D. Murphy 1989).

Left to their own resources, the pioneering farmers, ranchers, and townspeople and their offspring devised their own local or regional versions of a proper dwelling, many examples of which have survived to this day. The relevant literature (for example, Finley and Scott 1940; Kniffen 1965; Kniffen and Glassie 1966; Rickert 1967; Glassie 1968; P. F. Lewis 1975; McAlester and McAlester 1984; A. G. Noble 1984a) is so large and detailed that there is not enough space here for even a skeletal account. Suffice it to say that readily recognizable regional house types developed early and, in many instances, have proved durable. That statement is especially valid for the Hispanic Southwest (Newcomb 1937),[5] the Mormon Culture Area, New England, and the Pennsylvania Culture Area; but, as we shall see, it does not apply to Hawaii and most of the present-day South, except perhaps for southern Louisiana (Kniffen 1936). The premodern South, however, was indeed home to a quite distinctive suite of house types (Scofield 1936; Zelinsky 1953; Vlach 1986 [1976]).

It is important to keep in mind that all the relevant literature thus far cited refers to folk or vernacular structures, the handiwork or commissions of working-class and middle-class homeowners. By contrast, the fortunate affluent few who formed society's elite dwelt in another architectural universe. They flaunted their status, then as now, by choosing the most elegant and trendy styles current in Europe or the country at large. Thus, for example, the fabled antebellum plantation houses of the Deep South were knockoffs of the most opulent, up-to-date residences of the Northeast (Bonner 1945; Zelinsky 1954). Needless to say, it is the homes of the wealthy that are now most zealously preserved and celebrated.

### Barns

Often the largest, most visibly striking object in the rural built landscape of yore (and even today) was the barn. Admiration for the ingenuity and inventiveness of their builders has bred a copious literature as well as sporadic efforts at preservation. Thus we have wide-ranging, detailed monographs and inventories spanning the continent (A. G. Noble 1984b; Zielinski 1989; Noble and Cleek 1995; Vlach 2003) and poetic tributes in the form of drawings and photos (E. Sloane 1954, 1985; Plowden 2003). The place-to-place variety of the structures is impressive. It reflects the localization of knowledge and skills transmitted from the Old World and place-specific innovation as well as the demands of particular crop systems and types of animal husbandry, so that we have, for example, studies of tobacco barns (Hart and Mather 1961; Raitz 1975) and dairy barns (Durand 1943).

In terms of regional coverage, the barn types of southeastern Pennsylvania may be the most intensively studied and gaped at (Bastian 1975; Ensminger 1992), but other localities have not been neglected (Francaviglia 1972; Carlson 1978; Raitz 1978; Noble and Wilhelm 1995). Of peculiar interest is the connecting barn that is such a conspicuous feature in much of northern New England (Zelinsky 1958). In a definitive study, Thomas Hubka (2004) has ascertained that the practice of joining farmhouse to stable and barn was not simply a response to climatic conditions but rather an expression of social values in the early nineteenth-century region.

Although the first generation or two of American barns has been superseded by modern types, many specimens have survived weathering and neglect when they have not been plundered of their timbers. Moreover, it is not uncommon to see handsome old barns used for storage or converted into dwellings, shops, or small factories. It is safe to assume much local and regional variation in the many outbuildings that accompanied house and barn on early and later farms—the corncribs, aviaries, icehouses, smokehouses, poultry coops, and pigpens, and an assortment of sheds—but the topic has yet to receive much systematic attention.

*Fences*

We do, however, have some scholarly notice of one essential feature adjoining virtually every farmstead, field, and pasture: fencing. It was an urgent matter for early cultivators and ranchers to keep livestock confined within designated areas and to keep marauders out (Mather and Hart 1954; Zelinsky 1959; Stilgoe 1982, 188–92) except in much of the South, where an open range system for livestock has long prevailed and may still be practiced in certain localities. The simplest, crudest temporary expedient, but one calling for backbreaking labor, was to line up stumps of uprooted trees so as to engirdle the newly created field or pasture. In glaciated tracts, notably New England, rocks cleared from the enclosed area could be heaped together to form an effective barrier, and one requiring little, if any, future care. In the case of the prospering Kentucky Bluegrass, where suitable trees were scarce, skilled craftsmen fashioned many hundreds of truly elegant stone walls from quarried materials (Murray-Wooley and Raitz 1992).[6] Then, in one stretch of the unforested Great Plains, north-central Kansas, settlers turned to quarried stone for fence posts after the arrival of barbed wire (Muilenburg and Swineford 1975, 6–7), thereby fashioning a unique landscape.[7]

More generally, however, landowners turned to a variety of wood fences after the initial clearing of land, and most especially to rail fencing in all its many geometries and varieties. The use of split logs or tree limbs suitably mounted, with or without supplementary rocks and a bit of wire, was quick, relatively simple, and called for no cash. A number of localized styles evolved and are still available for inspection today in some of the more remote corners of Appalachia and other derelict areas. Where local timber was not an option and the price of shipping lumber was excessive, as in the early years on the Great Plains, there was much experimentation with hedges, most notably Osage orange, but with unsatisfactory results, in part because it took several years before the plants matured to the point of effectiveness. Unlike the situation in western Europe, where hedgerows frequently dominate the scene, today on this side of the Atlantic they are common only in certain portions of Maryland and Virginia. Among the remaining choices for enclosures, we have only board fences, painted or otherwise, and iron fences and gates to consider; but, during the early period of settlement, none but the more pretentious of dwellings in city or village would be so adorned.

A thoroughgoing account of early rural America would necessarily include some discussion of the morphology of farmsteads and of field patterns. As for the latter, there is reason to believe that regional differences prevailed in the size, shape, and orientation of the various plots of soil plowed or hoed within a given farm, but the two solitary published ventures into this question (Hart 1968; McHenry 1986 [1978]) examine only limited areas. Similarly, two pathbreaking studies of the regional characteristics of American farmsteads (Trewartha 1946, 1948) have yet to inspire further inquiry into the historical geography of the complex assemblage of objects that comprise our farmsteads.

### Bridges and Other Necessities

Given the rudimentary development of roads and the usually abysmal quality of roadside accommodations, cross-country travel could be a fearsome ordeal during the earlier phases of American settlement. Not the least of the hazards was traversal of streams too deep or swift for wading. Where a river was broad and the traffic brisk enough, a ferry might be available. Elsewhere simply thrusting a log across the stream might do for the intrepid pedestrian; and, occasionally, someone might improvise a rope and wood-slat contraption that would provide a wobbly passage on foot. But, of course, such crude expedients were of no help for someone driving a wagon or coach.

Although documentation is sparse, we may assume that some communities were able to afford simple stone bridges or causeways or had carpenters capable of erecting usable, if fragile, structures from local timber and rock. A more general solution had to await advances in technology, as we shall see in this chapter. But, in the interim, Yankee ingenuity came up with a clever device: the covered bridge. As detailed in a classic account of the diffusion of an innovation (Kniffen 1951), an early nineteenth-century New England invention spread rapidly throughout much of the eastern portion of the country and even beyond to Oregon and Washington. A roof over a wooden carriageway served to weatherproof it and prolong its life, so that many—nearly a thousand in the United States and Canada and each of singular design—have managed to live on and become objects of nostalgic veneration and much tourist activity (R. Wells 1931; McKee 1997).[8]

The viability of every community depended on the operation of a gristmill and sawmill, preferably no farther than a day's journey from the customer, while tanneries were only a moderately less urgent resource. The siting of these facilities rested on the availability of timber, water, and water power. But another widespread enterprise—the distilling, legally or otherwise, of whisky and other strong spirits—was less discriminating as to location. Just how ubiquitous the industry may have been, or how uneven its distribution, remains a cloudy issue since we lack a detailed geographic inquiry. But is seems likely that the incidence of stills may have been relatively high in those frontier zones where conversion of corn and other grain into a more portable liquid made good economic sense when transport to long-settled communities was so costly. The political unpleasantness in western Pennsylvania in the 1790s suggests such an interpretation.

Pig and wrought iron for the fabrication of all manner of items has been another key commodity throughout American history. The initial geography of iron furnaces followed no easily predictable spatial pattern. Only select locations, many of them in the Appalachians, offered the necessary combination of adequate bodies of ore and abundant timber for producing charcoal, along with limestone and water (Bining 1938; Stilgoe 1982, 290–300). The resulting constellation of facilities, accompanied by small ramshackle settlements, all of which certainly accentuated place-to-place differences, operated at full blast from colonial times until the mid-nineteenth century. After being outmoded by more advanced technologies, they dwindled to extinction during the World War I era, but a number of the durable stone structures still receive tender loving care from preservationists.

### Cemeteries

An unavoidable feature of both town and countryside, in early years and today, is the burial place. Initially, the preferred site was in the churchyard, if space was available and accessible. It would be some years after the frontier phase before towns or villages would set unsanctified ground aside for general cemeteries.[9] But another practice that is now quite rare was interment in the vicinity of the home.[10] A more widespread pattern was the creation of informal community cemeteries—folk cemeteries we might call them—strewn throughout early rural America. Although many of these older burial grounds are no longer readily visible to the casual traveler, having been neglected and abandoned, most of the relatively durable headstones remain and old maps offer useful clues. Much fieldwork remains to be done, but we have enough information at hand to state that, in addition to quite real distinctions in style along ethnic and denominational lines, there has been, and still is, genuine regional differentiation in cemetery characteristics within the United States.

The most striking case may be that of southern Louisiana, whose primarily French deathscape closely resembles what we observe in Latin America, both areas with obvious antecedents in Mediterranean Europe (Nakagawa 1987). Within this region, one that I call Acadiana, interment in Catholic cemeteries is almost always above ground in structures that can be rather large and ornate and often bedecked with statuary. Contrary to popular belief, this practice is not related to drainage problems in this low-lying terrain; nearby Protestant and Jewish graves are usually dug well below the surface. The remainder of the South is also a place apart in terms of mortuary custom, with such distinctive elements as grave houses and shell-covered graves (Jeane 1969, 1989; Jordan 1980, 1982), and the sheer number of folk cemeteries.[11] The prevalence of scraped ground and the kinds of decorative objects on southern African American graves may suggest African influences (Vlach 1977). Then, no one examining graveyards in the Hispanic and aboriginal Southwest would confuse such places with a Connecticut cemetery. And, of course, the well-studied cemeteries and the gravestones of New England (for example, Ludwig 1966) are intimately associated with the culture of that region.

As an indication of how much remains to be learned about the necrogeography of our land, I can cite the outcome of an analysis I did of the number of named cemeteries (the great majority presumably old) per one hundred square miles by county based on data in the USGS's Geographic Names Information System. The resulting map (Zelinsky 1994a, 34) is profoundly puzzling. The clustering of high values throughout a swath of the Upper South from southern Ohio to northern Alabama and Mississippi stands in sharp contrast to a near-dearth in the South Atlantic states. No solution to the mystery is in sight.

*Town Morphology*

When we turn to the morphology of early American cities and towns, we fail to discern much consistency from region to region or even among neighboring places. Indeed many an agglomerated settlement came into existence without any preplanning at all, with Boston a prime example; they simply grew in response to the whim of property holders. Thus, in an era of ad hockery, the lack of any commonality in the essentially medieval street layouts of New England villages and cities and certainly throughout the South. But, perhaps thanks to the powerful example of Philadelphia, with its unique, widely applauded rectangular scheme structured around open squares, we find strong family resemblances among the street patterns of most Pennsylvania cities and towns founded before 1815 (Pillsbury 1968). On the other hand, Savannah's much-admired plan inspired no copycats in inland Georgia.

But once the founders of towns and cities had reached the territories surveyed in keeping with the federal rectangular system, the pressure to lay out streets and property lines parallel to section lines became irresistible, so that we begin to see a city-planning mind-set that transcends region (Reps 1965). One specific feature of the nineteenth-century American city must be mentioned, one that spread nationwide, but later fell out of fashion: the alley (Clay 1978; Borchert 1980). They furnished living space for servants and others, access to storage sheds, gardens, and garbage bins, among other things, and, at least in the case of the Pennsylvania alley, room for small business enterprises.

The authorities platting county seats faced a particular challenge: where to place the courthouse and how to design the space around it. In a definitive study, Edward Price (1968) was able to identify the date and origin of the basic schemes, their diffusion outward to the later locations, and a definite regionality in their distribution, a geographic pattern that endures.

Church buildings, overwhelmingly of the Protestant persuasion, claimed visual prominence in early American cities and towns by virtue of height and central, or near-central, placement. Their architecture reflected the ability of the congregation to adopt whatever style was fashionable in the Western world at the moment rather than any regional initiative. In the countryside, however, simpler structures prevailed; and, in the South at least, most of such surviving examples as we have, whether white or black, seem to be definitely regional in form. And, of course, in the Hispanic Southwest, houses of worship, then and now, bore little resemblance to those in the remainder of the nation.

Elementary and secondary school buildings were not conspicuous elements in earlier America. Indeed many classes were held in churches or other public buildings. Eventually, the now-vanishing one-room schoolhouse, the object of much latter-day sentimentalizing, dotted rural landscapes (Harker 2008). No one has suggested any regional variation in their utilitarian design. However, as noted elsewhere, from the outset college campuses managed to assert their individuality. William and Mary would never be mistaken for Yale or for the University of Georgia.

## Modern Technology Takes Over

The preceding pages have sketched the landscape of a still essentially premodern, if decidedly non-medieval, America, a period drawing to a close by the 1840s or 1850s. Thereafter, and especially after the Civil War, the built landscape underwent profound revision as the telegraph, railroad, telephone, and other new technologies, mass education, maturation of the business corporation, mass production of a broad range of commodities, the publication of manuals and plans for builder and householder, and an ever more potent centralized political system became decisive factors in the life of the national community.

### The House

Perhaps the best way to begin surveying the changing scene, as modern technology and nonlocal forms of social organization come to the fore, is to consider the buildings we call home. In doing so, we confront an uncomfortable fact: that the reality departs so drastically from a coveted ideal. As Douglas Kelbaugh puts it in a rousing, but defensive, manifesto dealing with dwellings designed individually by architects:

> Architecture is in a rare position to embody and express regional differences—more so than manufactured products like cars, chairs, shoes, or even clothing. Perhaps only food is local, although regional food products are now shipped far and wide. Because architecture is one of the few remaining items in modern life that is not mass produced and mass marketed for the masses [a debatable proposition!], it can resist the commodification of culture. Because it is site-specific and one-of-a-kind production, it can resist the banalization of place. And because it is one of the few handbuilt items left in the industrialized world, it can resist standardization. Architecture can still be rooted in local climate, topography, flora, building practices, architectural types, cultures, history, and mythology. (1997, 52)[12]

But, unfortunately, what we actually see in so much of the world, and especially in the United States over the past century and a half, is a standardization of dwellings from place to place, the repetition en masse, of a set of designs that varies more over time than it does over territory. Indeed, if we restrict our gaze to domestic structures, the case for placelessness seems irrefutable. But why is the argument so particularly persuasive in the American case? Part of the explanation is the remarkably meager emotional and symbolic investment restless Americans make in their residences (G. W. Pierson 1973). In contrast to a number of other countries, it is the rare individual in the United States that can claim the same address from birth to death or who can trace house ownership across two or more generations.[13] Leaving aside the substantial percentage of the population that rent apartments or houses or live full time in vehicles, homeowners (with or without mortgages hanging over their heads) usually find only temporary comfort and pride in their real estate. Fundamentally, they consider their dwelling place to be a financial proposition, a commodity they hope will appreciate over the years. Thus, for many, the property is simply a speculative venture they may not even live in, something to be "flipped" or razed for profit, for only the exceptional few, the place where they will spend their remaining years. For still others, it is one of two or more fungible items, including a second home or two, they may use in the course of a year. The same general observation about the superficiality of our attachment to the things we build and live in applies even more forcefully to commercial structures and other workplaces that only rarely are objects of genuine affection among proprietors or clientele or are candidates for indefinite preservation.

The standardization in question has come about through the efficacy of mass communications and mass production of commodities.[14] In an earlier America, knowledge of how to design and construct a dwelling, or other structures, was almost entirely local and traditional—except, of course, among the more knowledgeable elite—and the building materials came from the immediate vicinity. Although pattern books for architects and their well-heeled clients had existed since the mid-eighteenth century, if not earlier (Reiff 2000), it was only in the mid-1800s, with rising incomes and literacy, that such publications reached a large house-building public. The especially influential works of Andrew Jackson Downing (1842, 1861) had many competitors. Subsequently, American architectural journals began to flourish within the profession, disseminating plans and discussions of salable designs far and wide (Reiff 2000, 127–48). Then, during the twentieth century, we find on virtually every newsstand a number of periodicals devoted to shelter issues for the general public that are loaded with detailed plans and instructions for building one's dream home. Not to be ignored amid these developments is that clever American invention, the balloon-frame house, originating circa 1833 with number of carpenters experimenting independently, and becoming widespread by the 1850s (Boorstin 1965, 148–52; F. W. Peterson 2000). It rendered a process that had been slow, calling for much lumber and a certain degree of skill, into something fast, cheap, and easy.

In another inevitable development, shrewd entrepreneurs soon realized there was money to be made not only in selling house plans (T. W. Harvey 1981) but in actually manufacturing all the components of a limited number of models and then shipping them to the construction site along with the necessary instructions (Reiff 2000, 149–255). Sears, Roebuck was only one of several firms engaged in this profitable business. Discussing the 1906–40 period, Daniel Reiff concludes that

> the total for all these sources [precut houses and firms selling material to go with mail-order plans] could possibly be around 1,200,000 houses ... However, in the context of *all* privately owned dwellings (excluding farm-houses) erected ... from 1906 to 1940, which comes to 11,680,000, this is a reasonably small portion approximately 10 percent. We must remember, however, that the number of houses constructed by contractors and carpenters who ... simply referred to, modified, or perhaps at the time just pirated published designs from the catalogs of plan companies or firms selling precut dwellings was apparently considerable. (2000, 254–55)

The same author in 1984 conducted a unique inventory of all dwellings, some 2,239, in the reasonably representative town of Fredonia, New York, classifying them by type, and found that about 12 percent of the 1820–1890 houses were based on designs in books. But "there are ... for the period of c. 1890–1940 about 450 houses (roughly 75 percent) that can be linked, directly or indirectly, with designs in books. Clearly, the impact of these catalogs on the styles built in this typical village was profound, far greater than the estimated number of precut houses or mail-order plans sold would suggest" (Reiff 2000, 302).

The next logical step was another American invention, evidently in the 1920s (Hart, Rhodes, and Morgan 2002, 6), one that has spread, with less pervasiveness, to other parts of the world: the mobile home and its sibling, the motor home, both of varied size, design, and quality (Wallis 1991; Gellner and Keister 2002; Keister 2004; Trant 2005). These are items assembled in factories, then shipped to dealers or families to be bought or rented. They may be anchored to a given plot of land permanently, but always with the option of being wheeled away. The truly mobile domicile—the RV or motor home—is perpetually on the move with only temporary sojourns on permissible sites. "Virtually every place in the United States, no matter how small, has a cluster of mobile homes out at the edge of town. Larger places have more and larger clusters, many formalized as mobile home parks" (Hart, Rhodes, and Morgan 2002, 77). The increase in the number of such utterly placeless residences is impressive, and the number promises to keep growing: "In the single year 2000, mobile homes accounted for about 20 percent of all new single-family housing starts and about 30 percent of all new single-family homes sold, and enthusiasts predicted that mobile homes would soon comprise more than half of all new homes" (ibid., 1). And not to be overlooked is an interesting minority of Americans who dwell in manufactured boats which may or may not be docked indefinitely at a given location.

Nevertheless, the majority of single-family dwellings have continued to be built in the conventional fashion over the past two centuries. For those affluent enough to afford the current architectural fashion, there appeared a succession of styles without discernible regional differences, as related in any number of architectural histories: the progression from Georgian and Greek Revival to Gothic, Italianate, Queen Anne and other Victorian variants, a Georgian revival, various borrowings from overseas, including British and French villas, and Moderne.

But still standing in areas of premodern settlement, as in New England and Pennsylvania (Zelinsky 1977), is a substantial legacy of houses and other structures unmistakably indigenous to the region. However, as the population grew rapidly, and urbanization and suburbanization even more swiftly, builders have usually resorted to a limited repertory of geographically anonymous designs for working-class and middle-class clientele—with occasional local exceptions. There remains much opportunity for exploring late nineteenth-century and twentieth-century housing stock—the houses and apartment buildings in the city proper, excluding suburban developments—in urban places large and small and whether and how there may have been local deviations from national sameness.

The local exceptions we do know about are quite interesting, and suggest we give further thought to the inevitability of coast-to-coast conformity. The best documented exception may be the bungalow, a building type with an East Indian pedigree (Lancaster 1986 [1958]; King 1995), which enjoyed an especially warm reception in southern California in the early twentieth century. There "it came to capture certain qualities which were specifically Southern California" (Winter 1980, 7) and generated a number of appealing variants. A simplified offshoot, the small brick bungalow that dominates broad swaths of Chicago, but has yet to be celebrated by connoisseurs, flourished there in the 1910s and 1920s and perhaps in a few other cities in the same general region. As I can attest from prolonged exposure, Chicago builders also spawned their own special designs for two- or three-story brick apartment structures in a manner paralleling what happened in several cities in central New England with their distinctive wooden three-deckers with an individual family occupying each flat (Tunnard and Reed 1956, 59). In a similar fashion, much of early twentieth-century single-family construction in Brooklyn follows a locally distinctive style. In all such examples of local peculiarity we have cities large enough for builders and developers to invent something novel that appeals to their clientele, all this in keeping with the doctrine of *cultural drift.*

Then we have San Francisco, that compact city with its unbroken ranks of uniquely designed single-family wooden and stucco houses squeezed into narrow lots before and after the disaster of 1906. In recent years, many of the older frame structures with late Victorian gingerbread have become splendiferous multihued "Painted Ladies" (Pomada and Larsen 1978) to the delight of photographers. Such imaginative color palettes have spread to other cities, but only in a limited way. Color is also an issue elsewhere, as in northern New England, where French Canadian immigrants have shocked their Yankee neighbors by daubing previously white houses and barns with outlandishly bold pigments. In similar fashion, we see Mexican Americans in Los Angeles and elsewhere modifying the buildings and yards acquired from their Anglo predecessors (Archer 2005, 362), and Italian, Portuguese, and other immigrant families erecting religious images in front of their properties in various northeastern cities.

One of the more notable of localized architectural enthusiasms was the rage for Art Deco that flared up in several cities in the 1920s and 1930s, but most extravagantly in Miami Beach (Curtis 1982; Capitman 1988; Breeze 2003). Then, as in so many other departments of sociocultural behavior, the Southwest, despite a strong infusion of Anglos, has resisted national trends in all forms of architecture, jealously retaining or reinventing its Hispanic/aboriginal heritage. The most extreme example is that of Santa Fe, which, beginning in 1912, has systematically rather cynically reshaped itself into a simulacrum of an imagined past. "Santa Fe has methodically transformed itself into a harmonious Pueblo-Spanish fantasy through speculative restorations, the removal of overt signs of Americanization, and historic design review for new buildings" (C. Wilson 1997, 232; also see Markovich 1990). But the impulse is region-wide (Gebhard 1990, 140; also see C. Wilson 1990).[15]

Then, in the case of the Pacific Northwest, we detect stirrings of a serious trend toward fashioning a new regional style in keeping with the distinctive physical attributes of western Washington and Oregon (Woodbridge 1974; Kelbaugh 1997, 55–58; D. E. Miller 2005).[16] We broach here a topic to be explored in greater depth in another chapter, a rekindling of regional spirit as manifested in the choices of architects and homeowners. As Jim Kemp describes:

One of the focal points of this movement back to the future is the reacquaintanceship by architects, designers, and homeowners with a long-neglected realm—regional architecture and design. Rising out of and, in a sense, embodying a particular location and cultural tradition, each of America's native housing styles—from the New England Saltbox and the New Mexico adobe to the Southeastern Dogtrot—is being enjoyed once again for its inherent beauty and practicality. (1987, 8; also see Dixon 1974; Speck and Attoe 1987)

And he goes on to provide many examples, region by region.[17] It is interesting to note parenthetically that this trend is clearly associated with a more general retro mood as shown, inter alia, in the widespread recent appearance in suburbia of replicas of the American farmhouse of the late Victorian era and other styles from the past (Dostrovsky and Harris 2008).

When we turn to suburbia and exurbia, spatial realms that now claim an ever larger share of the national population, it is to find—at least outside the Southwest and certain enclaves of tradition along the Atlantic seaboard—an overwhelming sameness from coast to coast. Within any single developer's project one usually encounters a remarkable poverty of architectural imagination. No single house style dominates, while one is benumbed by the profusion of ranch houses or "ramblers," along with variants on a basic tri-level design, simplified Georgians, Neoclassical themes, Norman chateaus, and cookie-cutter McMansions (Gowans 1986; Archer 2005). Such differentiation as is visible appears in terms of date, that is, the coming and going of building fashions, rather than location.[18]

Thus, in scanning post–World War II dwellings in the younger tracts of our cities and the spaces beyond, an emphatic repetitiveness appears in their outward physical presence. Because of the increasing number and size of the indispensable auto, gone is the freestanding garage in the rear (Clay 1978, 13–14). The automobile now claims its sovereign station as an integral, streetward-facing part of the house, with room for one, two, or even three vehicles and miscellaneous storage—or, at a minimum, a carport—and a paved driveway that may also harbor an RV or motorboat.

Also gone, with scant regret, again thanks to modern technology, is the formerly universal outhouse, an artifact that apparently lacked any regional aspect in its design (Strombeck and Strombeck 1980; Booth 1998),[19] along with the chicken coops and pigpens of yore and most woodpiles. Only occasionally can we glimpse a clothesline, its function now taken over by the electric dryer in the bowels of the dwelling. With some frequency, especially in the non-South, the national flag may be flying from a pole in the front yard or on a staff attached to the house. Applying an artistic fillip to the face of property, we find a flourishing recent fad in the hanging aloft of colorful, decorative banners with or without verbiage.[20] The front yard often sports playful wooden or ceramic objects, while whimsicality may run amok in mailbox design (Epstein 1996). Then, as noted elsewhere, most self-respecting citizens will decorate house and lawn with appropriate items for the Christmas, Easter, and Halloween seasons, and pious immigrants and their offspring set up effigies of divinities (Curtis 1980; Sciorra 1989). Depending on the affluence of the owner and size of the backyard, it may contain a swimming pool, tennis or badminton court, jungle gym and other kinds of juvenile play apparatus, barbeque setup, utility shed, and doghouse (the last item a venerable adjunct to the American homestead).[21]

Despite the various deviations noted above, there is no avoiding the obvious overall appraisal. Over the past 150 years, sense of place has been drained from our American houses and their grounds. The forces of *cultural diffusion* and *the modern market system* have crushed the life out of an older diversity. If we need further confirmation for such a claim, look at what we do with the space between building and street.

### The Great American Lawn

Today nothing is more universal or quintessentially American than the (hopefully) well-manicured lawn adjoining every single single-family dwelling with any amount of available soil. Obsession is not too strong a term to use in discussing the phenomenon (Steinberg 2006). Lawns do occur in other lands, of course, but are generally treated rather casually except among the nobility and gentry of the British Isles and northwest Europe. The American lawn as a sine qua non of respectability, and indeed legally mandated in the codes of many municipalities, is a relatively late development. It may have been "a pre-Revolutionary feature common to all the Northern colonies and well established by the early national period of the United States" (T. O'Malley 1999, 65), but only among the likes of Washington and Jefferson and other members of the elite.[22] Thus "in the 1840s, Downing reported that although the horticultural skill of lawnmaking was still not commonly found in America, the situation was improving" (T. O'Malley 1999, 81).

> The idea of cultivating grass around homes did not become popular until the Civil War. Before then, most people in towns and cities either maintained small fenced-in vegetable gardens or simply left the area alone, allowing it to revert to dirt interspersed with whatever vegetation flourished. "The well-trimmed lawns and green meadows of home are not there," wrote Charles Dickens on a tour of New England in the eighteen-forties. And as for the back yard, with its outhouses, no one would dare think of planting turfgrass and holding a family occasion there. (Steinberg 2006, 11–12)

After the Civil War, with increasing wealth, a rising middle class, and a series of technical advances, the well-kept grass lawn began to form an essential element of the American Dream. "In the eyes of the new American leisure class, for which higher cost meant higher beauty, the lawn conferred signs of acquired nobility" (Teyssot 1999, 9).[23] The invention of, and constant subsequent improvements in, the lawnmower (replacing the occasional horse or sheep) made lawn maintenance relatively painless. Some entrepreneurs soon realized that much profit was to be garnered via the selling of the lawn idea, and proceeded to exploit the potentialities through skillful advertising and development of new and better seeds, fertilizers, herbicides, tools, and methods of lawn care, a story quite effectively chronicled by Virginia Scott Jenkins (1994). Finally, "with the housing boom following the Second World War . . . the idea of perfect turf became a national pre-occupation" (Steinberg 2006, 13).

What we behold today, then, through individual aspiration, common social assent, and governmental surveillance, is a land in which virtually every single-family dwelling (apart from beach houses and wilderness cabins), apartment complex, public building, office park, modern cemetery, ceremonial space, and municipal park features a more or less carefully tended grass lawn. All this despite the enormous expenditure of time, labor, and cash, the demands on an increasingly burdened water supply, and the demonstrably heavy damage to the environment and ecosystem (Steinberg 2006). There has been a certain amount of backlash. Despite all the ingenuity of plant breeders, acceptable grass lawns are difficult to grow and maintain in such places as Florida and southern California and almost impossible in Arizona without excessive investments of money and attention. Thus the growing acceptability of desert landscaping in communities like Tucson (Hecht 1975) and the appearance here and there of maverick householders who flout neighbors' scorn by letting their yards revert to prairie or whatever local conditions may produce.

### Second Homes

Up to this point we have bypassed a largely unprecedented, constantly accelerating development in the American (and world) residential scene: the second home. Although even as early as the colonial era the well-to-do could afford to maintain a seasonal retreat for their families amid pleasant surroundings (in addition to frequenting spas), the notion of owning or renting a summertime vacation cabin, or perhaps even something more sumptuous, at some distance from one's regular residence did not become widespread until well into the twentieth century. An even later, quite logical development was conversion of the second home into a year-round domicile on retirement. We have here the combined effects of *demographic change* and *the pleasure principle* and a phenomenon rendered possible for the working class as well as the middle class in general and for the elderly in particular by rising incomes, improved transportation, and advances in communication media. Thus the census counted 1,050,466 second homes in 1959, or 2.28 percent of all residences, but more than three times as many, 3,604,216 in 2000, some 3.11 percent of the total in question (Shellito 2006, 196). Furthermore, "nationally, in 2001, approximately 5.5 percent of all homes sold each year were second homes" (ibid., 195), with Michigan, Wisconsin, California, Arizona, Texas, New York, and Florida as the most popular destinations.

This seasonal, and eventually permanent, shifting of several million Americans has resulted in a sharp intensification of regional diversity as well as sociological complications. The migrants in question have sought out amenity-rich locations with access to ocean, lake, forest, desert, scenery, or other attractions, but often, as in the Ozarks or hilly tracts of southern Illinois, in areas where the indigenous folks are economically distressed. Most of the inland second homes are architecturally unpretentious, not usually facsimiles of standard suburban styles. On the other hand, the often opulent beach houses that line the Atlantic, Gulf, Pacific, and, occasionally, Great Lakes waterfronts display wide departures from conformity in design (Irvine 1990; McMillan 1994). Indeed architectural ingenuity and playfulness run riot along these sandy or rocky strands, so that we are constantly surprised by the most venturesome experiments in postmodernity as well as ramshackle huts, all devoid of reference to region. But the significance of the second home reaches beyond demographic and architectural considerations. In a world where many persons feel placeless, the recreational cottage "provides continuity of identity and sense of place through symbolic territorial identification with an emotional home" (Williams and Kaltenborn 1999, 223; also see Gustafson 2006, 29).

## The Modern American City

It would take many volumes to document and interpret fully the shaping of American cities over the past century. For present purposes, however, suffice it to say that, since the 1840s, the evolving morphology of the newer ones and accretions to older places followed much the same general scenario (Reps 1965, 1981). "Overall . . . one must be impressed with how effectively standardized architecture and design (e.g., building form, street pattern) created a readily identifiable 'American town' appearance from coast to coast in the nineteenth century" (Francaviglia 1996, 127). Not the least of formative forces behind the standardization of so many street plans was the advent of the railroad, especially as the founder and sustainer of railside communities (J. B. Jackson 1972, 67–69; T. W. Harvey 1982, 1983; Hudson 1985).

The central business district calls for special comment. A commercial downtown, or Main Street, however lively or ailing, has been a universal, persistent feature of all American urban places, and they share a strong family resemblance throughout the country (Rifkind 1977; Macdonald 1985; Liebs 1985).

Richard Longstreth is apparently the only scholar to date to have attempted a typology of urban commercial architecture. A key observation of his merits quoting at length.

> A third important difference in this typology is the absence of pronounced regional distinctions. Whereas early house typologies were developed as a means of delineating cultural regions, there is no comparable basis for classification of commercial architecture. Locational variations certainly can be found in the use of materials, elements, and historical references. Some types may be more prevalent in certain parts of the country than others. But when viewed from a national perspective, these aspects are minor compared to the basic similarities that exist . . . Competition among the communities further stimulated the tendency to conform . . . cities strove to upstage one another in a battle for economic hegemony. Architecture offered a potent symbol in these contests. Through commercial buildings, towns sought to look like cities, small cities to look like larger cities. Examples in the major metropolises set the standard. Under the circumstances, the conspicuous presence of ethnic roots or regional peculiarities in a commercial district was the last attribute community boosters wanted. (1986, 14–15)

The facades of street-level shops and offices may change over the years to keep up with fashion, even if the upper stories may not, but, again, outside the self-consciously regional Southwestern, Southern California, and Florida cases, all our Main Streets are as interchangeable as pieces in a Tinkertoy set. Elsewhere within the city or its periphery we encounter the same predictable series of chain or franchise enterprises, each with its readily recognizable design (Vieyra 1979; Lohof 1974; Hirshorn and Izenour 1979; Langdon 1986; Jakle, Sculle, and Rogers 1996; B. L. Thomas 1997; Jakle and Sculle 1999). Perhaps the sturdiest of these images over time and territory has been the hamburger-dispensing White Tower system. "In more than fifty years of development the White Towers have formed a particularly complete and sophisticated set of stylistic variations on one strict symbolic theme—a white building with a tower over its entrance" (Hirshorn and Izenour 1979, v). Then McDonald's highly standardized Golden Arches have become so widespread as to be inescapable.

But there is one intriguing regional exception: the diner. Originating in Worcester, Massachusetts, in 1898 as a lunch wagon (Gutman 2000, 18), it became quite popular in much of New England, then in New Jersey, New York, and eastern Pennsylvania. In the 1960s, some five thousand of these roadside converted railroad cars or fancier, but still distinctive, mutants were still in business, usually with Greek American proprietors and heavy on Italian and Greek menu, while approximately two thousand remained extant in 2000 (Gutman 2000, 170, 245–69). Explaining just why the genius loci was compatible with this novel form of eatery only within a restricted territory could tell us much about the essence of American cultural regions.

There is also a temporal exception: the movie palace (Pildas 1980). From the 1910s to about 1930, every sizable city was the proud possessor of one or more ornate, exotic movie theater. The gaudiness and occasional brilliance of marquee, box office, and entrance, as well as auditorium, all usually totally bereft of regional reference, added a flash of architectural unpredictability to otherwise routine Main Streets.

We also have the question of whether railroad stations have contributed to the individuation of cities. Unlike industrial or warehouse architecture in general, which seldom, if ever, offers any hint of regional affiliation (Bradley 1999), the railroad depot, standing as it does close to the heart of the city, can be the object of considerable civic pride and even a symbol of local identity. Indeed the grander railroad stations were once regarded as modern cathedrals. "The lavishness of the new stations [1860–90] . . . so often reminded their contemporaries of medieval cathedrals—stations which embodied the triumph of the picturesque eclectic aesthetic in complex massing, bolder symmetry, pointed vaults, and towers" (Meeks 1956, 90). And indeed the grandeur of such edifices as New York City's 1869 Grand Central Station—the first American example "capable of standing comparison with the finest European ones" (ibid., 49)—and later its Pennsylvania Station, Washington's Union Station, and Chicago's cluster of downtown depots did bolster a sense of place during their heyday. How much they added to the regional cause is another matter. In his study of sixteen stations build from 1885 to 1939, Christopher Brown (2005) identifies only three exhibiting a regional style. It was in the Southwest, again, that architects celebrated a Hispanic tradition.[24]

The widespread availability of electric power by the late nineteenth century enabled every city of a certain size to replace its horse-drawn transit system with motorized cars rolling along steel rails. Although virtually all the trolleys have been superseded by buses, many of the rails remain. Less durable was an extensive light-rail electric interurban network that flourished, largely within the northeastern quadrant of the nation, during the early twentieth century carrying commuters and interurban passengers at a leisurely pace (Hilton and Due 1960; J. E. Vance 1986, 392–95). With the ascendancy of the auto and bus, this landscape feature has been abandoned, leaving few traces behind.

It was within the modern American city that civil engineers, exploiting the newest technologies and materials, and often a liberal imagination, designed and erected a number of signature bridges (Plowden 1984; D. C. Jackson 1988; DeLony 1993). Several firms with a national reach had already replaced the rather primitive items local craftsmen had devised with a set of standardized designs for structures crossing lesser streams in the hinterlands. It was the majestic bridges spanning grander water bodies in metropolitan settings that stirred the popular imagination, enriching the placefulness of their places, and generating symbolic messages. Thus one can hardly visualize San Francisco without its Golden Gate Bridge or St. Louis without the Eads, or even Chicago without its relatively modest, but photogenic, Michigan Avenue Bridge. But no city has more fully basked in the engineering glory of its bridges than New York, with its girdle of spans serving Manhattan, and most especially the iconic Brooklyn Bridge, which has inspired so much art, photography, and literature, as well as birthday celebrations (Trachtenberg 1965).

But even more decidedly than bridges, we have in the case of that towering technological marvel, the skyscraper, the ultimate metropolitan statement. Rendered possible by improved steel, concrete, and glass technology, electric-powered elevators, and, less obviously, the telephone, it was Chicago architects and engineers who invented the skyscraper toward the close of the nineteenth century (Starrett 1928, 1–44). Although it may have been safe to say in the 1920s that "the skyscraper is the most distinctively American thing in the world" (Starrett 1928, 1), that distinction rapidly became obsolete. Not only did every up-and-coming American city (except Washington, D.C.) hasten to emulate the Chicago pioneers, but eventually just about every ambitious metropolis in Europe (aside from stodgy London and Paris), Russia, Asia, Australia, Latin America, and Africa have joined the competition (Goldberger 1981; Huxtable 1984).

Some of the bolder efforts have succeeded in serving as unique visual slogans for the locality. Thus, within New York City, we have had at least four powerful examples: the Woolworth Building, Empire State Building, Chrysler Building, and the late, lamented World Trade Towers—skyscrapers that so often serve to establish the site during the opening frames of a film. Similarly, in the cases of Boston, Pittsburgh, Chicago, Detroit, and San Francisco, each has had at least one instantly recognizable skyscraper that became emblematic of its surroundings. On the other hand, large cities everywhere are becoming crowded with a profusion of anonymous, placeless high-rise office and apartment buildings and hotels, still another symptom of globalization. Or else they exhibit flamboyant eccentricities that capitalize on the latest international trend but say nothing specific about geographic identity.

Another elevated structure, but on a much humbler scale than the skyscraper, has punctuated the modern American urban scene: the water tower or tank. Although the oldest example dates back to 1754–61 in Bethlehem, Pennsylvania (Hazlehurst 1901, 5), with two stand pipes presumably fed by gravity, apparently this water supply system did not come into general use until the advent of electric motors. Thus, as of 1901, we have a report of some 992 elevated metallic storage tanks throughout the land, 535 of which were erected in the 1890s (Hazlehurst 1901, 6). Their number has grown since then, of course, with their acquisition by virtually every municipality and many a factory, college, and other institution without any regional differentiation except for the popularity of water towers clad in wood in certain of California's coastal tracts. In smaller towns, the water tank may be the tallest artifact present, and we often find it emblazoned with the name of the place along with some choice facts or sentiments. It has also proved to be an irresistible target for the more audacious of graffiti artists.

If skyscrapers have lost much of their place-making magic, modern technology has afforded at least a few cities the opportunity to assert their special personalities via the medium of startling electronic advertising signs, often with moving images and blazing colors. Although Los Angeles and perhaps a few other metropolises have toyed with the strategy, clearly the two champion cases are Las Vegas (Venturi 1972) and New York City's Time Square (Levi and Heller 2004; Berman 2006, 3–19). In fact, it is difficult to think of either place without an automatic mental image of their astonishing billboards.

What can our airports tell us about the place-making possibilities of advanced technology and architectural cunning? After their modest, fumbling beginnings in the early twentieth century, engineers and architects found no earlier models to turn to, unlike earlier designers of the larger railroad stations who could quote the language of traditional public buildings. In any event, no consistent pattern has ever evolved. But, as it happened, one of the earlier expedients was the regional theme. Thus the first Atlanta airport sported a Confederate motif (Gordon 2004, 62) and "a [1930s] terminal for El Paso, Texas, was designed in an Alamo-meets-Buck Rogers style of faux ruined stucco and stonework. In 1936, San Francisco built a Spanish-style terminal with terra-cotta tiles and coffered ceilings. Albuquerque's new terminal, opened in 1939, was modeled after Pueblo Indian architecture with adobe walls and rustic timbers" (Gordon 2004, 62; also see 60–61).

Airports lack one of the crucial advantages enjoyed by railroad stations: near-centrality of siting and thus a certain pride of place. If downtown workers, shoppers, and other pedestrians may be unable to avoid viewing these imposing structures, recent generations of airports are located far outside city centers. One never approaches them on foot or bicycle, and, although some are genuine architectural gems, but with no regional flavor, others may be little more than functional sheds. The harried passenger seldom can pause on the approaching highway to evaluate them or is in the mood to do so. Rather than acting as an anchor of local identity, our larger metropolitan airports are non-places par excellence inadvertently symbolizing the rootlessness and impersonality of so much of contemporary existence.[25]

But these grander airports have begun to transform the anatomy of metropolitan areas by creating a novel sort of edge city.

> Airports of the 1960s offered urban planners a new template for the modern city—one that would resolve the problem of the old city center by ignoring it altogether. Gigantic new complexes . . . were no longer like cities, but were real, self-contained urban nodes, servicing millions of passengers a year and hiring thousands of employees . . . Jet-age airports would have their own police and fire departments, power plants, fuel dumps, dentists, doctors, hotels, conference centers, and, in some cases, theaters, nightclubs, and churches. (Gordon 2004, 184)[26]

Also occupying outlying sites are the newer cemeteries serving our urban populations. Many, possibly most, of the current generation of these burial places, often operated as commercial enterprises, are of the modern lawn species, smooth expanses of mechanically mown and watered grass (technology strikes again!) with a minimum of flowers or shrubbery, within which small metal or stone markers, flush with the surface, record the final resting places of the deceased. Whatever regional connotations one can glimpse in the older cemeteries are absent here.

In contrast, the final component of our relatively late urban scene has little, if anything, to do with modern technology but much to do with modern networks of communication and organization. Urban community gardens (or Victory Gardens in wartime) have claimed a significant portion of vacant land within many larger American cities since the 1890s, for example, some 398,593 acres in 1934 (Lawson 2005, 149). "Unlike European allotment gardens, American urban garden programs have not had the singular goal of providing land to workers for food production. Garden programs have been established for many reasons—educational, social, economic" (ibid., 4) and as a tactic in the recent environmental movement. Their fortunes have waxed and waned in response to historical conditions—multiplying during depressions in the 1890s and 1930s and especially during the two world wars and with varying levels of support by governmental agencies and voluntary local and national organizations. Indeed, although it may be an inflated estimate, "at the peak of production in 1944, 20,000,000 victory gardens yielded 40 percent of the fresh vegetables consumed in the United States" (Bassett 1981, 7). Case studies of four localities (Hynes 1996)—Harlem, San Francisco, Chicago, and Philadelphia—did not disclose any meaningful place-to-place differences. However, one may conjecture that detailed research on the characteristics of domestic gardens in an earlier America might well reveal regional patterns that have failed to endure. In addition, further work on contemporary urban vegetable and flower gardens might enlighten us as to the extent that a plethora of gardening periodical and books have lessened or accentuated territorial diversity.

## The Countryside

Like so many other items in the latter-day built landscape, newer farmhouses have generally lost much or all of whatever regional distinctiveness they may have displayed previously. Many are simply trailers or standard suburban types. In the case of barns, cheapness and modern efficiency have trumped reverence for the local ingenuities of the past. Harper and Gordon's (1995) threnody for the passing midwestern rural scene applies nationwide.

> Equally telling, at least in terms of their effect on the historic rural landscape, are the ever-increasing numbers of single-story, wood and metal, prefabricated agricultural buildings. Like the ranch house, their suburban equivalent, these structures are ushering in a homogeneous leveling of the landscape . . . there is little to distinguish these utilitarian structures from similar buildings constructed in urban areas for commercial use. The uniform design of such modern agricultural structures has led one author to predict "a national rural landscape of repetitious buildings." (1995, 232)

Then, in discussing the artifacts gracing the burgeoning agribusinesses across the land, John Michael Vlach is even more emphatic in the same vein.[27] Paralleling the fate of older barns has been the demise or modernization of its bulky adjunct, the silo (A. G. Noble 1981). Many of the older locally designed structures, fabricated mostly of wood and brick, have disappeared. Their standardized replacements, manufactured by one or two national firms, are sheathed in gleaming steel.

Formerly as essential to the farmstead as barn and silo, and almost as eye-catching, has been the windmill, at least for those farmers lacking easy access to streams or springs. Although windmills had been in operation in the Old World for millennia, they were generally large, clumsy, relatively inefficient affairs requiring close attention and beyond the means of most early American tillers of the soil. Once again, Yankee ingenuity came to the rescue with the invention in 1854 of the first commercially successful self-governing windmill (Baker 1985, 5). It was soon adopted far and wide by farmers, ranchers, occasionally for town supply, and, in drier sections of the land, by railroad companies. Indeed the improved windmill made farming, ranching, and railroading feasible in the western two-thirds of the United States.

As of 1889 there were seventy-seven factories turning out this essential device (Torrey 1976, 88), but "already by the 1890's the makers of gasoline engines were claiming that their products were taking the place of wind mills" (Torrey 1976, 106). But it was the electric motor that doomed wind-generated water supply to near-extinction. "Rural electrification . . . created new competition. As the power lines spread into the countryside, farmers and ranchers bought not only lighting systems and radios but also electric pumps" (Baker 1985, 107). Consequently, "by 1973 only two factories in the United States were still well equipped to make complete old-fashioned farm windmills" (Torrey 1976, 115). "Although a half million windmills were reported to be still upright a few years ago in the United States and Canada, many were in sad shape" (ibid., 10). Predictably enough, "the ranks of windmill collectors . . . are growing" (Baker 1985, 111; also see Torrey 1976, 148–49).

Shortly after modern technology had solved the water supply problem for the American countryside, it also discovered the answer for the perennial challenge of cheap, effective fencing for farm and ranch: barbed wire. As related in a definitive account by Alan Krell (2002), several inventors in New Jersey, Ohio, and New York, almost simultaneously in the 1860s, hit on this ingenious notion.[28] Then, almost immediately, manufacturers leaped at a golden opportunity, and, aided by vigorous, adroit publicity, barbed wire soon conquered the national scene, along with less injurious forms of woven wire fencing. As already noted, the older, regionally diverse walls and fences have been abandoned or are on life support.

With the advent of modern technology and modernity in general, the hundreds of thousands of miles of road in rural, as well as urban, America underwent many changes. Along with better bridges and fencing, the availability of tax dollars and new earth-moving and paving machinery and snow plows meant transformation of dirt, log, or gravel tracks into two- or multiple-lane thoroughfares with macadam or concrete surfaces for rapid, all-weather movement of autos, trucks, buses, and motorcycles. All these improved roads adhered to strict federal, state, county, or municipal specifications, the applicable set of rules depending on their status within the transportation hierarchy. In this transformative automotive era, a number of novel items materialized along the right-of-way: telephone and telegraph lines and poles; seasonal fruit stands; rest stops; automated signals at railroad crossings; strings of nonfarm suburban dwellings; emergency telephones, sometimes operated with the aid of nearby solar power collectors; personal monuments; nighttime lighting for some major interchanges or heavily traveled sections; and an array of official signs informing, cajoling, or warning the motorist.

But it is unofficial signs that have flourished in greatest profusion. In a process that began in horse-and-buggy days, with the daubing of advertisements on barns, trees, rocks, and cliffs,[29] national billboard corporations moved in profitably, planting their signs, large and small, within or next to the right-of-way wherever possible and, when not possible—as along the Interstates—at some still legible distance (Gudis 2004; Jakle 2004). Sometimes the signs, which can be amusing or seductive, are aligned in a series at strategic intervals, sometimes ranging hundreds of miles from the place of business, as with Wall Drug Store or South of the Border, those elaborate tourist traps in the middle of nowhere, or, most memorably, the playful Burma Shave jingles (Rowsome 1961), with no particular destination in mind. Clearly the most extravagant, indeed outrageous, of these roadside artifacts have been the colossal three-dimensional sculptures or inflatable constructions depicting beasts (for example, dinosaurs) or superhuman heroes (for example, Paul Bunyan) looming over the highway (Marling 1984). (Only in America?) An intriguing post–World War II innovation has been the welcoming sign, greeting the visitor and extolling the wonders of the town or state (Zelinsky 1992c). The geography of American roadside signs lacks any regional component. In general, it is simply the modern market system running amok.

But both the past and contemporary American countryside have contained many phenomena that occur sporadically and unevenly over space in response to environmental or economic factors or some combination thereof. One of the more obvious examples is the archipelago of mines and quarries whose locations are determined by deposits of marketable gold, silver, lead, copper, nickel, uranium, bauxite, marble, coal, slate, petroleum, natural gas, iron ore, gravel, and other such resources. Their extraction may not only leave behind permanent, or long-lasting, gashes on the earth's surface but also the mine superstructure, tipples, waste heaps, abandoned railroad tracks, oil derricks, discarded machinery, and associated company towns, which, may or may not survive cessation of mining activity (Rohe 1984; Francaviglia 1991; D. Robertson 2006). Given the geological realities, one could hardly expect the grosser regional aspect of mining activity to vary in any major way over time. What can be said, however, is that, as demand grows more desperate and exploratory techniques become more advanced, new locations may go into production and older ones could experience even more intense exploitation.

But, in another instance, newer technologies have rendered redundant what was once a widespread, if irregularly distributed, highly visible necessity in our national, state, and private forests: the lookout tower. Aircraft, satellite imagery, GPS, and other new communication media have largely eliminated their utility. "Gradually, the lookout tower has become an anachronism in a technological world. Aerial reconnaissance planes have taken over the job of spotting fires . . . Of the thousands of towers that once guarded our forests, approximately one-third remain . . . Some have become useful for communication relays, including telephone microwave relays, police agency relays, and aerial navigation aids" (Kines 1979, 26–27).

In still another case, one operating in the opposite direction, evolving technologies have led to the emergence of a spectacular new addition to the American countryside: the wind farm. Since the first successful operation of a wind tower on a Vermont mountaintop feeding energy into the utility company grid on October 19, 1941 (Torrey 1976, 130–39), clusters of these giant contraptions, usually sitting astride ridges and hills, have begun to materialize in a patchy pattern throughout the country, but only where the proper combination of topography, wind patterns, and power lines make their operation economical. For obvious reasons, one can confidently predict considerable future proliferation of these contributions to increased territorial diversity hither and yon despite some local resistance on aesthetic, ecological, or political grounds. Another recent novelty in the built landscape, one that also takes advantage of altitude, are the microwave relay towers spread at wide intervals across the countryside. Then, there is still another example of advanced technology amending the visible scene in the solar energy farms already in operation in the Mojave Desert that may soon be joined by others in the sunnier, emptier tracts of the Southwest and possibly elsewhere.

Arguably the most heroic alteration of the American countryside has been the construction of huge dams, accompanied by power stations as well as the resulting artificial lakes, some of vast extent (D. C. Jackson 1988, 41–54). Enabled by advanced technology, these great achievements are twentieth-century affairs, but few, if any, future projects are likely. In fact, there is now a strong movement afoot to decommission and remove many of our medium-sized and small dams. It hardly needs pointing out that hydrology and terrain are governing factors in the geography of dams—and of aqueducts.

Economic calculation and modern technology have combined with the environmentally conditioned geography of grain production to produce the regionalism of one of the most imposing and photogenic objects in the American countryside: the grain elevator (Grain Elevators of North America 1942; Gohlke 1992; Maha-Keplinger 1993; Becher and Becher 2006). Although relatively crude small elevators, build of wood, brick, and tile, had appeared railside by the 1870s (Gohlke 1992, 96), "the earliest reinforced concrete silos were built around 1900" (Becher and Becher 2006, 5). Greatly admired by painters and photographers, this American invention attained its apogee in the mid-1900s. Since then, the abandonment of many rail lines, availability of trucking, and the shifting economics of the grain trade have led to the demise of many elevator operations (Gohlke 1992, 22–23), but their hulking presence still dominates the scene across many a mile in the midriff of the nation.

A much more recent innovation, center-pivot irrigation, has radically revised the look of certain tracts of farmland. Although it has begun to show up in a wide array of locations, wherever the quantity of ground water and boost in productivity justify the investment, the resultant pattern, one resembling an abstract painting, is most likely to capture the attention of the transcontinental air passenger while crossing the Texas Panhandle or other sections of the Great Plains. On the other hand, the huge—and visually and aromatically unavoidable—huge feedlots that have sprung up recently and sporadically within the central grain-growing states are sited where they are as a pure business proposition with no reference to the environmental setting.

## The Impress of Central Authority

How effective is the landscape expression of central authority within the nation-state in solidifying its hold on the mind and hearts of the citizenry and thus helping create a homogeneous domain? Or does it matter much in the larger scheme of things given the fact that the virile state has so many other devices in its toolkit? The American experience offers us an especially useful test case.

The impress of central authority operates at several territorial or jurisdictional scales, from the federal level down through the fifty states, more than three thousand counties, and, finally, among many thousands of municipalities and townships.[30] It goes without saying that it is the federal presence that is most pervasive today in a multiplicity of visible and tangible ways. But that was hardly the situation in the early years of independence when, after its earlier peregrinations, the national government settled down in a then quite unimpressive District of Columbia, a place whose transient residents and visitors looked on as something of a purgatory (J. F. Meyer 2001). In fact, the only tangible early clues to the existence of a national regime outside Washington, other than the occasional fort, naval shipyard, or post office, was a string of lighthouses along the coast (Holland 1981; Craig 1984, 72–77; D. L. Noble 1997: Grant and Jones 1998).[31] From 1789 to 1820 their number grew from 12 to 25, and "by 1852, there were 331 lighthouses and 42 lightships" (D. L. Noble 1997, 7, 12), while others were to be constructed in later years. Eventually, however, most lighthouses have been rendered obsolete with the advent of such electronic improvements in navigation as Loran and GPS. Although some 426 still existed as of 1997 (ibid., 184–221), many were no longer operational and had become tourist attractions and objects of antiquarian solicitude. In any event, for all their picturesqueness, the viewing of a lighthouse is not calculated to stir the souls of patriots.

In the course of time, however, the District of Columbia and its environs did become the place that has succeeded, quite emphatically, in injecting a unifying statist faith into the bosoms of Americans by means of its built landscape (J. F. Meyer 2001). "Although the visible impress of the state is inescapable throughout the length and breadth of America, it is in the nation's capital that we encounter by far the most concentrated and powerful expressions of statist ideas. And indeed, the City of Washington was designed with that purpose in mind" (Zelinsky 1988a, 179).

In implementing that program, the single preeminent structure, occupying as it does a commanding height, is, of course, the Capitol.[32] After its completion in something like its present form in 1863, it has been mimicked by many a state capitol and county courthouse. But this noble edifice is only one of a potent throng of awe-inspiring features, a list that includes the Supreme Court Building, the three Library of Congress structures, the National Archives (with its holy writ), the various imposing departmental and congressional headquarters, the mighty Pentagon, the White House, the Smithsonian and the National Gallery museums, Arlington Cemetery and various tombs, the Mall and other promenades, all of which dazzle the pilgrim. Adding to the dazzlement are scores of inspiring memorials and monuments, large and small, the most visually effective of which are those dedicated to Washington, Jefferson, Lincoln, and FDR. The overall impression is unmistakably Imperial Roman.

Beyond the capital city we encounter an archipelago of structures purely federal in origin and function. Leaving aside all those lines and boundaries over so much of the country produced by the rectangular survey graticule that may remind us only subliminally, if at all, of their origin, there are the mints, the federal courthouses in major cities, a series of custom houses, all grand in bulk and style, and lookalike VA hospitals. But lacking in architectural artifice are the usually small international border stations (which have yet to claim scholarly attention), as well as the fence and associated gear being erected along much of the Mexican border. A few of the widespread National Guard armories are hefty, imposing structures, something that cannot be said about the recruiting offices operated by the armed forces and found in countless cities. Even though they are not designed to generate nationalistic zeal on the part of observers, the many visually obtrusive military installations throughout the land also most decidedly ratify the reality of the federal presence. So too, if only indirectly, is the effect of the stylistically heterogeneous veterans' halls—American Legion and VFW—that are essential components of the social life of virtually every small city and town.

Amid this array of uniquely federal buildings, what is more ubiquitous than our post offices? Throughout most of the nation's history it was the local post office that served as the universal reminder that a benevolent, overarching federal apparatus was mindful of the welfare of all, as well as often functioning as a popular gathering place for its patrons. Although initially the post office might occupy a nondescript building or just the corner of a shop, by the twentieth century many places had acquired standardized, vaguely classical structures to house postal business and perhaps other governmental functions. But, quite recently, what had long been a federal monopoly has met serious competition from a number of commercial firms, most notably Federal Express and UPS, handling documents and parcels out of unprepossessing offices.

If there was ever a single period during which the central regime stamped its image most firmly on the built landscape, it was most decidedly the stressful years of the Great Depression and the New Deal.[33] "From field terrace and picnic shelter to ski trail and water garden, the New Deal left a panoply of monuments to itself. Public works popped up in every nook and cranny of the country" (Cutler 1985, 150). For a variety of compelling reasons, but principally to employ the unemployed, the federal establishment engaged in a heroic series of building and maintenance projects. Thus, during the period of 1933–39, in addition to the efforts of other agencies, the Public Works Administration either fully or partially funded and helped design the construction of an amazing total of 34,752 buildings (Short and Stanley-Brown 1939, 671; also see Leighninger 2007, 35–42, 80–101).

In addition to the pervasive PWA accomplishments, we find, within the alphabetic maze of the New Deal, several other important landscape-altering agencies: the Civilian Conservation Corps, 1933–42 (P. H. Merrill 1981; Cutler 1985, 67–71; Leighninger 2007, 11–34); the Civil Works Administration, 1933–34, and the Works Progress Administration, 1935–43 (Leighninger 2007, 43–54, 55–79), and, most obtrusive visibly and widely celebrated or excoriated, the Tennessee Valley Authority, 1933–present (Creese 1990; Leighninger 2007, 102–17). In the TVA we have a case where an entire region, the Tennessee River Basin, has been altered profoundly for better or worse and where one cannot be oblivious to the might and majesty of federal authority. It is also an exceptional instance in which that authority has augmented, rather than diminished, territorial diversity at the macro scale. Then, one might also include another creature of the federal government, the Corps of Engineers, as an agent working toward great place-to-place differentiation. Its heroic feats in building dikes, dams, canals, and other projects at or along specific sites have canceled, to some degree, other trends toward homogeneity.

In addition to the libraries, museums, schools, hospitals, prisons, post offices, airports, dams, and bridges, a novel category of governmental agency enters the scene in the 1930s: public housing (an innovation later adopted by several major cities), apartment complexes with an unmistakable government-issue appearance (Leighninger 2007, 118–35). As indicated in Short and Stanley-Brown's (1939) exhaustive inventory, there was heavy reliance on the Hispanic theme in many of the buildings in California, Arizona, Florida, and, occasionally, Texas, but otherwise classical and other traditional styles prevailed, so that the regional movement that flourished in other venues during the New Deal era failed to make much headway in these construction projects.

Meaningful though the impact of a looming federal presence may have been on the look of structures, it is with the manipulation of something less substantial, namely symbols, that the sovereignty and place-erasing power of central authority have been manifested most triumphantly. Indeed with the current ubiquity of flags, eagles, red-white-and-blue motifs, shields, and various mottoes, one could make the case not only for the homogenizing effect of the central regime but also for the exceptional status of the United States of America among all the nation-states of the contemporary world. Although the national flag did not attain widespread display and reverence until the Civil War period, it then proceeded to become ever more pervasive in every imaginable venue (Zelinsky 1988a, 197–99; Marvin and Ingle 1999).

Thus nowadays we see the flag flying next to, or on, all public buildings, as well as many residences, churches, factories, and shops, and emblazoned on trucks, autos, clothing, many an epidermis as a tattoo, and a wide range of advertisements, and, of course, draped over many a casket. By the many millions, small flags are brandished in the hands of loyal citizens at public events. The occasional appearance of other national flags, such as those for Italy, Greece, or Mexico, or the device used by those still championing the cause of those mythical Vietnam War MIAs represents the feeblest sort of competition, and state or municipal flags virtually none at all. No other country I know of offers anything to match this degree of flag mania. Then, beyond the flag itself, we find a remarkable universality of the red-white-and-blue theme in the logos of business firms and in their ads. If the bald eagle, the national totem, and the shield, a figure derived from the Great Seal, with those familiar three colors and a band of stars, are not as inescapable within the public landscape, they are still widely present.

Within each of the fifty states—all jealous of their contested degree of sovereignty—we discern a certain replication of the federal example in the official phase of the built landscape. If we begin with the state capitol, the homogenizing effect of the national capitol is readily apparent (Goodsell 2001, 79–79). "Although each statehouse is unique, almost all of them share certain key characteristics, such as prominent building site, park-like setting, monumental size, cruciform ground plan, dome and rotunda, and classic temple front" (ibid., 4). Indeed only two of them—New Mexico's and Hawaii's—offer any allusion to region.

Then, in simulation of the Washington model, the state capitol structure is accompanied by a courthouse, cluster of government offices, monuments, library, and museum, all within carefully landscaped sites, and attaining the ultimate in grandiosity in Albany, New York. The extent to which such landscape manipulation leads to heightened affection or allegiance to the individual state is still another question that awaits investigation.

The urge toward monumentality in public buildings continues down through the county and municipal levels. It is especially evident in county and other courthouses which, in general, slavishly followed national fashions in design and only belatedly utilize local or regional themes (Seale 2006).[34] Although we still lack any comprehensive account of city halls, in his examination of 114 structures, Lebovich (1984) found, once again, reflections of general temporal shifts in architectural taste with virtually no reference to region.[35]

*To summarize a pervasive development, we find in the physical presentation of the key administrative and judicial operations of the land, consciously or otherwise, a replication or overlapping of statist motifs from the national level down to the county and municipality all serving to drive home the message of centripetal loyalty.*

There are at least three other types of public buildings with some architectural aspiration toward symbolic indoctrination and statefulness: museums, libraries, and colleges. As of the 1920s, virtually all museums had been built in the standard classical mold, while public libraries, except those in predictably Hispanic-leaning California, were classical or Georgian in character (R. W. Sexton 1931, 129–64, 165–90). Subsequently, there may have been more variety and imagination in design. As for college campuses, there was and is such riotous diversity in building styles that it is difficult to divine any consistent message relevant to the central question of this study.

Leaving aside all those public buildings exhibiting some yearning for grandeur or edification in their visual presentation, we have several kinds of necessary facilities that make little fuss about architecture and which may compete with the private sector for patronage. With rare exceptions, hospitals, prisons (Hoyt 1980, 72–85), retirement homes, and cemeteries fall into this category. Police stations comprise another essential component of the settlement fabric. With no consistency in design or any apparent need for such (ibid.), they fit into the political hierarchy from the federal (with the single rather grotesque FBI building in Washington) down to the village level. Here again, in recent years, with a boom in commercial security services, operating out of almost invisible quarters, we have the *modern market system in alliance with the state.*

The firehouse occupies a special niche in this catalog of public facilities. During the infancy and childhood of American urban life, volunteer fire companies, working with or without buildings of their own, did their best to safeguard the community. Such organizations still persist in many sections of the country, and, in addition to their stated purpose, often function as vital components of the local social life, but "when municipal governments took control of the fire service after the Civil War, the fire station became a public building and its design and funding reflected political decisions" (Zurier 1991, 13). The resulting structures, either embodying national shifts in fashion or opting for a delicious eclecticism, but with only the rarest reference to region or locality, were often objects of civic pride. But eventually, as Rebecca Zurier has chronicled in her wonderfully definitive study, modern technology led to greater functional efficiency and standardization of forms, so that the firehouse has lost much or all of its civic cachet.[36] Many of the older ones have been abandoned or razed, while, predictably enough, a number of decommissioned firehouses have been converted to homes, cafes, shops, neighborhood centers, and studios and workshops (ibid., 257–69).

Finally, rounding out this roll call of public buildings, we have those that are normally out of sight and out of mind: waterworks, sewage disposal plants, and animal shelters. Expressions of localized central authority, to be sure, but with zero impact on our perceptions of regional particularity or national identity.

## A Summing Up

Our review of the built landscape, past and present, quite unsurprisingly has yielded the general conclusion telegraphed at the outset of this chapter. If there was a notable degree of regionalization and localization in the ways Americans manipulated their surroundings during the early decades of the republic, such place-to-place differences have since been greatly diluted or erased as the central political regime and its subaltern jurisdictions have exerted ever greater control over the doings of the citizenry and especially as modern technology has revolutionized virtually every aspect of American life.

But the story line is not altogether straightforward. Other forces and processes, as well as simple inertia, complicate the picture.[37] It is important to note that in this chapter we have scanned the built landscape pretty much in its totality, disregarding the distinction between structures located at predictable sites and those whose addresses are not governed by any geographic formula. We have also been concerned with a rather intermediate category of objects that can come and go in rather methodical fashion through the interplay of environmental, technological, and economic factors. This group includes, inter alia, lighthouses, dams, mines and quarries, grain elevators, wind farms, center-pivot irrigation, and lookout towers.

Much of the older landscape in tracts of initial pre-Revolutionary occupation retains its special appearance, mainly as a matter of practicality but also through the exertions of preservationists and opportunistic business folk. But in the territory settled after 1840 there has been a near-extinction of grosser artifacts with some degree of regional or localistic flavor: house types, barns, fences, bridges, cemeteries, churches, mills, and the pitiful roads. *Modern technology, hand in hand with state and market, has generally succeeded in flattening the look of the land.* Thus in such elements as dwellings, urban morphology, commercial and industrial structures, fencing, highways and all their accouterments, and the Great American Lawn a certain national sameness has come to pass. Moreover, whatever initial promise railroad stations, airports, and skyscrapers may have held forth as architectural statements of local individuality has, with few exceptions, not been realized. But among the most massive of exceptions to the smoothing over of the settlement landscape is something that could have been rendered feasible only through modern technology (including advances in medical know-how): the second home phenomenon. We can attribute this major, ongoing reshaping or undoing of the American population map and housing panorama to latter-day transportation and communication media—in conjunction with social developments, of course.

We can also observe in our cities regional and localistic exceptions to the dominant trend (a topic considered more fully in another chapter). Thus the diners in some northeastern cities, indigenous styles of apartment buildings and single-family dwellings, and the extravagance of advertising signs in a handful of metropolises. Then, an entire category of irregularly located cities—those catering to vacationers and pleasure-seekers—are creatures of modern technology and have developed their own special landscapes.

But the evidence adduced in the preceding pages points to central political authority in league with the market, of course, as a most effective agent in promoting uniformity in the built landscape. At play here is, above all, the power emanating from the national capital, along with secondary impulses radiating out of state capitals and municipal and county headquarters. The federal imprint is too broad, varied, and complex for simple recapitulation here. Suffice it to say that it functioned most energetically during the New Deal era, but has become ever more conspicuous with the passing years. If the most eye-catching of the effects is in the design and placement of structures, even more efficacious has been the manipulation of symbols. The saturation of the American scene with the national flag, the red-white-and-blue motif, the national shield, and the eagle has generated a mind-set unified to a degree probably unparalleled in any other nation-state. And such a mind-set is a prerequisite for standardized landscape.

But if central authority—primarily at the federal level but, in lesser degree, in subsidiary jurisdictions—has worked so well to homogenize the built landscape, it has also produced some contrary results. As we shall see shortly, the power residing in Washington has created hundreds of military facilities, parks, forests, historical landmarks, hospitals, prisons, and other eminently noticeable constructions at unpredictable sites, in accordance with the process of *arbitrary governmental/corporate/individual locational decisions.* But thus far the boldest expression of such place-making potency was the piecing together and molding of a veritable quasi-region, the Tennessee Valley Authority, from portions of seven states.

The only sensible conclusion to this pondering of the built landscape is that it sends mixed messages—for the most part powerful testimony as to the vigor of forces fostering homogeneity, but also minority reports of healthy deviation.

# 4    The Theater of the Unpredictable

As WE have seen, much of the humanized landscape of the United States is explainable in terms of rational, even "scientific," decisions and actions on the part of government agencies and by business firms operating nationally and regionally, programs calculated to maximize profit or power. The result has been progression from a relatively simple and homogeneous early agrarian American landscape, one rather nicely in accord with central place theory and the cluster concept, toward a much more complicated type of territorial predictability or repetitiveness. Thus the pattern today, the coast-to-coast backdrop, so to speak, is something dynamic and intricate: the tendency toward recurrent grouping, or tessellation, of approximately similar tiles along with an emphatically homogenized built landscape. If such were the entire story, this account would have to come to a screeching halt at this point. But the reality is a good deal stranger and resistant to even the most relaxed of geographic formulas as we begin to observe a huge assortment of arbitrary places scattered across the land and we follow in the footsteps of our imaginary traveler as he or she ventures into the past and present byways of the nation.

All the unexpected places or objects appearing in this journey are by-products of the modernization process. And it has been far from a simple process. If it has spawned the nation-state and the modern market system with their powerful drive toward conformity, it has also uncorked a veritable explosion of human cravings and possibilities while generating most of the means for pursuing them. The outcome has been an extraordinary proliferation of novel commodities, services, and experiences. An obvious example is the supermarket with its tens of thousands of choices in contrast to the meager inventory of the old general store. Or consider the unlimited variety of costumes, male and female, to be seen on the streets of any thriving

117

metropolis as compared to the drab wardrobe of nineteenth-century farm folk. Then, inter alia, there are the hundreds of cookbooks available in the well-stocked bookstore as well as dozens in many a household. Is it surprising that such inventiveness has spilled over into the world of place-making?

Thus, beyond the realm of rectangular townships and sections, cunningly located superhighways, time zones, railroad towns, factories, warehouses, truckstops, shopping malls, all those franchised motels, eating places, and the like there lies a vast array of other visible, tangible features that resist logical geographic formulation. Indeed there is no possible way to predict their existence or siting. If economic logic firmly dictates the location of filling stations or banks, it is of little use in telling us where to look for a state park or a retirement colony. Consequently, if a single generative process—the *modern market system in alliance with the state*—suffices to account for most of the phenomena treated in the preceding chapters, when we enter the theater of the unpredictable, we must recruit at least three other processes to make much sense of the scene: *pursuit of pleasure; arbitrary corporate/governmental/individual locational decisions;* and *self-conscious place-making.*

Given the enormous variety of singularities in question, perhaps the best way to proceed is to partition them into several general categories and, then, to discuss each group. The earliest, and an especially crowded, category, is:

## Pleasuring Places for the Multitudes

Although we can discern similar developments in other first world countries, they are far fewer in number and less varied in character than in the American case. The explanation may lie in three factors: the exceptional prosperity of Americans, a potent streak of individualism in the national character, and the availability of a vast tabula rasa on which to act out personal and group impulses unhindered by the detritus of the past. The one quality all these wildly diverse pleasuring places have in common is the temporary character of their usage. These are places/events that Americans frequent for a matter of hours or days or for a certain season of the year or special fraction of a lifetime. They are not lifelong residences or (for the visitors) workplaces.

These are facilities or events meant to afford fun, excitement, uplift, relaxation, sociability, or better health, or some combination thereof, and, in any case, a reprieve from the daily humdrumness of home and workplace. After an initial phase of exclusivity, they began to appeal to the population at large or rather all those who could afford the trip and price of admission or lodging (but initially excluding Blacks, Jews, Native Americans, Asians, and other disreputables). Their creation was historically contingent. Although there may be earlier instances of such facilities being created on behalf of Old World royalty and nobility, pleasuring places in Europe and America became commonplace only from the seventeenth century onward with the rise of a substantial middle class and even more numerous in recent times as a certain degree of affluence, and paid vacations, began to be enjoyed by ordinary wage-earners.

Another obvious consideration, of course, is the advent of improved and cheaper transportation. In many, perhaps most, instances, the physical and other special attributes of the site are critical to the success of the enterprise. They include a permissive climate, potable water, interesting terrain, particular kinds of geology, ease of access, historical connotations, and a pliable local government. But even if the necessary conditions are met, they may not be sufficient for success or survival.[1] The capabilities and energy of local entrepreneur(s) and a large dose of serendipity may be relevant, while the vagaries of the business cycle or warfare can play havoc with the best-laid schemes.

### Spas

Following European fashion, the earliest form of site-specific recreation involving transient visitors was the spa, a place blessed with springs or wells yielding mineralized water with presumed medicinal benefits when imbibed or bathed in and also having suitable lodgings on the spot or nearby. Appropriate sites in Virginia, Pennsylvania, and Massachusetts enjoyed popularity not long after initial colonization.[2] Indeed, "taking the waters had been popular among America's upper classes since the late seventeenth century," and "by 1860 at least fifty-three springs establishments dotted western Virginia" (Chambers 2002, xvii, 2). In some localities more than a few hotels and boarding houses materialized around the springs; and the various forms of entertainment they offered, as well as social opportunities, added to their allure. Saratoga Springs, New York, was, and is, so successful, in fact, that it was "the first village in the nation to base its continuous prosperity and growth on its ability to become a center of entertainment" (Corbett 2001, 59; also see Sterngass 2001).[3]

Such early fashionable spas and resorts were consequential in ways well beyond their impact on the settlement landscape. "For much of the early nineteenth century, South Carolina planters and Boston abolitionists drank the same waters and placed their common social interest above political issues. From these experiences might have emerged a sense of shared interests and thence a class-based common culture of leisure and privilege. The springs may have been one of the few social institutions that united elite Americans during the early republic, as well as during the heightening political tensions of the 1850s" (Chambers 2002, 182). But, alas, whatever rapport may have been forming beforehand began to unravel in the 1850s and the traumatic years that followed. Later on, however, "the springs proved vitally important to the cultural and economic unification of the late nineteenth-century America" (ibid., 185).

The popularity of mineral water spas grew robustly from the colonial era until reaching its apogee in the 1890s (Valenza 2000, 35; also see H. W. Lawrence 1983) with such enterprises in virtually every state in the Union. But it is important to note again that not every eligible site underwent development. Thus, when we compare two maps for Missouri, one for mineral water locations and the other for the state's eighty-three mineral water resorts (Bullard 2004, 8, 66), there may be an emphatic spatial correlation, yet no resorts at all in some twenty-one counties that did report springs.

In any event, the spa was a significant component of the late nineteenth-century American scene. "In 1886, Dr. Albert Peale of the U.S. Geological Survey counted 634 mineral water spas in the United States, an average of seventeen per state. To put this number in perspective, however, one should realize that by this date there were thousands of spas operating in Europe" (Bullard 2004, 23; also see Valenza 2000, 26). In any case, a meaningful fraction of the national population frequented such places, for example, Mineral Wells, Texas, a town of 7,000 which hosted 150,000 visitors annually (Valenza 2000, 40).

But, however important the American spa had been during the first two centuries of its popularity, from the early 1900s onward it dwindled rapidly in number and consequence, even as other types of resort flourished. Today this venerable industry is virtually extinct, with only the rare survivor, such as Berkeley Springs, West Virginia, and El Dorado Springs, Texas, that state's only current example.[4] The reasons are various. Perhaps as crucial as any was the consensus within the medical community that the curative or palliative efficacy of the waters is nonexistent. The dowdiness of the older establishments may also have been a factor. Even more potent has been competition from a variety of other resorts and electronic forms of entertainment (Valenza 2000, 139).

### Other Resorts and Attractions

Beginning in the early 1800s, America's elite discovered a variety of other locales in which to while away their leisure days, subsequently to be followed by hordes of the less privileged (Sears 1989). Two types of environment aroused the greatest interest: mountains and the seashore. "By the late 1830s,

significant numbers of well-to-do Americans had developed a taste for mountains" (K. Myers 1987, 66). And, fortunately, picturesque mountains were
relatively close at hand for residents of the Atlantic Seaboard, from the
White Mountains of New Hampshire to the Appalachian highlands of Virginia and the Carolinas. Soon enough steamboats and steam railroads made
various mountain localities relatively accessible. Some canny entrepreneurs
capitalized on the yearnings of restless city folk and rural gentry, so that "by
the end of the 1820s the [Mountain House] hotel [in the Catskills] had
joined Niagara Falls and the springs at Saratoga as a regular stop on the
American equivalent of the European Grand Tour" (ibid., 37), and the first
hotel in Pennsylvania's Poconos opened in 1829 (Squeri 2003, 2).

Once again, it is important to stress the fact that not every eligible mountain or seaside site underwent development. Trial and error on the part of
adventurous entrepreneurs was the rule. "There is nothing natural about
tourist attractions, even waterfalls. But why do tourists make the choices
they do? After all, plenty of waterfalls, fishing villages, and shopping malls
exist in the world. Why have some become famous and thus culturally desirable to 'do' while others have avoided the tourist gaze entirely?" (Dubinsky 1999, 5). In any case, among the upland pleasure zones, none was more
intensely exploited than the Catskills, given its proximity to New York City
and other major population centers and availability of relatively cheap land
and water transport (Evers et al. 1979). If certain of the resorts, hotels, and
rooming houses prospered, the general mortality rate was high both early
and late. After an initial phase as a gentile preserve, from the 1890s onward,
a massive seasonal Jewish invasion transformed the Catskills (Kanfer 1989).
Among other results in the so-called Borscht Belt was the development of a
veritable hotbed of up-and-coming young comedians and musicians who
were to enliven the twentieth-century American world of entertainment in
so many ways, a development that sets this locality apart as a truly exceptional case within our galaxy of pleasuring places. In recent decades the
Catskills may have suffered many vicissitudes and is constantly reinventing
itself, but it still manages to preserve its identity and something of its past
appeal.

During the nineteenth century, a number of resorts and associated towns
began to attract a summertime clientele along the Atlantic Coast and the
shores of Lake Michigan and, subsequently, the Pacific Coast. In only two
instances could one have prognosticated the precise location of these enterprises: Atlantic City and Coney Island (Funnell 1975; Sterngass 2001). In
the case of the former, its only special virtue was having the shoreline closest to Philadelphia, while, beginning in the 1870s and 1880s, Coney Island
offered quickest access to the cooling brine for the weary, overheated

throngs of Manhattan and Brooklyn (Weinstein 1984). But why the early success of Cape May—a popular destination by 1812 (ibid., 35)—rather than other promising coastal stretches in New Jersey (Stansfield 1990)? And, amid all the many scenic spots along the Maine coast, how and why did Bar Harbor achieve its special eminence? Then, what is behind the emergence of Newport, Rhode Island, as the ultimate expression of summertime luxuriation? Why so relatively little early exploitation of Cape Cod—certainly as compared to now—or the neglect of eastern Long Island beaches while Nantucket and Martha's Vineyard were heavily favored by the affluent vacationer (D. Brown 1995)?

There is, however, one towering exception, a peerless example of geographic predestination of a site as mighty tourist magnet (as well as a major industrial and power-generating center): Niagara Falls (Sears 1985; McGreevy 1994; Dubinsky 1999). "The tourist industry began in Niagara Falls immediately after the War of 1812" (Dubinsky 1999, 31). Then, after completion of the Erie Canal and parallel rail connections, it drew visitors from all corners of the United States and Canada as well as from Europe to become, by any reckoning, the most heavily patronized tourist site in North America, and also creating substantial urban centers on both sides of the international border.

But how could even the cleverest of early nineteenth-century fortune-tellers have foreseen that most extraordinary aspect of Niagara's tourist traffic: its near-monopoly of the honeymoon trade? This is something that began to flourish by the mid-1800s and climaxed in the middle of the past century. Karen Dubinsky struggles valiantly to explain this remarkable development (1999, 28–31, 153–175, 213–37), but her summary answer still leaves one wondering.

> Niagara Falls undoubtedly did make visitor after visitor think about sex, but the creation of the place as a honeymoon mecca was a complex process that brought together several strands: its reputation as an elite tourist resort; its proximity to a large, concentrated population; changing mores about the honeymoon itself in nineteenth-century society and family; cultural depictions of Niagara as an icon of beauty, which were more likely than not expressed in terms of gender and heterosexual attraction; and the forbidden pleasures of sexuality, romance, and danger that countless travelers experienced while gazing at, or playing with, the waterfalls. (53)

If so, why the sharp dwindling in Niagara's appeal to newlyweds in recent decades? And why was it overtaken by the 1960s by the Poconos, of all places, a region devoid of special sexual connotations or major scenic grandeur?[5]

During the late twentieth century, the aquatropic (-cum-heliotropic?) cravings of millions of solvent Americans have resulted in a virtually total filling in of the Atlantic, Gulf, Great Lakes, Pacific, and Hawaiian shorelines (Alaska, of course, belongs to another category)—except where interrupted by port cities, industrial plants, and tracts sequestered by federal and state agencies—with tourist-oriented cities and villages, marinas, tourist traps, second homes, motels, and other rental units. At a more modest scale, we can observe the same sort of land use along the margins of thousands of inland lakes large and small. Is it too fanciful to diagram the United States as a two-layered national landscape: a thin, voluptuous water-lapped epidermis enveloping a vast, intricately textured interior? This is not a peculiarly American phenomenon, of course; similar trends are afoot in several European countries, but not quite so far along.

There is still another species of pleasuring place catering to all manner of folks, one that occupies a substantial fraction of the national territory, whether littoral or inland: national and state parks. We have here a genuine American innovation and one eventually emulated far and wide elsewhere in the world. After a tentative start at Yosemite in 1864, the national park system began its auspicious career with the establishment of Yellowstone National Park in 1872 and has been expanding ever since, a tale expertly related by Alfred Runte (1997; also see Nash 1970). In recent times, the federal government has also designated and managed other varieties of controlled environments for the delight and edification of all visitors, namely, National Seashores (Dilsaver 2004, 79–81), Lakeshores, Scenic Riverways, and various recreation areas (Runte 1997, 224–29, map facing 96).

Inspired by the success of the national park system, individual states have followed suit. New York may have begun the first of the series with its dedication of Niagara Falls Reservation and the Adirondack Forest Preserve in 1885 (Runte 1997, 57; also see: T. R. Cox 1988, 4; Binneweis 2001), but Minnesota claims to have initiated its first park in the same year (R. W. Meyer 1991, xvii). If "few state parks existed prior to the twentieth century, then they came with a rush" (T. R. Cox 1988, xi). Especially impressive is California's elaborate system (Robinson and Calais 1966).[6] Then, in a parallel development, we have the sanctification and touristification of a number of major historical military sites, notably Gettysburg (Patterson 1989: Weeks 2003), Valley Forge, and Little Big Horn.

The official christening of these cosseted tracts is decidedly not a matter of divine predestination. The creation, as well as delineation of specific boundaries, of these parks and other protected areas has called for considerable lobbying, haggling, and political strife. Moreover, there is still many an eligible site awaiting anointment. Be that as it may, we encounter here a widely scattered array of places that, resisting the stigma of placelessness, stand apart from their surroundings.

There have been many other durable developments serving pleasure-seeking Americans that do happen to be predictable in their siting. Thus every self-respecting town of a certain size felt compelled to establish a park, usually with bandstand, playground, and other recreational facilities. Every truly large city would also acquire an amusement park operated as a commercial enterprise, along with a municipal zoo and botanical garden. Commencing in the late nineteenth century, many hundreds of counties inaugurated their annual county fair, predictably at a site peripheral to the county seat (Schlereth 1989a, 339–75), while, at a grander scale, virtually every state began to stage its state fair—at the capital city, of course.

Concurrently or earlier, the next logical upward step in this progression was the international exposition, the world fair, a spectacle that began its meteoric career on both sides of the Atlantic in the 1850s. Americans were enthusiastic players in these orgies of nationalistic promotion, mass entertainment, and earnest instruction in science, art, and technology (Burg 1976; Allwood 1977; Badger 1979; Rydell 1980; Benedict 1983). The choice of venue followed no discernible geographic logic. Why Chicago (twice!) and never Los Angeles? Why Seattle, but not Denver? Or Philadelphia rather than eligible Boston? But the question becomes moot with the recent global demise of the event and a not so grand American finale in 1984 in New Orleans. Equally grand, however, in terms of prestige and patronage since 1896 have been the quadrennial Olympic games designed to attract a wide cross section of humanity. Whether any American metropolis, or which particular one, will win its bid to host the summer or winter competitions is a matter of intense political and commercial intrigue. The landscape aftermath for the winners can be substantial.

If such grandiose events—whose siting obeys no formula, it must be stressed again—are rarities of limited duration, such is not the case for that late twentieth century phenomenon, the theme park, which operates during most or all of the year for an indefinite run of years (Starbuck 1976; Gottdiener 2001). Although meant to appeal to a broad public and usually offering all manner of fun, such enterprises may style themselves on a specific motif, such as wildlife, the Wild West, celebrities, American history, Bible stories, film and the comics, or technology. Their sole locational requirement is access to heavy highway traffic, so that proprietors can exercise utter personal whim as to where to break ground. What other explanation for finding Dollywood at Pigeon Forge, Tennessee (Sears 1989, 214; Gottdiener 2001, 126–30) or Hershey Park at Hershey, Pennsylvania, or the eponymous Disneyland and Walt Disney World in their particular settings (Findlay 1992, 52–116; Foglesong 1999; Cross and Walton 2005)? At a more trivial level, locational randomness prevails in such roadside excrescences as Wall

Drugstore and South of the Border, the latter at the line separating the two Carolinas.

On a track paralleling such businesses, the more ambitious shopping malls adorning every sizable American city have also acquired a carnivalesque flavor. But if they have become standardized, predictable items in the contemporary American landscape, at least one, Minnesota's Mall of America, has taken a quantum leap upward to become a mini-metropolis, a mecca of glorified consumption of goods and pleasure, drawing hordes of the faithful from throughout the land and from abroad (Goss 1999; Gerlach and Janke 2001). (And what logical explanation for a Minnesota location?) Such enterprises, including Disney World and Canada's West Edmonton Mall, "point the way to a strategy of creating a sense of placeness out of whole cloth, with no reference to the surrounding context at all" (Judd 1999, 52). Prime products of *self-conscious place-making*!

The logical culmination of this trend to capitalize on the craving for fun and frolic on the part of a huge national and international customer base has been the appearance of entire cities whose only raison d'être is to assuage such desires. Branson, located haphazardly in the heart of the Missouri Ozarks, with an emphasis, inter alia, on country music with a religious flavor, is a relatively humble example of such places and, though landlocked, is akin to Britain's seaside resort towns and those on the French Riviera. But, of course, unrivaled, even at the global scale, is our ultimate exhibit: Las Vegas. So much has been written about this extraordinary creation (for example, Gottdiener, Collins, and Dickens 1999; Gottdiener 2001, 105–15; Rothman 2002; Raento 2003, 242–47) that further comment would be superfluous.[7] In the context of this discussion, however, it is worth noting that the city's site is a leading candidate in any competition for America's worst: remoteness, lack of nearby support facilities, absence of any redeeming scenic features, a fearsome climate, and a perpetually nagging concern over water supply. Could even the zaniest of nineteenth-century prophets have foretold the fate lying in store for Clark County, Nevada? The selection of Las Vegas, initially a small, obscure rail junction, was simply a random ploy by a handful of entrepreneurs in the gambling industry, but one that paid off, in large part because of its relative accessibility by highway to the southern California market. Over the years the city has broadened its appeal to become a general entertainment center with something, or even too much, for everyone.

At a much more modest scale than Las Vegas, Disney World, and the Mall of America, the twentieth century has witnessed a remarkable proliferation of localized annual festivals. If they are quite numerous, and Robert Janiskee has tallied over 20,000 (1996a; also see Geffen and Berglie 1986;

Janiskee 1994, 1996b), they are by no means universal or predictable as to location, theme, or timing. Many are simply celebrations of the history or general glories of the locality while others are themed to food, music, plant life, native heroes, sports, manufactures, or other specialties, as they aim to draw in a large unspecialized public.

A penultimate species of more or less pleasurable places catering to the populace in general—in this case, part-time or ephemeral places and the least pretentious in our series—is the flea market. Although it has received remarkably little scholarly attention (the exceptions being Maisel 1974 and Clay 1994, 204–6), they have sprouted in all manner of likely and unlikely spots and are not to be confused with that other latter-day, ubiquitous development, the garage sale (Littlefield 2007). Flea markets are to be found, perhaps seasonally, usually under rude shelter, at unpredictable points along well-traveled highways or, in their fullest flowering, on large open lots, such as defunct drive-in movies. The most impressive of them may be "The Whole 900-Mile Yard Sale" "strewn every August since 1986 along 450 miles of U.S. Highway 127 from the outskirts of Cincinnati to Gadsden, Alabama" (Clay 1994, 205; also see Littlefield 2007, 132–39), although the huge annual affair at Quartzite, Arizona may be its rival in terms of size and variety.

Left for last in this catalog of pleasuring places fashioned for Everyman and Everywoman is a peculiar, distinctly nontraditional latter-day sort of temporary residence: the cruise ship. Only in the last quarter of the twentieth century did the now-thriving cruise industry here and abroad contrive to build and operate floating palaces for the masses. A study published in the late 1990s noted that cruising had "grown phenomenally in the last 25 years—from a mere half a million passengers a year in the 1970s to over 5 million in 1995" (Dickinson and Vladimir 1997, 37), and in 2009, according to an industry website, almost 9 million cruise passengers embarked from U.S. ports. Thus at any moment a significant fraction of all Americans (along with foreign visitors) are gliding along in North American, Caribbean, or more distant waters within these generically similar, terminally placeless temporary places.

The reason—and it is admittedly a wild conjecture—for including this set of vessels in an account of unpredictable geographies is that we *may* thereby reduce the conformist, leveling tendencies the passengers might otherwise exert on the spatial irregularities of their native turf. Whether the ships add or subtract from the uniqueness of their ports of call is another question we had best avoid.

## Places Attracting Specialized Pleasureseekers

If we can detect a surprising variety of unpredictable places/events that re-strict their appeal to particular segments of the American population, for most categories thereof there is no clear historical sequence in their ap-pearance and development. Consequently, I am obliged to take them up in random order, as follows.

### Retirement Colonies

"Before World War II, there was, broadly speaking, no such thing as an age-segregated community and no such concept as "retirement living." Until the mid-fifties, in fact, "housing for the elderly" generally meant church-run homes for the very poor" (FitzGerald 1986, 209–10) or the county home for aged indigents. But, during the latter part of the twentieth century, a large, rapidly growing percentage of the national labor force and general popula-tion had reached retirement age and also enjoyed the means to transfer to places where they might, hopefully, enjoy their "golden years" to the full. The result has been, as noted earlier, a significant recent shift in the spatial patterning of the national population at both macro and micro scales, a phe-nomenon that has yet to receive the thoroughgoing analysis it merits.

What is clear, however, is that in certain regions the absolute and relative number of seasonal or full-time elderly residents has grown quite markedly, among them northern New England, the Cutover Region of northern Mich-igan, Wisconsin, and Minnesota, the Ozarks, and much of Florida and Ari-zona (Stroud 1995; Valerio 1997; Suchan, Perry, and Fitzsimmons 2007, maps 4.14, 4.15, and 14.50). The visible impact on the built landscape may not be especially striking, as is also the case with retirement facilities in urban settings. But one can hardly ignore the large, distinctive creations that are Sun City, Arizona, and Sun City Center, Florida (FitzGerald 1986, 203–45), or their offshoots and imitators, places that house multiple thou-sands of retirees, exclusively fifty-five and older (Findlay 1992, 160–213). Then we also have some totally novel landscapes consisting of closely spaced RVs, those large tracts of land inhabited by elderly snowbirds which abound in Arizona and Florida (Mings and McHugh 1989; McHugh 2006). But, what-ever the local details, there is no doubt that the seasonal and long-term spa-tial reshuffling of older Americans, as well as younger folk in quest of the good life, is leading to pronounced disparities, a serious unevenness in the social geography of the land. This is not the road to placelessness.

It may be useful at this point, during our tour of the mostly modern Theater of the Unpredictable, to cast a backward glance at the placement of the elderly in a fledgling America. There is every reason to believe that any organized spatial segregation of the aged would have been both unthinkable and infeasible then in a society where nuclear families would customarily continue to dwell under a single roof. The only available alternatives, under dire circumstances, might be shifting of a parent or grandparent to other kinfolk or kindly neighbors. Such is the situation that still prevails among communities in less developed portions of the world.

### The Music and Art Scene

It is not clear when, where, or how the notion of staging music festivals originated in the United States (there were European precedents, of course), but they have certainly flourished during most of the twentieth century. By the 1980s, no fewer than 170 art music festivals were in operation in forty-three states (Rabin 1983, 8; also see: Hopkins, Wolman, and Marshall 1970). If many or most of these events took place on college campuses or in urban auditoriums lacking dedicated venues (Kupferberg 1976, 13–16), quite a few eventually sought out bucolic settings or created them.

The most celebrated case may be that of Tanglewood in western Massachusetts, an annual summertime affair from 1934 onward. The selection of a site that now contains a complex of special facilities, including an academy, was a perfectly haphazard occurrence, the offhand largesse of generous benefactors (Kupferberg 1976, 17–18). Incidentally, the choice of a farmstead in nearby Lee for the annual Jacob's Pillow Dance Festival seems to have been equally fortuitous (ibid., 25). In any event, as of 1931, four music camps dedicated to instrumental instruction of young students in classical music were in operation: Eastern in Maine; two others in Lagrange and Marion, Indiana; and, most consequentially, Interlochen on the eastern shore of Lake Michigan (Boal 1998, 54). And, once more, the acquisition of real estate at Interlochen was largely a stroke of good luck (ibid., 34–36). But, again, the outcome, as at Tanglewood, has been a major, lasting transformation of what had previously been an undifferentiated landscape.

Other "serious" music festivals have flourished, or come and gone, recently, such as those at Marlboro, Vermont, New Mexico's Santa Fe Opera, and Glimmerglass Opera in upstate New York, with or without some enduring imprint on the landscape. Far outnumbering such highbrow examples of place-making is the latter-day explosion of festivals devoted to popular music—to jazz, folk, blues, country, rock, and whatever else is in vogue, including "womyn's music" (Dowd, Liddle, and Nelson 2004). As of 1969, ten thousand assorted festivals were being held (Hopkins, Wolman, and Marshall 1970, 5). At the risk of redundancy, we must note that their locations could not have been predicted. "In 1965, the first bluegrass festival was held in Virginia. In 1996, 516 bluegrass festivals will be held in an amazing array of locations, including five on winter cruise ships" (J. Wilson 1996, 88)

By all odds, the largest—and certainly most notorious—musical gathering in American, and perhaps world, history took place in August 1969 on a six-hundred-acre farm near Woodstock, New York, with some 350,000 persons assembled for three days of music and carousing, creating all sorts of aftershocks for American society and culture (Clay 1994, 78; Landy 1994).[8] Can one possibly imagine a more consequential transient place, whose unpredictable siting came about through the indulgence of a single landowner?

Under the heading of music, we dare not forget musical pilgrimages to New Orleans and Beale Street, Memphis, and similar shrines, most famously perhaps the steady stream of the faithful performing their place-making rites at Elvis Presley's Graceland (Sears 1989, 210–11), or all those paying customers at Grand Old Opry near Nashville. Then, although music fails to dominate the proceedings, this account would be sorely lacking if it did not take note of a truly extraordinary place/event, the weeklong Burning Man festival held every year in the Black Rock Desert near Gerlach, Nevada, originating in the early 1980s (Kozinets 2003; Gilmore and Van Proyen 2005). "In 1995, four thousand citizens made Black Rock City; in 2003 around thirty thousand showed up" (Doherty 2004, 6). Only in America? Between festivities, the bleak terrain is restored to some semblance of wildness.

Less audible and visible than this plethora of musical orgies (though occasionally related thereto) is a fascinating constellation of art colonies where the gifted arrive to spend days, weeks, even months or years learning, sharing, and expressing their creativity. These retreats—again eluding any predictable spatial patterning—more often than not combine two or more modes of activity: music, writing, drama, dance, crafts, and every variety of art. The inspiration for the American ventures undoubtedly came from France's mid-nineteenth-century rural art colonies, frequented by some of the most noted figures of the period (M. Jacobs 1985, 167–79).

Dating can be a problem since origins were often casual and undocumented. However, William Morris Hunt initiated one of the earliest at Magnolia, Massachusetts in 1877 (M. Jacobs 1985, 168–69), while there is a case to be made for a colony at North Conway, New Hampshire, in the 1850s and at Cragmoor, New York, and the Gloucester-Rockport area in Massachusetts in the 1870s (Shipp 1996, 37–42, 63–70).[9] A fair number have evolved from the late 1800s up to the present, sometimes with important results for American music, art, and literature. An outstanding example is the rich harvest reaped at the MacDowell Colony at Peterborough, New Hampshire, which, thanks to the munificence of the composer and his wife, began to take shape in 1907 (Levy 1998, 233–28; Wiseman 2007). Equally consequential for the progress of American arts and letters was the early twentieth-century establishment of Yaddo, a most opulent haven for the creative elite in a mansion at Saratoga Springs (Waite 1933). These oases of the muses have occupied varied locations, sometimes striking in appearance, often unobtrusive, sometimes urban but more often rural and remote, on farms, ranches, and other out-of-the-way sites, but, once again, observing no set pattern.[10]

## The Tug of History

For that considerable fraction of the American population with more than a passing interest in the nation's past, we find an impressive array of places, buildings, and signs calculated to satisfy their curiosity. And if such facilities chance to catch the fancy of all the John Q. Publics, all the better. If we exclude from this account the hundreds of predictable institutions—state historical museums and libraries, invariably in the state capital, and their county-level equivalents in county seats, along with several thousand other historical museums of all sorts, large and small, that may, or may not, figure conspicuously within the built landscape (Wheeler 1990), there is still much for the footloose history buff to reckon with.

Beginning in the late antebellum years, high-minded voluntary organizations, overwhelmingly female in composition, became deeply concerned about the rescue and preservation of homes and other sites associated with the founding fathers. Their great initial success, the salvation of George Washington's Mount Vernon in the 1850s (P. West 1999), inspired a series of similar campaigns. The result has been restoration, embalming, and museumization, with varying degrees of historical fidelity, of the birthplaces, residences, and other locations associated with each of our chief executives. If the likes of Washington, Jefferson, Jackson, Lincoln, and Theodore Roosevelt have enjoyed especially lavish attention, even such relatively obscure characters as Buchanan and Hayes have become stops along the touristic circuit (Haas 1976).

In a latter-day elaboration of the quasi-deification of the presidency, we encounter an important innovation: the presidential library and museum. This is a notion we can attribute to FDR and zealously perpetuated by all his successors, however questionable their achievements, and their champions (Kumar 1983; Hufbauer 2005). In some instances, the siting is preordained by the biography of the honoree, as is the case with Hyde Park and Truman's Kansas City, but hardly so in choosing locations for Eisenhower and Nixon.[11] The outcome, one that obviously adheres to no geographic law, can be a startling addition to, a fillip in, the urban scene, for example, the striking Clinton edifice in Little Rock or the hulking LBJ Library on the University of Texas campus in Austin.

But far outnumbering presidents and the very occasional vice president is the throng of other statesmen, generals, inventors, business tycoons, writers, artists, and other heroes and celebrities memorialized via house museums. Indeed it is difficult to offer more than an informed guess as to their total number today, a figure certainly in the many hundreds. We do know that "by the [eighteen] nineties, house museums were being established at the rate of about two per year" (P. West 1999, 43) and that in 1932 Laurence Vail Coleman reported two hundred small public museums in historical houses (1932, iv). Then, "the . . . DAR achieved a remarkable record of accomplishment in the field of historic preservation with more than 250 houses in its custody by 1941" (P. West 1999, 45; also see Herbst 1989). The following list is a mere sampling of authors and painters so sanctified: Mark Twain, Thomas Wolfe, Joel Chandler Harris, Frederic Edwin Church, Emily Dickinson, Robinson Jeffers, Ernest Hemingway, Edith Wharton, John Steinbeck, Norman Rockwell, William Faulkner, and Henry Thoreau.

In terms of acreage, however, our various museum villages greatly overshadow the stochastic archipelago of house museums (Haas 1974). Their genealogy is obvious. The contemporaneous initiators of the movement in the 1920s were John D. Rockefeller Jr. with Colonial Williamsburg and Henry Ford with his eclectic Greenfield Village (an arbitrary location). Following their example, we have had such serious educational efforts at historic reconstruction or reimagining as Old Sturbridge; Plimouth Plantation (Burnham 1995, 28–34) and Old Deerfield Village in Massachusetts; Old Salem, North Carolina; Old Bedford Village, Pennsylvania; Mystic Seaport in Connecticut; St. Augustine, Florida; Shelburne Museum in Vermont; Shaker Village of Pleasant Hill, Kentucky (Burnham 1995, 127–31); Farmer's Museum in Cooperstown, New York; and New Harmony, Indiana (Zook 1971). In a similar vein, there have been heritage landscapes, such as the mummification of Mark Twain's Hannibal; Steinbeck's Cannery Row; Old Tucson; Conner Prairie Settlement, Indiana; Nauvoo, Illinois; and Old World Wisconsin, all earnest exercises in education and veneration (Francaviglia 2000). Closely allied in spirit to such pious gestures is that recent innovation, the living history farm and farmstead, an operation that replicates as faithfully as possible the crops, artifacts, and practices of yesteryear. As of 1975, thirty-two existed in widely scattered locations (Morain 1979, 550); in the 1980s, some sixty living history museums were open to the public (Leon and Piatt 1989, 65; also see J. Anderson 1984; Goodacre and Baldwin 2002, 65); today there are doubtless more.[12]

Within the same general category of synthetic nostalgia are those fairly recent places combining history and ethnic themes with more than a gesture at authenticity, as in New Glarus, Wisconsin, and its evocation of Swissness (Hoelscher 1998, 2005); New Sweden (Lindsborg, Kansas) (Schnell 2003); and four German ventures: German Village, Columbus Ohio; Hermann, Missouri; New Ulm, Minnesota; and Fredericksburg, Texas. A general point to be stressed once again is that such enterprises could have taken root in any number of other plausible localities; but it was here, in these specific communities, that convergence of civic pride, effective go-getters, and the vision of economic benefit made possibility a reality. Less authentic— except for the forlorn Chinese coolie village at Locke, California (Burnham 1995, 182–86)—are the tourist-oriented Chinatowns in our larger cities, essentially realizations of what Westerners believe such places should be like rather than replicas, or survivors, of the actuality (K. J. Anderson 1987; Upton 1996).

The historic preservation movement has steadily gained major momentum over the past century and a half at local, state, and national levels (Lea 2003; Stipe 2003; Murtagh 2006). The critical culmination of these efforts came about in 1966 when Congress passed the National Historic Preservation Act and established the National Register of Historic Places to be administered by the Department of the Interior's National Park Service. As of 1994, the Register has listed approximately 62,000 places or objects, in addition to an uncountable number of other items officially recognized by municipal, county, and state agencies (National Park Service 1994, x). Some 73 percent of the federal roster consists of buildings created principally to shelter human activity. But also included are such structures as bridges, tunnels, and dams; historic sites and districts; and small historically significant objects such as sculptures, monuments, boundary markers, and fountains (ibid., viii). Can there be any doubt that the grand total of such entities enjoying some degree of community care and protection has increased substantially since 1994 and will keep on growing indefinitely?

The location of federally designated and preserved items is a matter of no small interest. As indicated in table 4.1, there are enormous disparities in their degree of spatial concentration. Even though we cannot ignore the factor of zeal and adroitness on the part of local advocates in negotiating

Table 4.1. National Register of Historic Places Listings, 1966–1994, by State, in Order of Territorial Density

| | No. of listings | Square miles per item | | No. of listings | Square miles per item |
|---|---|---|---|---|---|
| District of Columbia | 309 | 0.2 | Louisiana | 938 | 46 |
| Rhode Island | 613 | 1.7 | Michigan | 1,245 | 46 |
| Massachusetts | 3,441 | 2.3 | Illinois | 1,118 | 50 |
| Delaware | 621 | 3.1 | Alabama | 940 | 54 |
| Connecticut | 1,194 | 4.1 | Florida | 960 | 56 |
| New Jersey | 1,231 | 6.0 | Minnesota | 1,412 | 56 |
| Maryland | 1,121 | 8.7 | Missouri | 1,128 | 61 |
| Ohio | 3,218 | 13 | Washington | 1,082 | 62 |
| Kentucky | 2,750 | 14 | Oregon | 1,313 | 73 |
| New Hampshire | 603 | 15 | Utah | 1,048 | 78 |
| New York | 3,122 | 15 | California | 1,857 | 84 |
| Pennsylvania | 2,678 | 17 | Oklahoma | 814 | 84 |
| Vermont | 524 | 18 | South Dakota | 817 | 93 |
| Hawaii | 276 | 23 | Idaho | 853 | 97 |
| Virginia | 1,640 | 24 | Nebraska | 728 | 106 |
| North Carolina | 1,850 | 26 | Texas | 2,380 | 110 |
| Maine | 1,163 | 27 | Arizona | 981 | 116 |
| South Carolina | 1,127 | 27 | Colorado | 863 | 120 |
| Tennessee | 1,517 | 27 | Kansas | 618 | 132 |
| Arkansas | 1,584 | 33 | New Mexico | 905 | 134 |
| Indiana | 1,056 | 34 | Montana | 719 | 202 |
| West Virginia | 667 | 36 | North Dakota | 310 | 222 |
| Wisconsin | 1,510 | 36 | Wyoming | 370 | 262 |
| Georgia | 1,446 | 40 | Nevada | 264 | 416 |
| Mississippi | 1,057 | 44 | Alaska | 306 | 1,869 |

*Source:* After National Park Service (1994), x.

the complex process of gaining official anointment, we do have here a crude, but meaningful, index to the level of "historicity," the localized sedimentation of remembered meaning, as it varies among the states. Thus the casual visitor to Washington, D.C., or Rhode Island can hardly help stumbling across several historic places, while the traveler in Nevada or Alaska would endure a long, hard slog to the closest of the sites. Such gross unevenness in placement adds still another component to the unpredictability and placefulness of the American scene.

More meretricious than the foregoing are such perversions of the ethnic past as Cherokee Village in western North Carolina. Then, seeking to snare the innocent motorist, are those desperate towns that have fabricated an ethnic/historic identity out of whole cloth, such as faux-Bavarian Leavenworth, Washington (Frenkel and Walton 2002), or from the barest remnants of an ancestral past, such as Danish Solvang, California. Finally, there are those bald-faced grabs for the tourist dollar just about anywhere along the highway, jerry-built whatevers that may have only a short shelf life. For a case study of such a retroscape there is the sad tale of the creation and disappearance of Hayward, Wisconsin's Historyland, the brainchild of a single entrepreneur (Troester 2003).

A final species of history-laden place that seems to be rare or nonexistent outside North America and has recently won touristic notice is the ghost town. These are abandoned or nearly derelict settlements mostly situated at highly irregular intervals in the American West that owed their brief existence to mineral or livestock enterprises (Florin 1971; Steinhiber 2003). A lucky minority are enjoying a second life as tourist destinations. "Whereas abandoned mining camps had once been derided, by the mid-twentieth century ghost towns were being celebrated and protected . . . Ghost towns had gone from detritus to heritage" (Delyser 2003, 285).

## Sport and Spatial Serendipity

For the sport enthusiast, the surface of the United States is not a flat, uniform plane, nor is it a set of repetitive spatial boxes, each with its predictable complement of lookalike athletic attractions and facilities. The irregularities of the sportscape derive from two causes: the inherent regionalization of certain sports (a topic to which we shall have occasion to return), and the diversity of landscape expression within most sports.

Turning to the first of these causes, several athletic activities are obviously environmentally constrained, notably skiing, hang gliding, water polo, iceboating, and (at least outdoor) ice hockey. Others tend to be concentrated in specific parts of the country because of cultural, economic, or social history, for example, lacrosse and harness racing in the Midwest and Northeast, bowling in the north-central states, rodeos in the Rocky Mountain states, stock car racing in the South (Pillsbury 1995a, 1995b), rowing in Megalopolis, English-style fox hunting in Megalopolis and the Northeast in general (Raitz 1995c, 370), and what Karl Raitz terms "yeoman fox hunting" in the South (1998), all such regionalisms ably documented by Rooney and Pillsbury (1992). On the other hand, the traveler today may stumble across facilities for a variety of unconventional sport spectacles of rather recent invention almost anywhere in the country where an entrepreneur is willing to try his luck.

When we look at a sample of the sports whose popularity is spatially constricted, we find that their physical facilities and the patronage of their participants most decidedly contribute to particularized place-making. Nowhere is this more evident than in the case of ski resorts (Rooney and Pillsbury 1992, 122–23; E. J. B. Allen 1993; Harrison 2006, 163–82). After a sluggish beginning in the late nineteenth and early twentieth century,

the ski industry came into its own during the post–World War II period
(E. J. B. Allen 1993). Once again, we must remind ourselves that not every
climatically and topographically suitable locale will necessarily spawn a
ski resort or cluster thereof. Much depends on local politics, access to metropolitan markets, transport facilities, and the shrewdness of entrepreneurs. But when such facilities do materialize and prosper, each ski complex
is sui generis. With their hundreds or thousands of acres of play area, elaborate lifts and tracks, lodges, restaurants, motels, and support facilities, the
visual, economic, and social impact on the surrounding area can be drastic, albeit seasonal (Harrison 2006, 163–82).

Quite different in origin, history, and landscape impress is the case of
rodeo (Fredericksson 1985; Rooney and Pillsbury 1992, 112; Okrant and
Starrs 1995). Initiated in the small towns and countryside of the ranching
West, it remained in that region until well into the twentieth century when
traveling shows and a few of local origin (such as the anomaly of New Jersey's
Cowtown) began to draw crowds in the Northeast and the South. But, unlike ski resorts, rodeos do not call for special facilities. Their role in place-
making is that of the transient spectacle, the loud and raucous place/event
that would startle any unforewarned traveler. The situation is closely akin
to that of another intensely rural avocation: English-style fox hunting
(Raitz 1995c). When the ebullient chase is at full tilt, the onlooker can have
no doubt that here is a truly special place/event. Afterward we are left with
an ordinary, placid countryside.

A related enterprise, another that is quite unevenly spread across the land
and also calls for some athletic activity, is the dude ranch (Borne 1990).
Originating in 1882, they were confined "in the mid-1920s . . . within fifty
miles of Cody, Sheridan, or Jackson (Wyoming)" (Borne 1990, 21). As of
1973, there may have been as many as 1,800 distributed widely throughout
the western states along with a small number of alleged dude ranches in the
East (ibid., 209).

If the argument for locational uniqueness and landscape differentiation
seems to have a certain force when we consider such sports as skiing and
others that are region-specific, wouldn't any such pleading collapse when
confronting the truly national sports—baseball, football, basketball, golf,
tennis, thoroughbred racing, wrestling, boxing, track and field, soccer—
with their rigid sets of rules and standardized playing surfaces? Don't we
find these games being played on every college campus and in every town
above a certain threshold size and in much the same sort of facilities? The
answer is a qualified no.

Countless towns and colleges have multipurpose stadiums and sport arenas
that are undistinguished in appearance and seem cast from the same molds.

But, as Karl Raitz has pointed out, "as a sport becomes commercialized, beginning in high school and college and culminating in professional games, the structures built to accommodate spectators increase in size and distinctiveness" (1995a, 5)—and thus contribute to place-making. Such a process is evident in the grander football stadiums, which, with their special architectural statements, may well be the largest, most assertive and iconic structures on campus and possibly in the town as well (Gumprecht 2003b). Perhaps no single project better epitomizes the recent drive toward such visual bullying than the addition of a grotesque postmodern upper deck on Chicago's venerable Soldier Field, a stadium formerly limiting itself to the sort of neoclassical style so often seen elsewhere. The latter-day compulsion to create unique emblems of the individuality of a metropolis is well illustrated in our newer baseball parks.

> Just as the wider society, in the 1980s, had finally rejected the claim and goals of the international style in architecture and urbanism with its unrooted universalism, so has the generation of ballparks built in the 1990s (in Baltimore, Cleveland, Denver, and Arlington, Texas) returned to an earlier construction idiom. Based on the postmodernist ethos of free eclecticism, the reappropriation of earlier forms and symbols, and a highly textured contextualism, they are decidedly *baseball* parks, not multipurpose stadiums; they are unabashedly architectural. (Neilson 1995, 69)

Such an individualistic turn in building design has also been appearing in other structures of civic import: the art museums and libraries, once so predictably and staidly sheathed in neoclassical garb, not to mention our recent megachurches and convention centers.

Among national sports, perhaps none has become more territorially pervasive or voraciously demanding of acreage than golf (Napton and Laingen 2008). Like skiing, but to a much greater degree, it has generated an enormous set of highly individualized landscapes. By the very nature of the sport, "an aesthetically effective golf course design cannot be achieved through a standard plan or formula but must be shaped by local circumstances and tastes" (Raitz 1995a, 25). Not only must the golf course be responsive to terrain, climate, hydrology, and biota, but, to attract a better clientele, it must also be cunningly designed, a parkland unlike any other. Thus the jet setter, weary of airports, superhighways, and shopping malls, can enjoy therapeutic relief by feasting his or her eyes on a series of country clubs and their wondrously varied vistas. Even more rewarding and singular are the various golf resorts with their multiple facilities and delights, another late twentieth-century innovation that has become widespread, but with especially luxuriant development in Pinehurst, North Carolina, and South Carolina's Hilton Head and Grand Strand (Adams 1995)—none of them geographically predestined.

Still another sport with a quite special imprint on the American landscape is horse racing, but its territorial presence is much more restricted than golf's. The construction and operation of racetracks and associated betting facilities are strictly controlled by the individual states and local authorities, with the result that the one hundred American tracks are confined to only thirty-five states (Raitz 1995b, 330). But where they do occur they are utterly distinctive components of the locale. "The racetrack is not unlike a small town that will include as many as 100 buildings of different functions tightly grouped at trackside. . . . The older, traditional tracks tend to be unique, real places that are readily distinguishable from the other sports places, or, for that matter, from other racetracks" (Raitz 1995b, 354, 356).

Among the landscape consequences of American prosperity and an insatiable craze for sport has been the late twentieth-century creation of many hundreds of sport camps and clinics for youngsters and adults, and for professional as well as amateurs, a development involving all major sports. Pure happenstance seems to be the rule in their siting, so that they are likely to pop up in any rural or suburban tract. In the case of tennis camps, the first such commercial venture materialized in 1957 but was preceded in the mid-1940s by day camps for kids. As of 1986, 307 of the former were in operation (Ryan 1995). In this general context, another quite special institution merits mention: the spring training camps maintained by major league baseball teams, largely in Arizona and Florida, and patronized each year by hordes of fans.

Finally, we encounter still another recent manifestation of the American passion for sport and its heroes and histories in the establishment of no fewer than 342 sports halls of fame and museums (Danilov 2005, 207–14; also see Jones 1977; Soderberg and Washington 1977). "Sports museums had their origin in Europe during the second half of the nineteenth century and sports halls of fame first emerged in the United States in the 1930s" (Danilov 2005, 5), the most celebrated—and most decidedly place-making— of which has been Cooperstown's (however historically spurious) dalliance with baseball (Grella 2003).

Once again, we must note the strong element of chance and unevenness in the spatial array of these sports meccas, with only a single representative apiece in Maine, Nevada, Utah, and West Virginia but forty-three in New York State, while more than a few addresses give one pause. Is Lincoln, Nebraska, really the absolutely inevitable choice for the National Museum of Rollerskating? And what geographic wisdom lies behind designating Holyoke, Massachusetts, as the ideal spot to erect the Volleyball Hall of Fame (Danilov 2005, 207–14)?

So, on balance, does sport do more to engender placelessness or to counteract it by begetting new and diversified places? Evidently only a single scholar has confronted head-on the question of organized sport as a factor in the phenomenon of placelessness. John Bale directs his observations to cricket, a sport of minimal concern to Americans, in a passage entitled "Authentic or Placeless Places," but his Scotch verdict can be applied to other spectator sports. "The multifaceted nature of cricket makes the notion of placelessness and dehumanized landscapes inappropriate as a generalization about all cricket environments . . . Cricket's landscapes are not homogeneous; while in some cases the attitudes and outcomes of placelessness are obvious, in others authenticity of place clearly remains" (1995, 96).

## Summer Camps

It may be excessive to claim that "organized camping is a uniquely American cultural phenomenon" (Zola 2006, 1; also see Eells 1986, v) since there are twentieth-century offshoots in Europe and elsewhere, but in no other country are summer camps for lads and lasses in bucolic rural and exurban settings (whose precise locations resist prediction) so numerous and consequential. "The American Camping Association (ACA) estimates that today there are about 11,000 organized camps in the United States; these camps serve 4,000,000 children and thousands of adults each summer" (Eells 1986, 4; also see Van Slyck 2006, xxxv).

The summer camp movement, which did indeed originate in the United States, was an outgrowth of social ferment and evolving environmental attitudes in the late nineteenth century which were most in evidence in the Northeast. "Summer camps . . . grew out of this new appreciation for the wilderness and out of turn-of-the-century anxieties about the disappearance of the wilder parts of nature. Such concerns help explain why the summer camp phenomenon began in the East, and why eastern camps outnumber the many camps established in the Midwest, while western camps remain comparatively few" (Van Slyck 2006, 4).

The earliest camp to be documented was founded by schoolmaster Frederick William Gunn in August 1861, to be followed by a Dr. Rothrock in 1876 and Camp Chocorus in 1881 (Eells 1986, 7). Rapid acceleration followed, so that "in 1905 *World's Work Magazine* listed 700 private camps, diverse in character and purpose, but almost all in New England" (Eells 1986, 59). These seasonal enterprises served various philanthropic, religious, racial/ethnic, and commercial ends and were housed in permanent rustic, often spartan, facilities generally in woodlands and preferably alongside lakes or streams. One of the more interesting studies "identified 191 camps that have a Jewish owner or sponsor, are largely populated by Jewish campers, and self-identify as a Jewish camp" (Sales and Saxe 2004, 21), but it excluded Hasidic and ultra-Orthodox entities. An accompanying map and table (ibid., 29) display the predictable clustering in New England, the Adirondacks, Catskills, Poconos, and southern Wisconsin, but also, rather far removed from source areas, a fair number of camps in North Carolina's Great Smokies, north Georgia, northern Michigan and Wisconsin, and the Sierras, and a single isolated example in the Texas Panhandle. If a certain expected regionalization is manifest here once again, I must insist that, when it comes to the specific siting of these camps, places that do not resemble any other features in the countryside, randomness prevails.

## Gambling as a Place-making Phenomenon

Not all Americans are compulsive gamblers, but when one adds such unfortunates to the much greater multitude of those who indulge on occasion in games of chance, we have an activity that has been a significant part of the country's life since early colonial days, however much conventional morality may have frowned on it, and one that, in recent times, has begun to transform the look of the land. Indeed among all the items in this roster of the unpredictable, few have so abruptly and radically altered the built landscape and socioeconomic scene of so many localities over the past quarter century or so as has the gambling casino.

Legal wagering, once confined to certain racetracks and off-track betting facilities in cities, has always been controlled by state-level agencies. "Until New Jersey authorized casinos in Atlantic City in 1978, American casino gambling was confined to Nevada" (Janke and Gerlach 2002, 14). If any form of gambling was and is prohibited in Utah and Hawaii, the remaining states permitted various levels of unostentatious wagering. "However, between 1989 and 1995, licensed casinos came into existence in more than 20 additional states, appearing in a variety of forms and hybrids" (Eadington 1998, 4–5; also see Morse and Goss 2007, 16–17), and, at the time of writing, at least two other states were seriously considering the legalization of casino gambling. Thus, in keeping with a major shift in the mind-set of contemporary Americans, there has been a rapid, staggering growth in the number of customers and in revenues and profit with still no end in sight. (These developments are concurrent with widespread adoption of state-run lotteries, a revenue-raising device with scarcely any impact on the visible face of the country.)

In certain areas, the advent of casinos has meant fundamental restructuring of what had previously been predictable, humdrum patches of territory.

Nowhere has such a transformation been more thoroughgoing than along Mississippi's Gulf Coast, where one is seldom out of sight of casinos or their billboards (Meyer-Arendt 1998).[13] But riverboat gambling along the Mississippi River has also done much to shake up, in ways both good and bad, many a placid or floundering municipality (Deitrick, Beauregard, and Kerchis 1999). But perhaps the single most dramatic example of the phenomenon is the extraordinarily successful Foxwoods Resort, a tribal casino at Mashantucket, Connecticut, reputedly the world's largest, a facility that has redefined life and landscape in much of the eastern part of the state (Carmichael 1998; Lawlor 2006, 41–46).

The siting of casinos offers an ideal example of the operation of *arbitrary governmental/corporate/individual locational decisions* as state-level legislation, and much local politicking and regulation have dictated acceptance or denial of applications by aspiring entrepreneurs. I might add that belief in the placelessness of contemporary America is in serious jeopardy when, driving south from Idaho or west from Utah, especially at night, one is jolted by the blinding light and din pouring out from those garish casinos just shy of the Nevada state line (Jackson and Hudman 1987; Raento 2003, 239).

What is particularly astonishing about the casino boom is the role being played by Native American organizations (Davis and Otterstrom 1998; W. Leach 1999, 105–8; Janke and Gerlach 2002; Lawlor 2006). "Indian gaming has grown rapidly, starting with a single high-stakes bingo parlor in 1979, and reaching approximately 200 casinos and bingo parlors by early 1995" (Davis and Otterstrom 1998, 65), thanks to shrewd lobbying and subsequent federal judicial decisions and congressional legislation. The ongoing rate of growth staggers the imagination. Thus "there are 405 tribal gaming facilities in the United States in 2004 compared to 385 in 2003" (Morse and Goss 2007, 19).

Their location is neither random nor predictable, even though "Indian casinos can, in theory, emerge anywhere in the United States, and non-Indian neighbors will only have an indirect say in the matter" (Lawlor 2006, 32). In actual fact, however, their distribution is highly irregular, as *self-conscious place-making* comes to the fore, so that, as the maps so vividly demonstrate (Davis and Otterstrom 1998, 60; Raento 2003, 239), we find prominent clusters in Wisconsin and Minnesota (Janke and Gerlach 2002, 15), the Dakotas, Upper Michigan, Washington, Oklahoma, California, New Mexico, and Arizona, but none at all in some twenty-two states. Where they do appear, the structures housing these establishments are not always prepossessing, but a good many are attention-grabbing: large, flamboyant, and ostentatiously aboriginal, as, for example, Sky City Casino at Acoma Pueblo, New Mexico (Lawlor 2006, 145–51).

Gay and Lesbian Retreats

Until fairly recently, the significant minority of Americans who are gay or lesbian and strive to live accordingly have had to lead an underground existence with no discernible effect on the visible scene. But the situation has been changing in notable fashion from about 1970 onward. Today every major metropolis has at least one neighborhood where gays and lesbians maintain a palpable, if not always dominant, presence and where bars (Weightman 1980) and a variety of specialized shops and entertainments make that fact visible to the casual onlooker. Indeed the gay and lesbian ingathering and efflorescence has been an important factor in the recent gentrification phenomenon (Lauria and Knopp 1985). Nowhere has this development been larger, stronger, or more notorious than in San Francisco's Castro district (FitzGerald 1986, 25–119), which, like its counterparts in Manhattan, New Orleans, and elsewhere, draws gay visitors as well as housing permanent residents.

Although it can be argued that the emergence of such tracts is predictable in the light of enlightened, up-to-date urban theory, no such argument can prevail when it comes to vacation sites. As far back as the 1930s, New York City's gays and lesbians sought out and began developing reasonably secluded Fire Island on a stretch of Long Island's southwestern shore as a weekend and summer retreat—a rather arbitrary choice—until today nary a straight family or couple is to be seen (E. Newton 1993). In the face of homophobia, remoteness was key in selecting such vacation spots as Provincetown on the tip of Cape Cod or end-of-the-world Key West, Florida. Nowadays, however, greater openness is possible, so that such relatively accessible places as Saugatuck/Douglas, Michigan; Guernerville, California; Rehoboth Beach, Delaware; Jeffersonville, New York; Pahoa, Hawaii; and Ogunquit, Maine—all apparently arbitrary choices—have come out of the geographic closet (Greenfield 2006).

Nudist Camps and Beaches

We have here a phenomenon that not even the most clairvoyant of eighteenth-century American prognosticators could have foreseen and another indication of how profoundly our American mentalité has mutated in recent decades. Originating in Germany during the early twentieth century (Ilfeld and Lauer 1964, 25–27), nudism, or naturism, claimed its earliest foothold in the United States in 1929 (Ilfeld and Lauer 1964, 27–40), although "by 1915, several intentional farm-based communities in New England quietly practiced nudity" (Baxandall 1995, 20). From that date onward (Selth 1985,

41), commercially or cooperatively managed nudist camps began to appear in many parts of the country, while, by means of word of mouth, a number of remote, physically appealing unorganized spots in mountain and desert country also drew the unclad.

The nude beach movement was launched by the 1960s (Coleman and Edwards 1977, 147–55; Selth 1985, 41–42), predictably enough in California. "By 1967, San Gregorio [California] was described by *Time* as the country's first nude beach" (Baxandall 1995, 20). "California is the center of this social movement, but, as in so many other things, it already seems to have set the pattern which other areas are following, especially the beaches of Cape Cod in Massachusetts" (Douglas, Rasmussen, and Flanagan 1977, 29). It must be added that, although some municipalities have officially designated certain tracts for nude bathing, many other beaches, usually rather inaccessible ones, are sought out for that purpose without official blessing.

The general state-level distribution of commercial or organized nudist colonies is a reasonably predictable one, although specific locations are much less so. According to Lee Baxandall's *World Guide to Nude Beaches and Resorts* (1995), California was in the lead with fifteen and Florida in second place with ten. Arizona, Texas, New York, and Washington followed in that order. Twenty-two other states reported three or fewer nudist camps, while they seemed to be totally absent in the remaining sixteen.

## Schools

Schools of one sort or another—public, private, or parochial, large and small, comprehensive or specialized—have been ubiquitous within America for well over three centuries and in numbers possibly unmatched in the remainder of the world. Indeed as soon as any community attained a certain level of viability its citizens would usually take it on themselves to initiate an elementary school, with or without tax support, while individual pedagogues might set up their own academies, and religious congregations could fill in any remaining gaps. As towns and cities grew larger and more affluent, a system of secondary schools would materialize and eventually some sort of community college or technical institute. So far the scenario is one of inevitability, or predictability, while the visual aspect has been generally unremarkable. Classes, offices, gyms, and labs are almost always housed in single structures (or even some private residences initially) with only modest architectural aspirations on relatively small plots of land indifferently landscaped.

But atop this universal substratum of educational facilities accessible to the masses there exists a populous constellation of quite irregularly located private prep schools and private or state-related colleges, something originating early in the colonial era and in numbers far beyond anything seen in foreign lands. Then, in a further demonstration of American exceptionalism, we find scores of college towns, places where social and economic life and landscape are powerfully affected, if not dominated, by an institution of higher learning. Among many examples, we have Amherst and Williamstown, Massachusetts; Manhattan, Kansas; Oberlin, Ohio; Iowa City; Chapel Hill, North Carolina; Ithaca and Clinton, New York; and Davis, California. But the supreme example of a metropolis totally dependent on a college for its existence and eventual prosperity is State College, Pennsylvania, where the Pennsylvania State University (initially College) was established in the middle of a cornfield in 1855.[14]

Oddly enough, to date we have had only a single scholar seeking to understand these atypical, intellectually arresting localities, Blake Gumprecht, with his exemplary exploratory study (2003a) and subsequent comprehensive monograph (2008).[15] The college town is distinctive in its demography, economy, and social and political attitudes, in having its special business zone, along with a fraternity row, student ghetto and faculty enclave (Gumprecht 2006). Furthermore, each of the many campuses has its very own personality.

As it happens, a majority of American colleges are either to be found in a bucolic setting or have fabricated a parklike setting. On the other hand, a goodly minority of these schools, such as the University of Pittsburgh, Penn and Temple in Philadelphia, and Georgia State in Atlanta, find themselves on crowded sites at or near the center of the city. Although most colonial colleges, including Harvard, Yale, Brown, and William and Mary, appeared within what were then major urban places, as time went on, the anti-urban bias that has been for so long so potent a strain in America's psyche manifested itself in the siting of colleges or in their internal design. To cite just a pair of cases, there is the sylvan-cum-meadow expanse that is the University of Chicago's domain in the city's South Side, something utterly out of kilter with the prescriptions of the Park and Burgess model of urban zonation, and the expansive park that is Stanford enfolded within Palo Alto.

To pursue this theme a bit further, "the most common explanation for why the United States has so many college towns has been the perception that college founders believed that a quiet, rural setting, away from the evils of city life, was the only proper environment for learning (Gumprecht 2003a, 56). Accordingly, the selection of Charlottesville for Virginia's first state-supported college, Amherst in the case of Massachusetts, Urbana for Illinois, and State College far from the iniquities of Philadelphia and Pittsburgh. Overall, when we survey all fifty states, thirty-three of them have planted the initial mother campus of their university system in a town that is neither that state capital nor its largest city, as had been the almost universal practice in Europe (although branch campuses may have sprouted there later). In the most extreme example, the University of Rhode Island, the school is literally townless, in the middle of nowhere. In only five instances—Hawaii, Minnesota, Oklahoma, South Carolina, and Utah—do we find the flagship school in a state capital that also happens to be the most populous city. If Nebraska, New York, Texas, and Wisconsin have placed their first state universities in a capital city that is not their largest (another interesting American peculiarity), New Mexico, Vermont, and Washington contrariwise have made do with their largest cities, but places without political preeminence. For an even more extreme expression of antipathy toward big cities, there are the late, lamented Black Mountain College nestled in a townless western North Carolina valley (Lane 1990) and Deep Springs College in a truly remote corner of California.

Within each of these middle landscapes called college campuses we see an array of buildings of varied number, vintage, and architectural style and quality (and sometimes quite adventurous), even though Gothic and classical themes are seldom missing, artfully or not so artfully set within whatever land is available. After having ogled many scores of colleges across the country over the years, I must confess failure to identify a single pair that would qualify as either identical or fraternal twins. Thus any traveler zigzagging across the land can never foretell when, where, or whether he or she will stumble on one or more of these singular entities that ornament our landscape in so many surprising ways.

There may be even greater locational caprice in the placement of the many prep schools that have catered to privileged youngsters for many generations. The most comprehensive of available rosters (*Handbook of Private Schools* 2005) lists some 1,551 of these relatively small institutions, frequently blessed with a quite handsome and distinctive physical setting. There may be others in operation, in addition to those that have fallen by the wayside, since this compilation is unabashedly elitist in its criteria for inclusion.

In any event, the addresses of these places are quite varied, including cities and towns of all sizes as well as the completely rural, another example of entrepreneurial initiative and the process of *self-conscious place-making;* but what is immediately striking is a strong, durable regional imbalance. As one might anticipate, the notion of a rich, special educational environment for pre-college pupils originated, as did so many other advanced social, cultural, and technological ideas, in the Northeastern states. Thus, of the 1,551 schools in question, 717, or 46.2 percent, are located in New England,

New York, New Jersey, Delaware, Maryland, D.C., and Pennsylvania, states accounting for only 23.3 percent of the nation's population. We find only a single listing for Idaho, only two for South Dakota and Alaska, and a measly three for Nebraska, Iowa, Montana, and Nevada. (The canny reader will have noted by now that such a regional imbalance in the more desirable types of unpredictable places, one favoring the northeastern corner of the nation, is observable in other items covered in this chapter.) In a quite separate category of private schooling, we have some 1,200 or so one-room Amish ventures offering classes for the elementary grades (Kraybill and Bowman 2001). Small and plain though these structures may be, and confined to just a few states, they stand apart vividly from the standardized elements in the American scene.

Among the many institutions not listed in the *Handbook of Private Schools* are all those private secondary schools (not to mention the elementary ones) for Caucasian youngsters, presumably numbering in the many hundreds, that were established in southern states after the Supreme Court struck down racial segregation in schools in 1954. I have been unable to locate a comprehensive listing of such. An analysis of their historical geography could prove to be a worthy task for the scholar.

## Communes

"The utopian tradition is an unbroken motif, not an erratic and fragmented experience. There was never any extended period of time when an important experiment, or experiments, was not under way, from the Ephrata Cloister to today's more than 500 intentional communities. True enough, there were times when community building flourished and times when it was less vigorous, but the quest for utopia has never ceased" (Sutton 2003, ix–x). And indeed, since the early eighteenth century, if not earlier, there have been many thousands of these experiments, self-governing communes socially and physically set apart from the American mainstream and driven by the quest for social, political, or religious perfection (Veysey 1973; Porter and Lukermann 1976; Fogarty 1990; Berry 1992; Pitzer 1997; T. Miller 1998, 1999; Sutton 2003).

If sequestered religious communities have abounded in the Old World, there is nothing in Europe or Asia to rival the development of American communes with largely secular motives. Following an initial heyday in the 1850s (Fogarty 1990), there seems to have been rather less of such activity in the late 1800s and early 1900s, but, then, an absolutely astonishing burst in the late 1960s and early 1970s, with an estimated 10,000 or more of these experiments (Pitzer 1997, 12). Despite a high casualty rate, quite a few of these enterprises have survived (T. Miller 1999, 228), and many new ones are constantly arriving on the scene.

As is true for so many other phenomena accosted in this study, there has been considerable regional unevenness in the distribution of communes, at least initially. Porter and Lukermann (1976, 202) ascertained a primary clustering in the Northeast (again!) and a secondary one in the East Central States, but little activity in the Deep South, as did Brian Berry (1992, 7), for the 1787–1870 period. Since then, communes have tended to go national, even if the South still lags somewhat behind. "Although not as many communes still exist today as did in the early 1970s, several thousand of them still do operate in the United States—more, almost certainly, than at any time in American history other than the 1960s era" (T. Miller 1999, 228).

However distinctively and complexly the communes may punctuate the social geography of the land past and present, their physical presence is visually obvious in only a minority of cases, most of which are religious in character. By far the most recognizably exceptional in appearance are the Hutterite colonies. Spatially isolated and distinctive in their layout of dwellings and work buildings (Rinschede 1999, 153–55), there were 116 of these settlements as of 2001, with a primary concentration in the north-central sector of the nation including 52 in North Dakota and 46 in Montana (but significantly more across the border in Canadian provinces) (Kraybill and Bowman 2001, 22; also see T. Miller 1998, 6–8). With their remarkably high fertility rates and powerful social cohesion, we can safely anticipate a multiplication of Hutterite sites still further diversifying the American landscape.

Other religious groups also play their part in contributing unique visual accents to the scene, as in the early example of Ephrata Cloister and the initial cores of Bethlehem, Pennsylvania and Salem, North Carolina (Reps 1965, 443–53; Rinschede 1999, 156). Following the great immigrant influx from continental Europe in the mid-nineteenth century and thereafter, a goodly number of Roman Catholic religious communities materialized throughout the nation, but with greatest representation in the northeastern quadrant of the nation (McCrank 1997, 220). Quite impressive is a map displaying scores of "Major Benedictine and Cistercian Monastic Communities," one in which only six states are blank (McCrank 1997, 214–15). More recently, there have been reports, largely journalistic, of more than a few Buddhist ashrams and similar non-Christian retreats, but evidently no scholarly treatments to date. They seem to favor rural isolation. Also worthy of note, although they do not provide housing, are the 120 Roman Catholic pilgrimage sites in the United States, some of them quite elaborate and largely arbitrary as to location (Rinschede 1990), along with a smaller number of Mormon, Hindu, and Sikh sites.

## Camp Meetings

We have in the extraordinary cultural complex called the camp meeting something originated by fervent evangelical Presbyterians in Scotland and Ulster, then transferred to America by emigrants, but eventually dying out in the British Isles (Schmidt 1989). In their American original form these were summertime events, lasting several days or even weeks, drawing swarms of Protestant worshipers and the curious from throughout a wide area for non-stop preaching, hymn-singing, testimonials, conversions, and not a little frolicking. The physical setting was, and is, sui generis. We have in the camp meeting what may be a unique exception to the rule that the early unpredictable places tended to cater to the uppermost strata of society. That was clearly the case with spas and colleges—or, in the realm of predictable location, the earliest museums and libraries. According to an early eyewitness:

> This latter house of worship, in construction, more strikingly resembles the city market . . . than it does a church, as it consists merely of a roof of great extent everywhere supported by pillars standing at regular distances from each other.
>
> On every side of the square, all fronting the center, the fathers of the principal families constituting these assemblies, have each their own family residence. These little habitations are built of logs, having a piazza in front, and their number is sufficient to enclose the entire square, while in the background are arranged all the outhouses belonging to each. (Burke 1850, 238)[16]

But the permanent affair Miss Burke describes might have been outnumbered by the crude temporary brush arbors consisting merely of a simple pulpit and some benches under a lattice of leafy boughs that offered shelter from the sun if not rain and wind. There is a strong likelihood that both types of facilities had their source in the building practices of the aboriginal nations of the Southeast (Swanton 1979, Plates 99–104).

Fortunately, we have an excellent study of the American camp meeting that identifies 1,800 surviving examples of these strikingly unusual landscape features (K. O. Brown 1992; also see C. A. Johnson 1955). The most celebrated and elaborate of these places is assuredly Wesleyan Grove, founded in 1835 on Martha's Vineyard and eventually ornamented by Oak Bluffs, the adjoining resort with its astonishingly original cottages (E. Weiss 1987). But Wesleyan Grove is atypical in terms of both grandeur and location. The great bulk of early camp meetings were situated in the Southeast. A map depicting 103 of those extant as of 1850, whose founding date is known (Gaustad and Barlow 2001, 334), with the earliest circa 1790 (preceding the Great Revival of the early nineteenth century), has 49 of its symbols placed in northern Georgia and all but 16 of the remainder in other southeastern states, with a decided cluster in south-central North Carolina.

The number and fervor of the traditional camp meetings may have diminished somewhat over the years, although "there are nearly 120 live encampments around the nation which were established in 1876 or earlier" (K. O. Brown 1992, 25). Other related types of activity, such as temperance and Chautauqua events might keep the facilities occupied at least seasonally. The number of these unpredictably located places/events remains far from trivial, but it is difficult to guess whether it is growing or declining. "No one knows how many camp meetings, assembly grounds, Bible conferences, and Christian retreat centers actually do exist, but if the count included children's, youths', and the specialty camps (denominational, associational/organizational, and interdenominational), the total number might well exceed six or seven thousand encampments per year" (K. O. Brown 1992, 45).

In any event, if we examine Kenneth Brown's (1992) most recent tabulation of church-related camp meetings, some 1,770 in all, it is clear that the phenomenon is still alive and well. Among the 919 whose founding year is stated, 1935 is the median data, and no fewer than 78 were established in the 1970s. But much more surprising is a massive locational shift in these places/events (table 4.2). The South no longer monopolizes the scene now

Table 4.2. Extant Religious Campgrounds, 1991, by State

| Pennsylvania | 174 | Wisconsin | 31 |
|---|---|---|---|
| Ohio | 119 | New Jersey | 29 |
| California | 98 | Massachusetts | 20 |
| Michigan | 94 | Nebraska | 18 |
| Indiana | 93 | Montana | 17 |
| Georgia | 70 | South Dakota | 17 |
| New York | 68 | Idaho | 16 |
| North Carolina | 59 | New Mexico | 16 |
| Illinois | 57 | New Hampshire | 15 |
| Texas | 54 | North Dakota | 12 |
| Florida | 44 | Connecticut | 9 |
| Virginia | 44 | Wyoming | 9 |
| Alabama | 43 | Alaska | 8 |
| Missouri | 40 | Delaware | 5 |
| Colorado | 38 | Rhode Island | 4 |
| Tennessee | 37 | Vermont | 3 |
| Kentucky | 36 | Hawaii | 1 |
| Washington | 36 | Utah | 1 |
| Kansas | 33 | Arizona | 0 |
| West Virginia | 33 | Nevada | 0 |
| Oregon | 31 | TOTAL | 1,770 |

Source: After K. O. Brown 1992, 141–238.

that the camp meeting has gone national. Quite perplexing are the major concentrations in Pennsylvania, Ohio, Michigan, Indiana, and Illinois, accounting for 30 percent of the total. No explanation is forthcoming.

## The Military Scene

There is a great yawning gap in our coverage of the American story. Perhaps some day an intrepid historical geographer will set forth in detail and meaningful perspective the ways, the where, when, how, and why our multitude of military facilities came into being, persisted, or faded away and how they have interacted with the civilian landscape and society (but see Rhyne 1979).[17] Until then, we have, of course, maps aplenty of individual sites and a huge, literally immeasurable mass of maps and printed matter on the battles, campaigns, and personalities involved in warfare on American soil over the past four centuries. It is plain enough, however, that a considerable fraction of the total national territory is devoted to military purposes or memorialization, to army camps, forts, proving grounds, airfields, naval shipyards and facilities, ordnance works, ammunition dumps, laboratories, service academies, prisons, military hospitals, Veterans Administration hospitals, national cemeteries, historic battlefields, Coast Guard stations, office complexes, museums, recruiting stations, and recreational sites for service personnel. The list grows a good deal longer if we include NASA's quasi-military establishments and the manifold imprint on the landscape of the Army Corps of Engineers.

Some of these war-related items are small and inconspicuous, blending into the general scene, while, at the other extreme, we find others to be gross and obtrusive, visually at odds with their surroundings and occupying thousands of square miles of fenced-off territory. It is also quite apparent that there is great unevenness, a high degree of the arbitrary, in the distribution of these installations and that, while physical geography has dictated a number of choices, in most instances political clout, guile, and chicanery have trumped other considerations. Thus an atlas plate depicting "Major Military Installations" (Rand McNally Commercial Atlas & Marketing Guide 2002, 34–35; also see Military Living Publications 2002) has none of them appearing in Iowa, New Hampshire, Vermont, and West Virginia. Similarly, a comprehensive listing of 953 military bases within the United States (Evinger 1998; also see Crawford et al. 1999) documents California, Virginia, and Florida as the winners in the competition with 88, 76, and 49, respectively. In contrast, Delaware and Vermont have to make do with only 4 each.

A similar degree of spatial disparity prevails in the location of national cemeteries with their distinctive design—in part a consequence of the sites of major battles and venerable camps—so that Virginia claims ten of them and Kentucky, Illinois, and California six each as against nine states with none at all (Holt 1992, 462; also see Steere 1953–54). It is also important to note that, whenever a major military base adjoins a city or lies nearby, it inevitably imparts a special character to that locality or at least to a distinctive commercial strip. In a manner somewhat analogous to the effect colleges have on their towns, the presence of thousands of armed forces personnel gives rise to loan offices, specialized shops, bars, and various other sleazy enterprises.

The military element has formed part of the American landscape since the earliest days of European occupation. Some of the pioneering fortified sites survive today only as place-names, for example, Chicago's Fort Dearborn and Fort Worth, or as museumized tourist attractions (Haas 1979). Over the years, the number and heft of military installations has waxed and waned in accordance with historical circumstances. The accompanying tabulation (table 4.3), which lists the 478 bases extant in 1991 whose date of origin is known, clearly reflects the effects of the Civil War, World War I, and especially World War II. There is no question but that 1945 was the year in which the military achieved its greatest prominence ever in terms of acreage and visibility.

Some of the World War II facilities were necessarily temporary in nature, such as the 370 sites (some merely sections of generic military bases) housing prisoners of war, the eleven relocation camps for Japanese Americans (in Arizona, California, Colorado, Idaho, and Utah), and several facilities for enemy aliens. The curious geography of the POW camps merits looking into (Osborne 1996). Why 120 in Texas, with South Carolina's 20 a distant second, and none at all in Alaska, Connecticut, Delaware, Hawaii, Minnesota, Nevada, and Vermont?

Table 4.3. Extant Military Bases, 1991, by Date of Establishment

| | | | |
|---|---|---|---|
| 1700s | 4 | 1900s | 15 |
| 1800s | 5 | 1910s | 60 |
| 1810s | 2 | 1920s | 27 |
| 1820s | 3 | 1930s | 41 |
| 1830s | 3 | 1940s | 192 |
| 1840s | 3 | 1950s | 32 |
| 1850s | 7 | 1960s | 21 |
| 1860s | 11 | 1970s | 11 |
| 1870s | 6 | 1980s | 9 |
| 1880s | 8 | TOTAL | 478 |
| 1890s | 8 | | |

*Source:* After Evinger 1998.

Although a significant batch of new bases have appeared in the post World War II period, they are far outnumbered by various closures, usually mandated by Congress for budgetary reasons despite fierce local resistance. We are ignorant of the fate of this large class of places, a topic calling for comprehensive scholarly inquiry. Apparently many have been turned over to local authorities and private entrepreneurs to be operated for nonmilitary purposes; still others may simply lie derelict and forlorn, a distinctive, if not particularly attractive, facet of a throwaway civilization.

### Indian Reservations

We have here an archipelago of many scores of quasi-sovereign territories that fall outside the rigidities of the *modern market system in alliance with the state* and the nation-state system in general and interrupt whatever geographic regularities we have learned about in Chapter 2. In sum, they account for a significant fraction of American space, around 2.3 percent, an area roughly equivalent to that of Idaho. The distribution of Indian reservations within some forty states is extremely irregular (U.S. Geological Survey 1970, 256–57; Confederation of American Indians 1986; Russell 2001), and so too is their shape. In terms of size, they range from the miniscule, places only a few hectares in extent, to the largest, the Navajo reservation, which is a good deal more spacious than New Jersey.

The Indian reservation system has had a long, tortuous, contentious historical geography, as expertly set forth by the geographer Klaus Frantz (1999), one beginning in the 1830s and seemingly attaining some sort of stasis recently. In addition to the unpredictability of their location, size, and shape, as yielded by *arbitrary governmental locational decisions*, there are the nearly universal contrasts between what lies within and outside their boundaries. The demography, sociology, economy, and built landscape of the typical reservation hardly resemble that of mainstream America.

### Company Towns

The most succinct definition of the company town is "a community inhabited chiefly by the employees of a single company or group of companies which also owns a substantial part of the real estate and houses" (M. Crawford 1995, 1). Such places have usually been identified with manufacturing, mining, and forest industries, and, because of the nature of their economic activity, they may be transient affairs, whether carefully planned or haphazard assemblages of structures. In any event, although they fail to share any common morphology, they do tend to look different from the generality of settlements, those based on a variety of commercial, transport, manufacturing, management, and other functions. One might argue that there are a few exceptional durable places that might qualify as company towns. Thus many observers would fit Washington, D.C., into this category, along with a number of college towns. And, then, we have such extraordinary, durable federal creations as Los Alamos (Hunner 2004), Oak Ridge, and Norris, Tennessee, the model TVA town (M. Crawford 1992, 165–68).

It is not quite right to state that "despite the extent and importance of company towns, a general history of American company towns has yet to appear" (M. Crawford 1995, 4) because Margaret Crawford's extended chronicle begins to fill that need (also see Reps 1965, 414–38; Garner 1992a). If their colonial origins are obscure, lumber camps in New England and later in the Great Lakes region (Rohe 1985) and turpentine camps in the piney woods of the Southeast did come and go sporadically. What qualifies such places and others to be treated presently in a chapter devoted to locational unpredictability is the fact that, although many suitable sites may have abounded, specific choices for development depended on the whim or resources of entrepreneurs.

A certain degree of permanence characterized the scores of small, unplanned villages that sprouted along New England streams that furnished the energy for textile operations (Coolidge 1993, 9–17; also see M. Crawford 1995, 19). Eventually the proprietors realized it was to their material advantage to bring about some rational order, to provide housing, shops, schools, and other amenities to attract and retain a labor force, creating villages that being "easily recognizable by their distinctive morphology became places set apart from the larger community" (M. Crawford 1992, 152). Subsequently, Earl Draper became the leading figure in an early twentieth-century reshaping of the industrial-residential landscape. "Beginning with the Spencer Mills in Spindale, North Carolina, his office planned more than one hundred villages, developing, extending, or improving mill villages in every southern textile state" (ibid., 194).

In several notable instances, civic-minded or relatively benevolent captains of industry took it upon themselves to plan, build, and manage distinctive model communities, occasionally with utopian aspirations. One of the earliest, and probably the most celebrated, was Lowell, Massachusetts (Coolidge 1993). Other examples include Chicopee, Georgia, another textile town; the steel-making town of Vandergrift, Pennsylvania (Mosher 2004); and the railroad-related experiment of Pullman on the former outskirts of Chicago (M. Crawford 1995, 3, 37–40). Of more recent vintage are the Dow Company's upscale city of Midland, Michigan, Reader's Digest's Pleasantville, New York, and the genuinely exceptional Hershey, Pennsylvania, a location lacking any economic rationale aside from proximity to the founder's birthplace.

Setting aside such unique and thriving survivors as Midland and Hershey, the sun has set on the era of the company town. "In 1930 the Bureau of Labor Statistics estimated that more than two million people were living in the company towns. But shortly after, the effects of the Depression and changes in labor laws decreased their number and the company town gradually disappeared from the American landscape" (M. Crawford 1995, 2, also see 201–3). A significant increase in working-class incomes, at least until the 1970s, and virtually universal access to autos, along with highway improvements, provided employees with a much broader territorial range for home ownership or rentals (J. B. Allen 1966, 145). Thus, in the densely settled sections of the country, former company towns may or may not retain their distinctive appearance but now accommodate a general population or the elderly retired. Such is the story of Pennsylvania's anthracite district with its dwindling mining enterprises but location within commuting distance of other opportunities (Marsh 1987).

A harsher fate has befallen most of the relatively remote company towns in a thinly occupied American West.[18] Abrupt rises and declines in the sales price of ores, resource exhaustion, and technological changes have meant a boom-and-bust economy and much trauma (Rohe 1984; Roth 1992; M. Crawford 1995, 210; Amundson 2002; Robertson 2006). Some of these places have turned into ghost towns; others have become tourist attractions or destinations for snowbirds or the retired.

## State and Federal Prisons and Their Ilk

The United States can claim an indisputable, if dubious, championship: having the world's largest prison population, as well as a record incarceration rate that is steadily rising.[19] It should be minimally surprising, then, that "correctional" facilities of all sorts have been occupying an ever more noticeable niche in the built landscape.

A good many of these installations—those operated by municipal and county authorities—now, as in the past, are just where one would expect to find them: in or near the county courthouse or city hall or at some appropriate site in or next to town. But state and federal penitentiaries are a totally different proposition, being subject to complex political and administrative negotiations (Travis and Sheridan 1983; Sechrist 1992; Gilmore 2007). The federal system is surprisingly recent in origin, the oldest specimens being those at Leavenworth, Kansas (1895), and Atlanta (1899–1902) (Keve 1991).[20] Several of the eighteen or so other federal prisons appear at rather unpredictable sites, including Marion, Illinois; La Tuna, Texas; El Reno, Oklahoma; Terre Haute, Indiana; and Butner, North Carolina. In at least one instance, however, a methodical search process did occur, one that ended with a decision favoring Lewisburg, Pennsylvania (J. W. Roberts 2006).

The fifty states encounter a set of constraints in locating and constructing their prisons rather different from those governing U.S. Department of Justice decisions. If the practice of placing these installations in major cities, obviously the principal generators of felons and other miscreants, was feasible enough in the nineteenth century, that is no longer the case. Quite aside from the NIMBY factor (which also applies to other types of detention or special treatment centers), there is the prohibitive price of real estate. An adequate state prison nowadays is a large affair housing up to thousands of the unfortunates, not a minor blip on the landscape like flea markets or house museums. In addition to cell blocks and other essential features, the ideal situation is one in which there is an adjoining prison farm and various workshops, recreational facilities, and ample parking lots, along with an elaborate system of floodlights (another annoyance for neighbors).

The obvious solution has been to site these prisons on relatively inexpensive rural tracts near welcoming small towns that expect (perhaps unrealistically, as it turns out) to enjoy economic benefits in the form of new jobs and supply contracts for local merchants. The fact that these locations are quite inconvenient for the great majority of visiting family members and friends does not enter into the equation. What does matter is a complex set of political and economic considerations (Travis and Sheridan 1983; Gilmore 2007, 102–7).

Beginning in the late twentieth century, the nation has experienced a veritable frenzy of prison construction by various states, with no end yet in sight, in response to a widespread perception of a law-and-order crisis, despite the actuality of falling or steady crime rates. Nowhere is this more evident than in California, our most populous state and one with grossly more than its share of prisoners. Fortunately, we have an exemplary account of the California situation (and the only such to date) in Ruth Gilmore's (2007) monograph.

> Since 1984, California has completed twenty-three major new prisons . . . at a cost of $280–$350 million dollars apiece. The state had previously built only twelve prisons between 1852 and 1964. The gargantuan new poured-concrete structures loom at the edge of small, economically struggling, ethnically diverse towns in rural areas. California has *also* added, in similar locations, thirteen small (500-bed) community correction facilities, five prison camps, and five mother-prisoner centers to its pre-1984 inventory. By 2005, a hotly contested twenty-fourth new prison designed to cage 5,160 men will, if opened, bring the total number of state lockups for adult men and women to ninety. (7–8)

And, as already suggested, these ninety facilities are negatively correlated with the state's population map. "The concentration of new prisons in the Central Valley, and along the state's southern and southeastern perimeter from Rock Mountain (southern San Diego County) to Blythe Valley (Riverside County), is the result of the confluence of political and economic forces embedded in, and built on, the historical power of agriculture and resource extraction in the state" (ibid., 105).

The outcome can be some startling experiences for the unsuspecting motorist cruising through the nonmetropolitan stretches of California and some other states, especially at night. The blaze of light from these massive installations—in a manner reminiscent of the casinos hugging Nevada's borders—is vivid confirmation of the growth of certain forms of unpredictability on our national stage.

The incarceration, or institutionalization, of individuals has been a practice that, for more then two centuries, has gone beyond suspected or convicted criminals. If counties and municipalities have assumed the responsibility of housing and tending to orphans, the aged, and the indigent, there are other unfortunates who fall under the jurisdiction of the fifty states. They have included the mentally deranged, feebleminded, and juvenile delinquents. As the individual states rose to the challenge, they erected a number of large, special, often architecturally impressive structures, especially those for the insane (Grob 1973; Yanni 2007). "About three hundred were built in the United States before 1900" (Yanni 2007, 1).

Initially they were sited in or next to major cities, as was the case for "the first freestanding hospital for the insane . . . built in 1770" (Yanni 2007, 14) in Philadelphia. Subsequently, as had happened with prisons, it proved more practical to farm out such facilities to nonmetropolitan locations (Grob 1973, 369–70). Thus, to take the representative case of Pennsylvania, as of 1963 the Commonwealth contained twenty-seven mental health institutions, either in use or under construction (Pennsylvania, Office of Mental Health 1963, map facing 16). Only seven of these facilities were in, or next to, major cities, namely, Philadelphia, Pittsburgh, and Harrisburg. The remaining twenty were to be found in small towns or the countryside. Once again, there is no geographic formula to invoke in explanation of a spatial pattern.

## A Medley of Uniquenesses

Clamoring for our attention are a varied lot of visible, tangible features in the contemporary American landscape that may not be as numerous or far flung as the preceding sets of items, but also eluding locational predictability, yet have much to tell us about the evolving character of our national community. Even though most of these phenomena merit monographic treatment, the present discussion will be brief, mainly because, with a couple of exceptions, the literature is sparse or localized and the fieldwork negligible.

### "New Towns"

Even though one can trace their ancestry to such exclusive suburban projects as Frederick Law Olmsted's Riverside, Illinois (Frantz and Collins 1999, 57–58), Tuxedo Park, New Jersey, the Garden City movement in Great Britain, and such New Deal experiments as Greenbelt, Maryland (Knepper 2001), and others (Cutler 1985, 116–32), the quite recent crop of nostalgic or futuristic new towns are a breed apart. Their creators, with motivations ranging from the crassly commercial to the utopian, have sensed a widespread disenchantment with life in central cities or standard suburbs and a yearning for genuine community and have striven to fill the void. They can pop up almost anywhere. "All across the country, neotraditional towns have begun to spring up. In Fort Mill, South Carolina, and Newport Beach, California. Outside Scottsdale, Arizona, and bordering Sarasota, Florida. In Gaithersburg, Maryland, and DuPont, Washington" (Frantz and Collins 1999, 313).

Perhaps the most influential of these ventures has been Seaside, Florida (R. Sexton 1995, 96–157), with its highly sophisticated evocation of the near-mythical nineteenth-century American small town. But, as is the case with all the other phenomena covered in this chapter, its siting is arbitrary; there is nothing especially inviting or preordained about this specific stretch of the Gulf Coast. The jury is still out as to the eventual social or economic success or wider impact of these special places, decidedly so in the case of Paolo Soleri's (1987) idiosyncratic Arcosanti, "an urban laboratory," on the outskirts of Phoenix. The more conventional experiments, such as Reston, Virginia (Macdonald 1994), Columbia, Maryland and Irvine, California (Bloom 2001), have been reasonably successful, along with such neotraditional places as Sea Ranch, California (R. Sexton 1995, 31–91), and Rancho Santa Margarita in southern Orange County (Till 1993). Perhaps the most ambitious to date, and also the one most thoroughly described and analyzed by a pair of participant-observers, is Disney's Celebration, Florida (Frantz and Collins 1999), a carefully crafted simulacrum of the Good Life of Middle America.

### Conference Centers and Research Parks

Creatures of the late twentieth century (the earliest dating from the 1950s (Luger and Goldstein 1991, 1). these usually pretentious facilities have sprung up in a wide variety of minimally predictable locations. Many conference centers are affiliated with universities and may claim campus sites, while the remainder are to be found in suburban or rural settings (Laventhol and Horwath 1987, 1989) but always in tasteful parklike ensembles or recycled mansions.

Research parks, which may also contain conference facilities, numbered 116 as of 1991 (Luger and Goldstein 1991, 1) and "are distributed across all of U.S. Census regions and among forty-two states. They are located in urban areas of all sizes, ranging from the largest metropolitan areas to small cities hundreds of miles from the nearest metropolitan area" (ibid., 2). In appearance, they bear a strong family resemblance to the fancier industrial estates and bucolic corporate headquarters. But the latter are almost always predictably located in posh metropolitan peripheries, with much less of the element of the unexpected.

### Scientific Facilities

Their numbers may not be great, but research centers not situated within university campuses, industrial complexes, or research parks stand apart from other features on the American landscape at their unpredictable sites. Thus we find astronomical observatories and weather stations on *some* of the mountaintops and hills meeting the necessary physical requirements and, at sea level, a handful of oceanographic institutes. More widely scattered are the experimental forests, farms, grasslands, and fish hatcheries and various animal sanctuaries and study centers. And can you guess the location of the largest American research facility for subatomic physics?

### Special Highways and Trails

The overwhelming majority of American thoroughfares are designed and built to precise, highly standardized specifications, whether federal, state, county, or municipal, so that one seldom sees much variation in the look of most of our roads across the land. But we have an interesting minority of exceptions, highways specially designed, landscaped, and controlled because of their scenic virtues or historic connotations. Thus New York state has maintained its uniquely attractive Taconic Parkway and Palisades Parkway (Binneweis 2001, 213–38), and several states cooperated in planning and creating the Blue Ridge Parkway winding its splendid near-ridgetop Appalachian route over hundreds of miles (Jolley 1969).

The National Park Service has been deeply involved in such matters. "The Natchez Trace Parkway was established in 1983 [completed in 2005] in order to commemorate the Natchez Trace. It is one of nine parkways in the National Park Service (NPS) (S. A. Leach 2006, 100). The others are the George Washington Memorial Parkway, Baltimore-Washington

Parkway, and Suitland Parkway in the Greater Washington, D.C., area and the John D. Rockefeller Jr. Memorial Parkway and Colonial Parkway [near Jamestown and Williamsburg]" (ibid., 112).

The NPS has also designated a system of other national historic "trails" along various highways, with the Oregon Trail, Mormon Pioneer Trail, Lewis and Clark Trail, and Iditarod Trail as initial components (Runte 1997, 234), but the only landscape impact thus far has been signposting. Also worthy of note is the growing vogue for bike paths in or near our cities, often along abandoned railroad rights-of-way, but unpredictably so.

Not all the irregularities in our transportation landscape are vehicular in character. If thousands of informal hiking trails exist in the United States, an increasing number, especially in the more rugged portions of the Atlantic seaboard states and the West, have received official designation and enjoy a certain degree of care and maintenance. And, once again, we are in the realm of the random since their institutionalization comes about through the vagaries of community, governmental, and individual initiative. The most celebrated, and justly so, is the heavily patronized Appalachian Trail stretching all the way from Maine to Georgia and largely the doing of the remarkable Benton MacKaye (L. Anderson 2002). There is every indication of future expansion of such amenities.

### Waste Landscapes

We tend to avert our eyes, noses, and feet from another essential component of the humanized landscape and, again, one of sporadic incidence: waste sites. The most visible of these are the huge refuse mounds, irreverently dubbed Mount Trashmore, a "label . . . first applied in 1965 . . . in the Blackwell forest preserve in DuPage County near Chicago" (Engler 2004, 85086). But not all of these eyesores are situated in metropolitan peripheries. Much refuse is being hauled to remote, needy localities in Texas and other states. Indeed there are two "Recycletowns" in Petaluma and Healdsburg, California (Engler 2004, 146).

An escalating crisis in the generation and disposal of hazardous wastes led in 1980 to legislation that enabled the Environmental Protection Agency to identify, sequester, and oversee the treatment of Superfund sites, which in 2010 totaled 1,263 in the United States and an additional 17 in its territories. These tracts vary greatly in size, visibility, and notoriety, though few have inspired as many headlines as Love Canal, Times Beach, or Rocky Mountain Arsenal. There is also extreme irregularity in their distribution, with 111 in beleaguered New Jersey but just a single site each in Nevada and the District of Columbia and none in North Dakota (table 4.4).

Table 4.4. Superfund Sites, 1997, by State, in Order of Number

| | | | |
|---|---|---|---|
| New Jersey | 111 | Delaware | 14 |
| Pennsylvania | 95 | Connecticut | 14 |
| California | 94 | Oregon | 13 |
| New York | 86 | New Mexico | 13 |
| Michigan | 67 | Nebraska | 13 |
| Florida | 54 | Alabama | 13 |
| Washington | 48 | Rhode Island | 12 |
| Texas | 48 | Maine | 12 |
| Illinois | 44 | Vermont | 11 |
| Wisconsin | 38 | Kansas | 11 |
| North Carolina | 35 | Iowa | 11 |
| Ohio | 34 | West Virginia | 9 |
| Indiana | 32 | Arizona | 9 |
| Virginia | 31 | Oklahoma | 8 |
| Missouri | 31 | Louisiana | 8 |
| Massachusetts | 31 | Arkansas | 8 |
| South Carolina | 26 | Idaho | 6 |
| Minnesota | 25 | Alaska | 6 |
| New Hampshire | 20 | Mississippi | 4 |
| Maryland | 18 | Hawaii | 3 |
| Colorado | 18 | Wyoming | 2 |
| Utah | 16 | South Dakota | 2 |
| Montana | 15 | Nevada | 1 |
| Tennessee | 14 | District of Columbia | 1 |
| Kentucky | 14 | North Dakota | 0 |
| Georgia | 14 | TOTAL | 1,263 |

*Source:* www.epa.gov.

## Militias

What may prove to have been an ephemeral or episodic national phenomenon, the Militia, or "Patriot," movement, seems to have originated around 1994 as local groups of ultra-right, super-nationalistic individuals of a militaristic bent organized cells and began rituals and training in preparation for an apocalyptic future. Given their semi-clandestine character, we have no way of knowing just how many succeeded in arranging regular physical facilities, which would presumably not be readily visible from the highway, or simply made do with irregular, temporary meeting places. The one detailed account, covering the impressive installation of Montana's Church Universal and Triumphant, may be of an atypical organization (Starrs and Wright 2005).

The movement attained its peak in 1996 with 858 active militias, and maximum numbers in California, Texas, and Michigan, then rapidly dwindled to 217 in 1999 (Potok 2000, 17, 19–20), then 152 in 2004 (ibid., 66), but, at the time of writing (2010), seems to be roaring back. Whatever its fate, this phenomenon is of interest because of its irregular spatial distribution. Why, for example, no chapters in Wyoming, Vermont, or New Hampshire in 1999?

### Hillside Letters

"Giant capital letters adorn hillsides near many cities and towns in the American West. These letters, typically constructed of whitewashed or painted stone or of concrete, are cultural signatures" (Parsons 1988, 15). So wrote James Parsons, the solitary student of these peculiarly American artifacts, after collecting nearly 250 examples, virtually all west of the 104th meridian. The tree-covered slopes of eastern hills and mountains discourage such boosterism. The practice of creating and maintaining these huge initials that identify town or college began in 1905 and has persisted ever since thanks to the zeal of college and high school students. Whether or not they meet our definition of place, these hillside artifacts do add a definite touch of diversity for the transcontinental driver or airborne passenger.

### Personal Expression

If there is a strong individualistic streak in the American national character and its rich landscape expression as a consequence, there is no lack of Old World antecedents. The noble and mighty of Europe could create grandiose one-of-a-kind castles and mansions—Mad King Ludwig of Bavaria and Louis XIV's Versailles may be extreme examples—and elaborate parks and hunting grounds. Their American counterparts eventually followed suit with the extravagances of Newport and the Hudson River estates, and, as the ultimate thrust in this direction, we are awed by William Randolph Hearst's San Simeon fantasy. Relying on rather more modest means, Frank Lloyd Wright placed his unique and remarkable signature on the Wisconsin and Arizona landscapes with Taliesen East and Taliesen West. Then, even though public funding was involved, I must classify the bas reliefs on Stone Mountain, Georgia, and Mount Rushmore (Fite 1952) as manifestations of Gutzon Borglum's quite special, obstinate ego.

But determined individuals with even the slenderest of means can leave their mark for all to see, as so dramatically demonstrated by Los Angeles's astonishing Watts Towers. In the same general genre, those who wander the byways of America will occasionally happen upon the most amazing biblical gardens or other fanciful displays by visionary artists (Beardsley 1995) to a degree rare or absent in other lands, or front yards overflowing with displays of religious or political items or dolls, shells, ceramics, carvings, and other bric-a-brac. Then there are those temporary Christmas extravaganzas in American cities and suburbs, where the householder has gone to such extremes that traffic jams of gawkers can result. Individual whim or passion is also the explanation for the scores of large crosses erected in groups of three accosting one unexpectedly along the highways thanks to a born-again West Virginia millionaire and the countless other hilltop or roadside crosses and billboards paid for by ultra-devout individuals. (Everett 2002; Carver 2006).

### Wind Farms

Something quite novel and impossible to ignore has been erupting on the American scene. More and more frequently nowadays, the traveler is startled by phalanxes of huge power-generating windmills whirling away along ridgetops hither and yon. The safest of predictions concerning the American landscape is that, despite local controversy, such wind farms will continue to proliferate, but just where is beyond the ken of the prognosticator. The number of eligible sites is vast, but decisions to construct and operate are contingent on local regulations, public opinion, and politics, in addition to the courage of entrepreneurs and the vagaries of the energy economy. One can confidently await more scholarly attention by students of the landscape than the minimal amount currently available (Clay 1994, 219–20).

### Fireworks Stands and Their Ilk

Small, piquant, garish, and often ephemeral though they be, the opportunistic roadside stands clinging to some of our international, state, and municipal borders enliven the national scene by their unpredictable occurrence. These casual businesses traffic in near-contraband commodities, such as liquor, fireworks, and margarine (the sales of which are outlawed in some jurisdictions), or goods more costly or heavily taxed on the other side of the line.[21]

## A Summing Up

There is at least one sensible, immediate inference to be drawn from this review of an array of the unpredictable visible, tangible components of our landscape: that they do indeed contribute—along, of course, with more immaterial items—to some degree to whatever place-to-place diversity prevails in the human geography of the United States. But large questions remain. Has the role of these features become stronger or weaker with the passage of time? How do they factor into the overarching problem addressed in this study: the reality or illusion of a placeless land?

Given the wildly incompatible attributes of the forty-odd kinds of place-making items scrutinized in this chapter—their number, age, duration, and range in bulk and acreage—there can be no direct or rigorous quantitative approach to the first question. But, resorting to the crudest type of arithmetic, suppose we divide the phenomena in question into three categories: those that have essentially vanished; others that have fluctuated in their salience over time; and the remainder that have grown in number and significance over time or reached some sort of stasis.

As it turns out, there are only two valid entries for the initial category: spas and world fairs. Rather more numerous are the candidates for the second group: camp meetings, communes, company towns, fireworks stands and their ilk, and military facilities, and, with less certainty, militias, rodeos, and Indian reservations. We are left, then, with the numerous residue, listed here in alphabetical order:

art colonies
colleges
conference centers and research parks
dude ranches
flea markets
gambling casinos
gay and lesbian neighborhoods
gay and lesbian vacation areas
ghost towns
golf courses and resorts
hillside letters
historical museums and houses
local festivals
museum villages
music camps
music festivals
national and state parks
"New Towns"

nudist camps and beaches
other resorts
personalized places
prep schools
presidential libraries/museums
racetracks
retirement colonies
scientific facilities
ski resorts
special highways and trails
sport camps
sports halls of fame
state and federal prisons
summer camps
theme parks
waste dumps
wind farms

OF MORE than incidental interest is the fact that 22 of these 35 entities are of twentieth-century origin. It would not be too surprising if there were future unpredictable additions to the ranks of unpredictable elements in the American landscape. Furthermore, given the fact that the late eighteenth-century observer would have encountered only four of the phenomena under discussion—colleges, religious communes, military facilities, and spas—and those in meager numbers, there is no avoiding the conclusion that, insofar as the variety and quantity of locationally unpredictable elements in the visible scene is concerned, the United States today may be a more territorially diversified, a more complex panorama, than it has ever been in the past, and that there is every likelihood that it will become even more so in the future.

In any event, after reviewing this large and varied mass of relevant data, we can now propound a lawlike generalization in the realm of human geography, one that has previously eluded detection, namely: *the number and variety of places whose location is unpredictable is positively correlated with level of modernization, or socioeconomic and technological development, in a nation, while, correspondingly, the number and variety of persons who use or visit such places, once limited to the privileged, will increase even as the mean socioeconomic status of the general population rises.*

But perhaps we can reflect even further on the deeper implications of the evidence visible in the American landscape. Does it not seem plausible that the burst of human energy at the core of the modernization episode begets not only the regularities of the nation-state but also a cornucopia of hitherto unknown things? Consider how a catalogue of the contents of the typical middle-class American house, basement, attic, and garage would vastly outnumber the variety of objects that the richest medieval baron could have assembled. Such latter-day exuberance of contrivance and acquisition escapes the control of business managers and government bureaucrats to spill into the general landscape. Hence the unpredictability of the American scene.

# 5  Territorial Diversities in the Cultural Realm: Yea and Nay

AFTER OUR tour of the visible, tangible, and readily countable features of the American landscape in Chapters 2 and 3, we could affirm that the conventional wisdom does have some basis in fact. There has indeed been a pervasive homogenization or, more strictly, a repetitive patterning, a tessellation, of places, of modes of work and consumption. The *modern market system in alliance with the state* has been triumphant, and decidedly so. The main business of America is business: making things, providing services, getting, spending, and, in collusion with government, arranging spatial matters so as to optimize the accumulation of capital and its profitable investment.

But we must also attach to any such statement a major proviso. Other processes have grafted both major and minor modifications onto what would otherwise be a predictable social and economic geography. In a country thickly speckled with aberrations from the expected, as set forth in Chapter 4, *demographic change* complicates the scenario, especially with the introduction of unfamiliar ethnic groups. The *pursuit of pleasure* can be ever so fickle in its geographic expression. Then, of course, neither *arbitrary corporate/governmental/individual place-making* nor *self-conscious place-making* submits to systematic formulation. Thus, rather than a smoothly predictable vista, we can begin to characterize the American land concisely, if in admittedly rather ungainly fashion, as a Tessellated-cum-Aleatory Space, or, in less lofty terms, as a flawed mosaic with random patches.

But further complicating an already complex scene, what we must consider now are other usually less visible or countable levels or facets of American life that may not be responsive to the forces of homogenization but matter mightily in immediate thought, feeling, action, and personal and place identity and, ultimately, in fashioning grander regional identities. I have in mind cultural attributes that not only are not necessarily obedient

164

to centralizing processes but can also fail to impede their operation. The Powers That Be are not annoyed by the existence of regional dialects so long as the masses can communicate efficiently via a single language. Similarly, they scarcely notice the preference of some folks for hush puppies as against clams or mountain oysters or for a Queen Anne residence versus a McMansion. Nor do they care much whether customers buy bluegrass rather than the blues so long as they keep shelling out for enough recordings, or whether they attend Lutheran rather than Assembly of God services. There are more important issues to ponder in the counting house.

The cultural attributes in question here—with the exception of dress and ornament and folk arts and handicrafts—are at best marginally visible or tangible. We are dealing, then, with patterns of behavior. Thus our imaginary traveler would have to sojourn for protracted periods in a number of localities, observing and listening attentively, before being able to plot the territorial range of these sets of cultural practices, ones that do pry places apart in a serious way. As already suggested, the cultural phenomena in question usually bear significant emotional weight and are not evaluated in dollar terms, unlike dwellings, for example, where affection may be contaminated by monetary considerations. Perhaps we are most deeply involved emotionally with language, religion, and political beliefs. Let us begin with

## Language

None of the cultural attributes we might examine may be more fundamental to defining personal, group, and place identity than this quintessential human acquisition. As we have noted earlier, one of the basic facts about the United States is that it has its very own national language, one of the many more or less mutually intelligible dialects of English, a fact that promotes ethnic self-awareness, especially whenever a Yank converses with a Scot, Jamaican, East Indian, South African, or even a Canadian. "When the Thirteen Colonies became the United States, there were already indications that American English was becoming a separate entity from British English" (Wolfram and Schilling-Estes 1998, 105; also see Montgomery 2003) and also that regional variants of the new colonial tongue had already begun to emerge (Simpson 1986, 101–6).

If, as I have also pointed out earlier, printed materials certainly promoted national uniformity in vocabulary, orthography, and grammar, it is not clear how the spoken language attained its past and present form. The circulation of schoolmasters, preachers, statesmen, and lecturers may offer a partial answer. In recent times, of course, phonograph recordings, movies, radio, and television, as well as massive internal migrations of ordinary citizens, have intensified the process. "Many critics urged the adoption of an official standard of radio pronunciation in the United States . . . By the 1930s the fully established networks and the advertisers who controlled much of radio programming *did* impose a standard of radio pronunciation. Diction contests on the air set norms for announcers and listeners" (Douglas 2004, 103; also see Metcalf 2000, x). And television networks may have followed suit. Nevertheless, the extirpation of regional and local dialects has not come to pass.

The U.S. Congress has never made English an official language by legislative fiat, but in recent years there has been widespread, as yet unsuccessful, agitation on the part of xenophobes for just such a statute (Baron 1990; J. Crawford 1992). The proponents do not specify what particular variety of English they have in mind. Evidently any version will do. As it happens, some places, such as New Mexico, are officially bilingual and many others have become so de facto. Paralleling early efforts to standardize a distinct American language was a later brief, ill-fated campaign to engineer something of the sort for the Confederacy (Faust 1988, 11).

Whatever the aspirations of earlier and later pedagogues and public figures may have been and the latter-day effects of the mass media and the conformist pressures of our educational system, American English persists in branching out in riotous diversity in keeping with the primordial puissance of *cultural drift* and the lingering effects of initial settlement from a wide variety of European source areas. If usage varies in important and interesting ways in terms of the age, gender, class, ethnicity, and social situation of the speaker, it is only the spatial aspects of the utterances, the place-to-place differences, that need concern us here. We are quite fortunate in having access to massive amounts of relevant data collected over the past several decades by devoted linguists and others by means of interviews, maps, and other documents (McDavid 1958; Detro 1982; Cassidy and Hall 1985–; D. R. Preston 2003). A series of regional linguistic atlases initiated by Hans Kurath (1939–43) may be completed in the foreseeable future (Kretzschmar 2003).

But the most laudable achievement may well be the *Dictionary of American Regional English* (DARE) (Cassidy and Hall 1985–), an eventual five-volume publication based primarily, in addition to a ransacking of printed sources, on extended questionnaires administered in some one thousand localities across the country. It includes a multitude of cartograms depicting word choice and pronunciation. In a preliminary analysis of DARE materials, Craig Carver (1987) has been able to regionalize the dialects of American English based on phonology and vocabulary. Inter alia, Carver's work confirms the areas delimited in the northeastern states solely through an analysis of place-names (Zelinsky 1955). DARE's huge data bank could well offer the means for ascertaining whether or how there has been interregional convergence or divergence over time in the vocabulary of American English. To date, however, no one has initiated such a herculean project.

Although there have been many highly technical studies of temporal shifts in the syntax or grammar of American English, unfortunately, to date none have viewed the topic from a spatial angle. But superseding or refining earlier efforts at regionalizing the language, we now have at hand the results of a massive recent, methodologically elegant study of phonetics, phonology, and sound change in the United States and Canada by William Labov and his associates (2005). The summary map they have generated merits close attention. It is no surprise that Canadians inhabit their own distinctive linguistic realm or to have the particularity of the South (with two subregions, but lacking virtually all of Florida) and New England stoutly confirmed. But it is most important to note the nonexistence of any midwestern region. Instead we find that speakers within the territory traditionally defined as such are deeply split between two dialects, each with its own subdivisions: the North and the Midland, the latter stretching from Pennsylvania and New Jersey to Nebraska, Kansas, and Oklahoma. Further confirming the sharp areal distinction between the Midland speech region and the conventional Middle West are studies by Ash (2006), Frazer (2006), and Murray and Simon (2006a).

It is also noteworthy that the Labov map, as does Carver's, assigns the western half of the country to a rather vague or shallow Western category. What our maps fail to reveal is the very lively existence of metropolitan subdialects in such instances as Boston, New York City (where there are even finer localizations), Charleston, Cincinnati (Labov, Ash, and Boberg 2005, 304), Philadelphia, Pittsburgh, Baltimore, and New Orleans. As a native Chicagoan, I can recognize fellow natives with their unique cadences the moment they begin speaking.

The findings of the Labov project are surprising, if rather complex, indeed in direct contradiction to the perceptions of the general public and many scholars.

> One important result of ANAE [Atlas of North American English] is the confirmation of the earlier finding of sociolinguistic studies that change in progress is continuing, a result that has aroused a great deal of interest in the general public. Given the uniform exposure of speakers everywhere to the broadcast standard of the mass media, it is difficult for most people to believe that sound change is continuing at a rapid rate. *On a larger scale ANAE finds that the diversity of regional dialects in North America is not diminishing, but is increasing over time.* (Labov, Ash, and Boberg 2005, 304; emphasis added)

However, "this increasing diversity does not apply to smaller units within the major regions. Within most of the regional boundaries, linguistic (changes in progress) have the effect of solidifying and developing the regional patterns. Many local dialects are indeed disappearing, but they are assimilating to larger regional patterns rather than to a national or continental model" (ibid., 119).[1]

There is no easy explanation for such a startling counterintuitive finding, one that our imaginary traveler would not have had the expertise to detect no matter how many trips over the decades. We have learned that human languages do evolve constantly, responding to their own deep, mysterious internal laws that are beyond our conscious control but not necessarily beyond our ultimate comprehension. Thus linguists now have an increasing grasp of how vowels and consonants shift over time and some inkling as to the evolution of grammar. But just how the mechanisms of *cultural drift* bring about divergences in the expression of linguistic laws in spatially separated communities remains an enigma.

Another approach to the linguistic dimensions of regional diversity is the exploitation of names. This is a strategy employed to good effect in analyses of place-names appearing on maps (Zelinsky 1955, 1967) and names of enterprises as listed in telephone directories (Zelinsky 1980). But the great drawback in this research is the fixity of such names, which, once given, change seldom or never.

Overcoming that limitation, I executed a study (1970) that examined personal names over time, one of the rare attempts to gauge diachronic convergence across territory. It involved factor analysis of variance in the 179 most popular forenames of males with presumably British surnames in sixteen widely separated counties along the Atlantic Seaboard in 1790 and then again circa 1968. The 1790 data came from census records, while the later material was gleaned from telephone directories. The working assumption was that the choice of given names for the newborn is as close to an ideal cultural metric as is available to us.

The statistical manipulation of the data generated no fewer than twenty-five factors and a multitude of interesting insights into the historical geography of naming practices; but, for present purposes, the most important finding is in a graph delineating "taxonomic trees, the stepwise grouping in taxonomic space of the 16 counties." Its message is clear. The taxonomic distances—the degree of similarity among the places in question—were decidedly shorter in 1968 than in 1790. This led to my conclusion that "the results reported in this inquiry generally lean toward my convergence hypothesis" (Zelinsky 1970, 769).

In retrospect, however, I am less confident of the soundness of this assertion. In addition to the obvious difficulties of inferring the shape and direction of the arc of nationwide change from just two distant points in time and from a narrow slice of national territory, I now realize a failure to take into account a significant factor: the increasing role of fashion. Although it is highly likely that patterns of personal naming changed only slowly and imperceptibly in young America, the situation is quite different today. Given the pervasiveness of mass communication and entertainment media, with our widespread celebrity-worship nowadays, fads in given names can come and go swiftly. Thus one can look forward to reading a news story every year reporting the top ten names given to infant boys and girls during the preceding twelve months—and to being startled by the shifts in the rankings.[2] But, if the claim for given names as the ideal cultural metric may have been overstated, there is still much to be learned through further empirical work.

## Religion

Although we may regard language and religion as both being critical to molding personal, group, and regional identity, there is an important distinction in the ways they operate geographically and otherwise. First, every inhabited portion of the world can be said to have a linguistic geography worth studying, whether more than one language exists therein and whether anyone has as yet troubled to examine it. On the other hand, there are entire countries so dominated by a single faith or denomination—Italy, Greece, Spain, Sweden, Thailand, Libya, and Tibet come to mind—that mapping religious affiliation (but certainly not local nuances of practice) would be an exercise in futility. Furthermore, an increasingly large fraction of first world populations lack any sort of religious affiliation.

Second, the language(s) and dialect we acquire unconsciously during childhood normally last a lifetime and tell the trained listener who we are and whence we come. It takes considerable effort and perhaps professional coaching to switch from a localized dialect to standard national speech or another tongue. On the other hand, in first world countries in general, an individual may be born into a specific faith or none at all, but can later enjoy the option of changing his or her affiliation any number of times or dropping out entirely from any kind of religious connection. Consequently, we might anticipate much ampler opportunity for rapid place-related religious convergence or divergence than seems to be the case with relatively stable, slowly evolving speech patterns. What do the data tell us?

Unfortunately, in the case of the United States, the analyst must deal with exasperating problems in the availability and quality of data and truly major challenges in making sense of them (Zelinsky 1961, 141–44). No small part of the difficulty is the sheer number of faiths, denominations, and congregations in question. Quite emphatically, within this realm of social reality, the claim of American exceptionalism is unassailable. No other nation is within haling distance in terms of relevant numbers. Another major obstacle is a questionable interpretation of the Constitution that prevents the Bureau of the Census from collecting any information from individuals or households on church membership or religious preference or practice, something done periodically in a number of other countries.[3]

As a result, such recent statistics as we do have were assembled and published by nongovernmental organizations that are obliged to rely on the ability and willingness of central denominational offices to provide data. Some of these offices lack the capability or are unwilling to offer any figures on membership or other attributes of their flock. Moreover, we are totally in the dark when it comes to the many thousands of independent or unaffiliated congregations. The upshot is that it is not simple to interpret the significance of the numbers we do have by state, metropolis, county, or whatever, if only because membership criteria vary so greatly from one group to another. Then, even if membership statistics were comparable cross-denominationally, information on actual attendance at church services and other indications of personal religiosity are woefully scarce and unreliable. Opinion polls and other sources furnish material only at the grossest areal level and have other serious shortcomings. Consequently, whatever numbers and maps we have for the American religious scene at any given point in time are fuzzy approximations, and inferences as to change over time and space must be ever so tentative.

But, turning away from membership and survey data and using a totally different approach to the regionalization of religion or, rather, personal religiosity, in a recent project (2007) I collected relevant data in scores of cemeteries in a number of widely separated American localities. The evidence is in the form of the incidence, by date, of verbal, pictorial, or symbolic statements of religious sentiment on gravestones. The pronounced variations over time in the Gravestone Index need not detain us here. But what was unforeseen and most perplexing—and relevant to this discussion—is the absence of any significant interregional differentials in the index from the 1850s (earlier data are too fragmentary) up to the present. Thus, for example, the South, past and present, registers as being no more pious than the non-South. Such a finding of early and, in this instance, durable national homogeneity ties in with certain other observations offered elsewhere in this study, especially in Chapter 2, where I tendered the notion of a premodern commonality in livelihood patterns and social arrangements pervading early American life throughout the land. The question awaits future investigation.

But setting aside all qualifications, there is no doubt as to the existence of religious regions in the United States at least as defined in terms of claimed denominational membership. Evidently the map I drafted using 1952 data (1961, 193; also see J. R. Shortridge 1976) was the first cartographic effort to document the reality. Subsequently, Edwin Scott Gaustad and Philip Barlow (2001), in their magnificently comprehensive treatment of the historical geography of American religions via scores of maps and graphs, have offered us a series of multicolor plates displaying "Regional Denominational Predominance" at the county level for the years 1790, 1830, 1850, 1870, 1890, 1916, 1936, 1952, 1971, and 1990. Although there is no explicit delineation of regions in this series, the reader can readily visualize the existence of the major ones. Especially noteworthy is a persistent southern region that has received both scholarly and, as the "Bible Belt," popular attention (Heatwole 1978). In another interesting approach to regionalization, James Shortridge (1977) has plotted by county five "Religious Types" (Transition; Intense Conservative Protestant; Diverse Liberal Protestant; Catholic; and Super Catholic), but without drawing regional boundaries.

My 1961 depiction of "Major Religious Regions" and other relevant maps establishes the existence of several that, for the most part, coincide nicely with the general cultural regions I consider later in this study. Thus we have the South, New England, a Pennsylvania-German Midland, the Mormon Region, and a heavily Catholic/Hispanic Southwest, along with a Catholic southern Louisiana, or Acadiana. But it is notable again that there is no singular Middle West. The territory so conventionally delimited is split between two major regions. Furthermore, we can discern no western religious region as a cohesive entity.

So what do the available maps and statistics tell us about any increase or decrease in place-to-place differences in America's outward religious characteristics? Whatever quantitative or territorial shifts have occurred over time are relatively minor; near-stability seems to be the rule, even in the face of the recent appearance of many new homegrown and exotic religious creeds from overseas. And, incidentally, the data do not support any significant secularization of American society as would be expected by the majority of students of modernization.

The one scholar who claims "Regional Divergence in Religious Affiliation" has been Roger Stump (1984) in his state-scale analysis of the membership of major Protestant and Roman Catholic congregations over the period 1906–1971. But, on the other hand, in a more recent study based on his own analysis of earlier writings, Thomas Crawford concludes that "the literature . . . suggests that, to a large extent, the U.S. religious landscape has been fairly stable during the second half of the twentieth century" and "traditional regional patterns remain imprinted upon the landscape" (T. Crawford 2005, 52–53, 82; also see Newman and Halvorson 1984). Similarly, Samuel Hill (1985) argues strongly for the persistence of those established patterns on the part of both native and immigrant populations.[4]

We are left with a frustrating situation. In contrast to language, where a single mode of speech dominates the scene and for which we have adequate data, the religious landscape is a multilayered tapestry, for which we have incomplete and flawed information. Although we can track a leading denomination or two, we cannot begin to capture the complex actuality in all its many dimensions.

If forced to draw a conclusion, I must state, yes, we do have persistent, meaningful gross religious regions—another demonstration of the ever-lasting power of cultural inertia. But one cannot assess their strength or say with any confidence that they are becoming more strongly or weakly defined or whether, overall, in spatial terms American religious practice has been more convergent than divergent. Then, casting a glance at the future, there is every likelihood that such questions will become more difficult to answer as additional millions of immigrants bring with them both traditional and unfamiliar faiths and settle in a rather irregular territorial fashion. (Perhaps a glance at ongoing developments in northwest Europe may offer some enlightenment.) Then a final puzzle is how to unpack the relationship between conventional churches and the American civil religion, something notable and durable, and how it has fared over time and space.

## Political Belief and Behavior

If our available evidence concerning language and religion, two of the most central components of any cultural system, fails to support the notion of convergence, or cultural homogenization, within the United States, what do we find in turning to another key element, political behavior? Fortunately, geographers, historians, and political scientists have expended a great deal of effort in exploring the spatiotemporal aspects of the ballots cast by American voters. Less fortunately, scholars have paid much less attention to other equally revealing facets of political sentiment. Our libraries do not contain a single serious study of the important topic of the historical geography of voter turnout. Similarly, scholars have failed to examine how voter registration varies over time and space by party or as a percentage of the eligible electorate.[5] A single partial exception, a map depicting registration by party and minor civil division in Pennsylvania as of 1983 (Cuff et al. 1989, 182–83) vividly illustrates the sharp intrastate discontinuities that must also prevail in the many other states having a complex social geography.

Then, although the United States does not conduct nationwide referenda, a number of states do so within their borders, and analyses of the results could tell us much about how the political landscape has shifted over the years in some crucial corners of the nation. Unfortunately, national opinion polls posing political questions are not too enlightening since findings are reported just for the past few decades and by only three or four gross divisions of the country. A final approach to the political regionalization of the United States has been the plotting of congressional votes on selected politically or geographically sensitive legislative issues (Martis 1989, 1993; Mellow 2008). The resulting maps and graphs are interesting and useful but only to a limited extent, for two reasons. First, the territory and population represented by congressional districts can be highly irregular in shape and heterogeneous in sociocultural composition. Second, the elected member's decisions on given issues may reflect personal views or various political pressures that may not correspond with the interests of his or her constituents.

We are left, then, as our major resource with a series of penetrating studies and ambitious atlases that delineate American political geography by scanning voting patterns, almost always for presidential candidates, at state or county levels from 1788 onward. The undisputed pioneer in this enterprise was Frederick Jackson Turner (Archer et al. 2006, 24–25), beginning with an essay in 1914, then a fuller fleshing out of the method in 1932 with maps and discussion that argue for the relevance of "sections" and other geographical factors in the spatial patterns of national elections. In that same year, Paullin and Wright produced a monumental historical atlas that, inter alia, painstakingly documented in maps and commentary all the presidential elections (and votes on some other political questions) up to 1928 (1932, 88–104, pls. 102–11), and did the same for some crucial congressional votes (ibid., 104–24, pls. 112–22). Subsequently, other publications have updated the cartographic chronicle (Archer and Taylor 1981; Archer and Shelley 1986; Archer, Lavin, Martis, and Shelley 2002; Menendez 2005; Archer et al. 2006; Morrill, Knopp, and Brown 2007). Only rarely are midterm elections mapped (Morrill, Knopp, and Brown 2007, 28). Archer et al. 2006 may well prove to be *the* definitive documentation and critical discussion of presidential elections.

These volumes do not always seek to recognize or map regions explicitly, although Turner is consistent in his vision of North, South, and West as sections. But in an elaborate factor analysis of voting data at the state level that did not result in drawing definite regional boundaries, Archer and Taylor (1981, 99–113) identified three regional factors that support Turnerian doctrine: Northerness, Southerness, and Westerness (their spelling) in addition to a Uniqueness factor. These factors fluctuate in strength but materialize with some consistency during the period 1872–1980. "That the sectional basis of American politics does consist of three distinct sections is conclusively shown through our regionalization by S-mode factor analysis" (ibid., 208). But their concept of regional factors that stretch or shrink over space as relevant conditions change is a wholly economistic one.[6] No consideration is given to historical, religious, ethnic-racial, or other attitudinal factors that may impinge on voting decisions.

Taking a quite different approach, Daniel Elazar (1966, 1994; also see C. A. Johnson 1976) has delivered an alternative geographic perspective on the structure of American political behavior. After assembling masses of data on local political policy and practice, community and ethnic history and ideologies, and other social and cultural variables relevant to political behavior (Archer and Shelley 1986, 20), he formulated and mapped another three-way system, but one at best only partially coincident with the Turner/Archer/Taylor scheme. The three subcultures in question are the Moralistic, Individualistic, and Traditionalistic. When the subcultures are mapped, there is coincidence with only one, Southerness, as proposed by Archer and Taylor. It is noteworthy that, in the eastern half of the nation, Elazar's three subcultures tend to occupy east-west state-level swaths corresponding crudely to our three major early, and persistent, culture areas. On the other hand, a distinct West fails to materialize. The states in question, along or beyond the 100th meridian, display a medley of the trio of subcultures.

The most recent political regionalization of the United States is that used by Earl Black and Merle Black (2007) in their analysis of the shifting fortunes of the two major parties from the 1950s to 2006, simply five blocs of states as follows: Northeast; South; Midwest; Mountains/Plains; Pacific. (Note again the absence of any unitary West.) They fail to offer any rationale for their system, simply assuming it to be self-evident. Also lacking is any explicit inquiry into convergence or divergence among their regions.

Unquestionably, then, political regions, as perceived through the cloudy lenses of Elazar and others, have existed in the United States for the past two hundred years or so. But it is also obvious that, unlike the situation with respect to language and religion, such entities have been rather volatile over time, subject to shifts in boundaries, character, and intensity. Perhaps the only near-constant feature of the various maps has been the solid southern political region, at least since the end of the Reconstruction, a predictability interrupted only during the transition in the 1950s and 1960s from Democratic to Republican solidity.[7]

In the recent past, journalists and the general public have become fixated on a highly simplistic binary carving up of the country: Red (Republican) states vs. Blue (Democratic), a formulation that glosses over more sophisticated approaches and lacks continuity with a complicated past. It also ignores the actual mood of the great majority of voters.[8] "Although the Red and Blue division is real, it is at the same time the case that most of the electorate is not at the ideological extremes, and a significant share are somewhat in the middle" (Morrill, Knopp, and Brown 2007, 29).

But we have yet to confront the political dimension of the central question of this inquiry: has the United States been experiencing convergence or divergence, or possibly a complex stasis, in the territorial aspects of its social and cultural life? In lieu of any other test of the political material, I have contrived a Diversity Index, a version of the familiar Segregation Index, one that states the percentage of aggregate national ballots cast in presidential elections for Republican, Democratic, and all third party candidates lumped together that would have to be shifted to other parties so as to achieve identical shares in all states, and applied it to data for the period 1856–2004 (table 5.1). The year 1856 is the starting point for that was when our two dominant parties first emerged on the scene in tandem and began their long-lasting rivalry. The reasons for omitting 1864, 1868, and 1872 are obvious enough, while the inclusion of 1876 is debatable.

The results are thought-provoking. After the traumatic elections of 1856 and 1860, the index has fluctuated erratically, displaying no clear long-term trends. Moreover, since the 1928 election, it has moved up and down within rather narrow limits: 3.58 to 9.05. But, taking the figures at hand to a higher level of abstraction, we find that the index averages out at 10.01 for the 18 elections held from 1856 to 1936, but only 5.58 for the 17 dating from 1940 to 2004. Does this suggest a modest degree of state-level convergence in political sentiment over the long run? We can only conjecture. The only general conclusion to be drawn from this exercise is that, insofar as partisan preferences exhibited in presidential elections reflect the political composition of the general population, the place-to-place differences therein are relatively minor and show no sign of profound change.

Other scholars have failed to recognize any signs of national convergence in voting patterns at the regional or section level (Sharkansky 1969, 78; Archer and Shelley 1986, 54; Murauskas, Archer, and Shelley 1988, 81; D. H. Fischer

Table 5.1. A Diversity Index* of State-Level Popular Vote in Presidential Elections, 1856–2004

| | | Popular Vote | | |
|---|---|---|---|---|
| | D.I. | R | D | Others |
| 1856 | 17.87% | 33.13% | 45.31% | 21.56% |
| 1860 | 33.76 | 39.79 | 29.49 | 30.72 |
| 1876 | 5.24 | 47.93 | 50.87 | 1.20 |
| 1880 | 7.07 | 48.31 | 47.89 | 3.80 |
| 1884 | 5.45 | 48.24 | 48.54 | 3.22 |
| 1888 | 5.35 | 47.85 | 48.65 | 3.50 |
| 1892 | 11.18 | 42.47 | 46.06 | 11.06 |
| 1896 | 8.40 | 51.07 | 46.69 | 2.24 |
| 1900 | 6.29 | 51.67 | 45.51 | 2.82 |
| 1904 | 9.99 | 56.42 | 37.60 | 5.98 |
| 1908 | 7.10 | 51.50 | 43.08 | 5.36 |
| 1912 | 11.25 | 23.18 | 41.82 | 35.00 |
| 1916 | 7.26 | 46.08 | 49.27 | 4.65 |
| 1920 | 9.28 | 60.55 | 34.29 | 5.16 |
| 1924 | 14.17 | 54.18 | 28.89 | 16.93 |
| 1928 | 6.38 | 58.01 | 40.82 | 1.17 |
| 1932 | 7.55 | 39.59 | 57.32 | 3.09 |
| 1936 | 6.56 | 36.54 | 60.19 | 3.27 |
| 1940 | 5.74% | 44.77% | 54.69% | 0.52% |
| 1944 | 6.65 | 45.87 | 51.64 | 2.49 |
| 1948 | 7.00 | 44.99 | 49.57 | 5.43 |
| 1952 | 3.60 | 54.88 | 44.38 | 0.73 |
| 1956 | 4.79 | 57.36 | 41.50 | 1.14 |
| 1960 | 3.42 | 49.55 | 49.72 | 0.73 |
| 1964 | 6.21 | 38.47 | 61.05 | 0.48 |
| 1968 | 9.05 | 43.41 | 42.72 | 13.87 |
| 1972 | 5.65 | 60.69 | 37.46 | 1.85 |
| 1976 | 3.58 | 48.00 | 50.06 | 1.94 |
| 1980 | 5.21 | 50.75 | 41.01 | 8.24 |
| 1984 | 4.02 | 58.77 | 40.56 | 0.67 |
| 1988 | 6.76 | 58.83 | 40.56 | 0.61 |
| 1992 | 5.36 | 37.45 | 43.01 | 19.54 |
| 1996 | 5.25 | 40.71 | 49.03 | 10.05 |
| 2000 | 6.33 | 47.87 | 48.38 | 3.75 |
| 2004 | 6.18 | 51.39 | 46.27 | 0.34 |

*Percentage of aggregate national ballots cast that would have to be shifted to other parties to achieve identical shares in all states

1989, 884–89). But if we take table 5.1 at face value, it is hard to avoid a verdict of at least a mild degree of long-term convergence while also affirming the longevity of those venerable sections first identified by Turner.

The most explicit attack on the question of geographical change in American political behavior, at least in recent decades, may be that by Nicole Mellow (2008, esp. 164–79) in a study charting patterns of congressional votes over the past half-century on socially and economically sensitive issues. After an analysis, based on four large regions—North, South, West, and Pacific Coast—she affirms the durability of regional distinctiveness.

> One of the most often cited political aphorisms of late is that place-based differences are disappearing ... [I]s there an inevitable march toward convergence or toward progress, as American cultural mythologizing (from both left and right) would suggest? If the recent past is prologue to the future, the answer is, Not necessarily. This book argues against popular wisdom, citing how modernizing changes and new ideas during the last fifty years have been differently incorporated by, and indeed have reinforced, America's distinctive regions. (173)

Then, if we scan the partisan scene at a finer spatial scale, that is, by county, as Bill Bishop has done (2008, 10, 45–47), we discern more than simple regional persistence of voting patterns. Instead the territorial segregation of Republicans and Democrats shows unmistakable signs of intensification in recent decades.

Finally, if we conjecture further, we must also puzzle over some urgent issues. Is political allegiance as meaningful an index of personal or place identity as language or religion, given the fact that so many individuals can change party affiliation repeatedly and that we may be witnessing a significant increase over time in the number of independent or swing voters? Then, as indicators of place identity, is it not plausible that choices in national (as well as local) elections may be less sensitive to general regional characteristics than to immediate ethnic/racial, class, religious, moral, and immediate pocketbook considerations or to residence, that is, urban vs. rural or inner city vs. suburban? Obviously we are still a long way from any adequate understanding of how our political leanings do, or do not, contribute to erasure or maintenance of place-to-place difference in the United States.

### Foodways

For human beings, food and drink amount to much more than mere biological imperatives. Particular comestibles and potables, whether sought after or taboo, can bear powerful emotional or symbolic weight and can serve as markers of personal and group identity. If dietary complexes are products of climate, soils, available fauna and flora, along with technology, economics, ethnic and religious heritage, and *cultural diffusion*, one would logically expect some sorting out into discrete regional parcels. And that is indeed what has long prevailed in such countries as India, China, Italy, France (Bell and Valentine 1997, 158), and Mexico, as well as in a bygone aboriginal America. So what is the situation in the United States? Is there a distinctive national cuisine? Does the country contain a set of recognizable dietary regions? And, if so, has their vitality been waxing or waning?

The answer to the first pair of questions is a qualified yes. The early colonists along the Atlantic seaboard bore with them the dietary preferences of the homelands, and finding, at least in New England and the middle colonies, only partially alien physical conditions, they were able to maintain some semblance of traditional eating and drinking patterns.[9] But only to a degree. If familiar grains, fruits, and vegetables flourished throughout most of the freshly settled land, colonists soon learned that, when planted to the maize so eagerly borrowed from Native Americans, their fields yielded much greater caloric bounty than when they essayed wheat, oats, rye, or barley. Then, if cattle, chickens, and especially hogs found New World fields and forests much to their liking, that was not the case for sheep, while milk and meat from goats virtually disappeared from the kitchen. Although northwest Europeans had always consumed fish and other marine foods in rather large quantities, in America it proved impractical to transport them inland farther than a single day's journey, with the predictable outcome for the standard national diet.

This cuisine, which has prevailed over at least two-thirds of the conterminous United States, is based on beef, pork, and poultry, milk and milk products, maize (and later soybean) products, breads based on wheat, oats, and rye, a variety of fruits and vegetables (especially white potatoes), water, coffee, various distilled spirits, and, eventually, carbonated beverages. The aboriginal contributions to this mix are not trivial. In addition to the all-important maize, we have our New World predecessors to thank for a variety of beans and squashes, sunflowers, pecans, maple syrup, the clambake, and knowledge of an abundance of wild edible and medicinal plants, in addition to the potato, peanut, tomato, and turkey that arrived on these shores from Latin America via Europe. In sum, then, while akin to its Old World antecedents, this dietary complex is specific to the United States or to most of its territory.

After the standard Euro-American dietary complex had solidified and spread across the continent, there were, of course, local and largely temporary modifications with the influx of immigrant Germans, Scandinavians, Jews and other Eastern Europeans, Italians, Cubans, and a varied lot of others. Eventually, their descendants would join the majority population in matters of taste, reverting to ancestral foodways only at holidays and other sacred occasions or at ethnic food festivals. In some isolated cases, however, the Old World edible has managed to survive, if only in local niches. Thus the availability today, if one knows when or where to venture, of borscht, the knish, bialy, lutefisk, haggis, polenta, and the pasty (the last in Michigan's Upper Peninsula (Lockwood and Lockwood 1991). There may also be a notable exception in the persistence, after more than three centuries, of Pennsylvania-German cookery in portions of the commonwealth. Less persistent may be a wide variety of local recipes, indigenous or imported, items that may have vanished but still recalled by residents, or at least the names thereof, when DARE fieldworkers quizzed them. Thus there are no fewer than eighty-eight state- or region-specific items (for example, apple slump, Bob Andy pie, alligator bread) among just the A and B entries in volume 1.

The outstanding regional exception to the standardized Euro-American cuisine is, of course, to be found in the South, whose distinctive dietary regime has been set forth authoritatively by Rupert Vance (1935, 411–41) and Sam Hilliard (1972, 37–69) as well as in many other publications and learned conferences. Early British colonists from Virginia southward to Georgia, as did their later inland successors, encountered a much less familiar physical setting than did their neighbors to the north. The long, hot summers and mild winters, unfamiliar soils, and exotic plants, insects, and other animal life presented serious challenges to the cultivator and rancher, and thus to the spouse who set the table. The early solution has basically lasted to this day. It involves heavy reliance on pork, corn bread, along with hominy, grits, and other corn products, molasses (derived form sorghum or sugar cane), hot wheaten biscuits, turnip greens, sweet potatoes, with the occasional chicken, rice, and, where available, catfish, all washed down with distilled spirits or coffee and, more recently, iced tea or buttermilk. Beef, fresh fruits (aside from watermelon), and most vegetables are, at best, marginal to these staples.[10] It is worth noting that some crucial items, namely sorghum, rice, and sugar cane, arrived directly or otherwise from Africa, as did the less vital okra, watermelon, and guinea fowl. Arguably, the most authentic southern food complex is that practiced by African Americans, the soul food later transported north and west into urban ghettos.

Covering such a broad territory as it does, it is hardly surprising to learn that the Southern dietary region has its subregions. Thus "outside the cotton belt, mountain and coastal diet areas are clearly marked" (R. B. Vance 1935, 430). Nor should we be taken aback by the ceaseless operation of *cultural drift* and local invention. Thus, as a largely twentieth-century innovation, pork and beef barbeque, probably of West Indian origin, has settled in firmly throughout the South with many a local or personal variation. For example, Kovacik and Winberry (1987, 209; also see H. L. Preston 1991a, 194–95) have mapped just within South Carolina four distinct barbeque subregions, each characterized by emphasis on either tomato, ketchup, mustard, or vinegar and pepper sauce.

Furthermore, despite the saturation of the nation's groceries and eating places with mass-produced edibles and menus, "not only have traditional southern foods survived, or at least the best of them, but dishes peculiar to regions within the South still thrive. Texas still prides itself on barbeque and chili. Kentuckians still make burgoo, and south of the Kentucky line Brunswick stew is a favorite. Virginia and North Carolina still produce superb hams; South Carolina and Georgia still use leftover rice for delicious rice puddings. Spanish bean soup and eggs Malaguena are still favorites in Florida" (J. G. Taylor 1982, 154).

In sections of the mountain South, the garlic-like ramps are celebrated at special festivals (Hufford 2005), while elsewhere in the region many small restaurants specializing in catfish are still in business (H. L. Preston 1991a, 194), and many Louisianians dote on crawfish (Gary 1973). Then, on the very edge of the South, there is the intensely parochial "Cincinnati chili culinary complex," recently originated by Greek immigrants and lovingly devoured in great quantities by loyal locals (Lloyd 1981).

In addition to the Southern region, we must not overlook two other sections of the country that stand apart from mainstream America in matters of the palate: southern Louisiana's Acadiana and the Hispanic Southwest (and, as a possible third, portions of Florida with their heavy influx of Cubans, Haitians, and others from the West Indies and beyond). No one would dare dispute the singularity—and glory!—of the Acadian complex, the product of French, Caribbean, African, Spanish, and Native American contributions and so loudly, joyously acclaimed in many a cookbook and restaurant review. Then, when the Spanish and Mexicans colonized the borderlands from California to Texas, they automatically introduced their own dietary preferences, but occasionally adopted some Native Americana recipes and foodstuffs.

The Southwestern region shows little sign of serious attrition, aside from the loss of Anglicized California, reinforced as it is by constant streams of newcomers from Mexico and Central America. But, like the Southern region, the Southwestern is not a monolithic entity. In his delineation of Tejano South Texas as a distinctive Mexican American subregion, Daniel Arreola distinguishes one critical product. "The flour tortilla taco is the regional icon of South Texas Mexican food and more than any single item distinguishes this ethnic foodway from other Mexican American food traditions . . . One ethnographer who studies Tejano migrant farmworkers claims that 'the tamale has no serious rival' in the array of artifacts with which these people identify themselves" (2002, 171–72). And he proceeds to furnish us with a map of the Taco-Burrito and Taco-Barbeque lines as defining the western and eastern limits, respectively, of his South Texas Mexican food region (2002, 175).

I trust that the canny reader can visualize the location of the four dietary regions so far identified: the dominant coast-to-coast Euro-American; the Southern; the Southwestern; and the Acadian. But, then, pursuing the second of our three central queries regarding foodways, the question arises: can we subdivide the largest of the four into meaningful subregions? The answer: conceivably.

We do have at hand an abundance of potentially relevant data, especially the surveys periodically conducted by marketing research firms that are area-specific as to what is being purchased by way of food and drink and thus presumably consumed near point of purchase. The difficulties here are multiple. Institutional food providers may not be quizzed; we have no way of knowing what dishes are assembled from the commodities being bought or the composition of meals; the surveys do not cover livestock, fruit, and vegetables or wine and other beverages produced privately by ordinary folks, then consumed at home or donated, exchanged, or bartered among various parties. Also missing are items purveyed at farmers' markets. Finally, the surveys probably omit most of the peculiar localized foodways practices that are most diagnostic of regional character.

What we do have in endless quantity are regional cookbooks that celebrate "indigenous" specialties of various localities but fail to inform us as to the extent of their popularity or familiarity. An ideal example is Clementine Paddleford's *How America Eats* (1960) with its hundreds of regional recipes. In addition, we have had recently a veritable explosion of food festivals that endeavor to glorify some local or regional product, in all too many instances items on life support or facing extinction (Geffen and Berglie 1986). In a collection of twenty-four essays, amounting to a requiem, extolling the delights of localized edibles and potables, including Indiana's persimmons, Brunswick stew and burgoo, hot Cajun sausage, black walnut, Tillamook cheddar, and chilis, Raymond Sokolov is dismissive as to their viability. "For the most part . . . the survival of regional foods and food customs in the United States is a token survival. Most regional foods never left home and are rarely served even there except in distorted, modernized versions warmed over for tourists in 'historic' restaurants or on special occasions sponsored by chambers of commerce and other groups dedicated to the promotion of local pride" (1981), 4).

But in a few notable cases, whether thanks to the persuasiveness of the marketers or the normal process of *cultural diffusion*, some regional or ethnic foods have become ubiquitous. Thus southern barbeque, chili con carne, wild rice, Key lime pie, and New England clam chowder are now on the national menu. On the other hand, non-southerners have resisted the charms of grits and okra and show only the mildest interest in hush puppies and other types of corn bread, while polenta, haggis, and Jewish stuffed kishkes and matzos remain ghettoized.

When it comes to the consumption of alcoholic beverages, we are blessed with a single pioneering study (Rooney and Butt 1978; also see Garwood 1988, 94) that strongly hints at the existence of meaningful regions. Thus bourbon—that great American invention—finds special favor in the Southeast, a region in which malt beverages are far less popular then elsewhere, while there is a distinct clustering of wine-loving states on the West Coast and in the Northeast. Then one can only gasp at the astonishing predilection for brandy among Wisconsin residents, whose per-capita guzzling outdistances the second-ranking state by a ratio of eight to one! Other studies dealing with moonshine whisky most decidedly bolster claims for the uniqueness of southern culture (Durand 1956; *Moonshine* 1971). But we remain woefully ignorant of the detailed geography, past or present, of beer consumption by the American masses, the amount, varieties, and brands of the mass-produced beverage.

In a totally different approach to just one narrow phase of the American foodscape—and assuming that choices in eating out are culturally nontrivial—I have studied the geography of ethnic restaurant cuisines, exploiting as data sources entries in the classified section of telephone directories (1985). The mapping of Italian, Mexican, Chinese, French, and Japanese restaurants by metropolitan area revealed marked place-to-place differences in the popularity or acceptability of their cuisines. Mapping the three dominant cuisines circa 1980 resulted in the depiction of Italian, Chinese, and Mexican regions that fill the entirety of the country, along with southern Canada (ibid., 66). But obviously any such patterning is quite evanescent in a rapidly evolving gastronomic scene and one governed to a decided degree by commercial enterprise rather than preexisting regional cultural configurations.

Since my 1985 article, the national and regional restaurant chains and some independent entrepreneurs have continued to level the gastronomic terrain while featuring their version of ethnic cuisine. Faux Mexican establishments are now virtually universal, as are various Italian operations, and Japanese eating places have appeared in every large city.[11] A craze for southern barbeque, or a reasonable facsimile thereof, has also swept the nation, with Cajun menus following close behind. And it is now a rare metropolis that does not have one or more cafes pushing the southwestern motif.

But it is important to note another basic spatial consideration in surveying the geography of exotic restaurant cuisines. While you can now patronize eating places featuring Chinese, Italian, Mexican, and perhaps southwestern or barbeque dishes in cities of even moderate size, you are likely to be disappointed if searching for Afghan fare in Peoria, Tibetan delicacies in Barstow, or Iranian offerings in Wheeling—or even an Italian eatery in those few and far between towns of eastern Montana. Although, as noted elsewhere, the deep historic dichotomy between town and countryside in America has been essentially shattered in recent years, it is still alive and well—Metropolis vs. Boondocks—at the more stratospheric levels of Culture (with that capital C).

It would not be fair to conclude this discussion of efforts to regionalize American food habits without mentioning another promising strategy. Embarking on a remarkable one-person project, Barbara Shortridge has been attempting to ascertain the food peculiarities of various sections of the country by means of mail questionnaires directed to housewives. There is a promising beginning in her report of the 744 responses and the resulting "Culinary Map of the Great Plains," covering the vast expanse from Montana to Texas and New Mexico, which does document decided North-South differences (B. G. Shortridge 2003, 525).

If our current knowledge of possible past and present subregions within the large Standard Euro-American Food Region remains hazy, we can be much more definite in responding to the question of whether there has been homogenization or convergence among putative subregions with an unqualified yes. As suggested earlier, as soon as modern means of transport and communication had been deployed throughout the land, the business community zealously set about producing, advertising, and selling highly standardized food products and meals from border to border. Then, although we have had countless regional cookbooks, their overall effect is to render regional practice universal, while the best-selling publications in this general genre are devoted to raising and standardizing culinary choices and expertise throughout the land, and may very well have done so. As Sidney Mintz has observed,

> Local variation in cuisine is under continuous pressure from commercial enterprise aimed at profiting by turning into a national fad every localized taste opportunity. Any natural product that is available in a place or season, and any distinctive cooking or flavoring method, excites merchants, packers, and processors intent on broadening their market. Of course not all of the products travel, and many do not travel well. In the view of food businessmen, it makes good sense to alter the nature of such foods in order to make them available elsewhere, even if they no longer are (or taste like) what they were at home . . .

Hence certain foods that are regionally distinctive become known to people elsewhere who have never eaten them except in the form of substitutes lacking any resemblance at all to the original. (2002, 27–28)

Another inevitable result of the rationalization of the food economy and the drive to extract maximum profit is the loss or near-extinction of the many varieties of fruit, vegetables, and livestock that had evolved over the generations in relatively isolated pockets of the land with their special physical conditions. Thus

in the United States, the nation's agricultural diversity, which had been rich in 1900, was vanishing from fields. A survey in 1983 found that, since 1903, the number of readily available varieties of cabbage dropped from five hundred and forty-four to twenty-eight; carrots dropped from two hundred and eighty-seven to twenty-one; cauliflower varieties fell from a hundred and fifty to nine; and varieties of pears fell from twenty-six hundred and eighty-three to three hundred and twenty-six. In many cases, the new commercial hybrids that replaced the traditional varieties no longer tasted as good—they were bred more for production than for flavor. (Seabrook 2007, 67)

Is there any need to reiterate the powerful impact of nationwide restaurant chains and their totally predictable menus ( Jakle and Sculle 1999), a development recounted in some detail in biographies of McDonald's (Fishwick 1978), White Castle (Ingram 1964), and Howard Johnson (Belasco 1979)? But the traveler who avoids standardized restaurant chains still encounters a remarkable repetitiveness in the bill of fare at independent, home-style eateries across the land—with the exception of those many southern businesses automatically serving up a dollop of grits.

The federal government has also been complicit in the campaign to standardize and unify the consumption patterns of the citizenry, most directly perhaps the Department of Agriculture. In addition to rationalizing the raising of crops and livestock, it has furnished guidelines to immigrant communities and the general public as to what constitutes healthful and nutritious meals (Perkin and McCann 1984). But perhaps even more influential in the long run has been the role of the military. The involvement of millions of American men and women in at least five major overseas conflicts during the twentieth century has meant not only large-scale mixing and mingling of volunteers and conscripts from every part of the nation along with the opportunity to be exposed to alien cuisines but, more directly, compulsory ingestion of thoroughly standardized rations. The effects linger on after demobilization. Writing about Howard Johnson, Paul Budra notes that "the typical meal they served (green salad, roll, steak, two vegetables, coffee, pie) was based on the Midwestern cuisine that came to dominate American tables after World War II, which had further homogenized the palate of the nation when meals based on this menu were served to American enlisted men fighting across the world" (2000, 234–35).

The tentative conclusion, then, given the fragmentary information at hand, must be that whatever regional or localized culinary particularity had prevailed in the United States in the past, with the notable exception of the South, Southwest, and Acadiana, has dwindled or faces erasure—a situation decidedly unlike what we have seen in the linguistic, religious, and political realms.

## Organized Sport

If a scholar had been tackling the central question addressed in this volume one hundred fifty years ago, he or she would have had little occasion to consider organized sport. Language, religion, and food are of primordial concern, and western Europe has developed a partisan political geography over the past few centuries; but place-making organized sport is a creature of the late nineteenth century, while coming into full bloom only during the twentieth. It is true enough that ever since human beings became human they have been playing games of one sort or another, but only slowly and gradually did organized competitions emerge—as happened with the ancient Olympics—events where specially trained athletes or teams perform before substantial numbers of onlookers. In the case of colonial and early republican America, there was the occasional horse race, wrestling or boxing match, or trials of strength or skill pitting individuals against each other and whatever informal team sports had survived the trans-Atlantic crossing, all such entertainments enacted before small crowds or perhaps none at all. But such activity had minimal place-making effect, and the only cash involved was in the form of private wagers.

The situation began to change substantially from the mid-nineteenth century on with revolutionary changes in transport and communication and as the general level of affluence rose and Americans enjoyed greater leisure. Among other developments in the mid-1800s, and as part of the nationalizing process, the United States, like a number of other nation-states, invented and accepted a national sport, baseball, which quickly became the rage for children and adults in every village and city (Voigt 1976) and began to attract large numbers of fans. Indeed, over time, this game, whose exportability has been limited to Canada, Japan, and a few Latin American and Caribbean countries, has acquired mythic, almost religious, status (M. R. Cohen 1946). Its enshrinement at Cooperstown attests to the fact (Grella 2003). On the other hand, some commentators would contend that American-style football now rivals or surpasses baseball as *the* great national passion. But, whatever the sport, it is in international competitions, especially the Olympics, where sport serves as a powerful agent for cementing American statefulness (Zelinsky 1988a, 107–12).

In any event, strong, sometimes hysterical, devotion to a particular sport and a particular team—one identified with a particular neighborhood, town, city, or state—has become a central element in the emotional life of a substantial fraction, perhaps even a majority, of Americans young and old. Local newspapers and radio television stations all strive energetically to inculcate team loyalty and, in so doing, create mappable fan sheds (Dow 1978). The high school teams are of local origin, of course, but it matters not that many or most of the nominally amateur members of the college squad or overpaid players in professional teams are recruited from distant parts of the land or even from overseas. What does matter mightily is winning, and thus shedding luster on the community and injecting meaning into our collective and individual lives.[12]

Do sport regions exist in the United States? Are certain pastimes exclusive to certain areas? Or are there pronounced emphases on some widespread sports in particular regions? A general answer to two of these questions is found in a unique map (Rooney and Pillsbury 1992, 15) that depicts eleven American sports regions, tracts within which a given sport or two is strongly favored but not to the exclusion of other major activities of national scope. It is important to note that none of the regions in question coincide with, or resemble, any of the culture areas that geographers and others have previously identified and mapped. (But the zeal of fans rooting for the New England Patriots and Boston Red Sox and Celtics has unquestionably quickened the vitality of the preexisting regional concept.) That finding is not unexpected in light of the fact that the presumable sports regions are so recent in origin and so often products of chance and the efforts of successful entrepreneurs and thus may not be rooted in deeper layers of culture.

A valid generalization is that the American athletic panorama is one in which a number of sports enjoy significant popularity rather evenly almost everywhere while others appear intermittently or with special vigor only in selected localities. The list of the former includes baseball, football, basketball (that hugely successful, now globalized, American invention), tennis, ping-pong, track, volleyball, wrestling, golf, and soccer (at least at the high school and college level) (Rooney 1974, 44–46.) One might add bowling to the list, although for reasons that remain mysterious, we find a pronounced concentration of bowling activity in the north-central states (Rooney 1974, 283; H. L. Preston 1991b, 198–99).

Environmental, historical, legal, and social factors help explain the spotty occurrence of certain sports. Thus climate, biogeography, and terrain have much to do with the location of skiing (Rooney and Pillsbury 1992, 122–23), fox hunting, iceboating, surfing, water polo, and whitewater racing. We must invoke history to account for the origin, diffusion, and current location of lacrosse (Ball and Loy 1975), the now nearly nationwide rodeo (Rooney and Pillsbury 1992, 112), fencing, squash, and crew (Rooney 1974, 278). State and local laws have restricted the range of horse racing and boxing, and shoved cockfights and dog fights underground in locations no one has been rash enough to map. The social factor is paramount in such elite diversions as dressage, imported English-style hunting (Raitz 1995d, 369–72), polo, and yacht racing. At the opposite end of the social spectrum we find the wild popularity, even passion, for "redneck" stock car racing in the South (Wilkinson 1980; Pillsbury 1995a, 1995b) and the indigenous southern style of fox hunting (Raitz 1998).

Geographers and sports sociologists still have much to learn about the spatial and cultural dimensions of sport. For example, among the remaining puzzles are such phenomena as the localized persistence of duckpin bowling in southern New England and Greater Washington, D.C., and rubberband duckpin bowling in Pittsburgh (Harmon 1985, 109; Rooney and Pillsbury 1992, 164). But, in response to the central question raised by this inquiry, it appears that the advent of any sort of regional patterning in American sport is so recent, the identity and boundaries of the regions still flexible enough, and information on temporal change so sparse that neither a nay or yea is an acceptable response as to the role of sport in the homogenization of the United States—or in its diversification.

## Music and Dance

Apart from the hapless tone-deaf or those suffering from amusia, all human beings seem susceptible to some degree to the charms of music—or at least to whatever forms of the art they have grown up with or later learned to savor.[13] Homo sapiens may be the only creature that is genuinely musical, but if the great majority of adult Americans utter words and sometimes complete sentences, worship, and vote, and all eat and drink, only a minor fraction of the national community are serious singers or instrumentalists—or dancers—on a regular basis (and those individuals are usually itinerant). Thus, if our near-universal affiliations with speech patterns, religion, foodways, and political ideology generally have territorial connotations, music and dance (the two are intertwined, of course) offer much more problematic challenges for the geographer.

Under premodern conditions, we can assume the existence of community- or region-specific forms of music and dance. But nowadays in the United States, as elsewhere, we are exposed to rapidly evolving musical experiences from anywhere and everywhere as new technologies shrink, stretch, dilute, and cross-fertilize previously discrete musical worlds, and individuals can be quite changeable in their enthusiasms.

Just as had happened in other realms of culture, the early European oc-cupiers of North America, as did African slaves, brought with them their familiar Old World musical instruments, folk and popular songs and dances, and elite art music, thus laying the groundwork for what would eventually become a distinctly American sound. But, given the diversity of musical traditions in the source areas, it is not surprising that Alan Lomax (1960, front endpaper) was able to map five regional styles of English-language folk songs, while Charles Gardner (1982, 239; also see Connell and Gib-son 2003, 33) plotted the ranges of the same number of Anglo-French-American fiddling styles.[14] Subsequent immigrants contributed other mu-sical and dance ingredients to the national and regional mixes, with greatest success in the cases of Germans, Irish, Poles, French Canadians, Jews, Mexicans, and Cubans. Particularly noteworthy is the durable polka craze, especially in the north-central states, and, by means other than immigra-tion, the widespread popularity of the Brazilian samba and other dances from that land. However, Native American music has failed to enter the mainstream either locally or nationally, remaining isolated wherever it manages to survive, and a twentieth-century fad for ersatz Hawaiian mu-sic was brief and superficial. The American masses have also been resistant to traditional Chinese, Japanese, East Indian, and Middle Eastern musical idioms.

It is not too far-fetched to claim that the very existence and perpetuation of an independent, unified United States would not have been possible without the prevalence of popular music that captured the ears and hearts of early citizens—and, most especially, military and patriotic songs and dances (V. B. Lawrence 1975; Zelinsky 1988a, 171–74). They were impor-tant, indeed arguably crucial, for the success of the rebels in the American Revolution (Moore 1846) and equally urgent—along with sentimental pop-ular songs—for the morale of Union forces in the Civil War (Stone 1941). Music also proved to be indispensable in the nation-building campaign for the abortive Confederacy. "The production of songbooks and sheet music outstripped every other area of southern publishing during the war, ex-panding dramatically in response to popular demand." Furthermore, "a number of Confederate songs served almost as catechisms in civics for the far-flung southern public" (Faust 1988, 18, 19).

Martial numbers continued to service the nationalistic, or statist, project quite well at least until the Spanish-American War or World War I. Perhaps more potently than any single orator or author, John Philip Sousa, with his remarkable military-style instrumental compositions quickened the pulse of the nation as he further solidified it (Harris 1983). His marches functioned "as 'a culture of reassurance' to a wide variety of Americans of all classes who felt threatened by industrial America's increasing, social, economic, and political unrest and violence" (Kenney 1999, 28–30). But, curiously enough, although each branch of the armed forces continues to this day to maintain musical ensembles of high quality, the original soul-stirring song or march may have fallen by the wayside since 1918 and certainly by 1945. If the Korean, Vietnam, or the two Gulf conflicts have generated any truly rousing musical number, I have yet to come across it.

Away from the battlefield, Americans had gathered together in musical communion by the early 1800s and throughout the later nineteenth century as publishers poured forth great quantities of nonviolent songbooks and sheet music, and every respectable middle-class household boasted a piano, harmonium, or organ, or aspired to acquire one. Absent too many other distractions, music-making at home, church, and other social gatherings was the general rule. Moreover, "the thousands of songs published between 1828 and 1860 in the United States . . . demonstrate that the song preferences of Americans from every part of the country were similar" (Tawa 1984, 19), thus fostering national singlemindedness.

Although the American musical language would never disown its western European ancestry, simple physical remoteness and cultural and social evolution have generated a unique nationwide musical realm. At the uppermost level, that of art music (a term much to be preferred over "classical"), Americans suffered through a long period of cultural cringe, as they had in literature, architecture, and the fine arts. In lieu of any outstanding models in the British Isles (at least until the twentieth century), elite music lovers turned primarily to the German/Austrian masters and, to a lesser extent, to French, Italian, and Russian repertoire. Ballet and dance aficionados also looked abroad.

Only belatedly did Charles Ives, Randall Thompson, Aaron Copland, George Gershwin, Samuel Barber, Duke Ellington, Stephen Sondheim, and a number of other young, gifted, up-and-coming composers declare aesthetic independence in the field of symphony, song, opera, and chamber music (Ross 2007, 120–56, 260–305). The result is that nowadays the discerning listener can usually detect the Americanness of a new composition on hearing just the opening notes, quite as German, French, Spanish, Czech, Russian, and Mexican art musics all have their distinctive aural fingerprints.

But in the United States any such national identity lacks a regional substratum. In their programming, our hundreds of professional, semipro, and amateur orchestras and the smaller number of dance companies seem oblivious to the regional resources of their surroundings. The occasional evocation of a specific place by a nineteenth- or twentieth-century American composer carries no larger regional message (Von Glahn 2003). As was so clearly the case with the fancier ethnic cuisines in American restaurants, the geography of art music and dance performed in concert halls makes little sense in regional terms. On the other hand, we run up against that durable cultural moat between elite metropolis and folksy countryside.

Within the field of popular music, Americans have quite successfully cultivated their own world of sound, one reaching from border to border via radio, television, singalongs, jukeboxes, and other media, an aural complex with little resemblance to what one hears in a British music hall or German beer parlor, and often with evocations of place (Gumprecht 1998). In the hands of such masters as Irving Berlin, Jerome Kern, Cole Porter, George Gershwin, and others, the popular tune entered the portals of genuine art, as did that glorious American innovation, the musical comedy. It is also noteworthy that jazz in all its many shades is a significant component of the nationally shared treasure that is American popular music. Despite its lowly origin in a corner of the Deep South and ultimate African heritage, it has permeated the mainstream culture and even made many a conquest overseas.

In a manner resembling the foodways situation, the pervasive standard American musical culture tolerates the existence of localized and regional exceptions.[15] Thus the large Latino communities of the Southwest and various metropolises elsewhere remain loyal to traditional or "norteno" music, and have even developed subregional variants, such as the "conjunto" played and sung in Tejano South Texas (Arreola 2002, 186–88), while a distinctive type of Latino music has been developing in south Florida (Curtis and Rose 1994). Similarly, the Cajuns of southern Louisiana have cultivated zydeco, their localized musical genre, and one that has captured the attention of outsiders (Kuhlken and Sexton 1994). Once again, as happened with some food items, the American South, which once had stood apart from the rest of the nation, eventually converted the entire nation to its "country" music.

It is to the poverty-stricken African American population of the Mississippi Delta, not the South in general, that we must turn for the gestation of the blues, a musical form that has gained the affection of a wide national audience (Ferris 1979, 1982; Cobb 1992, 277–305). In like fashion, the legendary birth of ragtime and jazz took place in some of the more disreputable black neighborhoods of New Orleans around 1900 before migrating to Memphis, Kansas City, Chicago, and the country at large (Ford 1971, 460). And, in the case of the local flowering of the Kansas City jazz style in the 1920s and 1930s, we have an ideal example of *cultural drift* in full spate (Pearson 1987). But it was at quite a distance from New Orleans in western North Carolina that white southerners invented bluegrass music (Carney 1974, 1996), a genre that has since spread far and wide (J. Wilson 1996, 88).

In still another example of the locational unpredictability of southern musical inventiveness there is the case of "beach music" in Myrtle Beach, South Carolina. "In Myrtle Beach beach music emigrated from the African American community to the mainstream. During the 1930s and 1940s African Americans were dancing the shag, a melding of the jitterbug and the lindy, and listening to swing music. Gradually a distinctive dance sound emerged with equal parts horns and rhythm, with roots in gospel and swing . . . The shag's popularity proved so enduring that in 1984 the South Carolina General Assembly adopted it as the official state dance" (K. Fuller 2006, 154, 163). Can this be the only instance of an official state dance?

Although most Americans are wont to conflate all forms of "country music" into a single entity and connect it with the entire South, as a matter of fact at least five really distinct substyles have existed (Carney 1982, 244; 1994, 125). In any event, those many radio stations throughout the land that have adopted a country music format don't make fine distinctions as to subtypes, thus projecting a blurred image of a unitary South as they play their part in what some commentators regard as the "Southernization of America" (Egerton 1974; Cobb 1982). Adding further momentum to the process is the popularity of both black and white gospel music, of presumed southern provenance, in all the numerous religious radio stations and programs.

If this chronicle has been composed a generation ago, it might well have terminated with the preceding paragraph and an added admission as to the impracticality of deciding whether territorial convergence or divergence had had the upper hand in the story of American music and dance. But, much more clearly than in the realms of language, religion, politics, or foodways, something novel and unforeseen has been going on of late in American music: an amalgam of postmodernism, globalization, and the rampant operation of *cultural drift* and instantaneous *cultural diffusion* that has been generating fresh forms of localism. As ragtime and jazz mutated to rhythm and blues, then to rock in all its subvarieties and, more recently, to punk, rap, and hip-hop, there was the concurrent immersion of the participants in the new space-shattering electronic media of communication, such as the Internet, and the ease and frequency of foreign travel. But, paradoxically, as happened in other economic, social, and cultural fields, "even under these circumstance of global integration, local identities and affiliations did not disappear. On the contrary, the transnational economy often makes itself felt most powerfully through the reorganization of spaces and the transformation of local experience—especially within and across urban areas" (Lipsitz 1994, 4; also see Connell and Gibson 2003, 102).

One of the results of all this musical cross-pollination has been the blossoming, often ephemerally, of musical "scenes" or place-based "sounds." Thus "we view a local scene to be a focused social activity that takes place in a delimited space and over a specific span of time in which clusters of producers, musicians, and fans realize their common musical taste, collectively distinguishing themselves from others by using music and cultural signs often appropriated from other places, but recombined and developed in ways that come to represent the local scene" (Peterson and Bennett 2004, 8).[16]

For obvious reasons, "port cities such as Liverpool, Hamburg, New Orleans and Oran (Algeria) became sites from where particular 'sounds' were said to have emerged" (Connell and Gibson 2003, 103), and port city Seattle, with its alternative rock scene, is another example (Bell 1996). But there have been many other venues. If college towns offer especially fertile soil for germination of localized musical scenes (Connell and Gibson 2003, 102–5), some major cities have also proved to be quite hospitable. Thus the Nashville Sound, Detroit's Motown, and a "Philly" Sound in Philadelphia (ibid., 98) as well as the development of sound and light shows in the Los Angeles of the 1960s (Rycroft 1998). In addition, black ghettos have been remarkably productive, issuing music that strongly insists on local identity (Forman 2002).

But all too often any local or regional success in creating fresh musical styles can prove self-defeating. As soon as tycoons in the music industry get wind of local breakthroughs, they will rush to commercialize the product at the national or international scale with scant regard for authenticity, a process documented in much detail in Joli Jensen's (1998) account of the Nashville Sound. But one must almost feel sorry for those tycoons, for what they are trying to do is to manipulate mercury. In any case, whatever the fate of latter-day local creativity, we are witnessing something essentially unprecedented: the interdependency of the parochial and the global. And, unlike the situation we face with language, religion, foodways, or politics, where only rarely can the lone individual register a regional or national impact, many a clever musical star can generate genuine microregions or have even broader impact. It is a democratic musical scene.

Then, beyond all the venues for commercial entertainment, one can be certain that, at any given moment, in dozens of American garages and basements, bunches of teenagers are gathered together trying to head out into virgin musical territory. "Beyond the dull compulsions of adult-organized activities and the terrors of everyday life . . . young people are carving out autonomous spaces and investing life with meaning. Innovating their own music scenes and secluding themselves in 'subcults,' kids manage to survive, thrive, and revive their spirits in the teenage wastelands of suburban America. People act, they react, they create and recreate, and sometimes they reach higher ground" (Gaines 1994, 64). Local cultural creativity is alive and well. With some confidence, one can predict a steady, stochastic eruption of novel popular musics hither and yon throughout the foreseeable future.

## Dress and Ornament

There is no need to equivocate here or to go on at great length. We have always had essential uniformity in style of clothing at the national, or continental, scale among Euro-Americans in North America from the colonial period on, and there is every indication this situation will persist indefinitely. Thus I need only repeat George Stewart's statement that "as opposed to the colorful history of American food and drink there is very little to be told about the history of American clothing" (1954, 125), while substituting the term "geography" for "history."[17] The unvarying practice in the past was to retain traditional European patterns of dress and ornament while hastening to adopt the latest in current fashion, initially from overseas. Today the United States is simply one participant and sometimes the leader in a global consortium of designers, tastemakers, and manufacturers in the garment and accessories industries.[18]

Such variation as we do observe in what Americans wear today is related to age, gender, weather and climate, social clique, and occupation, but only weakly to religion or ethnicity, and hardly at all to location per se. Whatever distinction once obtained in terms of social class or income has virtually vanished. In strolling through our central business districts, it is nearly impossible to distinguish the CEO from a pauper. But we might catch sight of an African American with a distinctive headwrap (Griebel 1995), an Indian American woman wearing her colorful sari, a recent African immigrant in traditional garb, or a Sikh gentleman sporting his turban. Then, in certain localities, we have the Amish in their eternally changeless garments and Hasidic men whose beards, earlocks, and black suits set them apart from a gentile world (Rubinstein 1995, 196, 198). We also find elements of non-Western dress and ornament in various Native American communities as well as Mexican pieces in the wardrobes of recent immigrants from south of the border. It is too early to tell whether such deviations from the general national pattern will survive much longer.

The single most boisterous claimant for regional recognition, the Western, turns out to be spurious. It may be true enough that we have an abundance of shops throughout the land purporting to sell "authentic" Western gear: boots, ten-gallon hats, fancy shirts, belt buckles, jewelry, and whatever.[19] But what they purvey is really the stage setting for a myth. As it happened, early westerners did their best to look like easterners. "Western merchants, manufacturers, trainmen, lawmen, saloon girls, teachers, and housewives did not look much different from their Eastern counterparts. Fashion and fashion sense were as important for people then as now . . . Being fashionable conveyed the mark of civilization; 'frontier' could imply lower social stature, backwardness, crudeness, romanticism, or even eccentricity" (Nottage 2001, 22). Moreover, "Some forms of clothing automatically associated with the West in fact did not originate there. So-called prairie dresses, worn by women whose faces were shaded by bonnets, seem like a frontier type, yet in reality they were simply day dresses just as commonly worn in the East" (Nottage 2001, 28).

But one clothing item—Levi's, or blue jeans—did indeed originate in the West, and during the past several decades has succeeded in saturating the entire country as well as much of the rest of the world. Although cowboys, who accounted for a minute fraction of the population of the western states, "usually did not think of themselves as anything more then men who worked hard from the back of a horse" (Nottage 2001, 34), their garments somehow became emblematic of the entire West.[20]

Emerging from its humble beginnings, we have the advent of an elaborate Western wardrobe by the mid-twentieth century. Its most flamboyant version is Rodeo Attire, a "style developed from a melting pot of clothing types: practical Western work wear, Native American costume, Mexican folk dress, theatrical Western costumes" (George-Warren and Freedman 2001, 129). That such a fictitious confection should appeal so effectively to a significant segment of the national population tells us something fundamental not just about the process of imagining a place that never really existed but, even more profoundly, about the not-so-well-being of our collective psyche.

What makes these clothes perennial, then, is that they are more than just a fashion statement . . . From playing cowboy to collecting cowboy, we dance between preserving and possessing dress of the West and wanting to be part of the West . . . As the iconographic symbols of the cowboy, this clothing represents independence, freedom, and individuality. And as more and more people spend time chained to their computers, there will probably arise an ever greater need for this sensibility in what they wear: if they can't roam the range, they can at least dress as if they were going to. (Ibid., 227)[21]

In summation, then, if there is still work to be done on the historical geography of Euro-American dress and ornament, it is unlikely to shed much light on the central question driving this inquiry.

What do we find when we contrast the geographic careers of foodways and clothing—those intimate ingredients of our daily existence—with the apparent regional stability of language, religion, and political behavior, three of the other basic dimensions defining our social or personal identity? In the American case, the former two—foodways and clothing—are decidedly susceptible to the blandishments of advertisers and merchants, as we also welcome the blessings of modern technology, a situation leading to substantial homogenization. In contrast, the territorial disposition of the ways we speak, worship, and vote—modes of behavior seemingly more closely entwined with our inner essence—seems relatively impervious to the pressures of modern media of communication and a good deal of proselytizing. But the differences between the two sets of cultural phenomena are a matter of degree and thus far from absolute. Can anyone imagine all American males going about in public wearing only loin cloths or favoring togas or women discarding everything except saris? Or is it conceivable that rice or manioc could become our dietary mainstay with two or three ample helpings every day? Some of us do become vegans, switch parties or denomination, and, within a single lifetime, most women have opted for slacks. But, however receptive we may be to a nationwide sharing of exotic accents in wardrobe or pantry, our basic systems of nourishment and bodily adornment repel radical de-Westernization.

## Informal Group Games

The subject is how American adults and children have been amusing themselves over the years with informal games involving two or more players which observe certain rules but seldom require referees or supervision and do not necessarily involve prizes. Left unexplored here are the many solitary pastimes, such as crossword puzzles, pinball machines, solitaire, stamp collecting, playing with toys, board games, handicrafts for fun, or the like and, of course, the organized sports treated earlier in this chapter.

Such social interaction and competition has been integral to human existence for millennia, whenever time could be spared from work, eating, sleep, and other urgent activities. Indeed some of the games youngsters still play today have been traced back to the ancient world.[22] Leisure time may have been at a premium in early America, but we have ample evidence that grownups and their offspring spent many of those precious hours in competitive games whether indoors or out in the open air. It is safe to conjecture that if many of these pastimes were traditional ones transferred from the Old World, local or regional variations in rules or nomenclature did develop during periods of relative isolation. Thus, in writing about the 1850–1900 period, Howard Chudacoff observes that "location—region and whether urban, small town, or rural—continued to distinguish play groups and play activities" (2007, 96).

Unfortunately, we have nothing in the United States to rival the mapping of "Children's Games in Street and Playground" in Great Britain so thoroughly executed by Iona and Peter Opie (1969). On the other hand, we do have evidence for the past, if not present, regional variety in such diversions within the United States in the vast compilation by DARE from documents and the recollections of older informants (but not yet analyzed to the point where we can decide on the presence or absence of regions). Within just the A and B entries, I have noted sixty-one children's games and seven played by adults that were specific in character and/or nomenclature in specific portions of the country. Whether they differed in more than name cannot be ascertained, but it is likely that migrants would develop new rules or nuances in practicing familiar activities after settling in distant destinations.

If I may wax autobiographical, let me recall the situation during my formative years (ca. 1927–37) in a Caucasian lower-middle-class/working-class neighborhood in Chicago. During school vacations and weekends, we kids would play outdoors from dawn to dusk stopping only for meals, errands, and the occasional storm (or the radio serials in early evening). Softball took up much of the boys' time, as we used the paved corners of a street intersection for bases and observed impromptu rules for strikeouts, home runs, and so on, and ignored traffic as much as possible while play went on for an indefinite number of innings. Another largely male endeavor was the occasional foot race, long jump, or wrestling bout, but the greatest excitement came from the heart-pounding, often hazardous, hide-and-seek games (with appropriate truce calls). Then, in empty lots, we would dig caves or build forts and improvise games to justify the effort. In wintertime, in addition to building snow houses, we would construct forts and wage fierce snowball battles. Kite flying was popular in the spring, but was usually a one-person affair. During the warmer months, there was mock warfare using homemade slingshots and wooden guns powered by heavy-duty rubber bands. We built most of our playthings ourselves, including soapbox scooters, since bicycles and other store-bought contraptions were beyond the means of most of us. Every week I would squander most of my allowance buying marbles and promptly lose all of them to my more adept competitors. As for the girls, they were preoccupied with jump rope competitions, along with the requisite chants, and with jacks and hopscotch.[23]

Let me ask the reader to recall the last time he or she witnessed boys playing marbles or girls engaged in hopscotch. As for myself, I have reconnoitered my old haunts a number of times in recent years without finding any juvenile players at large and indeed few pedestrians of any sort. Some alert colleagues of mine (Cross 2006; D. Wood 2006) confirm these impressions. On the other hand, one can still see traditional outdoor games and much street life in general in our more benighted Latino and African American neighborhoods (Chudacoff 2007, 201).

The statistical evidence is sparse but persuasive. Thus we learn that in the 1920s boys spent 58 percent of leisure time in streets and alleys, 6 percent in parks, schoolyards, and playgrounds, 7 percent in vacant lots, and 22 percent in private yards, leaving just 7 percent for other venues. Then a later study in the 1980s found that youths fourteen to eighteen devoted only 6 percent of leisure time to free play (Wartell and Mazzarella 1990, 176, 190).[24] Howard Chudacoff's general conclusion in a wide-ranging study of the history of juvenile play is in accord with the figures. "I believe that generally, and in a complex way, children's ability to play independently has eroded over time and that in the modern era this shrinkage has had unfortunate, if not perilous consequences" (2007, xiii). When it comes to adult games—a topic calling for much more research—my casual impression is that far fewer men and women today spend their spare time playing bridge, poker, pinochle, Monopoly, Scrabble, and other card and competitive board games. And indeed Robert Putnam has documented a recent decline in multihanded card games among adults (2000, 102–5).

The explanation is obvious, and it involves two powerful factors. First, since the 1950s, watching television has absorbed an increasing share of our waking hours, whatever our age, leaving less opportunity for other diversions.[25] Then, even more insidiously in the view of those who treasure spontaneity in play and place-to-place diversity is the immense popularity of video and other electronic games. Consequently, we now have old and young alike buying and playing the same universally shared repertoire of preprogrammed games throughout the nation and indeed the world, a phenomenon that tends to erase local identities.

The second, seemingly unrelated, factor is parental and general adult anxiety over child safety and achievement. We live now in an age when children have become a relatively rare and precious commodity, at least in emotional terms. In premodern America the average mother would produce eight to ten infants during her childbearing years. The more the merrier since the child could join the work force at a tender age and become an economic asset; and if some of the brood did not survive, as was often the case, the parents could adopt orphans from a nearby farm or village. Today, however, when the mean number of offspring barely reaches two, the emotional value of the child may have grown substantially even while its upbringing becomes ever more costly and any prospect of eventual economic return is problematic.

The consequence has been a severe restriction in the ability of children to play and amuse themselves on their own free of adult control or supervision. "In recent years there has been in this country a steadily growing tendency toward the regimentation of children's play . . . supervised play has taken the place of the earlier spontaneous and hence much more enjoyable playing and has made participation in games a mechanical performance instead of the delight which it once was and which it should be still" (Brewster 1953, xx; also see Chudacoff 2007, 154–81).[26] Thus we find parents, nannies and other child care workers, teachers, playground personnel, camp counselors, and coaches constantly hovering over the children, cheering them on in carefully organized contests and fretting about their safety. Such freedom as the child enjoys today is in the privacy of his or her own room and is mostly expended in homework, solitary reading, television viewing, telephone chatting and texting, exploring the Internet, and playing electronic games. Further comment on the impact of such behavior on American placefulness would be superfluous.

## Other Cultural Expressions

The preceding pages certainly fall far short of exhausting all the varieties of cultural practice that may find regional expression in the United States. Given the scarcity of relevant scholarship, I can offer no more than brief comments on three additional sets of phenomena.

### Folklore

For well over a century, folklore enthusiasts have been collecting and interpreting all manner of folklore throughout the land. But, unfortunately, "his

[William Lightfoot's] survey reveals that while the collection and study of regional folklore has a long history in American folklore scholarship, it has up until the present remained a minor stream in that scholarship" (B. Allen 1990, 184). The potential value of such data for the cultural geographer is suggested by E. Joan Wilson Miller's (1968) portrayal of an Ozark culture region as revealed by traditional materials.

Perhaps at some future date an intrepid folklorist will collate the great store of items from all the scattered locations and piece together their regional dimensions. Among the more promising fields of study are urban legends, local inventions that have roused much popular and scholarly attention (Brunvand 2001). The question remains as to how distinctively local or regional they are in origin and whether, in this age of instant electronic sharing, they promptly shed their original attributes. Such a concern is part of a larger question: is folklore in general, once confined to a limited territory, becoming emulsified within a national melting pot of communications?

### Folk Art and Handicrafts

Once again, we confront a field of study that has many practitioners, but few with any geographical bent. As an example of the potential for regional characterization, we have William Ferris's (1982) interviews with self-taught craftsmen (and musicians) in the Mississippi Delta.

One form of localized folk art that has generated a fair measure of scholarly interest is the outdoor mural movement, along with our generally surreptitious graffiti (Cockcroft, Weber, and Cockcroft 1977). The efflorescence of the murals, a late-twentieth-century development, and one inspired by Mexican practice, has been especially noteworthy in Mexican American communities (Arreola 1984). However, after crossing ethnic lines, murals have also flourished in several major cities, notably San Francisco (Drescher 1994), Chicago, and Philadelphia (Golden, Rice, and Kinney 2002), sometimes with official encouragement. The extent to which these productions— sometimes attaining dazzling virtuosity—are regional or localistic in style is a question awaiting methodical study. Golden, Rice, and Kinney (2002) argue strongly for the special character of the Philadelphia examples; and, in writing about "The Great Walls of Joliet [Illinois]," Jeff Heubner claims that "a 'Joliet style' is as recognizable and definable as other schools of painting in the history of art" (2001, 12). In addition, if I may add my own personal observations, Native American murals in some central Oklahoma towns have a decidedly regional flavor.

### Customs and Manners

We are all familiar with the fact that patterns of etiquette and social behavior, and customs of all sorts, vary a great deal from country to country.
Indeed they vary so much that a publisher has found it profitable to equip
the international business traveler with a manual coaching him or her as to
how to behave properly in some sixty different nations (Morrison and Conaway 2006). Is it unreasonable, then, to assume that in a land as vast as the
United States there may be some significant place-to-place distinctions in
the codes of social behavior followed by the locals? Such a field of study,
however, remains terra incognita for sociologists and geographers, but with
one inevitable exception: the South. Thus "since the late 1800s, an array
of novelists and promoters of tourism have depicted people in the South as
having a set of manners the rest of the country might admire, emulate, or at
least enjoy watching" (Ownby 2007, xi). For example, "throughout much
of the South, it is customary to make eye contact with passersby and then
to greet these people—perhaps several times a day. Hi, how ya doin'? C'est
tout. *C'est normal*" (Donlon 2001, 1).[27] Moreover, there may be different
levels of civility within the region. "People who claim the authority to
make such decisions continue to call Charleston, South Carolina, the most
mannerly place in the United States" (Ownby 2007, xi).

We are on somewhat less shaky ground when it comes to regional or
local customs, or at least we have the occasional factual tidbit. Thus, returning to the South again, we encounter the porch phenomenon (Donlon 2001).
Although socializing on and from the front porch has been practiced spottily in other sections of the country, especially in pre-TV days, it has been,
and remains, peculiarly important in southern neighborhoods, where it is
obligatory to greet passersby, familiar or strange, from the porch (Donlon
2001, 2) and to carry on prolonged colloquia therein with family, kinfolk,
friends, and neighbors. "One prevailing notion that spans cultural boundaries and characterizes the South as a whole is that the porch, though used
less frequently today than in the past, remains integral to a southern identity" (Donlon 2001, 19).

The general public may be acquainted with some of the special customs
of Acadiana: the Mardi Gras as celebrated throughout the region, the crewes,
and New Orleans's jazz funerals. But they are less aware of the sacredness
of Easter Monday in the South, the Juneteenth observances among Texan
African Americans, Detroit's Hell Night (October 31), the Goose Day (of
variable October occurrence) that still lingers on in central Pennsylvania,
or that commonwealth's immensely important Deer Day (the Monday after
Thanksgiving). Also worthy of investigation are the special rituals that

have originated on many college campuses, such as the Texas Aggie Bonfire at Texas A&M ( J. M. Smith 2007) or Mountain Day (the most colorful Tuesday in October) at Mount Holyoke College, occasions with significance only for the initiated. Excluded from consideration here are those annual, but quite unofficial, nationwide occasions for pranks, greeting cards, parties, guzzling, and gift-giving, such as April Fool's Day, Halloween, Groundhog Day, May Day, Mother's Day, St. Patrick's Day, and Valentine's Day. Whether such exceptional dates vary in popularity by region or are waxing or waning in significance is an open question.

The most thought-provoking of American customs with regional dimensions has to do with the marriage ritual. In the course of a study some thirty-odd years ago looking into the historical geography of choice of wedding date by month and day of the week in the United States and Canada during the period of 1844–1974, I stumbled across a phenomenon unbeknownst to participants, the wedding industry, and the scholarly community (1994; also see Sutton 2003). The general findings, after analyzing data at the state or provincial level, were generally in keeping with what one might expect in terms of modernization theory: mainly late fall ceremonies on weekdays in an earlier, predominantly agrarian America and a maximum in June and summer in general and on weekends throughout the year in our later modernized years. But totally baffling and unexpected was an intermediate development: the September Pattern.

It first surfaced in Michigan during the years 1905–14 when September weddings were exceeded in popularity only by those in June. Then, from the 1920s until the 1960s, September captured first place in the northeastern quadrant of the United States (and adjacent provinces in Canada) and occasionally in other states, indeed everywhere except the innovation-proof South. But by the 1970s the September Pattern had disappeared. Since then, a single calendric pattern prevails from coast to coast—further testimony for the Homogenization Thesis—a pronounced June maximum and a secondary one in August.

At this late date, I remain mystified. *Cultural drift* is the only process to be invoked here, but it is difficult to imagine precisely how it might have operated. How could all those brides and grooms, each couple independently pondering just when to schedule the most meaningful day in their lives—but possibly mindful of the obligations of friends and relatives—how could they have hit upon September rather than June or August for all those years for no obvious practical reason in so many states and provinces? In any event, calendric logic returned eventually, and in the passage from an early period during which one particular form of national uniformity prevailed to a later era when uniformity recurred, but for a different seasonal pattern, we have evidence that does nothing to tilt judgment for or against the convergence hypothesis. The serendipitous discovery of the September Pattern leads one to suspect that other customs with regional connotations are still hidden from view. How many more await the inquisitive investigator?

### Personal Preference Patterns

It is obvious to even the casual observer that the personalities and tastes of Americans, whether viewed singly or as communities, and however such traits may have originated, do vary significantly from place to place across the land. In the early 1970s, in an effort to plot the geography of such personal preference patterns, I perpetrated what may still be the only such investigation of its kind: a statistical-cum-cartographic analysis of the readership of special-interest magazines and membership in voluntary associations—some 163 entities in all—as recorded by state (1974). The 51 states (including D.C.) were regrettably coarse areal units, but the availability and nature of the raw data allowed no better alternative. The resulting 163 by 51 matrices and relevant census data were subjected to a series of factor analyses, and, as anticipated, several significant and interesting factors emerged, including, inter alia, an Urban Sophistication Factor, Sex and Romance Factor, Migrant Factor, and Midwest versus Southwest Factor.

Among the major findings, I discerned the existence of three macroregions: the "West-cum-Outer Megalopolis," the "Middle West," and the "South." In addition, several lesser aggregations of states emerged. Lest the reader jump to the conclusion that this analysis necessarily confirms the actuality of the Midwest and West, note the finding that the "Middle West Extended" embraced both Idaho and Pennsylvania, while the "West," which included California, wrested Texas and Oklahoma from the "South" and captured Arizona and New Mexico while excluding Nevada and Utah. The general verdict was that the data at hand only crudely suggested the reality of state-level culture areas.

The general conclusion to be drawn from this exercise is that there was, and undoubtedly still is, a genuine regionalized American geography of personality and personal taste, one that correlates with other social and economic geographies, but that data at a finer areal scale are needed before we can map it with any confidence. Unfortunately, this study still stands alone since no one else has tried to verify or update it, and the time and enormous effort it would take to provide a sequel has kept me from even dreaming about a later version. Consequently, it is impossible to speculate about whatever diachronic trends in personal preference patterns may have developed since 1970–71 and whether convergence or divergence in any regionalizations has been the dominant process.

## Adding Up the Incommensurables

Can we repeat the exercise that concluded the preceding chapter? Is it feasible to quantify and fuse together the evidence, albeit quite incomplete, for growth or decline in territorial diversity for a dozen or so categories of cultural phenomena within the United States and thus arrive at some verdict as to overall convergence or divergence within this realm of geographic reality? Perhaps the best way to begin attacking the question is to review briefly each of the categories treated above and to summarize whatever directional change the data and literature suggest.

Of all the topics under review, the judgment as to linguistic change is the most surprising. Although we lack studies of how the grammar of American English has evolved over time and space, recent analyses of phonology buttress the counterintuitive notion that not only has a set of speech regions persisted but that region-to-region differences in the sounds we utter have been widening and that there is no indication that such change will halt or be reversed. When it comes to vocabulary, the massive data set generated by DARE confirms the existence of a group of regions that apparently go a long way back in the nation's history. Unfortunately, however, no one has yet initiated the heroic task of ascertaining whether the distinctiveness of regional lexicons is currently declining or strengthening. The one body of relevant evidence—my study of the historical geography of male given names—suggests convergence but is too limited in number of localities and dates to be regarded as definitive.

Hampered though we are by flimsy and incomplete data, it seems safe to assume, on the basis of various studies, that the religious regions of the country, as delineated in terms of adherence to the leading denominations, show no sign of attrition or loss of spatial integrity. Although research remains to be done, one may speculate that territorial diversity may be on the rise with the advent of immigrant faiths in selected localities and the ceaseless contrivance of new theologies on the part of the native-born.

We are in a much better position to judge the spatial dynamics of American politics since the topic has enjoyed intense scrutiny by a number of scholars. What they have found is a set of regions, or sections (usually blocs of states or counties), as defined by partisan voting preferences by citizens and members of Congress, territorial entities that may be persistent or evanescent. But, whatever their identity or duration, there appears to be no definite diachronic trend in the depth of difference among them. Thus the United States would seem to exist in a condition of permanent heterogeneity politically and territorially, with neither convergence nor divergence ascendant.

Among the remaining facets of American cultural life, we suffer from a dearth of quantitative evidence. And indeed we have so little mappable information of any sort concerning folklore, folk art and handicrafts, and customs and manners that (except for the recent outbursts of murals) pronouncements as to whether their regional vitality has waxed or waned would be futile. Similarly, the availability of only a single study means that we have no idea as to whether or how personal preference patterns may have been evolving over and time and space. In another instance, that of dress and ornament, the persistence over the centuries of a nationwide sameness renders our central question moot.

Then, despite the absence of meaningful statistics, one can say, with some assurance, that, overall, there has been a drastic suppression of whatever regional or local particularity once prevailed in American foodways, despite some rearguard action (to be noted later) and the lingering on of minor pockets of special dietary tastes. Even more emphatic, despite, again, the meager fund of hard data and our uncertainty as to the existence of early regionalization, has been the fate of informal group games, especially all those juvenile pastimes now on the brink of extinction, whose declining fortunes render irrelevant any questions as to current regionality. On the other hand, one must be cautious in offering judgment as to the diachronic and territorial shaping of organized sport given the recency of its emergence on the scene and the shallowness of whatever regions can be detected. Finally, if the historical geography of American music and dance is a tale of national and global cooption of various early and late regional developments that seems to confirm the convergence hypothesis, it is countered by an ongoing liveliness of local experimentation and the eruption of all those urban "sounds." In this case, a clear verdict is elusive.

Another way we could make some sense of the highly varied spatial careers of our dozen or so cultural phenomena is to look at how that most potent of all homogenizing processes—the *modern market system in alliance with the state*—has interacted with them. In doing so, we learn, as we did for the built landscape, that it has strangled and cast out whatever regional life may have existed in foodways, dress and ornament, and informal group games and has had much to do with the complicated story of music and dance as well as organized sport. But Leviathan is impotent, irrelevant, or simply standoffish in matters of language, religion, and, possibly, folklore, folk art, and customs and manners.

In any event, what happens if we try to merge the spatial careers of all these cultural manifestations, applying a nonexistent mega-arithmetic? The only sensible answer is that neither a yea nor a nay is appropriate. As far as cultural matters in toto are concerned, all one can venture is that no central tendency toward sameness or diversity over space is discernible.

# 6 The Regional Factor

THE ACCUMULATION of evidence in the preceding chapters leads to an unavoidable interim judgment: that the homogenization or rationalization of American territory and society has indeed been *the* dominant process in the historical geography of the nation since its inception. But we must also add some large qualifications to any account of this triumphal procession. As we have learned, accompanying such a grand convergence, this creation of a set of interlocking clusters bearing a strong family resemblance—along with the smoothing out of various cultural wrinkles—there has also been a lively eruption, ever greater in number and variety, of unpredictable places within the interstices of the grander system. Moreover, in at least three cultural realms—the linguistic, religious, and political—American place-to-place differences have shown little sign of vanishing. But there is still another major evolution we have yet to confront: a sea change developing over the past century in our sensibilities with regard to questions of space and place. More specifically, the notion of region has entered our general consciousness.

Thus we may now pose such questions as: do genuine regions exist within the United States? If so, how many and where? How old or new are they? How meaningful are these regions? How great are the differences among them? Are these differences increasing or decreasing? In short, what bearing do regions have upon the central concerns of this study?[1] But, before we can set about grappling with such questions, we must try to understand just what is meant by "region" and related terms and concepts.[2]

## On the Meaning and Fortunes of Place and Region

Perhaps the only unassailable claim concerning regions is that they are a certain kind of place. "We can begin by admitting that place and region are inherently complex, that they are messy ideas that resist easy characterization. Region is perhaps the most untidy, for nearly any description includes nagging exceptions and obdurate contradictions. Nothing seems to stay neatly packaged or bounded" (Lang 2001, v). But, fortunately, we have recently had major developments among the community of scholars who deal with human affairs which enhance the value, indeed the urgency, of dealing with place, if not region. The subsequent discussion would be rather superficial if these are not kept in mind.

First there is a "shibboleth among critical human geographers [and now almost everyone else!] that place and region are socially produced or socially constructed" (Entrikin 1996, 215), an understanding that has become universally accepted. Then, an even more fundamental reassessment of the role of place in the larger scheme of things has gained traction in recent years. "Mounting evidence of persistence and, in some instances, intensification of localist attachments and influences (even in highly industrialized societies) has prompted many to question the aspatial assumptions that have dominated the Western social literature in the twentieth century . . . With this development, the concepts of region, place, and locale have been accorded increasing attention in the social sciences and humanities" (A. B. Murphy 1992, 22).[3]

In a truly profound pair of volumes, the philosopher Edward Casey (1993, 1997) has trenchantly and lucidly explored the ongoing revolution, the emergent (postmodern?) paradigm that has begun to inform our current approach to social reality. It replaces an outmoded mind-set Casey has characterized as follows.

> In the past three centuries in the West—the period of "modernity"—place has come to be not only neglected but actively suppressed. Owing to the triumph of the natural and social sciences in this same period, any serious talk of place has been regarded as regressive or trivial. A discourse has emerged whose exclusive cosmological foci are Time and Space. When the two were combined by twentieth-century physicists into the amalgam "space-time," the overlooking of place was only continued by other means. For an entire epoch, place has been regarded as an impoverished second cousin of Time and Space, those two colossal cosmic partners that tower over modernity . . . By late modern times, this world has become increasingly placeless, a matter of mere sites instead of lived places, of sudden displacement rather than of perduring implacements. (1993, xiv–xv)

But ultimately a contradiction has ensued. As modernity seemingly flattens or diminishes place, our personal and scholarly concern with it has begun to rise sharply (Lutwack 1984, 182–83; Sack 1986, 218–19). In the preceding chapters, I have offered some indications of this recent transformation of sensibilities. Many more will follow.

There is no need here for an extended treatment of the concept of place in its various dimensions (a topic accosted in Chapter 1) since a number of scholars have dealt with it so extensively and productively (for example, Tuan 1974, 1977, 1980; Sack 1986, 1997; Massey 1995; Massey and Jess 1995a; D. Harvey 1996, 291–326; Creswell 2002, 2004). It is important to keep in mind the fact that places are four-dimensional affairs. They begin and end at certain times, having durations ranging from a few hours to millennia, and they change ceaselessly during their lifetimes. In a related field of inquiry we have had worthy explorations of sense of place in such publications as Gerson, Stueve, and Fischer 1977, Hummon 1992, Ryden 1993, and Rose 1995, which do not call for more than passing notice here, as well as explorations of the intimate details and perceptions of our dwellings (Bachelard 1969; Sack 1997, 8–10). The more immediate question is when a place—never to be confused with space, a purely physical construct!—is to be considered a region.

## The Regional Concept

When it comes to defining region for the purposes of this study, we begin wading through muddy waters. The only patch of certitude has to do with territorial magnitude. If it is legitimate to regard any bit of terrain ranging from a single room or inhabited cave up to an entire nation-state as constituting a place, the sort of region we are concerned with here—the social or cultural—is a sizable segment of the national territory, and certainly something too large to be perceived directly by the lone individual. It is also important to note that we are not concerned here with the many types of pseudo-regions created rather arbitrarily for operational or administrative purposes by business firms, governmental bodies, and religious and other organizations, entities labeled province, section, division, district, diocese, belt, zone, or whatever. More to the point, over the past two centuries, natural scientists have been able to define and delineate various regions—climatic, biotic, edaphic, physiographic, geologic—using rigorous, generally accepted criteria. No such luck for human geographers. It took until the middle of the twentieth century before they began to get serious about defining, recognizing, mapping, and anatomizing those culture areas, or regions, as may exist in the United States or elsewhere.

Such efforts, however, have an American prehistory in the early, persistent vitality of the sectional concept. As fully set forth in accounts by Fulmer Mood (1951) and William Hesseltine (1960), early statesmen and scholars were wont to perceive the nation as containing two or three state-based sections in apparently permanent contention over economic and political issues.

It was a concept most energetically and famously promoted by the historian and closet geographer Frederick Jackson Turner, who, writing in 1926, proclaimed that "the nation is now in reality rather a federation of sections than a federation of states" (1932, 198).[4]

With the passage of time, both scholars and the general public came to realize the inadequacy of state boundaries for characterizing human geographic realities. Thus we have the appearance of such enduring concepts as the Cotton Belt, Manufacturing Belt, Corn Belt, and Bible Belt, all ignoring state boundaries. Anthropologists may have been the originators of the notion of culture areas (Ehrich and Henderson 1968), which human geographers belatedly adopted. Surprisingly, however, it was a philosopher, Josiah Royce (1908), who pioneered its application to the modern American scene—though he used the term "province" instead of "region" in a quite straightforward, but debatable, definition. "For me, then, a province shall mean any one part of a national domain, which is, geographically and socially, sufficiently unified to have a true consciousness of its own unity, to feel a pride in its own ideals and customs, and to possess a sense of its distinction from other parts of the country" (1908, 61).

Much later, the sociologist Rupert Vance (another closet geographer) offered a similar definition and, again, one to which I must take partial exception. "A region is a homogeneous area with physical and cultural characteristics distinct from those of neighboring areas. As part of a national domain a region is sufficiently unified to have a consciousness of its customs and ideals and thus possesses a sense of identity distinct from the rest of the country" (1968, 377).[5] One could go on indefinitely in pursuit of an ideal definition of the sociocultural region, but, for the time being, the following skeletal characterization will have to suffice. "Any area of the earth's surface with distinct and internally consistent patterns of physical features or of human development which give it meaningful unity and distinguish it from surrounding areas" (Goodall 1987, 399).

If the quest for a definitive definition of regions may be never-ending—Roger Minshull cites at least forty as of 1938 (1967, 18)—geographers have adopted the regional method with much relish for teaching and research over the past several decades, despite its downgrading during the so-called Quantitative Revolution, and have also produced some detailed accounts and relevant critiques (for example, Whittlesey 1954, Minshull 1967, J. R. McDonald 1972, Paasi 1986, Starrs 1994, Ostergren 2005). They have also specified different types of cultural regions and explored their inner structure.

There is general agreement as to the existence of two basic types of region: the formal and the functional (Minshull 1967, 38–45; Jordan-Bychkov and Domosh 1999, 7–12). In the case of the formal region, we have an area distinguished from all others by the relatively uniform presence of a given attribute—physical, economic, social, or cultural—absent or rare in other areas. The functional region differs from the formal by being internally diversified, but, more specifically, by having some function, typically economic or political, directed or controlled from some central node. Newspaper circulation areas or beer distributorships are clear examples of such regions in which there are active transactions between a center and its outlying tributary territory. In the cultural variant of the functional model, which is one of the main concerns of this chapter, there may be no such immediately visible, ongoing movements of commodities and information, but rather the residue of a protracted period of influences and sociocultural interaction. Donald Meinig has most fully fleshed out the internal structure of the functional cultural area with its core, domain, and sphere, using the Mormon Culture Region as an ideal example.

> A *core* area . . . is taken to mean a centralized zone of concentration, displaying the greatest density of occupance, intensity of organization, strength and homogeneity of the particular features characteristic of the culture under study. It is the most vital center, the seat of power, the focus of circulation.
>
> The *domain* refers to those areas in which the particular culture under study is *dominant*, but with markedly less intensity and complexity of development than in the core, where the bonds of connection are fewer and more tenuous and where regional peculiarities are clearly evident.
>
> The *sphere* of a culture may be defined as the zone of outer influence and, often, peripheral acculturation, wherein that culture is represented only by certain of its elements or where its peoples reside as minorities among those of a different culture. (1965, 213)

As we shall see, the Meinig Model is applicable to two or three American culture areas in addition to the Mormon case, while the formal region formulation makes sense for the others. It is worth noting that for both types of cultural region—the formal and the functional—it is possible, in theory and occasionally in practice, to come across examples of nested hierarchies. Thus, in a manner analogous to the geometry set forth in central place theory, smaller regions encased within the larger may replicate some or all of the attributes of the grosser entity.

We must note in passing two other regional concepts that have received scholarly attention. First there is the Vernacular Culture Region, defined as "a region *perceived* to exist by its inhabitants, as evidenced by the widespread acceptance and use of a special regional name . . . They vary in scale from city neighborhoods to sizable parts of continents" (Jordon-Bychkov and Domosh 1999, 12). Their significance is usually much greater for the resident perceivers than it is for outsiders. There will be occasion to discuss them at a later point.

The concept of Homelands, as applied to the United States, has been most ardently championed by Richard Nostrand and Lawrence Estaville (2001), but much more weakly and fitfully by other scholars. We have as a definition the following.

> The concept of a "homeland," although abstract and elusive, has at least three basic elements: a people, a place, and identity with place. The people must have lived in a place long enough to have adjusted to its natural environment and to have left their impress in the form of a cultural landscape. And from their interactions with the natural and cultural totality of the place they must have developed an identity with the land—emotional feelings of attachment, desires to possess, even compulsions to defend. (Nostrand 1992, xvii)

If there are valid instance of homelands in certain parts of the Old World, unfortunately the relevance of the concept to the American scene turns out to be a matter of wishful thinking, with the possible exception of one or two aboriginal cases, long under threat of extinction. Michael Conzen in his commentary on the fourteen case studies assembled by Nostrand and Estaville 2001 effectively demolishes their sweeping claims for the United States.

> Any discussion of homelands in America needs to begin by recognizing how atypical the United States is in the world, as an immigrant state, in the fundamental relationship of its people to their form of government and territory. Like the relatively few other immigrant states, such as Canada, Argentina, Brazil, Australia, and New Zealand, localized or subnational homelands are at best cultural anachronisms, not part of the new national myth in the making . . .
> . . . Aside from the remnant homelands of Native Americans officially recognized as territorial reservations, and a couple of other historical cases of waning significance, most other subnational cultural groups today occupy geographic space in ways better articulated by such concepts as ethnic islands, ethnic substrates, and cultural regions. (Conzen 2001, 241, 271)[6]

If homelands fail to meet the test as meaningful American culture areas, what do we identify as the genuine article? Perhaps we can begin by looking at the fifty states that comprise the Union. But, before doing so, it is essential to keep in mind the fact that in its entirety the United States makes up a single culture area. Although this reality may not be obvious in tracts close to and on either side of our international borders, the sociocultural variability within the country as a whole is substantially less than the difference between the American nation and any other near or far. On the other hand, we dare not succumb to the delusion that the United States, or any other nation-state for that matter, is destined to endure forever. In his quirky, but extremely thought-provoking, sermon, Juan Enriquez (2005) forcefully demonstrates the past and present fragility and fissiparous possibilities of the United States, Canada, and Mexico. It is also necessary to note that the entities in the discussions that follow are all territorial and *relatively* durable in character. To be ignored for the time being are all the countless ephemeral places, or even mini-regions, such as the hundreds of conventions going on in the United States on any given day or the communities that exist only in cyberspace.

## The Fifty States as Culture Areas?

The United States defines itself, constitutionally and in practice, as a confederation of fifty quasi-sovereign states.[7] Over the course of more than two centuries, as a central national regime housed primarily in Washington has grown larger, more complex, much more powerful, and intrusive, a tug of war over powers, rights, and privileges between the individual states and the overarching central authority has never ceased (and, of course, actually erupted once into vicious warfare), and indeed promises to fester perpetually in the courts, state legislatures, Congress, and public discourse. "On the one hand, we seem constantly to be moving in the direction of a national community with one government. On the other hand, we seem never to get there. State governments persist. They retain vital functions. Important differences in public policies among states persist" (Derthick 2001, 74; also see Elazar 1984).

In the face of such persistent political differences can we also detect a carryover into the social and cultural realm such that at least some states can claim credibility as genuine, distinct, autonomous cultural entities, whether as formal or functional culture areas?[8] The desirability of such an identity manifests itself in the actual behavior of every one of the fifty jurisdictions in question. Thus within each state's capital city we encounter all the physical trappings of a sovereign state (perhaps most grandiloquently in Albany, New York): the visually overbearing capitol building; the structure housing the state's highest courts; impressive offices for all the many governmental departments; state museums and libraries; and historical monuments aplenty—not to mention the premises of attorneys and lobbyists and state-based associations.

Then the states have created and maintain their individual systems of colleges, parks, prisons, hospitals, forests, reformatories, and other such institutions, along with a police force and state-controlled National Guard, while at the unofficial level we have state athletic leagues and other organizations identified with the state. Each state flies its own flag, proclaims its special motto, nickname, holidays, and auto license plates, while celebrating its very own official anthem, flower, bird, mammal, insect, mineral, or whatever (Brunn 1974, 239–45). And dare we forget state fairs, state beauty pageants, spelling bees, and other such competitions? However, the impact of all these strategies remains problematic. Few residents ever recognize the state flag or motto, and truly rare is the person who can warble the official state song or point to its official flower—as against the throngs who can belt out "God Bless America" or "The Star-Spangled Banner."

On the other hand, the ability of each state to enact its own criminal code, marriage and divorce laws, income, liquor, tobacco, and other taxes, social benefits, educational policy, land-use regulations, highway speed limits, and countless other provisions results in meaningful interstate distinctions in the lives of citizens and in the visible landscape. This fact is most apparent at or near interstate borders where we come across fireworks stands (Puljak 2006, 215), gambling casinos (Jackson and Hudman 1987, 35), and shops purveying cigarettes, oleomargarine, liquor, and other merchandise either forbidden or overpriced just across the line. In addition, we cannot altogether ignore the possible effects of the agenda of various public radio and television networks with their state-oriented programming policies.

In light of all these considerations, just how many of our fifty entities are recognizably distinct in terms of cultural identity? How many recognize and cherish the specialness of their existence, a cultural or geographic personality that sets them apart from their neighbors? The answer is the result of history, territorial size, shape, and location, and internal human and physical geography. The number that clearly qualify is surprisingly small: a mere five—Hawaii, Oregon, Texas, Utah, and Vermont—plus three—Alaska, Oklahoma, and Wisconsin—for which a case of sorts could be made.[9]

The explanation for Hawaii, Texas, and Utah is clear enough: a period of political independence before joining the Union; and, of course, their cultural particularity also sets Hawaii and Utah apart from all other states.[10] In the case of Texas, a potent historical heritage suffices to smother its considerable physical and social diversity. Although late eighteenth-century Vermonters briefly flirted with the notion of political autonomy before becoming the fourteenth state, its current status, the recognition of Vermontness, is essentially a twentieth century development.[11] "Indeed, there is an undeniable mystique to the name Vermont—a mystique that . . . operates at the state scale, but one that has also made Vermont a powerful and enduring symbol of rural exceptionalism, both on regional and on national scales" (Harrison 2006, 6). A rather parallel situation prevails in Oregon (or at least its populous western portion), a kind of western counterpart of Vermont (the anti-California?) where we encounter a distinctive state-based self-consciousness or Oregonishness (Sarasohn 1983).

Alaska's status is hard to adjudicate. Any recollection of having once been the remotest province of imperial Russia has pretty much withered away. Instead, any claim to uniqueness relies on its isolation, sub-Arctic features, and perpetual survival as a frontier society. But how does such a situation differ from that in the Yukon, Kamchatka, or the northern reaches of Quebec? Oklahoma's tenuous case, in addition to its substantial aboriginal community, is based on its unique genesis as a territory and abrupt occupation, a mythologized origin sedulously cultivated by officialdom and the rank and file. The state of Wisconsin is exceptional by virtue of being the only one to have the term "Idea" attached to its name (Doan 1947; Gard 1955; R. Davison 2006).[12] Whether the aura of political and social progressivism of yore still matters enough today to enough of its residents to make the state special is difficult to ascertain.

Of the forty-two states not yet considered, some twenty-odd are creatures of the national regime. And Congress seldom displayed geographic acumen in carving out new states from the national domain while they were being settled. Decisions as to size and boundaries were most often arbitrary and ill-informed. In the extreme cases, those of Colorado and Wyoming, we have simple bare rectangles. In any event, aside from the debatable instances of Wisconsin and Oklahoma, only Oregon (or its western fraction) seems to have achieved some level of sociocultural autonomy. As for the rest, shape, location, and internal diversity defeat any such aspirations.

As it happens, the most extreme example of state boundaries failing to recognize geographic realities is that of a grotesquely misshapen Maryland (the doing of the British Crown rather than Congress). Its only competitors—and distant ones at that—in any such competition would be Idaho and Florida. Maryland's Appalachian western extremity is utterly different in physical and human terms from its Eastern Shore, the coastal plain tracts draining eastward into Chesapeake Bay, or the island communities in the bay, while the intermediate Piedmont section belongs to a different world, as do the two large metropolises that account for the bulk of the state's population. Pity the poor publicist who must express the essence of Marylandishness in slogan and image!

The vagaries of boundary drawing have resulted in a number of other awkward intra-state nonconformities. Thus the sharp contrasts between north and south within Ohio, Indiana, Illinois, Missouri, Louisiana, Idaho, Delaware, and Florida and a comparable level of dissimilarity between east and west in Montana, Wyoming, Colorado, and North Carolina. Indeed, in the case of antebellum Virginia, the geographic incongruity was so unbearable that in 1863, shedding few tears, West Virginia divorced itself from the remainder of the state. Something of the same geographic discomfort is manifest in California where malcontents agitate periodically for dismembering the state into three or four meaningful units. By contrast, we have some states with a marked degree of internal homogeneity, for example, Iowa, West Virginia, and Nevada, but to no avail in any claim of distinctiveness since they share their physical and social characteristics with at least portions of their neighboring states.

Then, there is the dilemma posed by our smallest states. Squashed as it is between its two larger, potent neighbors, it is impossible to imagine tiny Rhode Island ever generating a personality of its own, a situation repeated by Delaware, lurking as it does in the shadow of Pennsylvania, New Jersey, and Maryland. And New Jersey, in turn, despite its less than glowing national reputation, has yet to evolve a singular personality of its own, given considerable internal diversity and the overpowering propinquity of New York and Pennsylvania. The real-world inadequacies of the current fifty-state subdivision of the United States has stimulated at least two scholars to suggest superior alternatives based on physical and social realities: G. Etzel Pearcy's (1973, 22–23) thirty-eight-state scheme; and Stanley Brunn's (1974, 423) sixteen-state arrangement—to no avail, of course.

But if, in sum, the current configuration of the fifty states is a feeble excuse for a serious sociocultural regionalization of the republic, there is still something to be said regarding the agency of federalism in promoting territorial diversity within the United States. As Martha Derthick has sagely observed,

> the social functions of federalism may be more significant than the political and governmental ones. By sustaining subnational communities with some residual degree of governmental independence and distinctiveness, federalism gives individuals choices about where to live. This gives inequality a spatial form, because of course the better-off use their freedom to congregate in communities that suit their tastes and use the power of local governments to protect their property, values and life-styles. Thus federalism in its social form, helping to give definition to distinct communities, is a leading ground of the continuing American battle between liberty and equality. (2001, 84–85)

With figure 6.1, I offer an updated and most carefully considered delineation of the contemporary culture areas of the United States, a drawing based on observation, reading, and much reflection.[13] In doing so, I supplant an earlier effort (Zelinsky 1992a, 118–19), a map that has attracted a fair amount of attention over the years.[14] But figure 6.1 is not a simple revision; instead it is an outright rejection of earlier misconceptions and a chastened approach toward geographic reality. In offering it, I disown the previous effort and, with considerable chagrin, confess its grievous faults.

**Culture Areas of the United States**

1. Hawaii
2. The Southwest
   2-a. Tejano South Texas
3. New England
   3-a. New England Extended, or New York Region
4. South
   4-a. Early British Colonial South
   4-b. Deep South
   4-c. Upland South
      4-c-1. Kentucky Bluegrass
   4-d. Texas
5. Acadiana
6. Pennsylvania Culture Area
7. Generic Euro-American Region
   7-a. Mormon Culture Area
   7-b. California Culture Area
   7-c. Peninsular Florida
   7-d. Pacific Northwest

⊛ Metropolitan Culture Area
☆ Possible Metropolitan Culture Area

Figure 6.1. Cultural regions of the United States.

But before making amends by offering an improved regionalization of the United States from a cultural perspective, one for which I invite comment and correction, it may be useful to review briefly some similar efforts by other scholars. After discussing earlier schemes, including Odum's state-based six regions (1936, 6), Raymond Gastil presented a map (1975, 29) depicting thirteen cultural regions, eight of which correspond more or less with those shown in figure 6.1. It is noteworthy that Gastil fails to recognize the West as a region unto itself, and also that, rather than having a unitary Midwest, he divides the territory in question into two distinct regions, an "Upper" and "Central." The most idiosyncratic of his decisions is the designation of a Rocky Mountain region, something missing from all other regional systems I am aware of.

Some years later, the historian David Hackett Fischer in his voluminous (946-page) opus, whose obsessive approach to the historical geography of American society is signaled by its subtitle, "Four British Folkways in America," identified seven cultural regions as existing in the late twentieth century (1989, 887–89). Oddly enough in a publication that abounds in maps, Fischer neglected to display these places cartographically, so that I am reduced here to a simple listing of names: the Northern Tier; Greater New York [City]; Midland America; the Great Basin; the Coastal South; the Southern Highlands; and Southern California.[15] The obsession in question is that we can quite effectively explain the essential past and present diversity of American society and culture in terms of four early culture hearths—southern New England, Virginia, the Delaware Valley, and the Appalachian backcountry—each occupied by settlers from particular portions of Great Britain and each batch of colonists arriving with their special cultural complex. The Fischer Thesis is that these four distinct bundles of persons and traits retained their separate characters to a marked degree over the past two centuries or so as settlement moved all the way across the continent. This notion parallels Elazar's mapping of three latitudinal strands in the political geography of the country.

Unfortunately, in his rather blinkered view of ground truth, Fischer ignores the work of geographers and sociologists as well as other processes and agencies that may have been operating over American space and time. But he did recruit an apostle, surprisingly enough from the ranks of psychiatry. Using a four-way state-level classification of the United States based on the Fischer scheme, Max Sugar (2004) reported that it provided a meaningful degree of explanation of regional differences in eight conditions: education; unwed motherhood; alcohol consumption; homicide; sexually transmitted diseases; child sexual abuse and homicide; and poverty.[16] To the best of my knowledge, no one has yet tried to replicate Sugar's interesting findings. The Fischer/Sugar hypothesis may have some merit, but only when embedded within a larger explanatory framework.

But, returning to my own shortcomings in drafting the 1992 map, the least of the faults was omission of Alaska and Hawaii, which was probably a simple case of absentmindedness. The most striking of the changes in the new map is the scuttling of two geographic myths—the presumed existence of a real Middle West and a real West—and, then, the incorporation of the relevant expanses, along with certain other territories, into what I call the Generic Euro-American Region. A much fuller explanation appears later in this chapter.

## Some Special Metropolises

Even more consequential in a conceptual sense than the blunders already noted was my past failure to recognize the obvious fact that a number of

American metropolises are genuine culture areas in and of themselves, with or without close kinship to their hinterlands. The seventeen places so identified in figure 6.1 are Baltimore, Boston, Charleston, Chicago, Cincinnati, Las Vegas, Los Angeles, New Orleans, New York, Philadelphia, Pittsburgh, Portland, Salt Lake City, San Francisco, Santa Fe, Savannah, and Seattle.[17] In addition, three other metropolises—Madison, Milwaukee, and Minneapolis–St. Paul—are marginal candidates for inclusion but will require further study. My oversight in dealing with a country where more than three-quarters of the population is urban clearly reflects an essentially subconscious rural bias, a Sauerian mind-set shared with many of my contemporary cultural geographers. The omission of these culturally distinctive places from the earlier map is inexcusable. I must point out that, not long after the initial appearance of the flawed earlier effort in 1973, both Raymond Gastil (1975, 29) and David Hackett Fischer (1989, 887) accorded New York City its rightful due as a legitimate culture area, but ignored all the other eligible candidates.

When can we regard a given city as constituting a valid culture area? We may classify it as such if and when it meets two criteria: (1) the possession of a set of cultural attributes not found elsewhere; and (2) an awareness on the part of its residents, indeed a proud acceptance, of not just the uniqueness of the place, all places being unique, but rather of some notable, precious qualitative differences worth cherishing. Just how a given metropolis manages to concoct the cultural chemistry needed to become a place apart, one nurturing and flaunting its one-of-a-kind mystique, is one of those puzzles we may never solve.

Several of these special places are distinctive by virtue of their local versions of American English as, for example, Pittsburgh (Donahue 2006) and New York. Others stand out from the rest of the country because of architectural styles, literary luster, street layout, particular dishes or cuisines, sports, musical dialects, the celebration of a noteworthy history, or some combination of these attributes.[18] It is altogether likely that, if the information were at hand, we would find some or all of these metropolises practicing their own peculiar manners and customs and value system (as in Las Vegas?). In the case of New Orleans, we have a city that harbors all of these attributes except sport. In one instance, that of Salt Lake City, it is religion that is an especially critical factor along with a history no one is permitted to forget.

In most cases, the process of cultural formation is spontaneous and unpremeditated. But in the case of Santa Fe, the least populous of the group, we have a town that set about in a coldly calculated way to achieve membership in the class of cultural singletons by making the most of its literary and artistic fame, architecture, and ethnic attributes (C. Wilson 1997; Cline 2007). In contrast, relatively laid-back Seattle and Portland (with nearby Vancouver as a competitor) came by their status rather recently in less flamboyant fashion. Their singularities are less a matter of regional architecture or pop music—though these attributes do help—than a certain social mindset. As capitals of an imaginary Ecotopia (Garreau 1981, 245–86), their residents partake, collectively and self-consciously, and however imperfectly, of a sense of separateness and ecological stewardship, and revel in their physical surroundings. They would abhor any hint of kinship with such interchangeable places as Charlotte, Indianapolis, or Omaha.

Over time, the special qualities of these special cities can merge into a particular mystique for each that outsiders can recognize and regard as either enticing or repellent, or both. Thus we have Chicago and its Chicagoness (Suttles 1990, 230–33), in the literary realm, inter alia (C. S. Smith 1984), and the universally acknowledged aura of New York City, San Francisco, and Los Angeles. Adding substantially to the particularity of such places and their national or international image is their exploitation and embellishment in fiction but especially in film and television, in addition to their celebration in popular song. Thus "from the mid-1960s to the mid-1990s more than five hundred feature films set wholly or principally in Los Angeles were released theatrically in the United States" (Carringer 2001, 247), and the total may be even greater for New York City, while San Francisco cannot lag far behind. On the other hand, among the many scores of metropolises lying outside the charmed archipelago of unique culture areas, fortunate are the few, such as Atlantic City, Dallas, Fargo, Kansas City, Nashville, and Yuma, that can bask in the spotlight of even a single movie or television series. We may have a long wait before witnessing a glorification of Denver, Knoxville, Providence, or Wilmington on our multiplex screens. The seventeen places designated as culturally special happen to account for a significant portion of the national population. The 21,410,000 persons inhabiting just the central city proper in 2000 made up 7.6 percent of the American total. But the figure would be more than twice as high if one were to include the metropolitan areas in their entirety.

The equivocal designation of three additional places—Madison, Milwaukee, and Minneapolis–St. Paul—as possible culture areas is the result of two considerations. Despite close acquaintance with Madison, Wisconsin, I am still unable to decide whether its rather aberrant political and social attributes are enough to qualify it for admission into the circle of Chicago and all the others with their ethnic and several other qualifications. As for the others, I simply lack the necessary intimate knowledge and leave the verdict to others.

I must also note that neither population size nor simple uniqueness suffices for membership in the fraternity in question. Thus figure 6.1 omits Washington, Detroit, and Atlanta, cities with which I am well acquainted. Although our nation's capital is featured in many an action thriller and film with a political theme, that is simply because it happens to be the seat of government. That fraction of its population not sojourning there temporarily has yet to evolve a coherent sense of itself as a community unlike any other or to develop its very own cuisine, fine arts, literary circle, dialect, architecture, or whatever. Detroit may furnish the setting for a dystopian horror flick or two, but one would be hard-pressed to distill any essence of Detroitness (except the evanescent Motown Sound?) from its beleaguered inner city or its more prosperous suburbs. If the reader is surprised at not finding Miami specified on the map, it is not because of a lack of uniqueness. Indeed it is quite twinless, lacking a sibling elsewhere in the world. The reason is the failure of the three or four strongly dissimilar Miami communities to fuse into anything like unity so as to create a singular Miaminess.

One of the questions posed at the head of this chapter is now within our grasp. Are the seventeen genuine metropolitan culture areas identified on our map growing or fading in their distinctiveness? On the basis of observation and reading, I am confident that each and every one remains imbued with its one-of-a-kind cultural personality and, if anything, is deviating ever further from its brethren despite partaking in all the outward trappings of supermodernity. This is part of the paradox permeating this entire inquiry: that while virtually all American places are participating to some degree or other in nationwide homogenization, as well as globalization and transnational acculturation, many are nevertheless able to invent or assert autonomy, to nurture a set of local variations on a cultural theme. It is indisputable, for example, that Las Vegas is becoming more Las Vegian by the day; that, despite its travails, New Orleans keeps burnishing its heritage and pushing it ever further; that it would be ridiculous to envision New Yorkers as ever becoming less New Yorkish or San Franciscans abandoning their eccentricities. Indeed these places, consciously or otherwise, are finding it to their material and psychological advantage to preserve and enhance whatever qualities enable them to stand out from the crowd. It is also worth noting, in pursuit of the central question of this inquiry, that, although they may not qualify as culture areas, such cities as Miami and El Paso keep deviating ever further from the standard American urban model.

Perhaps the most satisfying way to wind up this mini-essay on our special American cities is to quote at length from Gerald Suttles, the exceptional scholar who has thought deeply about such matters.

I argue that a fuller account of urban life requires more direct attention to the cumulative texture of local culture. We are becoming an older society; our cities are aging and the patina of local culture is more visible . . . This is a vast, heritable genome of physical artifacts, slogans, typifications, and catch phrases . . . Some places have a lot of such culture: songs that memorialize their great streets or side streets, homes once occupied by the famous or infamous, a distinctive dialect or vocabulary, routine festivals and parades that selectively dramatize the past, novels, dirty lyrics, pejorative nicknames, special holidays, dead heroes, evangelical moralists, celebrated wastrels, and so on. Other cities seem only the product of recent mass manufacture . . . some cities emerge quickly with a strong image of themselves often repeated in their appearential order and in the statements of outsiders. Others seem to remain practically nonentities no matter what their age. (1984, 285; also see 288–89)

## Authentic Conventional Culture Areas

The procedure to be followed hereafter is to discuss each of the several authentic culture areas of the country—those entities covering relatively broad tracts of both rural and urban territory and displaying a marked degree of cultural coherence—roughly in the order in which they appeared over time. Consequently, we begin with:

### Hawaii

Few geographic verities are more incontestable than the existence, over more than a millennium, of the Hawaiian archipelago as a distinctive cultural community, a subsection of the vast Polynesian cultural domain. If the past two hundred-odd years have witnessed a major transformation of the islands as they experienced fundamental economic alteration, substantial reduction and dilution of indigenous folk and cultural heritage, and the advent of many Asian and North American immigrants, Hawaii remains indelibly Hawaiian and far removed in character, as well as spatially, from any portion of the American mainland.[19]

### The Southwest

After their initial foray in the sixteenth century out of Mexico into what is now the southwestern quarter of the United States, the Spanish were able to secure a durable presence in New Mexico and Arizona by the close of the seventeenth century. Subsequently, they and their Mexican successors extended dominion into southern Colorado, California, and Texas. But it was a rather spotty dominion, involving small bands of European and Mexican clergy, troops, ranchers, and other settlers who intermingled, and often crossbred, with indigenous Native American communities, and left much territory unoccupied between nodes of settlement. Several scholars have delimited the extent of this hybrid culture area with some precision (Nostrand 1970, 1992; Meinig 1971; Garreau 1981, 207–44; Carlson 1990) and a significant subregion, Tejano South Texas (Arreola 2002).[20]

One of the abiding mysteries of Western Hemisphere historical geography is why so relatively few Spaniards crossed the Atlantic to settle in and exploit New Spain, then why they and their Mestizo descendants hesitated in claiming and exploiting more than scattered fragments of the productive California and Texas lands that they actually took over. The British, Russian, and indigenous groups off to the margins did not pose meaningful obstacles. The situation stands in strong contrast to the great swarms of Northwest Europeans entering the Atlantic and Gulf seaboards who soon hastened inward or westward as rapidly as conditions allowed. When the two surges—Anglo and Hispanic—met head-on on the plains of Texas in the 1830s and 1840s, it was no contest.

On the other hand, given their relative aridity and alien ecology, the two core states of the Southwestern Culture Area, New Mexico and Arizona, attracted only a modest trickle of agrarian Anglos throughout the century that followed the American conquest in 1848. But, during the last half of the past century, perceptions and attitudes have greatly altered, so that Americans of all sorts have gravitated in large numbers to the Southwest, the least culturally Euro-American segment of the mainland Union.[21] However, the Anglo invasion is now more than matched by a ceaseless northward drive, legal or otherwise, of Mexicans and Central Americans, so that the medley of three peoples, Native American, Hispanic, and Anglo, so ably portrayed by Donald Meinig (1971), promises to persist indefinitely.

What we find today in the Southwest is emphatically regionally distinctive. Its individuality is immediately visible in all manner of architecture and landscaping.[22] "The urge to cultivate a Hispanic–Native American regional architectural mode has now existed for well over three-quarters of a century, and it is as potent today as it ever was" (Gebhard 1990, 143). Regional character also appears in the clothing and ornaments worn by locals and newcomers alike, but especially by the Hispanics and Native Americans. Indeed there may be no other section of the nation where dress is so distinctively regional. The Southwest has also developed its own special cuisine, one beginning to find favor in other regions. And, anticipating a topic to be dealt with later, the region has cultivated its own literary and fine arts traditions.

Another way in which the Southwest differs from most other culture areas is localization of cultural identity and absence of any overt overall regional self-consciousness, political or otherwise.

> Peculiarly, the inhabitants of this area seem to be relatively innocent of regionalism. Whereas millions proclaim "I am a Texan," or "I am a Californian," almost no one boasts "I am a Southwesterner." Why I do not know. Perhaps because the phrase is too much of a mouthful. Perhaps because the Southwest is not and has never been a political unit, an office-electing unit, a taxing unit. Perhaps because it has had several local literatures instead of one that was as integrated as New England's. Perhaps because no single newspaper has ever spread its tentacles through the region as "The World's Greatest Newspaper" in the Midwest. Perhaps because the Southwest has never been embattled as was the South. (Caughey 1951, 184)[23]

Several decades later, these words still ring true. Nevertheless there can be little doubt as to the persisting, probably strengthening vitality of the Southwest as a regional concept, especially in the eyes of outsiders. It is also clear that it is a formal region, one that lacks core, domain, and sphere or an organizing center, as, in contrast, is the case with:

### New England

One may legitimately argue whether the South or New England should take chronological precedence here. But if the British settlement at Jamestown in 1607 antedates by a few years the enduring implantation of Europeans in Massachusetts, New England may merit pride of place in this account by virtue of earlier achievement of regional self-awareness.[24] "Decades before a powerful, defensive southern regional identity emerged, it was New Englanders who inherited, republicanized, and asserted in the context of national politics the new nation's most well-defined sense of regional distinctiveness and cultural superiority . . . [Jedidiah] Morse was the first writer to conceive of New England as a cultural region, the early republic's only cultural region" (Conforti 2001, 81–82).

The historical geography and cultural attributes of New England and its impact on the remainder of the nation have been so amply documented (for example, Rosenberry 1909; Wright 1933; Pierson 1955; McManis 1975; Garreau 1981, 14–48; Nissenbaum 1996, 1998; Cott 1997, 10–11; Conforti 2001; Kermes 2008) that not much need be added here.[25] The cultural distinctiveness of the region is quite apparent in its language, particular mix of religious denominations, dwellings, churches, barns (Zelinsky 1958; Hubka 2004), town morphology (J. S. Wood 1997a), and foodways. In addition, the list of New England "firsts" is long and distinguished, as the region, early and even today, has sought to wield political, intellectual, and artistic hegemony over the rest of the nation.[26]

In its internal structure, New England offers a convincing example of the Meinig Model, with Boston and environs, along with the older-settled sections of Massachusetts, Connecticut, and Rhode Island, serving as the core, the remainder of the census region as a domain, and an attenuated sphere stretching across much of New York as well as northern New Jersey and Pennsylvania (not to mention the Canadian Maritime provinces) but with some complications in the Dutch and Flemish tracts of the Hudson Valley and Long Island. Although not indicated in figure 6.1, traces of New England out-migration and culture are detectable across northern Ohio and indeed as far as the Mississippi and even beyond.

One of the more remarkable aspects of New England proper is how it has retained, and even intensified, its sense of regional integrity—and an image of rural and small-town quaintness—during its recent history de-spite massive urbanization, industrialization, and the arrival of great num-bers of non-British immigrants from Europe, Quebec, the Caribbean, and elsewhere as well as internal migrants, including African Americans, sea-sonal residents, and retirees, from elsewhere in the nation. Whatever the demographic contradictions, New England as a state of mind among resi-dents, but especially among outsiders, something sedulously cultivated by certain business interests, seems destined to live on indefinitely.[27] Essential to the hardiness of such prolonged existence is a semi-mythical Old New England. This was the result of

> a profound "sentimentalization" of New England, a new vision of the region expressed in an extensive literature—from history and journalism to novels and short stories—and in architectural and landscape reforms that began to trans-form the appearance of many towns and villages. Out of these diverse cultural movements emerged a mythic region called Old New England—rural, prein-dustrial, and ethnically "pure" . . . tourists discovered—indeed they helped to invent—a new myth of Old New England, a vision of the region that has proved to be extraordinarily tenacious and attractive. (D. Brown 1995, 8–11)

In any event, persistence of the New England Culture Area, whether real or mythological, is a fact, and convergence with the rest of the nation seems to be out of the question. But that is not necessarily the case with:

### The South

We have here the most universally acknowledged sociocultural subdivision of the United States and, in terms of both population and territory, the second largest of all regions under consideration. It differs markedly from

New England by virtue of being a formal region, that is, by displaying a set of characteristics present at various levels throughout its range, a unique complex of phenomena not found elsewhere, and by its lack of an organizing center or any resemblance to the Meinig Model. It also stands apart from the northeastern entity by containing distinct subregions. The South also far outranks all other American regions in the sheer volume of both scholarly and popular literature it has generated, which, in turn, is a measure of its exceptional prominence in the general imagination.

Despite the abundant attention the American South has enjoyed over the past two centuries among academics and others, we have only the vaguest sort of notion as to its origins. As Michael Zuckerman has noted,

> if, with Wirth, we define region as a "state of mind" or a domain in which residents achieve "a sense of common belonging," then the early South cannot be considered a region. Blassingame does not discover a single reference to the southern provinces as a coherent region in the entire era of imperial crisis. Degler says the region did not come to self-consciousness before the 1820s. Egerton maintains that it did not attain awareness of itself till even later. He insists on the embarrassing irony that "the Old South" was "created as a mental construct only a short time before it was historically eliminated as a material construct." (2003, 325)

How then did the American South originate?

*Cultural drift* is certainly in play, as it is eternally everywhere, but more immediately appealing is the operation of *interaction with the environment* (as is also the case with the Southwest). The concordance of the South with isotherms and isohyets is striking, so that we find here a warm, humid, quasi-subtropical, least Europe-like segment of North America with its peculiar set of soils, plants, and animals coinciding, not unexpectedly, with a distinctive way of life. Also entering the equation is the sociocultural background of the early European settlers, as argued by D. H. Fischer (1989) and McWhiney (1987). Significant though they may have been locally, the contributions of the unevenly distributed aborigines and African slaves and their progeny to the overall southern cultural mix remains problematic. In terms of pioneer settlement, the region was occupied by persons arriving via various ports along the Atlantic Seaboard and the Gulf and their offspring, but, for the Upper South at least, there was an important overland infusion of pioneers and cultural baggage from the Pennsylvania Culture Area.

Even before national independence had been achieved, it had become obvious that the economic and demographic composition of the colonies south of the Mason and Dixon Line had helped create a world quite unlike that of the North. Then the half century of political turmoil leading up to

the Civil War certainly contributed to a regional self-awareness, if not necessarily an accurate one. "The literature of the southern states reveals a . . .
romanticized vision of the Old South already being fully articulated in the
first half of the nineteenth century, and embellished by myths generated
by the Civil War and Reconstruction" (D. Brown 1995, 11). And, quite apart
from the military and political consequences of those events, warfare and
its aftermath produced a spatial churning that must have added to a broader
perspective of the South by its residents. But it was not until well into the
twentieth century that geographers and sociologists began serious description and analysis of the region (Odum 1936; Cash 1941; Parkins 1949). And,
most especially, our understanding of the South has been greatly enriched
by Rupert Vance's superb *Human Geography of the South* (1935) and by John
Shelton Reed's series of witty, thoughtful dispatches from the region (1976,
1982, 1983, 1990, 2005).

The picture that emerges is one of a regionally defined dietary regime
(Vance 1935, 411–41; Hilliard 1972; J. G. Taylor 1982) and, as noted earlier,
departures from the rest of the nation in political complexion, religious character, speech patterns, monuments (Martinez, Richardson, and McNinch-Su
2000; Martinez and Harris 2000), and, formerly at least, house and barn
types and other aspects of settlement morphology. Then, too, the South is
home to various folk and popular musical idioms. Within the realm of demography, a controversy still rages as to whether an exceptionally high rate
of homicide in the South is attributable to the general cultural milieu or to
other factors (Hackney 1969; Gastil 1971; Loftin and Hall 1974; Reed 1982,
139–53; Nisbett, Polly, and Lang 1995).

It is not too surprising to find distinctive subregions within a territorial
expanse as broad as the American South. The primary subdivision is that
between a Lowland, or Deep, South occupying the Atlantic coastal plain
and lower Mississippi Valley along with the adjacent Piedmont, and an
upland Upper South containing the ridges, valley basins, and plateaus of the
Appalachian system. Within the Lowland South we can discern a narrow
littoral stretching from Virginia to the Florida border with its own distinctive character owing to an early British and West Indian occupation and a
plantation economy unlike anything further inland. This subregion attains
its purest expression in the unique African American, or Gullah, culture of
the Sea Islands along the South Carolina and Georgia coast. Within the
Upland South, as so skillfully portrayed by Terry Jordan-Bychkov (2003), it
may be useful to consider the Ozarks and Ouachita areas as distinct offshoots of the broader eastern component of the subregion. However, there
can be no debate as to the distinctiveness of the Kentucky Bluegrass as a

subregion, something deeply cherished by its inhabitants and so ably delineated by Raitz 1980 and Alvey 1992.

In contrast, the cultural geographer confronts an insoluble dilemma in trying to fit Texas into any system of American culture areas. Straddling, as it does, the Southwest and the South, it seems fully committed to neither while loudly advancing its claim to a special Texasness. In addition, there is the Mexican factor. How to deal with the powerful impact, cultural and demographic, of our southern neighbor on the Texas identity (or, conversely, for the Mexican geographer, the Texas effect)? Incidentally, there is no such conundrum in regionalizing the places along our northern border since Canadian influences there are relatively subdued. We have in Texas a population with a strong sense of its precious unique identity, one it celebrates energetically in a variety of ways (De León 1997, 260), and a territory so extensive it merits nomination as a valid subregion. Donald Meinig has coped with the dilemma without fully resolving it by affixing his model to it (1968, 116), designating a triangular core cradled between Houston, San Antonio, and Fort Worth–Dallas and assigning the remainder of the state to a domain, and suggesting a sphere reaching into its neighboring states.

But let us return to the South as a whole, since, whatever the level of attachment to a given subregion, the native-born of the region generally tend to perceive themselves as generic southerners. So, given such a powerful salience and singularity in the past, as well as its tragic struggle for political sovereignty, how effectively has the South preserved, or possibly enhanced, its regional identity? How have its sociocultural contrasts with the non-South persevered over time? The question might have seemed trivial in, say, 1940, but today, after more than a half century of profound material transformation, can we still speak of the South as a place apart (R. Vance 1982, 211–13)? In posing these queries, concerns that have given rise to abundant academic and popular attention, we focus sharply and specifically on the central thrust of this inquiry. No other American region offers so definitive an opportunity to test the convergence thesis.

The modernization, or nationalization, of the visible scene is obvious to even the most casual of observers (Pillsbury 2006, 2–3). Industrialization, urbanization, suburbanization, higher levels of educational attainment, full participation in advanced forms of transport and communication, and especially, as noted elsewhere, air-conditioning have eliminated, or greatly reduced, the formidable gaps that once prevailed between the South and other American regions. Furthermore, a lively shuffling of migrants, black and white, into and out of the South, and often back again, has prevailed throughout most of the past century and has certainly had its impact on regional particularity, as has the recent significant influx of Latinos and other foreign-born.

The change in the built landscape has been truly startling, as I can attest from personal experience. The rural Georgia I surveyed in 1950–52, the regionally specific dwellings, church buildings, mills, barns, other outbuildings, wells, fences, and other such elements have either utterly vanished or are moldering away. If Georgia's smaller cities and towns still retain visible vestiges of the past, its countryside is now scarcely distinguishable from Indiana's or South Dakota's. Less visible, but certainly no less important, have been changes in social attitudes, ever so gradually approaching conformity with national standards.

The argument concerning survival of southern cultural authenticity follows two opposite directions: first, the contention that the South is being saturated and transformed by cultural baggage imported from elsewhere, the "northernization" of the region; and, contrariwise, the claim that, with the export of indigenous southern items and their eager adoption in the Non-South, we are witnessing the "southernization" of America, thereby rendering moot any discourse dealing with regional distinctions, a thesis most vigorously advanced by the journalist Peter Applepome (1996, 3–22). As far back as 1971, McKinney and Bourque concluded after examining all the standard socioeconomic measures that "the South has been changing more rapidly than the rest of the nation for the past forty years and moreover is becoming increasingly indistinguishable from the rest of American society" (1971, 399; also see Shafer and Johnston 2006). Additional support for this view comes from James Cobb (2000), who regards the erasure of North/South differences as a done deal.[28]

Perhaps some of the strongest evidence supporting the notion of convergence comes from the realms of cuisine and popular music and the recent national acceptance of southern country music (Egerton 1974, 206; Cobb 1982).[29] But if we turn to the quantifiable measures, we may have to settle for a Scotch verdict. As we have seen earlier, the available data fail to validate the perception of a vanishing South when we examine the linguistic, political, and religious scenes. The only halfway persuasive conformation of the homogenization argument appears in polling data. If only 75 percent of southerners indicated a desire in 2004 to be identified as such (as compared with 87 percent of New Englanders) (Cobb 2005, 328), the response to the question administered in the South "do you consider yourself to be a Southerner or not?" generated only 69.5 percent positive responses in 2001 as against 76.9 percent in 1991 (Griffin and Thompson 2003, 55), but in surveys involving a fair number of newcomers.

The most sobering of tidings for those who cherish the vitality of an American South, however, comes from the world of letters. Among devotees of southern literature, and fiction in particular, there has been a certain amount of hand-wringing over a possible loss of subject matter in the contemporary scene. If a brilliant galaxy of southern novelists, short story authors, and dramatists blazed away during much of the twentieth century, what are their successors to write about if the esoteric world of William Faulkner, Eudora Welty, Thomas Wolfe, Ellen Glasgow, Erskine Caldwell, Carson McCullers, and Tennessee Williams has given way to the blankness endured by Bobby Lee Mason's characters (Gray 1986, 2000; Kreyling 1998)? Are we permitted to hope, along with Louis Rubin (1988), that, although the Old South has been withering away, writers can still find rich raw material in the process of change?[30]

Despite the testimony of all those outward signs pointing toward obliteration of southern identity, several scholars continue to believe in its durability, albeit in altered form (Degler 1977; O'Brien 1979; Reed 1983, 2005; H. L. Preston 1991b; Grantham 1994; Carlton 1995; Ayers 1996; D. Roberts 2002).[31] Then, countering whatever trends toward regional erosion we might detect is a phenomenon unique to the South: the Neo-Confederate Movement (Horwitz 1998). We might regard it as rebel sentiment, the Lost Cause that has never quite died away among an underclass, a small, but significant, fraction of a defeated population, but now enhanced by the availability of modern communication media. In recent times, it has surfaced vociferously in public clashes over the display of Confederate symbols (Martinez and Richardson 2000; Poole 2005). The Neo-Confederates should not be confused with ultra-right militias and related groups elsewhere in the country who do not adhere to any regional agenda. Instead their program resonates in poignant fashion, and however malignantly, with a worldwide unease. "Although it is important to be critical of the neo-Cons and their narrow definition of southern heritage as conservative, white, and mostly male, their cyber-South does express a real desire for some type of social or community life that is less bound by distant and seemingly unresponsive government and more fully engaged in the local and the regional" (McPherson 2003, 114).

But, in a much more generalized, socially acceptable fashion, the South, or the image of the South, has taken on a new lease of life—as have all the other genuine and spurious regions of the land. We have here the manifestation of a latter-day regionalism, a phenomenon to be accosted in more detail later in this chapter. It has become commercially worthwhile and academically respectable to exploit the regional motif. Thus, throughout the twentieth century, we have had much lively imagineering of the South in film, popular fiction, radio, and television (Kirby 1986). And in such periodicals as *Southern Living* we are presented with a new southern lifestyle of fantasy with only the blurriest resemblance to the Old South, catering not to "someone linked to the South necessarily by family history, residence, or employment. Rather, a southerner is someone who participates in a southern 'lifestyle'" (Elias 2002, 257; also see P. F. Lewis 1993; Gray 2000, 357). So, whatever the reality on the ground, a synthetic region lives on in the world of consumerism. Ancillary to such marketplace hustle is the recent Southern Studies boom on college campuses.

> Because of growing statistical and anecdotal evidence of the South's assimilation into the American mainstream, interest in the southern cultural identity soared on southern university campuses in the 1980s and 1990s. As one journalist noted, "Institutes, centers, and programs for the study of the South are becoming as ubiquitous on Southern campuses as Wal-Marts are in Southern suburbia." Eric Bates of *Southern Exposure* magazine agreed that fascination with things southern is the biggest craze since miniature golf." (Cobb 2005, 229; also see O'Brien 1979, 217)

Thus, in conclusion, if the South offers an especially intriguing test of the convergence thesis—and an amply documented one—it fails to yield a simple answer. No single world or phrase can characterize the fate of southern regional identity. Neither requiem nor bill of health fits the case. Perhaps the most sensible assessment is that presented by Richard Gray.

> So, it seems, the essential paradoxes remain. The material culture has changed substantially since the Second World War, far more even than in the period when the Agrarians and their friends were taking their stand. But the nonmaterial culture, although altered, still enables Southerners to think and talk of themselves in terms of their regional identity, the inherited codes . . . Southerners may live in a predominately urban and suburban society and depend on an industrial economy; and the foundations of their lives may gradually be shifting under the impact of mass culture. They may watch television, eat at McDonald's, and listen to popular music. But old habits die hard; alterations in the material fabric of society are not necessarily or immediately accompanied by alterations in the consciousness of its members. So the cultural lag persists, even if in weakened form; and the war between the old codes and the new continues, with the new slowly but steadily gaining ground. The Southerner, in effect, still belongs in two worlds, two moral territories, even if he [*sic*] is turning back ever less easily or frequently to one of these; in terms of his mind or imagination at least, he remains an amphibious creature. (1986, 230–31)

### Acadiana

Roughly contemporaneous with the South is the much smaller, adjacent, but culturally alien Acadiana occupying the southern half or so of Louisiana. We have here a culture area and population of mixed origin, essentially French and black Caribbean but with some admixture of Spanish, aboriginal, and, belatedly, generalized Anglo-American elements (Kniffen 1968; Trépanier 1989; Estaville 2001). In addition, given proximity to the remainder of the lower Mississippi Valley, the most intensely Southern of Southern areas, we can assume a certain osmotic seepage of traits from that source. Excepting Hawaii, Acadiana may be the most exotic of the entire set of American culture areas, a claim bolstered by the character of its metropolis. New Orleans, with all its peculiarities of site and sociocultural attributes may be off the chart if we were to rank American cities in terms of conformity to a standard model (P. F. Lewis 2003; Colten 2005).

In any event, there is no question as to regional singularity in terms of ecology, economy, language, architecture, religion, cemeteries, cuisine, music, and manners and customs. It is equally clear that, despite much recent tourist traffic and the sharing of its music and cuisine with the rest of America, there is no immediate prospect of the crumbling of this remarkable tile within the national mosaic. "Louisiana Cajun music, language and culture, thought to be in imminent danger of demise thirty and forty years ago, are undergoing a revival and have been for some time" (E. Peterson 1996, 12).

### The Pennsylvania Culture Area

As the third and youngest of the major culture hearths along the Atlantic seaboard, the Pennsylvania Culture Area (PCA henceforth) may have been, it is reasonable to argue, the most consequential of the trio in the formation of the all-important Generic Euro-American Region. Occupying much, but far from all, of the Commonwealth of Pennsylvania, and extending southwestward into portions of Maryland, West Virginia, and Virginia, the PCA is comparable in area to the New England core and domain, but far smaller than the South.

But we find ourselves in something of a quandary in trying to squeeze the PCA into that broader, historically seminal expanse variously termed the Midland, Middle Atlantic, or some equivalent, that is, the states of New York, Pennsylvania, New Jersey, and perhaps Maryland and Delaware. What to do with upstate New York? Although calling it "New England Extended" makes a certain amount of sense, especially if we bypass utterly non–New

England New York City and the lower Hudson Valley, it did receive substantial numbers of settlers directly from overseas. Thereafter we find upstate New York's migrants and commerce running parallel with the PCA's but with minimal interaction. In any event, as we shall we, the broader region, dominated by Pennsylvania and New York, served as *the* crucial seedbed for the Generic Euro-American Region.

As it happened, it was in its ethnic genesis that the PCA differs from New England and the South and also offers us a rehearsal of the grander Melting Pot theme that is so basic to the American saga. The colonizers were English, Scotch-Irish, and German in roughly comparable quantities but with the addition of some smaller, possibly significant, numbers of Swedes, Finns, and Dutch from stillborn settlements along the lower Delaware (Lemon 1972). The interactions among these pioneers (*cultural diffusion* in full swing), bearing as they did varied sets of cultural baggage, and their dealings with an eminently exploitable territory gave birth to a distinctive culture area with its core centered in Cumberland, Perry, and Adams counties and an encircling domain and sphere in splendid accordance with the Meinig Model (Zelinsky 1977, 143).

The combination of cultural attributes in the PCA is decidedly specific to the region. Thus we find a particular speech pattern and vocabulary identified with it (Kurath 1949; Labov, Ash, and Boberg 2005, 148), an array of religious denominations in a mix found nowhere else on the continent (Zelinsky 1961), types of barns and houses specific to the region (Glass 1986; Ensminger 1992), and, perhaps most tellingly, a town morphology quite unparalleled elsewhere (Pillsbury 1968; Zelinsky 1977).[32] Then, whenever someone produces a proper map of the traditional dietary regions of the country, it is more than likely it will display a Pennsylvania region, one with a distinctly Teutonic flavor.

The foregoing thumbnail sketch of the PCA might suffice for present purposes except for a truly singular mystery: the fact that until recently both inhabitants and scholars seem to have been unaware of, or indifferent to, its existence. Historians have consistently given short shrift to Pennsylvania and to the Middle Atlantic states in general whenever they deal with the larger American story, while according ample attention to New England and the South (Shryock 1964; Zuckerman 1982; 2003, 324). Moreover, general geographic texts on North America have been totally oblivious to the region's existence. Although Henry Glassie in his treatment of material folk culture in the eastern United States (1968) gives us some intimation of its reality and Raymond Gastil (1975, 29) indicated the existence of a crudely, inaccurately bounded "Pennsylvania Region" on his map of culture areas, it was not until my 1977 essay on the Pennsylvania Town that detailed, explicit recognition and realistic mapping appeared in print.

That Pennsylvanians and other residents of the PCA are remarkably indifferent to their regional identity was disclosed by a study of vernacular regions based on geographic allusions in names of enterprises (Zelinsky 1980). It documented an almost total absence of the use of "Pennsylvania" or other regional references within the Commonwealth, a sort of "Zone of Indifference." Although there is a certain amount of tourist excitement involving the Amish, the Brandywine Valley, and such cities as Lancaster and Philadelphia, there is no broader exploitation invoking an overall regional theme. Consequently, there is no equivalent here to *Yankee* or *Southern Living.* The only meaningful explanation to be offered is that

> the failure to appreciate the full regional personality of the PCA stems largely, I suspect, from its "middleness." In many ways it is intermediate between the New England and New York cultural landscapes and those of the South, and thus is less aberrant from eastern seaboard and national norms. It has also been a major source, or at least channel, for the flow of migrants and ideas into the vast central and western reaches of the nation; and thus much that was to become national and "mainstream" later is found in the PCA, too prosaic and normal to stir up comment. (Zelinsky 1977, 146–47)

All that remains to be said is that, despite all the forces of massification that operate unimpeded in the PCA as freely as elsewhere in the nation, there is as yet no indication of regional disintegration, no trend toward disinheritance amid a citizenry notable for its cultural conservatism and latter-day disinclination to move out of the region.

### The Generic Euro-American Region

We have here the largest of our regions, accounting as it does for well over half the national territory and population: the essential, most typical America, indeed "Middle America" with a vengeance. Its origin is easy to trace. By the close of the eighteenth century, three vigorous streams of settlers had begun to traverse the Appalachian barrier from New England (and New England Extended), the PCA, and Upper South and to claim land in the upper Ohio Valley and vicinity and to mingle spatially and otherwise. Thus it came about in the early nineteenth century in the Old Northwest, and, more specifically, beginning in Ohio, that something resembling a general, or generic, American culture and nationality first saw the light of day.[33]

Although there was much mixing and smudging of the various migrational strands in the pioneer phase and later, we can still discern their origins across the state of Ohio and farther on into Indiana, Illinois, and even beyond. In addition to the three basic source areas, there was a fourth contribution from Canada and the northeastern states by way of the Great

Lakes, one that was significant in the peopling of portions of Michigan, Wisconsin, and Minnesota (Hudson 1984). Then, in addition to the westward fanning out of migrants from the Old Northwest, from the 1830s until the close of frontier settlement circa 1890, large numbers of highly varied immigrants from the British Isles, Scandinavia, and continental Europe crowding into canal boats, steamboats, and the new railroads leap-frogged over previously occupied territory to claim farmland, ranches, and other economic opportunities all the way across the continent to the shores of the Pacific and, rather later, even into Alaska.

In the course of time, all these newcomers and their predecessors have interacted or merged—not without some friction, of course—to form a relatively uniform cultural mind-set. A question that remains to be fully settled is whether traces of the triune (or quaternary) genesis of the Generic Euro-American Region (GEAR) are still in evidence across two-thirds of the national expanse, as maintained by Elazar (1984), D. H. Fischer (1989), and Sugar (2004), as opposed to the possibility that thorough fusion has been attained.

Whatever the final answer to that question, I must underscore the critical importance of this vast region in dealing with the central questions of this inquiry, quite apart from its impressive size and population count. We have here a robust demonstration of an ultimate obliteration of original difference, of the fabrication of a single central national ethos and modal way of life. If we were to limit our gaze to the GEAR, shorn of its subsequent offshoots, there would be no further debate as to the existence of a predominantly homogenized America. But such a simple solution to our quest eludes our grasp because, following the period of pioneer settlement, there have been further ethnic complications in this huge region and the partial or full formation of subregions. In addition to sporadic streams of easterners, migrants have arrived from the South and from Canada. Here, as elsewhere in the nation, Hispanics have begun of late to appear in appreciable numbers, and immigrants, refugees, and displaced persons from East Asia, Europe, and elsewhere have altered the character of a number of localities. Given the variety of physical, social, and historical circumstances, it is hardly surprising that at least four actual or emergent subregions have materialized, the earliest, the Mormon Culture Area, during the mid-nineteenth century and the other three during the twentieth century.

If I have not tried to characterize the specific cultural identity of the GEAR, it is because doing so is equivalent to delineating the United States as a whole—and a redundant exercise since such a portrayal is one of the incidental objectives of this volume. In effect, when outside observers generalize about American life, manners, or landscape, what they often have in mind is the GEAR, either taken as a whole or the intensification of its peculiarities in such subsections as California.

### The Mormon Culture Area

The history and historical geography of this truly unique territory have been examined so thoroughly and effectively (for example, Meinig 1965, 1996; R. H. Jackson 2003) that there is no need to recount once again the tale and what is also a classic example of still another place-making process or, rather, factor: the role of extraordinary individuals, in this case Joseph Smith and Brigham Young. What is extraordinary about this episode in the shaping of America is the rapidity and transparency of ethnogenesis, the sudden, well-documented creation of a novel society and cultural area within what had been a nearly empty expanse. Although clearly an offshoot of the grander Generic Euro-American entity, at least three processes have been at work to create and sequester the Mormon Culture Area from the parental zone: *interaction with the environment, demographic change*, and, uniquely within the American regional scheme of things, *religious tropism and repulsion.*

The outcome by the mid-nineteenth century was a huge tract of strongly or partially Mormonized territory—the inspiration for the Meinig Model—with a core in the Salt Lake area, a domain encompassing the remainder of Utah along with sizable slices of Idaho and Arizona, and a sphere once extending across Nevada into Southern California and north and south across the Canadian and Mexican borders. Both early and later what has so sharply distinguished this region—one so large and intensely developed it might seem to surpass the level of mere subregion—has been, of course, its religious composition. But there are other characteristics that set it apart. Its social and economic arrangements do not resemble anything found elsewhere in the nation, and its staunchly conservative, that is, Republican, political orientation has remained intact ever since Utah achieved statehood in 1896. Even more obvious is the Mormon built landscape (Jackson and Layton 1976; Francaviglia 1978; R. H. Jackson 1978). Early house types were indigenous to the area; the geometry and widths of streets and their adjacent ditches in Salt Lake City and other Mormon towns have no counterparts elsewhere, as is also the case for the farm villages with their large house lots and the houseless countryside.

But the purity and insularity of the early Mormon oasis could not endure, especially when its capital city lay athwart a principal transcontinental route. If the first generation of settlers in the region involved the ingathering of Mormons from throughout the northeastern quadrant of the

nation and significant numbers of Western European converts, their hegemony was later much diluted by an influx of gentiles and national enterprises and by political and social compromise. Thus, as Ethan Yorgason
(2003) has so thoroughly explicated, there has been a transition over the past
century and a quarter, not without serious tension, from a deviant, near-
outcast place to a supernationalist community with its communitarian
heritage compromised by capitalist doctrine. Thus

> today's . . . Mormon West consists of a dominant urban and suburban majority
> who share most of the socio-cultural characteristics of the larger Western
> urban/suburban milieu and a rural agrarian minority whose Mormon villages
> comprise relic landscape features in the region . . . Describing today's Mormon
> West, observers view a landscape . . . whose most typical Mormon features are
> the ward chapels and temples of the faith that dot an otherwise archetypical
> urban sprawl little different from that of many other parts of America. Even the
> ethnic character of the Mormon West is changing as Hispanic migrants flock
> into the cities and towns of the region. (R. H. Jackson 2003, 159)

But Jackson and Yorgason may well have overstated their case. What they
argue for the Mormon West parallels developments in other older culture
areas: a superficial overlay of the latest technology and landscape manipulation coexisting with an indelible mind-set and kit of sociocultural values.
In any event, we can assume that, if the Mormon Culture Area seems certain to endure far into the future, it would be as a watered-down version of
its pristine singularity but still notably distinct from other sections of our
mythical West.

### California

It is indisputable that the two most populous sections of California, both
adjacent to the ocean—a central tract anchored on the Bay Area and a southern one dominated by Los Angeles—now deviate so significantly from the
remainder of the nation as to comprise a valid cultural subregion. Whether
the two tracts in question differ sufficiently one from the other as to earn classification as separate entities remains open to debate. But, in my opinion—
and one that is certainly open to challenge—despite the obvious cultural
disparities between the two great metropolitan areas and even a certain
mutual dislike, they still share so much of an essential Californianess as to
qualify for joint membership in this distinctive cultural region.

What is clear is that a singular physical geography, the *pursuit of pleasure*,
and selective migration from other states and from East Asia, along with
a historic affinity to Mexico, especially in Southern California (Deverell
1997), and recent heavy infiltration from across the border are basic factors
in creating a super-Americanness, a sort of new world unto itself. Central

and particularly Southern California are ideal examples of the second of Laurence Veysey's regional types.

> On the simplest level, there are two distinct kinds of regions in the United States. The first depends for its character upon *continuing* qualities, upon traditions preserved over a long period of time. In this group naturally fall New England, Tidewater Virginia, the Hudson Valley, the Appalachian, and the New Orleans Creole cultures among others. The second type, especially indigenous to America, derives its character precisely from its social impermanence, from its shifting (which is, in the broad sense, to say *frontier*) characteristics. (1960, 43)[34]

By all appearance, this frontierish California cultural subregion continues to widen or, at the very least, to preserve its divergence from the norms of mainstream America, while, paradoxically, somehow epitomizing the very essence of the American spirit. But if the California subregion comforts us with taxonomic certitude, the situation is more problematic in the case of:

### *The Pacific Northwest*

Indeed the legitimacy of the claim of a firm regional identity for the Pacific Northwest, or Cascadia or other synonyms, is so cloudy that I have set a question mark over it in figure 6.1. Although Raymond Gastil accepts "detailed evidence for considering the Pacific Northwest to be a separate region deserving of further cultural analysis" (1974, 156), other observers reserve judgment or are downright skeptical. Thus William Robbins notes that "although there is general agreement that the Pacific Northwest has certain geographic characteristics, there is great confusion as to whether the region is a distinctive entity in an economic and cultural sense" (1983, 3).

And, in what may be the most serious effort to trap the elusive identity of the area, John Findlay writes that "at least until recently, the peoples who have lived in Oregon, Idaho, and Washington have generally neither defined themselves readily as belonging to the same region, nor, naturally, agreed on the meaning of that region . . . That is, regional identity over the years has tended to be somewhat dubious, artificial and ever-shifting" (1997, 38).[35] Brigitte Haehnle is even more dismissive. "Is Cascadia really a 'naturally grown' region, alive in the minds of people living in the territory? Or is Cascadia merely a construct invented by various agents and interest groups in pursuit of a constituency? . . . The outcome of this analysis suggests that Cascadia is an artificial construct conceived by a few inhabitants at the end of the 1980s in order to pursue their particular political and economic interests more easily under the general regional name of Cascadia" (2005, 225, 235).

Evidence supporting such a cynical attitude comes from a detailed account of an abortive campaign in the late nineteenth and early twentieth century to fashion the perception of an "Inland Empire" centered on Spokane and the Palouse Country off toward the eastern margins of Cascadia (Morrissey 1997). It was a culture area that never quite gelled in either fact or popular imagination. What we see, then, in the case of the Pacific Northwest is the especially overt operation of the regional ploy as practiced elsewhere by political, economic, and cultural promoters, sometimes, as we shall see, pushing a spurious cause. But here, as in the case of constructing the myths of New England and the South or such latter-day artifacts as Santa Fe, authentic raw materials are at hand.

Then we have the interesting possibility, one that has never been seriously investigated, that, as has apparently been the case for California and Anglos settling in the Southwest, internal migration into Washington and Oregon has been selective in terms of the social and psychological attributes of the newcomers, while an even more persuasive argument for the reality of the region is available from the realms of literature and architecture. As recounted by Nicholas O'Connell, a number of notable authors have anchored their writings in, and celebrated, the special physical environment of the Pacific Northwest. "They consider the split between the human and nonhuman as a dangerous illusion, which encourages the destruction of the environment and the spiritual impoverishment of human beings" (2003, 179). One might claim that nowhere else in the nation do we encounter such a critical mass of verse, fiction, and nonfiction developing such a theme. In any event, there can be little doubt as to the way that most influential writers of the region have endowed it with a particular personality.

> One may plausibly maintain that not until the post–World War II period has the Pacific Northwest produced a regional culture of fiction, poetry, art, and architecture that is truly of the first order. The recent cultural flowering of the Pacific Northwest, however, may well exceed all other regions in its combination of quality and coherence. It is strikingly evident that this achievement rests upon the creative inspiration provided by the Pacific Northwest environment of land, water, and climate. (R. M. Brown 1983, 68)

Most immediately noticeable is an architectural language specific to Washington and Oregon, building styles that began to emerge by the 1970s (Woodbridge 1974). Since then, regional architects have designed an ever-greater number of dwellings, as well as public and commercial buildings (inevitably with wood as the dominant component) that resonate with the natural environment, structures that have few or no counterparts elsewhere in the nation (Kelbaugh 1997; D. E. Miller 2005). It seems safe to conclude that, insofar as the Pacific Northwest is a genuine cultural entity, it is likely to preserve and probably increase its differences from the remainder of the nation.

### Peninsular Florida

The youngest of the subregions within the Generic Euro-American Region is an ongoing development of early twentieth-century origin. What had once been a remote, thinly settled, virtually wild territory whose physical attributes did not attract agrarian pioneers became a haven for great streams of pleasure-seekers, retirees, and other migrants once Americans had crossed a certain threshold of affluence and after railroad lines, modern highways, and airlines made access easy and relatively cheap. Indeed the lure of subtropical living has proved to be irresistible to millions of nonnative, full- or part-time Floridians.

Although a growing share of its twenty-first-century population hales from the Caribbean, South America, Canada, and the American South, the essential cultural tone of the subregion was set in the mid-1900s by persons coming from the northeastern and north central states, and especially the metropolises of those sections. (It is not uncommon to overhear New York City or Chicago accents in Miami or Tampa.) Thus, in a manner decidedly reminiscent of the Southern California experience, the essential Peninsular Florida is a composite of many of those demographic elements that went into the making of the greater GEAR. Although it may not be the purest sampling of that larger region, there is no question about its primary affiliation. Much work remains to be done on its fluid cultural geography, but further intensification of Peninsular Florida's regional peculiarities is a reasonable forecast.

### By Way of Summary

What light does this survey of what I regard as authentic American culture areas cast on the central question of this inquiry? Are we witnessing convergence, the spatial homogenization of our society and culture? The general answer is that our evidence suggests that we ought to be quite skeptical of such a judgment, but with one major proviso. For the time being we must omit from our balance sheet a Generic Euro-American Culture Area shorn of its subregions, a formidable tract in terms of space and population. The reason is simple. Posing and answering the question for this quintessentially American territory is really the central mission of this entire study. Arriving at a meaningful answer involves weighing the evidence offered in all the other chapters.

Leaving aside that huge qualification, note that the preceding pages contain no obituaries (except, of course, for the pre-Columbian culture areas and, arguably, the early Dutch-Flemish tract along the lower Hudson). Each of the valid entities I have identified, including those seventeen metropolises, still thrives and enjoys a certain level of cultural health. Indeed fresh new culture areas have appeared or are gestating, while some of the more venerable ones, such as Hawaii, the Southwest, and Acadiana, are enjoying a new lease on life, albeit with modern, or postmodern, modifications. The fact that all the areas in question—including the South, the most problematic and controversial of the set—are participating in the national playbook in so many outward ways does not override the persistence, or even enhancement, of regional peculiarity.

But if we are to gain an adequate appreciation of the salience of culture areas in the presumed homogenization of the American scene, we must cast a glance at the global situation and assess how the case of the United States appears within an international context. In doing so, one quickly realizes how gross or coarse-grained is the pattern displayed in figure 6.1, especially when set against the cultural regionalization of more venerable societies. With only fifteen first- or second-order regions—and just one of a lower order—the United States (as is the case also with Canada and Australia) is in a different league from that containing such nations as, say, Italy. It would be fair to claim that, with a population amounting to only 19 percent of the American total and a territory less than one-thirtieth of that occupied by the United States, one could readily list well over a score of larger Italian cities that qualify as bona fide culture areas, along with a much larger number of nonmetro tracts, within a nested hierarchy ranging down to the quite miniature (Griswold 2008, 104–6). Or, taking the quest to the extreme, we can turn to Mexico's Chiapas or highland Guatemala and see how each village claims its special identity in terms of costume and probably other less visible factors.

But, interesting as such disparities may be, much more relevant to the basic inquiry at hand is the fact that, with its relatively meager set of culturally distinctive places, the United States joins the rest of the world in terms of a key feature: their vitality and durability. Despite all the clamor about the omnipotence of modernization and globalization, has anyone seriously announced the imminent extinction of the many cultural subdivisions of Germany, France, or India? Is Paris about to lose its special identity? Or Venice, Edinburgh, Mumbai, Montreal, St. Petersburg, Bruges, Cairo, or Buenos Aires? *One of the rare unqualified predictions possible in this otherwise unpredictable world is that New York City, San Francisco, and other such distinctive metropolises are not going to become anonymous anytime within the foreseeable future.*

## Spurious Cultural Regions—and Others

Under this heading we consider some spatial concepts that most laypersons and many scholars erroneously regard as valid cultural regions for reasons that are worth considering, beginning with

### The Middle West

We have here a purported cultural region, one accepted by the general public and too many academics but lacking, nonetheless, serious geographic credentials.[36] Thus there is no specifically Middle West linguistic region. Moreover, the vaguely defined territory in question lacks any religious commonality, while also missing is any consistent political identity, dietary regime, unifying symbols, or vernacular architectural language. It displays none of the characteristics of either a formal or functional region.[37] Among the skeptics has been Max Lerner who observed that "there are some who feel that it [the Midwest] never was a region in a true sense and is not one now; that it has no geographic, economic, ethnic, or cultural unity. Certainly it is today less a region than, let us say, the Deep South or Northwest, the Far West or even New England. Its qualities have been fused and absorbed with the generalized qualities of America as a whole" (1957, 190). Joel Garreau is even more dismissive. "There is no such thing as the 'Midwest'" (1981, 5), and adds insult to injury by pasting the label of "Foundry" onto a large section of the conventional territory.[38]

But, moving past the bounds of rigorous cultural geography, the Middle West has enjoyed a robust life as a vernacular region, that is, a cultural area perceived to be real and meaningful by the public at large.[39] However, any such existence has been belated. The term "Middle West" did not materialize until the 1880s (J. R. Shortridge 1989, 13–26), long after the territory had been occupied. Furthermore, "Middle West came into its own as a major regional term about 1912" (J. R. Shortridge 1989, 24).

A further complication for anyone espousing the geographic validity of a Middle West cultural region has been the difficulty of defining its limits and the degree of midwesternness within those limits (Noble and Wilhelm 1995, 1–7). "When it comes to definition, the Midwest is a mushy place; experts cannot even agree on where it begins and ends. Is it the drainage area of the Great Lakes, or the upper Mississippi? What do northern Wisconsin and southeastern Ohio have in common with each other, or Cook County and southern Illinois, for that matter? Where are the shared events in the Midwest's past and present?" (Cayton 2001, 149).

As a practical matter, some scholars, for example, Hart 1972 and Slade and Lee 2004, have simply equated the region with a bloc of states.[40] On the other hand, the use of questionnaires has yielded more interesting re-sults. In the late 1950s, responses from 480 rural postmasters to the question as to whether their community lay within the Middle West generated a map for this vernacular region whose extent is virtually coincident with the dozen states classified as North Central by the census (J. W. Brownell 1960). (One must wonder what Joseph Brownell would have found if he had quizzed urban postmasters.) In testing regional perceptions of college students in a number of different states in 1980, James Shortridge (1989, 84–90) ascertained that their views were inconsistent in defining the heart of the Middle West, with differences largely dependent on state of origin, but with a consistent westward bias.[41] In addition, after reviewing the literature, Shortridge throughout his definitive 1989 volume stresses the periodic shifts in the location of the core of the region—westward, eastward, and back again—in the minds of the general public.

The strength or durability of our vision of the Middle West rests no so much on its averageness[42]—the most modal and representative of the national whole, as well as being the most centrally located of all our presumed regions—but rather on something much deeper and diagnostic of a national malaise. It is a place that, better than any other extended tract, embodies an imagined Middle Landscape, the transcendent theme of pastoralism, so vital, if subliminal, a component of the American Dream. Joanne Jacobson has stated it well.

> The Midwest seems, more than other rural landscapes in the US, to have become a constructed matter, conceived and sustained from outside the region itself. Continuing conflict over the geographical boundaries of the region (which expand and contract at points from the Ohio Valley to the Great Plains) reflects disjunction between idea and landscape in the Midwest. The Midwest has been so heavily mythologized, eulogized and satirized that its life as an idea seems, for a long time, to have dominated its experienced meaning: traditionally associated with the frontier values of movement and promise and with the rural values of fertility, order and stability, the Midwest has been invested in unique ways with the symbolic freight of national consensus, of the quintessentially "American." Conflict over that symbolic investment speaks, I believe, both for the impulse to invent a myth of commonality rooted in the physical landscape at the center of the continent and for the insufficiency of that myth as a response to the conditions of urban industrial culture. (1991, 243–22)[43]

The physical reality of whatever territory we deem to be the Middle West only weakly resembles the popular myth. To be sure, Minnesota, Indiana, Ohio, and the other states have their full complement of family farms and small towns, the latter still imbued with a nineteenth-century identity only modestly altered. But the great majority of residents in the twelve or so states in question are not engaged in growing corn, soybeans, oats, and hay, raising swine, or milking cows and making cheese. Instead they are mostly city dwellers and, if employed, working in factories, offices, retail shops, and schools and providing other services. Flint, Midland (Mich.), Duluth, Milwaukee, Toledo, South Bend, East St. Louis, Rantoul (Ill.), New Harmony (Ind.), the Wisconsin Dells, Cape Girardeau (Mo.), Vedic City (Iowa), or the Dutch American enclave in southwestern Michigan may not come to mind when we hear the words "Middle West," but they are essential components of whatever it is. The common perception of the region, this figment of our collective geographic imagination

> assumes a stable regional identity based in agriculture, clarity, and whiteness— none of which accurately represents the region. By folding regional history into national history, we risk losing sight of the genuinely complex past and present of a region which includes farmers and factory workers, members of all races, and cities and small towns. An oversimplified Midwest discounts and overlooks the race riots of Detroit in the 1960s as well as the rampant bank-ruptcies of farmers in the 1890s, 1930s and 1980s. It overlooks the region as both center of the Underground Railroad in the 1840s and ground-zero for the Ku Klux Klan in the 1920s. (Watts 2002, 219)

Given the spurious nature of the concept, the waxing and waning of the image of the Middle West is a phenomenon with little value in assessing the presumed convergence of our nation-state.

### The West

The American West is by far the grandest of our presumed cultural re-gions, real or imagined, accounting as it does for more than half of the territory of the continental United States if, as may be logical, we include Alaska.[44] But what are the West's qualifications as a genuine, unitary culture area? Although some geographers and historians, the latter perhaps best rep-resented by Patricia Nelson Limerick,[45] persist in viewing it as such, when we actually confront the geographic realities, the western half of the contiguous United States disintegrates into a collection of discrete cultural, as well as physically distinct, entities, and the holistic vision is recognized for what it is: a myth, but an exceptionally important myth, much like our encounter with the Middle West.

Where does the West begin? The answer depends on the date because perception of this vague area was for so long synonymous with a receding settlement frontier (Wrobel 1996). During James Fenimore Cooper's child-hood, the American West commenced somewhere in upstate New York. Even earlier "in the late sixteenth century, the West was New Jersey and

New Mexico; in the early nineteenth, Illinois and Texas. By the end of the twentieth century, white people had overrun the continent, and the last of the wests, stretching from the plains to the Pacific, has kept the name" (Klein 1996, 180). Clear-eyed observers have recognized the internal diversity of "the last of the wests," among them the late, great Wallace Stegner. "The West, which stretches from around the ninety-eighth meridian to the Pacific, and from the forty-ninth parallel to the Mexican border, is actually half a dozen subregions as different from one another as the Olympic rain forest is from Utah's slickrock country, or Seattle from Santa Fe" (1992, 45–46).[46] Donald Meinig has meticulously plotted the location of the valid constituent cultural tracts of the western portion of the nation in a map depicting six major regions and five secondary ones (1972, 169). Then we have an entire volume, appropriately entitled *Many Wests*, that richly develops the theme of western heterogeneity (Steiner and Wrobel 1997).

It should be unnecessary to run down the checklist, reviewing all the ways in which the West of the popular imagination fails to display cultural cohesiveness. Perhaps it will suffice to note that William Labov and his associates found the West to be an area too diffuse to define in linguistic terms (Labov, Ash, and Boberg 2005, 279). In the realms of art and literature we encounter the same failure of any comprehensive vision of westernness to emerge. Again, in the words of Wallace Stegner,

> though it has had notable writers since Gold Rush days, the West has never until very recently developed the support structures of the literary life. Neither has it ever produced a group of writers homogenous enough to be called a school. Why should it have been asked to? It is too various for that. How do you find a unity among the Pacific Northwest woods, the Basin deserts, the Rocky Mountains, the high plains, the Mormon plateau country, the Hispanic-and-Indian Southwest, the conurbation of the California littoral? What kind of school can you discern in writers so various as Ivan Doig, Frank Waters, Scott Momaday, Edward Abbey, Thomas McGuane, Larry McMurtry, Joan Didion, and Maxine Hong Kingston? (1992, 137–38)[47]

But if the West fails miserably to meet the criteria for a genuine, meaningful culture area on the order of the South or the Pennsylvania Culture Area, we do ourselves a great disservice if we ignore the potency of the Western Myth. For well over a century, it has permeated our collective and individual imaginations—and has even enjoyed some currency in western Europe—suffusing our daydreams with visions as to what must have been. Such visions are based on a blinkered perception of the actual scene. The actuality was that, insofar as conditions permitted, our western states replicated or improved upon the ways of life in the older, eastern portion of the country. We have here a curious sort of disconnect between yearning and reality, the contrast between the vision of an imaginary West as a holistic landscape and the reality of a vast area with an impressive degree of diversity and much overlap with the rest of the nation. Thus the Western Myth expresses a deep craving for spatial apartheid in a human world.

The mechanisms for creating and sustaining the myth are well known. Initially there were the overpowering landscape canvases created by Albert Bierstadt and others and Frederic Remington's exciting drawings of cowboys and Indians. Then there was the pulp fiction of the late nineteenth century and, later on, the novels of Zane Grey and his ilk. More recently, countless Western films and radio and television programs have celebrated an essentially fictitious region. But perhaps the single figure who was most effective in propagating the image of a West in which cowboys, savage Indians, bison, pioneers, and livestock dominated the scene was William (Buffalo Bill) Cody. His Wild West shows toured the entire country and much of Europe, for more than three decades until the World War I period, attracting enormous crowds (Reddin 1999; Kasson 2000; L. S. Warren 2005). His competitors were not far behind. But one must cast aside popular visions of a past or present Wild West if only for demographic reasons. From the outset, the area in question was dominated by its urban centers, while today, within the mountain states as designated by the census, more than two-thirds of the population resides in metropolitan areas.

The United States has been undergoing a process of westernization over the past few generations, a phenomenon older and stronger than the comparable southernization of the land, and one that shows no signs of slackening. We have already noted evidence of westernization in the world of clothing fashion (George-Warren and Freedman 2001; Nottage 2001), while Western-style gambling (Raento 2003), rodeo (Fredericksson 1985), and dude ranching (Borne 1990) have been working their way eastward. Rather recently, Western-themed restaurant chains have also achieved some nationwide commercial success.

One cannot exaggerate the importance of the Western Myth, one so integral to the national psyche and working to alleviate somewhat our anxiety over the question of national sociocultural convergence. In this respect, we stand united.[48] I would agree with Robert Athearn's insights.

> The myth's appeal goes far beyond [frontier nostalgia] . . . After all, each year carries us farther from that frontier heritage, yet the myth survives . . . Something more than modern frustration is keeping the myth alive. Perhaps the answer is to be found in an ever-more basic urge—a search for identity . . . The bewildering diversity of our society has deepened this urge. We are a stew into which the world has thrown whatever scraps have been at hand, and with so little in common, our people have reached out for something—anything—to

bind them together. In the Western myth, many have found exactly what they were looking for. Significantly the images and the simple story of the western legend first caught on in the early nineteenth century, those years when the young Republic, like a proud and gawky adolescent, was trying to decide who and what it was. This myth has been around ever since, simply because it has always done its job. (1986, 272)

### Appalachia

In contrast to the fuzziness associated with the genesis of the Southern, Middle Western, and Western regional concepts, we enjoy all the clarity one might possibly desire in accosting the history of the idea of Appalachia, another invention serving to palliate a psychic itch. "Appalachia is a creature of the urban imagination . . . [T]he making of Appalachia was a literary and a political invention rather than a geographical discovery" (Batteau 1990, 1). Taken as a whole, the Mountain South, along with other remote or backward areas, had initially served as an arena for local colorists. In part because of their relative accessibility to the larger cities and publishing houses of the Northeast, it was the communities in the valleys and coves of West Virginia, Kentucky, Tennessee, and western North Carolina that first attracted so many authors and do-gooders. "Reiterated in some 90 sketches and more than 125 short stories published between 1870 and 1890, it established Appalachia in the public consciousness as a discrete region, in but not of America" (Shapiro 1978, 18) and one inhabited by benighted creatures we can feel superior to and feel ennobled when offering them succor.

Because of the substandard living conditions of the relatively isolated mountain folk and the literary spotlight shone upon them and, not so incidentally, the opening of the territory to major mining and lumbering operations, the area soon received a remarkable amount of charitable largesse in the form of schools, medical clinics, and handicraft promotion (Whisnant 1983; J. S. Becker 1998). "Only because the social preoccupations of late Victorian Americans occurred with the industrial entry into eastern Kentucky and southern West Virginia did the Victorian public make the Southern Mountain Region into Appalachia" (Batteau 1990, 202).

In a rare instance of its sort, we can largely credit a single individual with the invention of this spurious region, or at least its name, although it was a development that would have been inevitable without him.

The architect of this new vision was William Goodell Frost, President of Berea College in Berea, Kentucky, from 1893, who coined the phrase "Appalachian America" in order to give the southern mountain region the name-of-its-own which it deserved as a "natural" region of the nation—and thereby made possible its identification as a cultural region as well—and who, by calling the mountaineers "our contemporary ancestors" thereby gave coherence to impressionistic notions that the population of Appalachia composed an homogeneous people. (Shapiro 1978, 119)

But, as it happens, the Appalachia that has had such a tenacious grip on the geographic imagination of twentieth-century Americans is an artificial, fallacious construct. The area in question is simply the frayed outer edge of the eastern portion of the Upland South, even as its residents, along with those farther west, are participants in a cultural subregion that ranges over a much broader territory than the conventional Appalachia. Henry Shapiro, the most lucid and persistent of the debunkers, states his skepticism plainly. "Do we seek to net a reality which is not quite there, which all the effort and all the sophistication which even *we* can muster can never quite enclose? Might it not be that Appalachia did not in fact form a coherent region with a uniform culture and a homogeneous population?" (1978, 265). And twenty-seven years later he was still of the same persuasion (Shapiro 2005).

On the other hand, Appalachia can claim a truly unique distinction as a would-be cultural region or reasonable facsimile thereof: the only portion of the United States to receive official designation as such. In 1965, in concert with the larger War against Poverty, the U.S. Congress established the Appalachian Regional Commission, and it has survived ever since despite a certain amount of political turmoil (Derthick 1974, 76–107). The official Appalachia administered by the ARC includes all of West Virginia and generous portions of Pennsylvania, New York, Ohio, Maryland, Virginia, Kentucky, Tennessee, North Carolina, South Carolina, Georgia, Alabama, and Mississippi. Although its core section (J. A. Williams 2002, 13) consists of a swath of counties that are indubitably distressed socially and economically, the ARC territory is areally bloated because of obvious political chicanery. Thus 36 of its 406 officially designated counties were downright prosperous as of 2001 (J. A. Williams 2002, 346), and the cultural affiliation of many others is certainly debatable. As of the most recent accounting, the ARC had expended $16 billion in federal funds (Abramson and Haskell 2006, 1569), resulting in significant physical betterment and, possibly, socioeconomic advancement for the places in question.

### Other Vernacular Regions

If the Middle West, South, and Appalachia are large, widely recognized vernacular regions, there are many others to be acknowledged that are smaller and usually scarcely known outside their immediate environs (Dunbar 1961; Zelinsky 1980). Such entities, "the product of the spatial perception of average people," to quote Terry Jordan (1978b, 293), have been mapped over the entire national territory by Ruth Hale (1971, 1984). Few of them begin to qualify as valid culture areas. Still others, such as the Sun Belt, Rust Belt, and Snow Belt (Sale 1975; Browning and Gesler 1979; Abbott 1990; Rice 1990), after having been concocted by journalists and other authors, have enjoyed a certain currency. However, "the fact was that most residents of the Sunbelt were not aware of their new regional identity or good fortune, and even the prime beneficiaries of the new trends did not recognize the Sunbelt as a real place . . . unless most people actually consider themselves residents of a region—as southerners and westerners—then the region does not, in a very real sense, exist. By this standard, the Sunbelt was a figment of the objective imagination" (B. A. Brownell 1990, 3–4).

Leaving aside such rare exceptions as the South or Bluegrass, which are genuine culture areas, the careers of our many vernacular regions have nothing to tell us that is relevant to our central question of sociocultural convergence. They are casual, often disposable, components of the mental worlds of the inhabitants—interesting, but always lacking staying power or meaningful emotional commitment.

### Regionalism

Up until our encounter with spurious cultural regions, this study has dealt with facts on the ground, with items that can be seen, heard, tasted, fondled, worn, and otherwise sensed and, in the best of cases, could be quantified. But when we turn to regionalism, we confront something quite insubstantial and much more elusive, an entity that resists direct interrogation. Whatever regionalism may be, it is decidedly a matter of mass attitudes and perceptions, and, as such, refuses to be pinned down in terms of numbers or other strict qualifications. But it does have a particular history.

Both the term "regionalism" and the concept it embodies are creatures of the modern age. The earliest documented occurrence of the word may have been in 1874.[49] "The word *regionalism* appeared in the literature in the late nineteenth century in response to the centralizing discourse of state-sponsored nationalism. The first recorded usage refers to the national unification effort in Italy, and more precisely to resistance to that unification effort on the part of the population of different regions of the country" (Ladd 2002, 51). It is essential to note that these "different regions" in Italy were well defined, widely recognized, and had had vivid biographies of their own over many centuries, a situation utterly different from the American case.[50]

Efforts at defining the term have been less than satisfactory. Indeed the *OED* attempt (with an earliest citation dated 1881 referring to Italy)—

"1. Tending to, or practice of, regional systems or methods; localism on a regional basis"—is quite disappointing. An effort by Edward Ayers and Peter Onuf is only slightly less mystifying. *"Regionalism, a sense of common interest and identity across an extended, if indeterminate, space, was a function of unpredictably changing circumstances and bears only a contingent relationship to the regions that scholars construct in order to organize and interpret a vast universe of historical data"* (1996, 9).[51]

And there is a comparable vagueness in Andrew Cayton's approach to the challenge. "If nothing else, regionality [regionalism?], or identification with a region, is about communities of human beings who decide that their sense of place unites them more than questions of religion, race, gender, class, or any other way of constructing identity" (2001, 143). Lothar Hönnighausen offers a more serviceable notion of regionalism. "The term *regionalism* addresses the function of regions in regard to home, identity, and pride in a specific culture—in other words, a wide spectrum of very emotional, value-charged, complex attitudes ranging from harmless regional sentimentality to bigoted provincialism to separatist terrorism" (2005b, 180).

Despite its European genesis, it is only in the United States that the generalized concept and practice of regionalism has ever really flourished, if only intermittently. Moreover, it has taken on an entirely different cast in America, where, at least initially, regionalism morphed into a creed, an ism, something resembling an ideology, encompassing all manner of regions rather than championing any particular one. In the European and other theaters, by contrast, the banner of regionalism has been raised exclusively in defense, or to further the interests, of specific, thoroughly venerable regions. In addition, whatever new regional stirrings have come to pass in western Europe (especially in France, Great Britain, Italy, and Spain) are primarily ethnic in nature and postdate the American phenomenon. The American experience is all the more curious insofar as our cultural regions are all relatively young, while some are weakly defined, and at least one (the PCA) scarcely recognized.

It is necessary to deal with American regionalism in our inquiry into the validity of the convergence hypothesis even though it is a state of mind rather than a phenomenon onto which we can paste numbers. Taking notice of emotional investment in regional identities, the nurturing of regionalism, is an essential component of our tale, as much as things that can be counted. Belief, fantasy, and angst do matter.[52]

### Regionalism I

As the drama of regional sentiment has played itself out in the United States, it is obvious it has been a two-act affair (but also with something of an encore), a pair of episodes, each distinct as to period and character. During the waning years of the nineteenth century, "a strange feeling of bounded-ness began to pervade the collective consciousness. A new era had begun" (Friedmann and Weaver 1979, 23). With the disappearance of the frontier, the triumph of industrialization and Big Business, the ugliness of class war-fare, recurrent spells of severe economic distress, and a perceived leveling of place-to-place differences, the boundless optimism of the past began to wither, and, among the intelligentsia at least, there developed a certain anguish over a perceived loss of national and regional identity. This malaise found full-throated expression in Hamlin Garland's *Crumbling Idols* (1960 [1894]), a passionate manifesto on behalf of both national and regional real-ism in American arts and letters.

In more scholarly fashion, the philosopher Josiah Royce, in addition to a jeremiad against "the leveling tendency of recent civilization" (1908, 74–79), produced a powerful brief on behalf of "Provincialism," his term for regionalism (57–108). "My thesis is that, in the present state of the world's civilization, and of the life of our own country, the time has come to em-phasize, with a new meaning and intensity, the positive value, the absolute necessity for our welfare, of a wholesome provincialism, as a saving power to which the world in the near future will need more and more to appeal" (62).

Such sentiments were echoed soon after by the eminent John Dewey (1920) and others. But more substantial effort did not come to pass until the 1920s.

> Perceptions of cultural fragmentation had emerged from the moral wreckage of World War I . . . More broadly, the sense of crisis grew out of fissures opened in older pieties and certainties by Einstein, Freud, Nietzsche, and other intellectual prophets of modernity, and by the disturbing new popular predominance of consumer values . . . To regionalists [in the 1920s] . . . con-temporary America was a nation adrift, inhumane, atomized, decadent, undemocratic, selfish, apathetic, materialistic, empty, and worsening. (Dor-man 1998, 2)

Responding to this alarming state of affairs, a group of regionalist schol-ars based in the Northeast, most notably Lewis Mumford (1928–29) and Benton MacKaye (J. L. Thomas 1990; L. Anderson 2002), began promul-gating the new gospel in many publications, lectures, and conferences, and eventually formalized the movement with the creation of the Regional Planning Association (Friedmann and Weaver 1979, 29–35). The program of these stalwarts was a redemptive, utopian one—ultimately akin to the millennial visions of some of our early thinkers and orators—the creation of a just, humane society based upon fitting the cultural and social needs of a community into the historical and ecological attributes of a given area. "The hopes of regionalists . . . were for restoration and preservation, for *reconstruction*, not only of the eroded landscape but of the fragmented culture and society of modern America" (Dorman 1998, 2). Apparently for the first time, we encounter here the stirrings of *self-conscious place-making*.

If Mumford, MacKaye, and company had been voices in the wilderness in the 1920s, the shock of the Great Depression of the 1930s pushed the masses—and the government—into serious flirtation with Regionalism I. What had been a subterranean strain in the American psyche rather abruptly broke to the surface and enjoyed its brief season of glory. "The *old regionalism* of the 1930s . . . against the background of economic collapse and the destruction of the American Dream, tried to invoke regions as havens of cultural permanence and purity" (Hönnighausen 2005b, 176).[53] For the zealots, it was their first and last opportunity to establish a regionalist civic religion. It is worth noting that nothing comparable was going on in Europe even though the Old World was also suffering from a worldwide depression.

Although the regionalist programs of the New Deal account for only a relatively small fraction of all the many frantic efforts of the federal establishment to revive the economy and spirits of the land, they enlisted many actors and impinged upon the lives and consciousness of a goodly portion of the general public (Dorman 1998, 291–303). Nowhere is this more evident than in the arts in general and the world of letters in particular.[54] The most far-reaching of the New Deal programs in question was the Federal Writers' Project (Kazin 1942, 501–2; Penkower 1977). In a giddy paean to a resurgent enthusiasm for the arts in the 1930s, Alfred Kazin declared that "a reawakening to the forgotten cultural resources of the country . . . developed out of the make-work program of the WPA; only when writers had gone on relief was America charted in the great New Deal Baedeker of the states and roads; searching only for facts, a whole army of social reporters and travelers recovered an American sense of history and began to chant the rich diversity and beauty of the country as if America had never been really known before" (1942, 500).

Then, in his truly exhaustive account of the FWP, Monty Noam Penkower reports that "with considerable scholarship, the federal writers uncovered a land which lay hidden behind billboards and boosterism. Their painstaking research reached far beyond the countless movie houses, highway restaurants, and chain stores to discover the nation's rich diversity. Cities and towns were found to have an individuality of their own. State pride quickened" (1977, 240).[55]

But, important though their output was, and still is, the Federal Writers' Project was actually only the most centrally organized component of a much broader development. In addition, more and more authors had begun, usually quite self-consciously, to anchor their fiction and other writings within some sort of regional or localistic setting (McWilliams 1930).[56] As Odum and Moore noted, "Restricting our titles to fiction and making the listings in *Publishers' Weekly* our source, it is possible to catalogue more than two thousand regional titles which have appeared during the last two decades" (1938, 185–86).[57]

In the realm of drama, the short-lived Federal Theatre espoused the noblest of regional ideals during its chaotic history. "The Federal Theatre at its best was working toward an art in which each region and eventually each state would have its unique, indigenous dramatic expression, its company housed in a building reflecting its own landscape and regional material, producing plays of its past and present, in its own rhythm of speech and its native design, in an essentially American pattern" (Flanagan 1940, 371; also see Sper 1948, 271–77). But, as it happened, this turned out to be an illusory goal. Never before or since has the American stage developed a distinctive or economically successful regional voice. On the other hand, the folk music movement, which is so inherently regional, became a force to be reckoned with in the 1930s and has prospered ever since" (R. M. Brown 1983, 39).

If I may digress a bit, the cause of American regional theater has always had a troubled history. "The regional theatre, everybody always said, might be regional but it rarely, if ever, belonged to the region. Whenever a regional theatre sought deliberately to become regional, either in its choice of play material or in its personnel, it was too provincial or too folksy" (Schneider 1973, ix). In his truly encyclopedic survey of the early twentieth-century regional theatrical scene, Felix Sper (1948) found much to scorn (especially the local color genre) and little to praise while holding out hope for the future. But, despite the heroic exertions of such zealots as Hallie Flanagan and Robert Gard (1955), the overall situation has remained one in which "regional theater is not seen as regional but rather as attempting to emulate or replace Broadway" (Zeigler 1973, 1). Only a handful of companies, such as Charleston's Dock Street Theatre (Datel 1990, 210), eastern Kentucky's Roadside Theater and the Dell'Arte in Blue Lake, California (Cohen-Cruz 2005, 51–55, 153–59) have managed, quite precariously, to manifest some sort of genuine regionalism.

The story of American regionalist art is a much blither one, at least during a certain heyday. Regionalism has always been a slippery, debatable concept in the world of art (Dennis 1986, 142–49), but, in the 1930s and early 1940s, it gained widespread currency and acceptance thanks largely to the canvases and propaganda of the mighty triumvirate of Grant Wood

(Corn 1983; Dennis 1986), John Steuart Curry, and Thomas Hart Benton (Richardson 1951; Guedon 1987), as well as the work of Georgia O'Keeffe and others in the Southwest (Goodstein 1990). But

> of the painters who gained lasting fame under the regionalist banner, only Grant Wood worked to organize a self-perpetuating movement dedicated to the prospect of establishing an internationally recognized American school. He alone formulated concrete principles and theories to validate "regionalism" as a term applicable to his art, a programmatic approach that corresponded in substance, if not in method, to the regionalist position adopted by a group of contemporary writers known as the Southern Agrarians. (Dennis 1986, 142–43)

During the New Deal period many lesser-known starving artists enrolled in various federal programs (McKinzie 1973), among them the Treasury Department's Section of Fine Arts, which did proclaim something of a regionalist vision.

> What emerges from its [the Section's] work is a geographic pattern that coexists with the patterns of national or purely local content. Section officials expected regionalism to develop in art as a force that would give strength and distinctiveness to a contemporary art as it had in Italian city-states during the Renaissance . . . that ideal informed a number of the murals and is sufficiently vivid to distinguish Section work from government commissions before and after the New Deal. (Park and Markowitz 1984, 68–69; also see Marling 1982)

The regionalist artists also enjoyed a brief spurt of popularity within the filmmaking community of Hollywood (Doss 1984) and, more consequentially, in the national advertising industry during the 1930s and early 1940s (Doss 1982).

Whatever triumph American regionalist art may have enjoyed was quite ephemeral, although, after its decline and fall, many of its works are still cherished by the general public and cognoscenti alike. Its loss of favor in the 1940s, as the abstract genre, surrealism, and other ultra modern modes of painting, sculpture, and design conquered the galleries of Manhattan and other art centers, coincided with the general twilight of Regionalism I. Unrelenting hostility on the part of right-wing politicians in Congress and elsewhere eventually effected the cutting off of governmental support of literature and the arts (to be revived cautiously in the 1960s). Following much the same scenario, the regionalist fervor in the sociological community stirred up by Howard Odum and his associates at Chapel Hill had lost its vitality with American entry into World War II.

The burst of nationalistic excitement and oneness during the "Good War," followed by years of unprecedented prosperity, spelled doom for the enticements of the local and regional. As far as regional planning was concerned, it had evolved from its messianic phase in the 1920s through the New Deal into its postwar technocratic, state-serving function (Friedmann and Weaver 1979). And "rather than the fulfillment of the 'wishes and dreams' of the regionalist movement, the TVA and other New Deal programs proved to be, by and large, their denouement" (Dorman 1998, 295). "Ultimately, regionalism was itself revealed to be a symptom of the passing of the older America, which after this brief renaissance, 'shrunk back to its own littleness' in the modern world" (ibid., xiv).[58]

### Regionalism II

If the eclipse of Regionalism I as a cohesive entity began during the final years of FDR's second term, the movement was effectively dead and buried during World War II and, if possible, became even more defunct during the 1950s when the *modern market system in alliance with the state* dominated the scene as never before. And be reminded that this was the decade when, as I have argued, the United States achieved its closest approximation of complete national sociocultural entropy. "Interest in regionalist theory declined in the 1950s. American culture in that decade tended toward consensus, stressing the continuities and unities within American historical experience. World War II had promoted the need for consensus and the Cold War reinforced that outlook" (C. R. Wilson 1998a, xi).

However, "regionalism, like that fabled cat, seems to have many lives" (Fishwick 1968, 400). Well, at least two. "Any notion of America as a seamless whole was shattered in the 1960s. The civil rights and anti-war protests, urban riots and environmental disasters, and the coming-to-consciousness of women and minority groups of all kinds have forced upon all of us a sense of the essential segmentation and pluralism of American culture" (Steiner and Mondale 1988, x).

If the first stirrings of Regionalism II were palpable by the 1960s, the phenomenon had matured by the 1970s.[59] It differs from its predecessor in terms of both chronology and character and also by virtue of being worldwide in occurrence. The following definition of the current incarnation of American (and, indeed, worldwide) regionalism may suffice: the recognition and use of regional (including metropolitan) particularities for sentimental, touristic, commercial, artistic, and scholarly purposes, *but* in the absence of any larger social or political agenda.[60] (If the distinction between the two regionalisms verges on the absolute, it is undeniable that isolated survivors from the earlier era may still be keepers of the flame.) We encounter here a mind-set that gazes upon regional features as pleasant curiosities to be analyzed coolly, hyped for gain in the marketplace, or simply enjoyed vicariously from time to time. Its practitioners are not about to begin reforming the country or the world.

Another major distinction between the two regionalisms is revealed by the latter-day popularity of tourism and long-distance vacations among the masses, activities previously confined to the well-to-do. Thus, during the late twentieth century, we have witnessed an ever greater dichotomization between the mundane ecumene of home, neighborhood, and workplace on the one hand and all those fetching other-places that promise pleasure, excitement, or at least difference on the other. Can the rise of tourism, now estimated to be the world's first- or second-largest industry, reflect, inter alia, a deep-seated craving for diversity? Regionalism I was for homebodies; Regionalism II catered to quite another clientele.

Regionalism II has made steady inroads into the academic domain recently. "Since the 1970s there has been a spate of new studies of region, in many disciplines, regarding many different places" (Ayers and Onuf 1996, 2). If, during the 1950s, "historians never abandoned the study of region, especially scholars of the South and West . . . other disciplines associated with regionalism, such as geography and sociology did seem to lose interest in it and followed new paths" (C. R. Wilson 1998a, xi–xii). But, after 1970, many groups of scholars again turned to interpreting regions, perhaps most notably the geographic fraternity in the United States and elsewhere. Such renewed interest occurred on a much more sophisticated "critical" level than the simplicities of regional discourse in early twentieth-century geography (Gilbert 1988; Pudup 1988; Sayer 1989; Claval 1998; Paasi 2003).

Even more convincing evidence of the resuscitation of the regional motif comes from the realm of formal institutions and projects. "Every major region of the country now . . . boasts a large research center" (Kowalewski 2003, 9; also see Conforti 2001, 314–15). A number of university presses have begun to specialize in regional themes, and, inter alia, they have produced, or are in the process of generating, impressive regional encyclopedias, atlases, and related reference works (C. R. Wilson 1998a, xii). Then, with the blessing and support of the federal establishment, the American Folklife Center housed in Washington has energetically promoted the regional cause over the past few decades.

In the world of letters, regionalism has gained a new lease on life recently in the output of American authors of both fiction and nonfiction (C. R. Wilson 1997; Crow 2003). "Regional writing in particular seems to be enjoying a renaissance of interest. New regional book awards honor local . . . talent. Regional book festivals, conferences, and benefits bring together authors and (often first-time) readers. New and old literary journals and magazine with a strong regional flavor (*Zyzzyva*, *Ruminator Review*,

*Northern Lights, Sewanee Review,* and *Great Plains Quarterly,* to name a few) continue to flourish" (Kowalewski 2003, 9). Then, as I have noted elsewhere, architecture with a regional accent has shown signs of vigor in certain parts of the nation (Lefaivre 2003), while the proliferation of local and regional festivals in recent years has been little short of astonishing.

An increasingly globalized American business community has exhibited no shyness in exploiting the selling power of modern-day regionalism, emulating the examples set by quasi-official organizations in both Europe and the United States. "Various regional authorities (e.g., planning organizations, chambers of commerce) have . . . started campaigns to try to make their regions into 'products' that can be sold on the market and that will attract tourists, skilled professionals and capital" (Paasi 2002a, 137). "It is to an increasing extent the international markets and regional political responses to global capitalism . . . that generate regionalism and accentuate the importance of regions" (Paasi 2002b, 803). "The perspective is that aspects of regional identities are used in the selling of products . . . regional identities may be used as commodities" (Simon 2005, 32).[61]

This sort of imagineering toward commercial ends tends to dominate such neoregional publications as *Southern Living* (Elias 2002), but it may also be part of a sales strategy of some national and global corporations usually regarded as the archvillains of placelessness. Thus "a McDonald's in Miami's Little Havana has a Spanish-style roof and feels more like a hacienda. Another in Freeport, Maine, looks like a quaint New England inn. The twelve-thousandth restaurant, which opened in 1991, is located in a restored 1860s white Colonial house on Long Island" (Ritzer 1993, 164). As Max Boas and Steve Chain observe, "McDonald's 'escape' atmosphere followed a general trend . . . a nautical theme in Boston, a campus theme near the University of California in Los Angeles, a chalet-type in Michigan, the replica of an artist's skylighted studio in New York's Greenwich Village, and a Western flavor in Dallas, with arches branded on hitching posts" (1976, 57; also see Sosnik, Dowd, and Fournier 2006, 88).[62]

Occasionally the Law of Unintended Consequences takes hold, and Regionalism I, or some aftershock thereof, takes us by surprise, despite the standardizing protocols of global corporations.

> Seemingly identical American street corners punctuated with Taco Bell, McDonald's, Texaco, and Wal-Mart franchises may have different patterns of association for different communities . . . Maybe Taco Bell is a center for youth cruising in one town while different youth cliques stake claims to a McDonald's or a Burger King in another. These chain businesses look the same and provide the same services and mostly the same goods, but their employees and consumers may interact in regional styles. Though shifts from local to national

or international merchandisers and restaurateurs obviously change regional lifestyles, regional interpretations are nonetheless imposed on what may seem standardized, generic, or even resistant to any local or regional cultural meaning. (C. Ray 2005, 81)

But it is perhaps within the world of periodicals that we find the strongest evidence for the profitability of the regional theme in recent decades. "Regional and city magazines have constituted one of the most dynamic sections of the United States magazine industry since shortly after World War II, the period in which mass circulation magazines began to lose ground to more specialized periodicals" (Riley and Selnow 1989, 3). And indeed Riley and Selnow were able to identify no fewer than 920 regional interest magazines that appeared between 1950 and 1988 (ibid., 4). In a chronological listing of such items from 1868 through 1988, a decided acceleration in their creation is obvious during the post–World War II years (Riley and Selnow 1991, 395–98; also see Moon 1970).

## Bioregionalism

This is a topic that poses a quandary for the student of the history and geography of American regions and their epistemology. Bioregionalism is certainly a significant, mostly recent body of thought and limited practice. Furthermore, it obviously has to do with regions, albeit of a rather nonstandard form. But the question is how to work it into the larger framework of this study given the fact that, unlike Regionalisms I and II, the national public is at best only dimly aware of, or affected by, the bioregional movement and hardly more cognizant of it locally in those few instances where it has had some success in land planning and management. We may define it as "a body of thought and related practice that has evolved in response to the challenge of reconnecting socially just cultures in a sustainable manner to the region-scale ecosystems in which they are irrevocably embedded" (Aberley 1999, 13). And thus "a technical process of identifying 'biogeographically interpreted culture areas . . . called bioregions.' Within these territories, resident human populations would . . . discover regional models for new and relatively non-arbitrary scales of human activity in relation to the biological realities of the natural landscape" (ibid., 22).

If "bioregionalism gestates in the culturally turbulent decades between 1950 and the early 1970s" (Aberley 1999, 14), it is clearly associated with the broader environmental movement that burst into prominence during those years. But it is also obvious that it has inherited the idealism of Regionalism I, along with the assertion of *self-conscious place-making* and the principles espoused by Lewis Mumford (Luccarelli 1995) and some of his colleagues.

Indeed we can trace its inspiration back to the mid-nineteenth century and George Perkins Marsh, the founding father, or honorary grandfather, of modern environmentalism.[63]

Only a curmudgeon could fail to praise the noble aspirations of the bioregionalists. To date, however, their preaching to the choir has generated little in the mappable world beyond the most local and isolated of effects. But if bioregionalism has yet to do much of anything to transform the face of the land or the ways in which nearly all its inhabitants perceive its diversity or lack thereof, it does fit into a broader, potentially significant set of developments we can call Neolocalism.

## Neolocalism

This spontaneous late twentieth-century development, originating largely without benefit of prophets or gurus, may be a distant echo of the idealism of Regionalism I, but, despite difference in spatial scale, Neolocalism is obviously somehow akin to Regionalism II, although something probably unrelated to what we might call "Paleolocalism," the earlier, largely subconscious attachment to one's surroundings that may have been effectively shredded by the forces of homogenization. In comparison with Bioregionalism, Neolocalism has enlisted a larger, if still rather minor, fraction of the citizenry and has effected quite a few tangible, mappable changes in the American landscape.

Robert Nisbet may have been the first observer to detect the emerging phenomenon when he noted in 1975 various signs and portents for "The Revival of Localism" (1975, 260–69). But Robert Thayer, in his introduction to a veritable bible on bioregional thought and practice, may have given us the most insightful briefing on this novel mode of behavior. "*Social trends are most often accompanied by their opposites.* A number of simultaneous movements toward 'relocalization' are now converging that challenge many of the basic and most dis-placed [*sic*] assumptions of postmodern culture: grassroots watershed conservancies, 'Friends of' groups for particular natural features, holistic ecosystem management efforts, coordinated resource management plans (CRiMPs), community-supported agricultural establishments, alternative local currencies, farmers' markets—even microbreweries that produce beer with proudly local labels" (2003, 3; emphasis added).

The most visible manifestation of American Neolocalism may be in the form of farmers' markets. Venerable though the institution may have been, with weekly assemblages dating back to colonial times and fitful local examples ever since, it is only during the past few decades that these markets have begun to enjoy widespread acceptance and patronage (Sommer 1980; R. L. Thayer 2003, 124–26). There is an obvious synergy here with the booming organic food industry, the general environmental movement, and an endless succession of food scares (Pyle 1971; A. Brown 2002, 173; Norberg-Hodge, Merrifield, and Gorelick 2002; Severson 2006). Thus, between 1956 and 1994, the number of farmers' markets in New York expanded from 6 to 172 (Lyson, Gillespie, and Hilchey 1995, 108), and "the number of retail farmers' markets in the USA grew from about 340 in 1970 to over 3,000 in 2001" (A. Brown 2002, 167; also see A. Brown 2001). Closely connected with this phase of Neolocalism is the remarkable growth of community-supported agriculture. The number of such formal arrangements between growers and consumers exploded from only two in 1986 to more than 1,700 in 2005 (Schnell 2007, 552; also see Norberg-Hodge, Merrifield, and Gorelick 2002; R. L. Thayer 2003, 124–26; Lazo 2007; Feffer 2008; Saulny 2008).

If farmers' markets cater to the cravings of more and more Americans for fresher, tastier, and presumably safer foodstuffs, these ephemeral places also help satisfy a social need. If "we have so few means of overcoming our solitude that even a discount superstore serves us as a temple of humanity" (Zukin 2004, 87), the farmers' market offers a superior venue for sociability. As demonstrated by ethnographic studies (McGrath, Sherry, and Heisley 1993; Gerbasi 2006) and, as I can attest from personal observation, these congenial events present growers, merchants, and the general public (often with pets) with splendid opportunities for banter, gossip, education, and social intimacy. "At the Midville Market, personal identities are communal currency. "Everyconsumer" rubs elbows with neighbors, politicos, ethnics, students, and other segments of the Midville social mosaic . . . For a few weekend hours, dispassionate and anonymous individuals coalesce into a little village" (McGrath, Sherry, and Heisley 1993, 308–9). If such place-making functions well below the regional level, it still works as a general antidote to placelessness. Might the same be said about the growing number of local food (and other sorts of) festivals (Geffen and Berglie 1986)?

Smaller and much less visible, but nevertheless laden with omens of some sort of turning point in our collective psyche, is another quite recent consumption-related development: the Slow Food movement (Kummer 2002; Miele and Murdoch 2002; Petrini 2002, 2006; Fernald, Milano, and Sarelo 2004). Spawned in Italy, appropriately enough, in the 1980s, this transnational phenomenon celebrates the joys of locally produced and leisurely ingested food and drink. "The largest . . . international growth has been in the United States" (Kummer 2002, 26), and "with more than 10,000 members and counting, Slow Food USA, in a few short years, has become perhaps the most dynamic of the international Slow Food movement's national progeny" (Petrini 2002, 142).[64]

But something even more indicative of the increasing vitality of Neolocalism is an amazing proliferation of American microbreweries in the late twentieth century. According to Wes Flack, who claims to have coined the term "neolocalism," "much of the appeal of a microbrewed beer is that it is a rejection of national, or even regional, culture in favor of something more local" (1997, 49). Steven Schnell and Joseph Reese concur. "During the 1990s, over 1,500 microbreweries sprouted and flourished across the country. This expansion of microbreweries derives, in part, from the desire of people to break away from the smothering homogeneity of popular, national culture" (2005, 45). The map they have generated, "Microbreweries by Zip Code, 2002" (Schnell and Reese 2005, 50), confirms their occurrence in all fifty states.[65] Especially striking are clusters in Megalopolis, along the Pacific Coast, and in Colorado, Wisconsin, and Michigan. The growing popularity of this localized beverage sends a persuasive message, as does the recent craving for locally oriented artisanal cheeses (Paxson 2006).

Still another line of evidence for the latter-day potency of Neolocalism is a phenomenon that, except for some incidental paragraphs by George Ritzer (1993, 15, 177), seems to have escaped scholarly scrutiny: B&Bs. These lodgings are, of course, a transnational development and one especially notable in Great Britain and Ireland, where both proprietors and clients seem to be motivated largely by pocketbook considerations. The story may be rather different in the United States, where they seldom cater to the frugal and where the recent boom in B&Bs could well be a reaction to McDonaldized motels (Ritzer 1993, 15).[66] The American places in question are frequently older, but recently converted, dwellings with a locally or regionally resonant architectural style, capitalizing not so subtly on the charms of the area. A study of their historical geography should be a rewarding, and not too difficult, project for some aspiring student.

Finally, we have another strictly late twentieth-century phenomenon: the welcoming sign (Zelinsky 1988b). Erected at the boundaries of municipalities and, occasionally, states, these declarations of parochial pride or ambition also speak of their yearning to be perceived as different, indeed unique.

Now that we have finished assembling and examining such a wide and divers array of evidence having to do with uniformities and variations over time and space in the sociocultural behavior of Americans and the manifold objects that comprise the American scene, what to make of all this material? What summary lessons can we find lurking within this motley mass of information? That is the business of our next and final chapter.

# 7 Is the Jury Still Out?

THE MOST immediate of the conclusions to be drawn from the evidence reviewed in this inquiry is that the conventional wisdom is essentially correct—but with some crucial qualifications. Superficially at least, the United States has become a monolithic, homogenized nation-state and, by any historical reckoning, a uniquely powerful one. This is hardly the outcome one would have foreseen for an infant republic with its loose confederation of thirteen former colonies more often than not at loggerheads with one another. Furthermore, what has resulted is a national community differing quite profoundly in the character of its homogeneity from a very real premodern version of geographical sameness prevailing in the late eighteenth century.

The combination of an ever more potent central regime, only slightly hindered by the limited sovereignty of the eventual fifty states, the unrestrained vigor of the modern market system, and the advent of advanced technologies in the fields of transport, communication, and manufacturing, along with deployment of a set of powerful nationalistic symbols, has produced a humanized landscape and a society that, at least to the casual onlooker, appears much the same from coast to coast. Thus, for the most part, our shops, dwellings, factories, office buildings, highways, the commodities we buy and use, and the news, information, and entertainment we absorb have come to vary little from one locality to another, and so too many of our personal characteristics.

Still further, although I have not explored the matter in depth, it is clear that, at a certain lofty level, Americans enthusiastically perceive their country to be a seamless whole, something quite distinct from the rest of the world, and one they take great pride in. But we must temper hasty acceptance of the Homogenization Thesis by acknowledging the importance (and visibility) of particular things we may be inclined to overlook: all those unique facilities whose locations accord with the dictates of physical geography and/or economic logic. Thus, for example, we cannot hope to find a steel plant in North Dakota, a large feedlot in New Hampshire, or a major hydroelectric plant in Florida.

This profound, but not total, leveling of the geographic scene has come about inexorably and gradually—aside from the hideous convulsion of the Civil War and its peremptory outcome. It is essential to note one of the more critical developments in the consolidation of our synthetic nation, and a gradual one again: the substantial elimination of what was once a stark, nearly absolute gap between the American rural realm and a once greatly outnumbered urban population thanks to universal postal service, mail-order firms, the auto and truck, telephony, electrification, and, more recently, the flight of city folk to the exurbs and beyond.

The might of the modern market system and the miracles of modern communications, along with a remarkably high level of mobility, have also eliminated, or thwarted, development of regional differences in certain departments of cultural behavior. Thus an essential leveling of whatever place-to-place differences may once have prevailed in dietary patterns, the failure of genuine regions to emerge in the garments Americans wear, the limited appearance of meaningful sport regions, and expunging of probable localisms in the informal group games Americans once enjoyed. Centripetal forces have also been at work in the field of music and dance, but that is a much more complicated tale. In addition, unifying processes have smoothed over the bumps in the demographic landscape, so that we now have greatly reduced territorial unevenness in sex ratios, age structure, literacy, educational attainment, fertility, marital characteristics, and income, at least at grosser areal scales.

But perhaps the single most noteworthy of the mappable achievements of our centralizing processes may be the creation of the Generic Euro-American Culture Region, that vast tract embracing most of the nation's territory and population and in sociocultural terms *the* most modal and central of areas. Originating largely from the three colonial culture hearths along the Atlantic Seaboard, it is here that the churning of migrants and their descendants has been especially vigorous and operation of economic and governmental pressures toward conformity least hindered.

If my observations are correct, it was in the 1950s that the United States most closely approached entropy in its sociocultural and economic geography, a time when sameness in phenomena mapped at a broad scale attained an all-time peak. The *modern market system in alliance with the state* had had its way with scant interference from centrifugal processes. It was especially noteworthy that a polyglot population had become much less poly with the virtual drying up of immigration and serious assimilation of earlier immigrants and their offspring.

But, when viewed at a finer scale, any homogenization as seen from afar becomes much less evident. Scale matters—and matters mightily! Indeed, at the local level, spatial differentiation has become the rule. In place of the "rummage" of classes, business activities, occupations, ethnicities, and ways of life that had typified towns and much of the countryside in colonial and early republican America we now find intense spatial segregation, often codified by ordinance, of functions, classes, and persistent ethnic/racial groups as well as in terms of taste. Such clustering of both urban and rural Americans was apparent by the 1950s and seems to have been intensifying ever since. The result has been a homogenization of sorts, but not one of blunt leveling. Instead we behold a repetition across the land of reasonably similar tiles, not without a few local modifications, within a grand national mosaic, a pattern for which I can coin no better label than the admittedly inelegant Tessellated-cum-Aleatory Space. Incidentally, the complexities of this clustering approach are among the manifestations of a truly fundamental change accompanying the progress of modernization worldwide as well as in the United States: an enormous proliferation and diversification of things, of commodities, services, occupations, diversions, and all manner of choices. This is a radical departure from the relative simplicities of premodern America, when local specialization in the economy, in crafts, livestock, fruits and vegetables, and cultural patterns in general had just begun to take off and there were few career choices for lads and almost none for lasses.

In any event, since the 1950s, and most markedly since 1965, the earlier trend toward nationwide conformity has been stalled or reversed. In part this has happened because the United States has been obliged to function as part of the larger world to a degree well beyond anything experienced during a younger nationhood. If, previously, one could adopt an isolationist stance in treating the human geography of the land (conveniently forgetting those massive infusions of European capital), now we must take account of transnational flows of ideas, forces, money, human beings, and certain illegal substances our central authorities seem helpless to control. Thus a major post-1965 influx of mostly unfamiliar immigrants from near and afar is a result of global processes no political agency can reverse. One outcome, as remarked earlier, has been a substantial and ongoing reshaping of the ethnic geography of the United States, a push toward diversification rather than uniformity. Then, another demographic development no nineteenth-century scholar could have foreseen—and also operating at an international scale—has begun to transform the social complexion of the land as it widens gaps between regions: the part- or full-time shift of millions of retired or elderly Americans to locales (including some abroad) they find appealing even though they may have little in common with the longtime residents. Absent a major economic debacle, these sharp new disconformities in the nation's social fabric are likely to intensify as time goes on.

But if this study has served to affirm, in however modulated a manner, the widespread impression of a homogenized nation, we have yet to deal with the question that leads off Chapter 1: "Is the United States of America becoming a placeless land?" The answer—and, I must confess, one that was hardly anticipated—is a qualified, but decisive, no! Indeed, quite to the contrary, this country is becoming ever more placeful as the number and variety of unpredictable places has persisted in growing at an increasing rate from early on and promises to do so indefinitely—even while a probably larger number of predictable places has also been materializing. If our imaginary traveler had been traversing all the highways, byways, and waterways of America in the 1790s, he or she would have encountered few unexpected features at unforeseen sites, aside from the occasional spa or iron furnace and perhaps the odd commune or camp meeting. Today an exhaustive canvas of the country would disclose a riotous profusion of all manner of places, large and small, that no geographic formula could have pinpointed.

As we dwell in this world of paradoxes, we have here in this, perhaps the most important of my findings, an apparent mind-bending anomaly: the coexistence of convergence and divergence, of the formulaic and the stochastic. But if this is a difficult concept to digest, it is one we must accept as an essential American reality. Thus, if the things nearly all of us confront in our daily rounds fit nicely into the model of a well-regulated machine, if we take time off to wander away from the quotidian groove of our personal cosmos, we replace the simplicities of a homogenized, repetitive world with something much more challenging and interesting. As it happens, although some are just a single structure or object, many of the unpredictable items to be encountered off the beaten path are massive in area and bulk, for example, national parks, Indian reservations, college campuses, military facilities, new towns, race tracks, and state and federal prisons. But one must append an all-important codicil to any consideration of such exceptional phenomena. With the possible exception of a number of communes and militia activities, these unpredictable facilities do nothing to detract from the overall American nation-state project. In fact, some, possibly most, of them actually strengthen Leviathan. Thus the spatial predictability of things need not be a necessary component of national togetherness.

But if the United States is not a placeless land, it is decidedly still a country inhabited by an ever more placeless population, a topic I have not deemed necessary to pursue methodically in this study. Suffice it to say that a decisive number of us shift from one residence or town to another multiple times in the course of a lifetime, as well as from job to job, school to school, one occupation to another, from one vacation haven to another, from one significant other to another, perhaps from one religious creed or congregation to another, all this without taking root perennially in one spot. It is difficult to think of another nation that begins to rival us in our fugacity.

If the *modern market system in alliance with the state* has managed to weaken seriously or erase totally place-to-place differences in certain departments of cultural behavior, it has met with defeat or stalemate in eliminating the regionality of certain other crucial elements in the cultural scene. It is here that we find the most formidable obstacle to any total triumph for the Homogenization Thesis, one even more fundamental than the proliferation of unpredictable places: old-fashioned cultural inertia and the operation of forces that transcend transient historical epochs. The most persuasive example of such failure to converge is the persistence, even divergence, of regional dialects of American English. Patterns of change in pronunciation, as well as grammatical structure, follow age-old laws that are beyond human control and perhaps even full understanding, but, in any event, are of no concern to Leviathan. Then, even though we lack data firm enough to track diachronic trends, the state and business community are at best only peripherally concerned with the apparent viability and stability of religious regions in the United States. Of more practical interest is the restructuring or dilution of shifting political regions in terms of voting patterns, which *may* have been eroding in recent decades at the state level but growing at the county or neighborhood level.

When we turn to culture areas, however, those extended tracts containing the total area-specific behavioral repertoire of fairly large communities, we behold durability and fecundity. Those primordial processes keep grinding away. Over the span of more than two centuries, none of the earlier entities has vanished or shows signs of doing so, aside from the enormously problematic case of the South, the subject of endless debate. On the contrary, they are all still with us, even though all but one have undergone significant modernization or postmodernization. In the single exceptional instance, that of the historically consequential Pennsylvania Culture Area, we see stasis, a conservative community that finds no reason to alter its traditional ways or to make a big public fuss about them. Moreover, a fresh generation of culture areas, including California, Peninsular Florida, and such cities as Seattle, Las Vegas, and Santa Fe, have begun to flourish in the twentieth century. It is altogether likely that others may be aborning.

Up to this point I have been summarizing and digesting the American scene as objectively observed. But rivaling objective fact in importance are the ways Americans perceive the geographic lineaments of their land. And such perceptions can lead to action or operate so as to modify whatever actual territorial uniformity may exist. Thus, if the general public takes great pride and comfort in the perceived cohesiveness and singularity of the United States and its unquestionable greatness, undermining any such satisfaction is gnawing uneasiness over the apparent emulsification of the country, with the seeming blandness, orderliness, and monotony of what most of us see about us in our daily routine or on the occasional long-distance excursion. Then, along with such perceived landscape predictability, there is subliminal grieving over the loss of physical frontiers, the passing of the age of limitless opportunity.

We have responded to such lostness in a variety of ways. The coping mechanism most widely shared is to cherish mythical or misperceived regions. Thus, since the late 1800s, an enduring love affair with a fabled West as the embodiment of all that was noble and adventurous in the American epic. Then we also revere a historically and geographically dubious Middle West, that heartwarming middle landscape with its sturdy yeoman farmers and virtuous small towns. Similarly, we take some satisfaction in looking down on a semibarbarous fictitious Appalachia or viewing New England or the South through tinted spectacles. Or we can seek genuine, full-time solace in one of those New Towns that strain to recapture an imagined past.

Need I note that such geographic questing is part of a grander syndrome, one expressed in the creation of two versions of regionalism and related developments? Gestating during the early twentieth century, Regionalism I enjoyed its brief springtime of glory in the 1930s as a redemptive cause seeking to nurture a healthy republic by honoring the worth of traditional regions and localities and, more immediately, by rearranging settlement, work, and leisure so as to conform with the realities of the ecosystem and human needs. After its abrupt demise in the 1940s, Regionalism I was succeeded by Regionalism II, a mind-set that dotes on the particularities of regions and places in general and exploits their commercial and scholarly potential without aiming to transform the American scene. Then, more fundamentally than the pair of regionalisms, there is that abiding, underlying kinship between our discomfort with placelessness on the one hand and, on the other, the historic preservation movement, the latter-day craze for antiques and genealogy, the passion for science fiction, and, of course, in a diffuse general way, with organic farming, bioregionalism, and an environmental movement that has been gathering momentum over the past century or so. And surely there is some sort of linkage with the spectacular recent popularity of tourism foreign and domestic.

Even though to date it involves only a small fraction of the population—but, arguably, an especially pivotal fraction—there is still another largely instinctive reaction to our perceived placelessness: the recent abrupt eruption of what I call Neo-localism. Suddenly we have all those microbreweries, the wild proliferation of locally themed festivals, the boom in farmers' markets and hundreds of thousands of locavores patronizing or subsidizing nearby producers. I also suspect some sort of subsurface connections between Neo-localism and the recent pandemic of localized scenes and sounds in the realm of popular music. It is too soon to know what to make of all this. Are we simply indulging in passing fads? Or are we witnessing a genuine turning point?

Can we extrapolate our findings to other countries and, in particular, to the most highly modernized of the lot in Europe, Asia, Australasia, and neighboring Canada? Only with the utmost caution and most severe of qualifications. The physical and historical circumstances of the American story are so special that any revelations regarding place and region are scarcely exportable. But what we can surmise is a profound underlying kinship between whatever is going on hereabouts and overseas: the playing out in spatial terms, as modified by local circumstance, of the mega-logic, the Pan-Process of Modernization, something that has been gaining momentum for some five hundred years and still has no end in sight.

What the nature of such a mega-logic might be is something well beyond my ability to discern. If, throughout this study, I have pursued a loosely reductionist modus operandi, by treating each discrete set of phenomena or formative process in relative isolation, there is no escaping the sense of some vaster, more intricate mechanism, newly emergent, that is reshaping human geography in this land and elsewhere, indeed at a global scale. Let us hope that someone cleverer than yours truly can someday clearly delineate the workings of this mega-logic.

In final summary, then, in returning to the central concerns driving this inquiry, we should realize at last that I have been confronting two separate, but inextricably intertwined, quandaries: has the United States been becoming a placeless land? And has it been becoming homogenized? Uncomfortable as we may be with what seems like a downright contradiction, the short answers again are a qualified but ultimate No! to the first question and a qualified but ultimate Yes! to the second. But one can, to a degree, reconcile these clashing verdicts by introducing the factor of geographic scale and the kinds of things being looked at.

Restricting our definition of place to those humanized segments of space-time that external observers can recognize, as I have striven to do throughout this enterprise, we find the vast majority of American places to be quite limited in size and falling into two grand categories. The first, and more numerous, consists of all those locationally predictable, repetitive entities—neighborhoods and "clusters," apartment complexes, strip malls, shopping centers, downtowns, and so on—that have come to resemble one another so closely that often they may be distinguished only by name. But in the case of the other category, all those places that are unpredictable as to identity, size, location, character, and other attributes, their numbers and variety seem also to be growing steadily ever greater.

Then, broadening the spatial scale, if we add those other larger phenomena—the grand, enduring regionalizations of language, religion, and political identity and the older persistent culture regions and emergent new ones—it seems fair to conclude that placefulness is still alive and well in this country. In addition, we have witnessed since the fateful year of 1965 sharper ethnic accents on the landscape and a sorting of places according to age of residents and the aspirations of skilled, well-educated footloose individuals seeking self-realization and/or the delights of special destinations. On the other hand, if we focus again solely at the national scale and examine the built landscape as it has evolved over the past century and a half, the argument for convergence and homogenization is compelling.

So, however wrenching the mental effort might be, we must come to terms with a paradox that will not go away: *ours is a land that is constantly becoming more uniform and more diverse at the same time.* The processes of convergence detailed in this volume also simultaneously set in motion processes of segregation, segmentation, customization, and thus extraordinary unpredictability in our landscape. No, the American world is not flat.

But what about the future? What is to become of American placefulness or placelessness? The only honest answer is that, as I have learned from bitter experience, it is foolish in the extreme to try forecasting the future geography of anything.

Setting aside our legitimate anxieties over impending economic and ecological crises for the world and nation, we can only speculate as to what impact our new, advanced modes of communication will have, and are already having, on the character and vitality of American (and other) places. For example, as direct interpersonal electronic messaging becomes ever more universal—and such a trend seems unstoppable during the first decades of the twenty-first century—will the embryonic cartography of cyberspace supplant our traditional plotting of things in Euclidean space? In any event, we can gain a certain perspective about the future by looking back through time.

What the historical record does reveal in no uncertain terms is the perishability or mutability of virtually all forms of political enterprise, whether chiefdom, barony, bishopric, kingdom, republic, empire, or whatever. If we look at the exceptional survivors, those polities that have lasted a millennium or longer—including China, Japan, Iran, France, and Great Britain (is Iceland the exception that proves the rule?)—we learn how radically governance has changed and how huge has been internal reorganization of population, economy, culture, and places in general. We can be reasonably confident of only one thing about the United States of, say, A.D. 3000, if it still exists then: that its human geography will be unrecognizable, utterly unlike what we have today.

My only counsel, then, in this parting benediction is of a humble sort. Let us glory in all the marvels of the American scene while doing our best to heal its blemishes. And, as we do so, keep eyes, ears, and the rest of our sensorium open and alert as long as we are able to make a difference. Then, of course, be prepared to expect the unexpected.

# Notes

## 1. The Argument

1. "Massification" is a term that enjoyed a brief season of popularity among social scientists in the 1960s and 1970s but has since sunk out of sight.

2. But it is difficult to lend much credence to an even earlier statement by James Fenimore Cooper in his *Notions of the Americans* (1828) because he had had much less direct exposure to the expanses of the young republic (or to the rest of the world) than our French visitor. "I have never seen a nation so much alike in my life, as the people in the United States, and what is more, they are not only like each other, but they are remarkably like that which common sense tells them they ought to resemble" (Holman 1995, 26).

3. Among the choicer examples, we have: Roszak 1972; Relph 1981; Lutwack 1984, 182–83; Schivelbusch 1986, 38, 41; Bradshaw 1988, 7; N. Jacobs 1992; Zuckerman 2003, 314. But I cannot resist adding Michael J. Weiss's concise indictment of a homogenized American scene. "In the last decades, social commentators hearing a Muzak drumbeat have complained that the country has homogenized itself into a monotonous two-lane highway, a land where gas station follows burger joint follows video store. Quaint New England towns boast Tex-Mex drive-ins where lobster shacks once stood. Newspapers like *USA Today* transmit the latest trends to readers in rural sections of the country, and syndicated talk shows have become national forums for debate on everything from racial unrest to child abuse. Across the land, shopping malls sprout overnight like concrete mushrooms" (1988, 6).

4. The thoughts of Edward Shils and Henri Lefebvre are worth pondering. "When, as in modern society, a more unified economic system, political democracy, urbanization, and education have brought the different sections of the population into more frequent contact with each other and created even greater mutual awareness, the central value system has found a wider acceptance than in other periods of the history of society. At the same time these changes have also increased the extent, if not the intensity, of active 'dissenses' or rejection of the central value system" (Shils 1975, 11). "The state is consolidating on a world scale. It weighs down on society (on all societies) in full force; it plans and organizes society 'rationally', with the help of knowledge and technology . . . As both the end and the meaning of history . . . it flattens the social and 'cultural' spheres . . . In the same space there are, however,

271

other forces on the boil, because the rationality of the state, of its techniques, plans and programmes, provokes opposition . . . State-imposed normality makes permanent transgression inevitable" (Lefebvre 1991, 23).

5. For splendid insights into the life and psyche of an incurable cosmopolitan, see Pico Iyer's *The Global Soul* (2000).

6. Augé would add to the list "extended transit camps where the planet's refugees are parked" (1995, 34). One could stage an interesting debate over that classification.

7. Also see Moran 2005. Joshua Meyrowitz has a somewhat different take on places and non-places and the muddying of the distinction between the categories caused by electronic media which "destroy the specialness of place and time. Television, radio, and telephone turn once private places into more public ones by making them more accessible to the outside world. And car stereos, wrist-watch televisions, and personal sound systems, such as the Sony 'Walkman,' make public spaces private. Through such media, what is happening almost anywhere can be happening wherever we are. Yet when we are everywhere, we are also no place in particular" (1985, 125).

8. But the cultural and visual impact of globalization is certainly apparent nearly everywhere. With his *Boring Postcards*, Martin Parr (1999) has given us all the evidence we need to recognize the banality and repetitiveness of much of Great Britain's latter-day built landscape and, inferentially, that of other first world countries.

## 2. E Pluribus Unum? The Mashing vs. the Sorting of America

1. Various types of political states had been in existence for millennia before modernization began to give rise to the nation-state. Wolfram Eberhard gets to the novel essence of this latter-day form of political organization. "In earlier societies it did not matter of which race, religion or culture the rulers were. They lived their own life in their palaces and cities. They did not interfere with the life of other groups, communities, classes, layers, except that they forced them to make contributions for their support—for which they promised 'protection'. And the members of lower layers, too, did not care who ruled them, nor did they care what people in other layers did, how they looked, which language they spoke" (1965, 6).

2. Possibly the single best treatment of the process is Eugen Weber's (1976) tale of how peasants were turned into Frenchmen. Also see Zelinsky 1988a, 7.

3. The case of New Zealand may fall outside whatever general scheme applies to the other British settler countries by virtue of its small size and population and the special prominence of the Maori minority.

4. "Neighborhoods were also mixed. There was some tendency for residents on individual streets to be concentrated in certain wealth brackets, but even the owners of Reading lots 1 through 32, which surrounded Penn Square and were the most valuable in town, included one man in the bottom 30 percent and four men in the middle 30 percent, along with seven in the upper 30 percent and eleven in the top 10 percent . . . other blocks likewise showed central tendencies in wealth and occupational characteristics of residents, but they, too, were economically mixed" (L. L. Becker 1992, 208).

5. "Gated communities in the United States first originated for year-round living on family estates and in wealthy communities, such as Llewellyn Park in Eagle

Ridge, New Jersey, built during the 1850s, and as resorts, exemplified by New York's Tuxedo Park, developed in 1886 as a hunting and fishing retreat with barbed-wire fence eight feet high and twenty-four miles long" (Low 2003, 14).

6. For an incisive critical review of the historiography of the subsequent transformation, the market revolution, see Stokes 1996. All of Charles Sellers's brilliant study of the market revolution in Jacksonian America merits close attention, as does James Henretta's fine account of the mentalité of the preindustrial United States (1991, 71–120). Also worthy of further consideration than it has received thus far is a four-stage model of territorial differentiation and societal change set forth by Sanford Labovitz (1965). Early nineteenth-century America would seem to fall into his second phase.

7. For further discussion of the semisubsistence economic and social system of early rural America, see Sellers 1991, 8–16.

8. Some years ago, during a nighttime flight over a snow-covered southern Wisconsin, I experienced strong visual confirmation of central place theory. I peered out the window to see countless tiny pinpricks of light, each marking a single farmstead and, then, just where theory would have set them, in approximate hexagonal array, the larger illuminations, each, in proper progression of brightness, representing the hamlets, villages, and towns.

9. The malaise we call boredom is a modern phenomenon (Goodstein 2005). Indeed the word and concept do not enter the scene until the nineteenth century. A proper treatment of the relationship of boredom to the central question attacked in this study would call for an extended essay, but one that I am not prepared to initiate.

10. It is important to stress that the creation of a national rail network required an incestuous relationship between government and private enterprise, a situation foreshadowed in the canal-building era.

11. "A whole way of life has passed, as Victorian diarists were fond of noting, a slower time of luxury and sociability, a chance to know the intimate landscape from the stagecoach window, when they swayed to the natural undulation of the horse. Obliterating inventions—railroad over the stagecoach, the automobile over the railroad, the typewriter over elegant handwriting, the computer over the typewriter—often unleash such sentimental reveries. Who wouldn't prefer a train, a sailboat, a bicycle, or cross-country skis to some jet-powered or motorized contrivance? Or a distinctive handwritten note from a fountain pen, to some standardized, ill-composed e-mail? We want more speed but we resent, or at least lament, the elimination of the slower and, arguably finer, more graceful experiences they replace. Railroad buffs, vintage-auto owners, beer-and-wine makers, fly-tying anglers, gardeners—*they* are the 'temporal millionaires,' who can afford to spend conspicuous amounts of time indulging their fancies, living partially in the past" (Blaise 2000, 145), along with the battle reenactors and the residents of living history farms (J. Anderson 1984).

12. "Standard time is the unexpressed operating system of all interdependent technologies. It can be said that the adoption of standard time for the world was as necessary for commercial advancement as the invention of the elevator was for modern urban development" (Blaise 2000, 18–19). The reader may recall the quite costly worldwide panic in late 1999—the infamous Y2K crisis—in anticipation of a breakdown in the global economy if clocks and computers did not meet the challenge of the arrival of a new millennium. Fortunately, nothing untoward occurred.

13. But a certain measure of localism does linger on. Individual states and municipalities can still decide whether and when to initiate and end daylight saving time.

14. There is, however, an interesting geography, as yet scarcely researched, in the regionalization of consumer preferences for different styles and colors, as well as types of vehicle (for example, pickup truck vs. station wagon) and, within a given type, for a specific brand.

15. Although the layout of the landing field and, specifically, the runways follows strict, federally mandated regulations, and, more often than not, the associated buildings are functional in design, we do have a number of highly individualized airport structures that offer bold architectural statements.

16. "The media through the sheer massiveness and pervasiveness of their popular appeal fulfill a culturally assimilationist, nationalizing function which patriotic exhortation and pluralistic politics before them could not accomplish. *E pluribus unum* is to be found in things besides money and constitutions" (F. Davis 1979, 131–32).

17. "National citizenship made sense because print culture gave many ordinary men and women access to news about the nation almost daily. . . . The mediation of action and experience by printed texts made the nation something more than imaginary" (Waldstreicher 1997, 110).

18. "The uniformity of the language in America is due to a very great extent to the great interest that Webster's activities and textbooks aroused in language" (Shoemaker 1966, 297).

19. For a map depicting the location of Chautauquas in 1912, see Canning 2005, 26.

20. LeRoy Ashby has shrewdly identified the paradoxes inherent in our national sport. "At first glance, much about baseball seemed alien to the new industrialized world and resembled a throwback to an earlier, pastoral era. After all, baseball, unlike the emerging economy, was outside the domain of the clock. Games moved according to their own momentum, working through outs and innings, not the number of minutes left to play . . . the playing area itself, especially the expansive outfield, summoned up images of rural America, uncrowded and leisurely. Yet, in major ways, baseball meshed well with the emerging corporate cultures. Like the urban, corporate world, it had rules, regularized procedures, and standardized areas. Play, it turned out, contained important lessons for work. Baseball players, like factory workers, learned the skills of particular assignments and played specialized positions. They also learned the importance of practice and discipline. Teamwork was crucial; indeed, the word *sacrifice* in baseball summed up a moment when the batter deliberately abandoned individual success to advance a teammate around the bases . . . it was, however, the emphasis on statistics that especially aligned baseball with the industrial mind-set. 'Almost from the beginning,' according to one baseball expert, 'the new sport of baseball was a mathematical wonder'" (2006, 96).

21. "The telegraph impressed early commentators as a pure medium that would surely act as a moral force in everyday life . . . but as a medium that transmitted and received coded messages from point to point, the telegraph had its most palpable effect on the modernization of America's press and commercial system" (Czitrom 1982, 30). In a prescient observation during the telegraph's infancy that continues to gather relevance in the twenty-first century, "the London *Spectator* looked dubiously on the net effect of electricity as an intellectual force. The crucial result has been the pervasive diffusion of news, 'the recording of every event, and especially every

crime, everywhere without perceptible interval of time—the world is for purposes of intelligence reduced to a village.' But was this desirable? 'All men are compelled to think of all things, at the same time, on imperfect information, and with too little interval for reflection . . . the constant diffusion of statements in snippets, the constant excitements of feeling unjustified by fact, the constant formation of hasty or erroneous opinions, must in the end, one would think, deteriorate the intelligence of all to whom the telegraph appeals . . . this unnatural excitement, this perpetual dissipation of the mind' was the legacy of the electric telegraph" (Czitrom 1982, 19).

22. "In the early days, it was thought that the phone had considerable potential for increased control and therefore centralization. History shows, however, that the phone made possible 'relationships at a distance' and that its centralizing power was much less than expected" (Katz 1999, 25).

23. But recorded as well as live military-style music did function "as 'a culture of reassurance' to a wide variety of Americans of all classes who felt threatened by industrial America's increasing social, economic, and political unrest and violence" (Kenney 1999, 28–30).

24. "But the contest between linguistic homogeneity and diversity found a fascinating territorial compromise, one that quickly became highly ritualized. Announcers for shows and those who read the commercials were indeed the custodians of 'official' English in America, as were newscasters and dramatic actors and actresses . . . but Americans were not going to abide such obvious, top-down, anti-individualist verbal encasements. For in comedy shows—and *Amos 'n' Andy* was the harbinger here—linguistic rebellion, even anarchy, reigned supreme. Radio comedians, in contrast to their linguistically staid, even pompous announcers, ran wild with the American language. Yes, radio would have standards and impose them. But 'nonstandard' English on the radio was where the laughs—and the profits—were" (Douglas 2004, 103).

25. At least one attentive listener confirms this overall impression. "In my own years traversing the country listening to car radios—my own and those of the people I hitched rides with—I was struck by profound regional difference. In the south and 'middle America,' all I ever heard—and when I had a car of my own, all I could ever get—were preachers and country musicians. I couldn't get top 40, jazz, rock, classical, R&B, or talk, just as there was then no country music in Philadelphia and no preaching except on a few black stations at the far end of the dial. To this day, conservative talk shows came very, very late to Philadelphia and are still only on one station, and country music and evangelicals are still rare rather than omnipresent" (Zuckerman 2008).

26. "Ad men attempted to convey a picture of the world in which small groups were no longer proper realms for the communication of values—it was within the corporation and the mass-industrial context that people might find a replacement for outdated communities and the substance they afforded" (Ewen 2001, 96).

27. For a detailed treatment of the inner workings of the advertising industry during a crucial period in its development, see Marchand 1985.

28. "Widely diffused images of goods also reduced regional difference, establishing shopping as a part of the foundation—after the English language, religion, and the U.S. Constitution—of national culture. Though these processes began with the early mass-circulation magazines, they speeded up and became more persuasive during the early days of radio, in the 1930s, and—even more spectacularly—with the universal acquisition of television during the 1960s" (Zukin 2004, 258).

29. Although the rather controversial issue is peripheral to my argument, the presumed interchangeability of manufactured parts—possible largely through the requirements of the American military (Cross and Szostak 2005, 110–13)—parallels the interchangeability of mass-produced commodities.

30. The centralizing, place-flattening impact of the major American corporations is not weakened by the fact that a good many of them—including airlines, railroads, banks, and supermarket chains—are only regional in scope. There is enough collaboration, imitation, and interdigitation among them to render the overall effect national.

31. The dictionary definition of uniforms—"an identifying outfit or style of dress worn by members of a given profession, organization, or rank"—is concise enough, but Nathan Joseph's is a bit more insightful: "The uniform identifies group members, helps insure that organizational goals will be attained, and orders priorities of group and status demands for the individual" (1986, 66–67).

32. "Uniforms are to be taken seriously, with suggestions of probity and virtue (clergy and nuns, judges when robed), expertise (naval officers, senior chefs, airline pilots), trustworthiness (Boy and Girl Scouts, letter carriers, delivery men and women), courage (U.S. Marines, police officers, fire-fighters), obedience (high school and university marching band, Ku Klux Klan), extraordinary cleanliness and sanitation (vendors of ice cream on the streets, operating room personnel, beauty salon employees, food workers visible to the public, and in hospitals all wearers of white lab coats)" (Fussell 2002, 3–4).

33. In contrast to other types of uniforms, the military versions, along with the costumes of royalty and the nobility, have received loving attention from a dedicated group of history buffs in the United States and other countries.

34. "Despite the issuance in 1861 of the Army's *Revised Regulations*, great diversity prevailed in the dress of Union volunteers" (Elting and McAfee 1982, v).

35. For an excellent broad-stroke treatment of the topic, see Abler 1975.

36. Thus, in an analysis of the 1870–1959 period, we learned that "within the United States, rates of natural increase generally decreased, with state rates tending to converge around the national average" (Eldridge and Thomas 1964, 63). Then, although the topic of inter-ethnic differentials is quite peripheral to this inquiry, it is interesting to note that "there has been both absolute and relative convergence of fertility across groups" (Haines 2002, abstract).

37. The matter of scale can be important. If convergence in income and other indicators of economic and social well-being may be progressing in a reassuring manner at the state or regional level, more localized pockets of poverty or affluence may be intensifying when we look more closely, as illustrated in a recent atlas of American poverty (Glasmeier 2003). Although not germane to the horizontal themes addressed in this book, it is difficult to ignore the seriously widening vertical, that is, class-based, disparities in income and related measures over the past three decades or so. Whether the gap is to become a persistent, long-term phenomenon or simply a phase in a cyclical swing is currently a question at the center of a heated academic and general policy debate.

38. However, we must not overlook at least three groups that obstinately rebut the idea of assimilation (and provides an ideal example of the process of *ethnic/racial/religious/class tropism and repulsion*) and is also breeding new members at a merry pace: the Amish (Lamme 2001), Hutterites, and Ultra-Orthodox Jews.

39. In a provocative volume titled *1959: The Year Everything Changed*, Fred Kaplan (2009) documents a number of striking events in that year which either foreshadowed or introduced the turbulent changes of the approaching decade.

40. Although the claim seems too melodramatic to be credible, Bill Bishop (2008, 86–90) does argue persuasively that a sudden unraveling of a placid America did occur abruptly during the frenetic summer of 1965. And is it mere coincidence that the transformative legislation that opened the gates to waves of new immigrants happened to have been enacted in that same year?

41. The philosopher Charles Taylor's insights into a remarkable cultural revolution merit attention. "Let's call this the Age of Authenticity . . . I believe, along with many others, that our North Atlantic civilization has been undergoing a cultural revolution in recent decades. The 60s provide perhaps the hinge moment, at least symbolically. It is on one hand an individuating revolution, which may sound strange, because our modern age was already based on a certain individualism . . . what is new is that this kind of self-orientation seems to have become a mass phenomenon" (2007, 473). "We see a steady spread of what I have called the culture of 'authenticity' . . . I mean the understanding of life which emerges with the Romantic expressivism of the late-eighteenth century, that each one of us had his/her own way of realizing our humanity, and that it is important to find and live out one's own, as against to surrendering to conformity with a model imposed on us from outside, by society, or the previous generation, or religious or political authority" (475).

42. "In a nation that prides itself on being a classless, egalitarian society, the cluster system reflects the roaring diversity of how we live . . . within each cluster of neighborhoods, inhabitants tend to lead similar lives, driving the same kind of cars to the same kind of jobs, discussing similar interests at similar social events—cocktail parties here, backyard barbeques there, stoop-sitting elsewhere" (M. J. Weiss 1988, 2). Also see his *Latitudes and Attitudes* (1994).

43. At some deep level there is some sort of kinship between central place theory and the cluster concept. Both of the systems posited therein are concerned with the spatial disposition of populations and of goods and services, and both countenance a certain degree of irregularity in pattern. But only the latter recognizes the reality of socioeconomic change and shifts in fashion and taste.

## 3. Pondering the Built Landscape

1. If we have a comprehensive account of sorts for the period up through 1845 (Stilgoe 1982), one apparently based in good part on the lectures and essays of J. B. Jackson, we still await a book-length treatment of the more recent scene. In the meantime, we have Jackson's many insightful snapshots and Robert Riley's (1980) brief, but thought-provoking, speculations on the new American landscapes.

2. We must not overlook the probability of some sort of African contribution to the southern built landscape (Anthony 1976). It may have appeared in the morphology of slave quarters, African American gardens and cemeteries, and—something yet to be studied methodically—the design of black rural churches.

3. One of the more makeshift varieties of log technology still barely survives in Wisconsin: "stovewood architecture," the use of chunks of round logs to form walls, with chinks filled in with clay or plaster (Tishler 1979).

4. "Personal descriptions of sod houses range from the mid-nineteenth century almost to the mid-twentieth: the latest soddy I have found was built in 1940 near Dunning, Nebraska by J. Dean Hersh" (Welsch 1968, 27).

5. The arrival of goodly numbers of Anglos in the Southwest from the mid-nineteenth century onward initiated a hybridization of domestic building styles that is still ongoing (J. A. Stewart 1974).

6. But most have suffered a sad fate. "A formidable combination of the law, science, technology, changing agricultural production, and alternative fencing materials acted in concert to clear the land of its rock fences . . . Anecdotal information from people who have lived in the region for decades suggests that only 5–10 percent of what was one of the most extensive networks of quarried rock fences on this continent remains." Recently, however, there has been an organized effort to preserve the fences (Murray-Wooley and Raitz 1992, 133, 134, 146–50).

7. "After 1920 the usefulness of the limestone fence post began to decline as the treated timber came into use . . . Despite all that, stone-post quarrying and setting did not halt in the 1920s or even in the 1930s, and annually at least up to World War II a few more miles of fence lines with stone posts were added in a few localities" (Muilenburg and Swineford 1975, 55, 57).

8. Their spatial pattern in the 1990s is a matter of some interest; the 842 covered bridges extant in 1997 were distrubuted as follows (McKee 1997, 149–52): Pennsylvania, 214; Ohio, 142; Vermont, 100; Indiana, 92; New Hampshire, 54; Oregon, 51; New York, 30; West Virginia, 17; Georgia, 15; Kentucky, 14; Alabama, 12; Iowa, 12; California, 11; Virginia, 10; Maine, 9; Connecticut, 6; Illinois, 6; Maryland, 6; Michigan, 6; Washington, 6; Missouri, 5; Wisconsin, 4; Tennessee, 3; Delaware, 2; North Carolina, 2; New Jersey, 1; South Carolina, 1; Texas, 1. Why no examples in Minnesota, Arkansas, or Mississippi?

9. For general treatments of the evolution of the American cemetery scene, see Francaviglia 1971; Jackson and Vergara 1990; D. C. Sloane 1991; and Linden 2007. Useful bibliographies appear in R. E. Meyer 1989, 329–39; and Linden 2007, 331–50.

10. Among many possible examples, there is the case of James Fenimore Cooper who buried a sister and a daughter in a plot adjoining his residence (Franklin 2007, 38, 181).

11. D. G. Jeane (1989, 109) has produced a map of Southern counties containing folk cemeteries based on the field observations of Milton B. Newton Jr.

12. Peter Fisher furnishes a much more sober assessment of what the great majority of architects have actually perpetrated in a statement that could be extended to other aspects of culture and environment. "The development of mechanical environmental systems during the twentieth century has denied to much recent architecture the symbolic role it previously played as a form of 'shelter' which by necessity responded to the prevailing local climate. It is now possible, at the expense of consuming greater levels of energy, for a building's form and orientation to ignore climate completely. Not only has this had a severe effect on emissions but it has also suppressed many of the experiential qualities that a concern with climatic factors had previously inspired, and can be seen as a part of a general progression toward an increasingly homogeneous world in which cities and buildings throughout the globe have begun to look the same, irrespective of location" (2004, 217–18; also see Shove 2004).

13. Meaningful international statistics are hard to come by, but it is generally agreed that, with an annual rate of shifting residence that has hovered around 20

percent for generations, the United States has the most mobile of populations. Indicative of this distinction is the appearance of special centennial plaques in front of farmhouses in Illinois and a few other states proclaiming that the same family has occupied the building for a hundred years or more. If I may cite my personal history, during my first forty-two years, I experienced thirty-seven changes of address, a fugacity that is certainly nowhere near the championship record. But after my late wife and I designed and built our current residence in 1963, I have developed a powerful passion for this final resting place of mine, so that I now fully appreciate the mystique, the "poetics of space," so artfully celebrated by Gaston Bachelard (1969), a mode of perception much more common in certain other parts of the world than in the United States.

14. For a brief, but insightful, discussion of the relevance of technology to the American landscape, see R. L. Thayer 1990.

15. Rather curiously, the "Pueblo Style" showed up occasionally in the 1920s in places well beyond the Southwest, such as Minnesota and Florida (Sheppard and Schreiber 1990).

16. I refrain from any meaningful comment on the architectural scene, vernacular or otherwise, in Hawaii and Alaska for lack of personal observation. But, as for Hawaii, the impression gained from two studies (Fairfax 1971; Sandler 1993) is of an eclectic mixture of borrowed styles without the development of any distinctive architectural language. Thus Geoffrey Fairfax tells us that "in the design of houses the tendency has been to borrow the California tract house concept, to add one lanai, subtract one fireplace, and to erroneously claim this equation results in an Hawaiian house" (1971, 15).

17. We have here an even more fundamental development in some architectural circles: the "reinvention of place," as enunciated by Susan Sirefman. "Today, much urban architecture seems interchangeable from city to city and country to country, while far too much suburban design consists of homogenous, cookie-cutter, neotraditional housing. Moreover, the latest digital technologies and information networks in our now global world have the potential to further disassociate architecture from place. Perhaps in response to this situation, there is a growing undercurrent across North America in the opposite direction—an exciting resurgence of interest in the architectural reinvention of place" (2004, 10).

18. One of the more curious recent developments is the widespread popularity of row houses in suburbia, a gesture at faux urbanity as well as an effort to economize on construction costs (Dingemans 1975).

19. But, predictably enough, the rapidly vanishing outdoor privy has inspired nostalgia and an association of aficionados (Booth 1998).

20. I have been told that the practice originated in Richmond, Virginia, in the 1980s.

21. But every so often the lucky landscape voyeur will come across the truly wonderful or grotesque lawn, porch, or house adorned with a wild assortment of objets d'art, sculptures, ceramics, shells, rocks, signs, junk, and bric-a-brac (Modra and Roberts 1998). This may well be another American idiosyncrasy.

22. "The status of the lawn as a realm occupied by the elite is attested to by a line in Charles Brockden Brown's 1798 novel, *Wieland* . . . This statement suggests that the experience was not available to or intended for anyone but the privileged and erudite who appreciated the luxury of the lawn" (T. O'Malley 1999, 80).

23. "The American lawn therefore was an amalgam of an elite ideal of romantic pastoralism and democratic communalism and can be understood as a construction shaped by intellectuals, social reformers, landscape architects, and civic leaders" (T. O'Malley 1999, 84–85).

24. "From Texas to California [in the 1914–56 period] the original . . . stations . . . were being replaced by larger and more pretentious ones in a style which sprang from the indigenous Spanish tradition. This group of mission-inspired depots with arcades, balconies, and belfries had counterparts in hotels and mansions" (Meeks 1956, 158).

25. In discussing the "apron building" or "loading arcade", now integral features of our busier airports, Alistair Gordon characterizes them as being "designed for the same purpose: to speed the transfer of human bodies and maximize profit. If architecture reflects something of the human condition, then these narrow sheep runs embodied the prosaic linearity of modern life: the treadmill of corporate employment, the narrow margin of profit, the anxiety of a salesman running for his flight. They were not designed to memorialize heroic deeds, but rather as antimonument to the likes of Willie Loman and Sammy Glick" (2004, 170).

26. "Airport terminals are the cathedrals of our age . . . as for landscape design, the airport, like the theme park, is a characteristic post-modern phenomenon. The green deserts between runways, the large turning and security areas, the ghostly lighting and the chain-link perimeter fence are what defines the airport as landscape. So if the airport itself is a new kind of city and the terminal buildings its cathedrals, then the whole assembly sits in a massive sterile green sward isolated from farming and other rural activities. This landscape setting, seen so clearly from the air, provides identity as sharply as the design of the buildings themselves. And it is an identity which distances man from nature, itself a metaphor for our age and the very essence of the airliner itself" (Edwards 2005, x).

27. "These corporate estates, now operating throughout the country—and especially dominant across the South—are essentially outdoor factories. That the barns on these properties resemble the sorts of storage shed and warehouses seen at textile and steel mills is not too surprising. Called 'pole barns,' these standardized buildings are raised on the grids of thin wooden poles that support prefabricated steel trusses. Compared to other barns, these structures seem cold, mechanical, and faceless, like the corporations that spawned them. That the pole barn is now becoming the structure of choice on the remaining family farms suggests the end of traditional barn designs in America" (Vlach 2003, 21–22).

28. Strangely enough, French inventors were granted patents simultaneously with their American counterparts (Krell 2002, 19). This episode eerily foreshadowed the multiple, widespread claims for primacy in the invention of telephony just a few years later.

29. "Itinerant sign painters had roamed the countryside propositioning farmers for the use of a side of their barn . . . most commonly they would paint the entire barn in exchange for the use of one side for an advertising sign. Products ordinarily advertised in this way were patent medicines and tobaccos. Mail Pouch tobacco was advertised regularly on the sides of barns and continues to be today . . . The once virgin landscape became progressively cluttered with signs painted on walls, posts, trees, and rocks . . . From the 1860s to the 1880s, painted letters from six inches to two feet high advertised home remedies on rocks and cliffs, barns, abandoned structures, and any other available surface" (Margolin, Brichta, and Brichta 1979, 35).

30. But we should not forget that singular twentieth-century expression of international authority, the United Nations Building in New York city. For a general treatment of the impress of central authority, see Zelinsky 1988a.

31. "Aside from the fortifications hastily thrown up during the Revolution, lighthouses were the first structures over which local communities had no control . . . They mark the new strength of nationalism over localism, the new power of new Government" (Stilgoe 1982, 111).

32. "The most defining feature of the capitol, the dome, may be viewed symbolically as a great archetypal head of authority. The temple front below the dome, imprinted on the Western mind as a universal sign of governmental power, was taken deliberately from classical antiquity to generate symbolic support of the new American republics [*sic*]" (Goodsell 2001, 186).

33. Lois Craig (1984) and Robert D. Leighninger Jr. (2007) have set forth and interpreted both the ephemeral and the lasting impact of the New Deal on America's built landscape.

34. However, "nativism became an important theme in courthouse design in the 1910s and 1920s, reflecting a certain hunger for the regional and local traditions that had seem obliterated by the European leanings of the Beaux-Arts" (Seale 2006, 56), and "rather apologetically, the skyscraper courthouse was always accompanied by a nativist art program, usually calling for murals representing Indian and pioneer life. These were very popular in western courthouses, but were present to an extent elsewhere" (Seale 2006, 57).

35. The three exceptions were Phoenix's city hall with its Indian motif and the Hispanic inspiration for those in Pasadena, California, and Coral Gables, Florida.

36. "While engineers and inventors have turned their attention to rationalizing the design of the fire station and improving the equipment inside it, the buildings themselves have lost whatever architectural distinction they once had. By the time the United States entered the space race, the American fire station, though filled with an impressive array of equipment, was likely to be one of the least impressive buildings in the community. And somehow the public—architects, city building departments, neighbors, and the firemen themselves—had come to expect no better" (Zurier 1991, 207).

37. Not considered here are the many one-of-a-kind items, the products of *arbitrary corporate/governmental place-making, personal expression, the pursuit of pleasure,* and *self-conscious place-making,* that are treated in Chapter 4.

## 4. The Theater of the Unpredictable

1. But, in some rare instances, a pleasuring place may thrive in spite of (or because of ?) thoroughly inhospitable conditions, as has happened with the wildly successful annual, week-long Burning Man festival in the completely bleak Black Rock Desert near Gerlach, Nevada (Kozinets 2003).

2. "The leading colonial spa was probably Bristol, Pennsylvania, located twenty miles northeast of Philadelphia . . . If Bristol was indeed the most popular spa, its patrons surely exceeded the estimated 2,000 people annually visiting the various Virginia springs in the 1770s and 400–600 guests staying at Berkeley and Yellow Springs at one time" (Weinstein 1984, 18).

3. But the operation of spas and their facilities has always been a risky business. "The precarious nature of the nineteenth-century resort economy was demonstrated

by numerous failures. The conditions that forced Ballston Spa to abandon resort life were common. After success as a spa in the eighteenth and early nineteenth centuries, Stafford Springs, Connecticut, lost its popularity and put aside its resort economy for one based on woolen-goods manufacture, pearl button making, and the mining and processing of iron. By the post–Civil War era, another resort, Clarendon Springs, Vermont, was on its way to becoming a ghost town. The construction of hotels would save Caldwell and White Sulphur Springs in Virginia as resorts but many others would not survive the nineteenth century" (Corbett 2001, 59).

4. But some of the villages and towns that initially flourished because of the spa industry survived its demise by turning to other functions. An especially interesting example is that of Sharon Springs, New York, which became a haven for a colony of ultra-orthodox Hasidim in the late twentieth century (Durlach 1980).

5. "As early as 1961, jet travel and the expansion of the Pocono Mountains resort region in Pennsylvania drew newlyweds away from the Falls . . . a U.S. marketing survey undertaken in 1970 placed Niagara fifth among honeymoon destinations, behind the Poconos, California, Florida, and New York City. Newlyweds of the 1980s and 1990s were even more likely to ignore Niagara, as honeymoon features in travel and wedding magazines extolled instead of the pleasures of Europe, Caribbean islands, and the Florida Keys" (Dubinsky 1999, 243).

6. For maps of state parks in Idaho, Washington, and Oregon, see T. R. Cox 1988, 21, 62, 88.

7. In their 1920s opera *The Rise and Fall of the City of Mahagonny*, Bertolt Brecht and Kurt Weill gave us an eerily prescient account of Las Vegas and its ilk.

8. The claim that Woodstock was "the largest spontaneous gathering of humanity in the history of the Western World" (Hopkins, Wolman, and Marshall 1970, 5) is a trifle excessive. I vividly recall witnessing an anti-war rally in New York City's Central Park involving at least 500,000 persons, and there have been other such enormous American political gatherings. The omission of such places/events from this study derives from the fact of their relative locational predictability: if not in Washington or a state capital, then in New York City, Chicago, San Francisco, or Los Angeles.

9. Steve Shipp (1996) provides us with accounts of some sixteen of the leading early art colonies and the artists associated with them. Also see T. Miller 1998, 42–65 and Jacobs 1985.

10. In the late twentieth century at least 79 colonies were operating in 31 states (Goff 1993; Snell 2000). Their distribution is interesting: New York 11; California 9; Massachusetts 7; Washington 5; Maine 3; New Mexico 3; North Carolina 3; Oregon 3; Vermont 3; Connecticut 2; Florida 2; Michigan 2; Minnesota 2; Montana 2; Nebraska 2; New Jersey 2; Wisconsin 2; and one each in Colorado, Georgia, Hawaii, Kentucky, Pennsylvania, Tennessee, Texas, Utah, Virginia, and Wyoming. What sort of appeal is lacking in the other 19 states?

11. At the time of writing, the prospect of having the George W. Bush library established at Southern Methodist University, not an inevitable choice, had stirred up serious controversy.

12. Is there any basis for the speculation that "behind the current popularity of the farms may be the quiet desperation of those who have begun to suspect that the world of their grandchildren may focus less on abundance and more on survival" (Morain 1979, 556)?

13. The near-total demolition of the bayside casinos—and virtually everything else in coastal Mississippi—by Hurricane Katrina in August 2005 has meant no more than a brief hiatus for the industry. Both the state government and the proprietors are intent on complete restoration.

14. It was a shrewd Centre County property owner who donated a fraction of his farm to the Commonwealth in the realistic expectation that the new school would greatly enhance the value of the remaining acreage for his heirs.

15. "Surely it is amazing that neither history, nor sociology, nor fiction, has given more than passing attention to the American college town, for surely it has had a character and a personality unlike other towns" (Canby 1936, 3).

16. For a similar description, there is Captain Frederick Marryat's of an 1838 campground near Cincinnati (C. A. Johnson 1955, 245–46).

17. We do have a much better grasp of the geography of the modern arms manufacturing industry thanks to a penetrating study by Ann Markusen et al. (1991).

18. For a map of company-owned and operated towns in the western United States, see Roth 1992, 174.

19. According to official Bureau of Justice statistics, a total of 1,512,823 persons were imprisoned in state and federal facilities (1,328,339 in the former, 184, 484 in the latter) as of mid-2005 (not to mention the many kept in county, municipal, and specialized facilities). In 1980 the total had been only 329,821. As of 2003, an astonishing number of individuals were, or had been at one time, incarcerated in these places, 5,618,000, as compared with only 1,819,000 in 1974 (Bonczar 2003). Maps recording the distribution of persons held in correctional institutions as of 1990 and 2000 (Suchan, Perry, and Fitzsimmons 2007, Maps 5–59, 5–60) reveal disparities between California, Texas, and Arizona on the one hand and all the other states (with much more modest numbers), on the other which one can only characterize as absolutely shocking.

20. "Before 1930, the Federal Prison System included only three penitentiaries—Leavenworth, Atlanta, and McNeil Island—as well as a women's reformatory in Alderson, West Virginia, a youth facility in Chillicothe, Ohio, and a detention center in New York City" (J. W. Roberts 2006, 6).

21. "One of the more unique characteristics of fireworks stands that distinguished them from most other commercial enterprises is that their location, appearance, and very existence are a product of the state, county, and local laws (Puljak 2006, 215).

## 5. Territorial Diversities in the Cultural Realm: Yea and Nay

1. Some scholars have accepted the conclusions of the Labov project and seek to draw larger lessons from it. "Dialect difference in America is by no means a thing of the past, and there is every indication that the boundaries whose foundations were laid when the first English colonists arrived in Jamestown in 1607 will continue to exist in some form long into the twenty-first century" (Wolfram and Schilling-Estes 1998, 121). "The reason for linguists' continued interest in regionalism is that, contrary to popular (and learned) belief that had assumed that regional speech differences were gradually vanishing due to the impact of job mobility and the mass media, regional dialects are not only surviving, but are actually diverging—owing, it is suggested, to the fact that regional speech constitutes an important part of regional identity" (Hönnighausen 2005, xvi).

2. Although the female choices may be more volatile, the relative popularity of various names for infant boys can also shift wildly and unpredictably during a short period.

3. Census officials did collect and publish religious statistics, along with the usual demographic and economic data, in the 1850, 1860 1870, and 1890 reports, but the information came from denominational offices rather than households. The same observation applies to *Census Reports on Religious Bodies* dated 1906, 1916, 1926, and 1936.

4. Hill merits quoting at some length. "Conventional wisdom has it that American society is becoming more and more homogeneous. Under the impact of television, the syndication of newspaper articles and even companies, and widespread travel, Americans are becoming more alike, so we are told. Regional differences thus should be decreasing in favor of greater national—American culture-wide—consensus. The religious life of the American people should reflect any such decline in regional peculiarity. To this supposition a second would be added by a number of observers— namely, the growth of secularism in its scope and in the power of its hold on our society under conditions of modernization. In other words, a growing proportion of American citizens is "practicing the absence of God'—a vest-pocket definition of secularism. They are taking religious faith less seriously, although without actually repudiating it and thereby becoming either atheists or agnostics. If these popular perceptions are in fact true, the strength of religion should be decreasing. It would follow that religion would be a less significant factor in any attempt to assess regional differences or similarities. On both points, the evidence disputes conventional wisdom. Religion is proving to be a more tenacious element in our national life than many have supposed" (1985, 133). "Zelinsky's classification of seven religious regions remains standard" (ibid., 132).

5. A map of voter registration in Garwood (1988, 191) displays values for only four census regions.

6. "The sections are interpreted as the geographical expression of broad materialist interests within the evolving American state. The sections and the interests being reflected change over time, but this geographical basis for economic conflict has been remarkably resilient over two hundred years" (Archer and Taylor 1981, 203–4).

7. For a detailed treatment of the political behavior of the South, particularly in recent times, and its relationship to class, race, and economic factors, see Shafer and Johnston 2006.

8. For a thorough debunking of the notion of a sharp division between the electorates in the so-called Red and Blue states, see Fiorina 2006, a volume that stresses the predominance of swing voters.

9. For a splendid account of the origins of American foodways, see George R. Stewart's *American Ways of Life* (1954, 102–31). It is interesting to compare the American experience with the analogous case of British settlers encountering the exotic Australian environment (Markey 1986). For a brief general survey of American scholarship in food matters, see Belasco 2002. For at least a tentative approach to American regional and ethnic foodways, see Brown and Mussell 1984 and Shortridge and Shortridge 1998.

10. But the South does feature one unusual indulgence in vegetables: sliced tomatoes for breakfast (M. B. Newton 1977).

11. An unsolved mystery is the failure of Chinese, Greek, Indian, Middle Eastern, and Jewish restaurants to thrive as chains or franchises.

12. It is simple enough to verify this claim by scanning American (or foreign) newspapers where the number of pages or columns devoted to sports every day far surpasses that for other forms of entertainment and rivals or exceeds the space allotted to politics, crime, warfare, gossip, religion, and food.

13. Although many birds sing—and some are remarkable mimics of human speech and song—and other creatures have distinctive cries, such behavior is governed mostly by instinct. Evidently only human beings are capable of creating and appreciating that mysterious phenomenon we call music. The task of defining music, a most elusive concept, strains the expertise of lexicographers. Thus the best *OED* can come up with in their initial effort is "that one of the fine arts which is concerned with the combination of sounds with a view to beauty of form and the expression of emotion." Professional musicians are tongue-tied when I pose the question to them. Dance poses an equally heroic definitional challenge, as shown again by a tortured *OED* effort: "a rhythmical skipping and stepping with regular turnings and movements of the limbs and body, usually to the accompaniment of music; either as an expression of joy, exaltation, and the like, or as an amusement or entertainment." Try telling that to devotee of modern dance.

14. Unfortunately, in devising its otherwise truly encyclopedic questionnaire, DARE did not include any query specifically requesting local music-related terms.

15. There is, of course, the persistence for at least a generation or two of musical traditions among immigrant Germans and others. More durable perhaps is the liturgical music performed in synagogues and Eastern Orthodox churches. Then, quite recently, one welcomes the surprising revival of the klezmer idiom.

16. "On the strength of my own ethnographic-based research into local patterns of music consumption, it does seem to me that consumers are in general more aware of the local arrangements around which their musical worlds are arranged than is generally acknowledged" (Bennett 2000, 67).

17. "One may say, paradoxically, that the strongest testimony for the undistinctive quality of American dress is the lack of testimony. Travelers from other countries, in their accounts, seldom mention clothing at all. They are full of comments upon other matters—food, drink, religious sects. They even tell not a little about housing. But when they mention how anyone was dressed, it is generally to write that he or she was 'well dressed,' or 'poorly dressed,' or 'fashionably dressed.' And even such comment is rare. It seems to be the same, no matter who the traveler or when he came, or what parts of the country he visited" (G. R. Stewart 1954, 126).

18. For an account of an especially significant component in a globally shared system of dress, the "Standard Suit" worn by all respectable adult males, see Zelinsky 2004.

19. "Smaller, specialized Western mail-order catalogues distinguished themselves from the large commercial books like Sears and Montgomery Ward by offering complete Western wardrobes, including clothing, accessories, gear, and equipment, as early as 1905" (Nottage 2001, 38).

20. "While styles, fabrics, and design elements eventually distinguished the brands favored in the West, early clothing preferred by working Westerners was similar to that of their Eastern counterparts" (Nottage 2001, 37).

21. Is there any need to waste space and time with a deconstruction of the fallacious image of the southern planter or "colonel"?

22. In discussing informal children's games in the United States in the 1900–1920 period, Elliott West claims nationwide similarity and inheritance from medieval

England. "Despite the differences between amusements in cities and in the country, there has always been a common culture of play throughout the United States. During the early decades of the twentieth century, children could be seen playing many of the same games in vacant lots in Brooklyn and in schoolyards in Arizona and Alabama" (1996, 20–21; also see Comeaux 2005).

23. For a vivid description of street play in the city, see Zerner 1977.

24. Social workers "in Cleveland, Ohio interviewed fifteen thousand boys and girls to find out how they were using their spare time in the summer of 1913. More than half spent their time on the streets, sometimes playing baseball and jacks or flying kites, but mostly 'doing nothing,' or rather engaging in shooting craps, teasing, stealing fruit, starting fires, writing on walls, or fighting" (Van Slyck 2006, 45). Unfortunately, a highly detailed analysis of "Sixty Years of Historical Change in the Game Preferences of American Children" (Sutton-Smith and Rosenburg 1961) carries the story only up to 1959, thus failing to reflect the full impact of television. The authors do prognosticate however, "Of a somewhat more speculative order is the . . . generalization that these historical changes imply that the majority of children's formal games may themselves in due course become anachronistic" (ibid., 31).

25. Writing in 2007, Howard Chudacoff reports that "a recent survey of the ways children spend discretionary time found that of the fifty-one non-school, nonwork hours kids had available to them each week, *only about one-half hour was spend in unstructured outdoor activities* while fourteen and a half hours were spent in indoor unstructured play and more than twelve separate hours were spent watching television" (2007, 189; emphasis added).

26. "But increasingly, the second factor, parental anxieties over child safety and child achievement, has intensified to the point that parents, supported by all types of public and private interests, have imposed formal activities on children's formerly unstructured and 'free' playtime. For underprivileged children, this movement— which some have called an 'invasion'—has meant after-school recreation and sports programs in boys' and girls' clubs, neighborhood clubs, YMCAs and YWCAs, and other such agencies. Among middle-class youngsters, karate and gymnastics lessons, homework and foreign-language instruction, soccer and baseball leagues, and school homework have replaced the informal 'scrub' baseball that the young Bruce Catton and Louise Dickinson Rich played, the 'side-yard' shows that Sylvia McNeeley liked to organize. Among all classes, many of today's parents tolerate extensive television viewing and video game playing by their children as alternative to unsupervised activity on city streets where, if the media are to be believed, perils of abuse, abduction, and assault stalk every corner. Even in supposedly 'secure' suburbs, many parents prevent their children from straying away from the house to play unobserved in the neighborhood. Thus, although precise data are difficult to come by, there are powerful indications that youngsters at present spend far more time indoors— mostly occupied by TV, the computer, and formal activity—than their predecessors did" (Chudacoff 2007, 218).

27. "Terms of endearment like 'honey' or 'baby' are commonly heard in the South but elsewhere can be considered inappropriate or demeaning, particularly when directed toward businesswomen" (Morrison and Conaway 2006, 552). Michael Zuckerman reports another interesting aspect of business manners. "I can't give you a citation—I heard it on the radio—but someone did a study of the time it takes businessmen to get to business in different parts of the country. The study measured the

time devoted to pleasantries (weather, wife and kids, the church picnic last Saturday, whatever) at the beginning of phone calls. The times that constituted good manners and expected/tolerable behavior varied a great deal, if you think thirty seconds versus three minutes is a good deal. (Even the most expansive chewing the fat would, of course, be impossibly impolitely abrupt in other places.). The South was, indeed, at the long end of the spectrum, but no more than small town businessmen everywhere, and Atlanta and Charlotte were just as quick as Philadelphia and Los Angeles. New York was at the thirty-second end, but so was Boston, which is smaller than Philadelphia and a pygmy next to LA" (2008).

## 6. The Regional Factor

1. One of the more serious claims for the uniqueness of the United States it that it seems to be the only country in which such questions should engage serious attention on the part of scholars.

2. For any student of the regional dimensions of the American scene the indispensable vade mecum is Michael Steiner and Clarence Mondale's *Region and Regionalism in the United States* (1988) along with Mondale's (1989) postscript.

3. Although "after 1970, scholars turned again to interpreting regions, and a new institutional structure emerged to do so" (C. R. Wilson 1997, 151), the shift in attitude is not limited to academics. "In contemporary American culture there is a strong longing for roots, for recapturing or restoring a sense of place. Widely held values such as technological progress, spatial mobility, and the achievement of a national culture are challenged . . . This movement, though only some fifteen years old, has had a remarkably broad impact. Academic and professional fields, such as anthropology and geography, architecture and planning, are affected by it. In the larger world we see its influences in people's concern with genealogy, in programs of neighborhood revitalization, and in the numerous efforts to designate and preserve historic buildings" (Tuan 1980, 3; also see Lowenthal 1985, 1996). Change is also afoot in the literary world, as documented later in this chapter, and for fundamental reasons. "In addition to a new interest in place as a formal element in literature, the twentieth century evidences a new interest in place as an important issue in general. This is a result of widespread public recognition that earth as a place, or the total environment, is being radically changed and perhaps rendered uninhabitable by more and more pervasive and powerful technologies . . . An increased sensitivity to place seems to be required, a sensitivity inspired by aesthetic as well as ecological values" (Lutwack 1984, 2). In "The Revival of Localism," Robert Nisbet (1975, 260–69) was one of the earliest commentators to detect a turning away from "Leviathan."

4. Patricia Nelson Limerick offers a key distinction between the two territorial concepts. "Regions unite . . . sections divide. Regions can both complement and compliment one another, sections can only compete. Regions have their roots in a warm and hearty connection between distinctive people and distinctive places; sections have their roots in a political and economic struggle for dominance" (1996, 84). For a detailed treatment of the essential differences between the two concepts, see Odum and Moore 1938, 35–51. As an interesting sidelight on the term "sectionalism," we have Donald Davidson's statement that "the word is peculiar to the United States. It is not an Anglicism" (1938, 7).

5. How prominent or critical a factor the subjective element may be in the existence of regions is not a simple problem. "Nothing is less innocent than the question, which divides the scientific world, of knowing whether one has to include in the system of pertinent criteria not only the so-called 'objective' categories (such as ancestry, territory, language, religion, economic activity, etc.) but also the so-called 'subjective' properties (such as the feeling of belonging), i.e., the *representations* through which social agents imagine the divisions of reality and which contribute to the reality of the divisions" (Bourdieu 1991, 226). For the etymology of the term "regional" and the history of its complex usage and implications, one may turn to Raymond Williams's invaluable *Keywords: A Vocabulary of Culture and Society* (1985, 264–66). He offers, in passing, the interesting observation that "*regional* . . . unlike *provincial* and *suburban*, has an alternative positive sense, as in the counter-movement indicated by modern uses of *regionalism*" (1985, 266).

6. Michael Conzen provides an arresting map of "Selected Ethnocultural Homelands in the United States" (2001, 260), one indicating numerous Native American territories, almost all now vanished or of only historical interest. The only non-Indian entities depicted are the Mormon and Hispanic.

7. For obvious reasons, I exclude from this discussion the District of Columbia and the Canal Zone, and other overseas territories administered by the federal government.

8. The situation in the United States stands in sharp contrast to the relationship between dominion and province in our northern neighbor. As Seymour Martin Lipset has noted, "given the much greater importance of their provincial governments in the lives of Canadians, as compared to the role the states now play for Americans, and the larger significance given to place in the literature and art of the northern country than in the southern, more commitment by the former to their subnational unit is to be expected. I have not been able to locate comparable surveys in the United States, testimony to the improbability of asking Americans to choose between state and nation as source of identity or loyalty" (1990, 210). In his *Nine Nations of North America* (only three of which fall entirely within the United States), Joel Garreau (1981) offers an intriguing regionalization of the continent, but one in which economic and other noncultural factors tend to overshadow the cultural. Only one of his "nations," Dixie, corresponds with any of the regions shown in figure 6.1. For other approaches to the cultural regionalization of the country, see Lerner 1957, 182–206; Glassie 1968; Gastil 1975; Zelinsky 1982; Bradshaw 1988; D. H. Fischer 1989. But the most far-reaching and illuminating introduction to the historical geography of the topic is to be found in Donald Meinig's monumental *Shaping of America* (1986–2004) and, most specifically, in volume 2 (published in 1993).

9. The case for the individuality of Texas is bolstered by the fact that, according to Labov, Ash, and Boberg 2005, 148, it is the only state, aside from Pennsylvania, harboring its very own subdialect of American English.

10. If each of the thirteen British colonies enjoyed a kind of quasi-independence before the Revolution, none of them has created or retained its own special sociocultural identity—even though some Virginians and South Carolinians might argue heatedly to the contrary. Pennsylvania is characterized by sharp intrastate regional contrasts, as is also the case for Maryland, Georgia, North Carolina, New York, New Jersey, and, in its miniature way, Delaware, while Massachusetts eventually spawned the incompatible state of Maine.

11. The notion of having Vermont secede from the Union has resurfaced quite recently and has gained the support of an estimated 8 percent of the population (Baldwin and Bryan 2007).

12. "The Wisconsin Idea was 'that continual sifting and winnowing' carried on not only in the classroom and laboratory but jointly in the classroom and government administrative office. It was the joint effort of the politician and the professor to serve the common interest of all the people rather than the special interest of particular groups" (Doan 1947, 15).

13. It is a curious, but important, fact that the United States is unique among all the nations of the world in having the need for its scholars to struggle endlessly with the chore of identifying and mapping its cultural regions. Throughout all the ancient communities of the Old World and in much of Latin America as well, deeply entrenched regional identities have prevailed time out of mind and are familiar to residents and neighbors alike. Because of the accidents of physical geography and history, aside from the United States, none of the European settler countries have had to worry a great deal about delineating the territorial parcels that compose their sociocultural map.

14. A similar map, "Traditional Rural Formal Cultural Regions of North America," appears as figure 1.6 in Jordan-Bychkov and Domosh 1999, 11.

15. For what they may be worth, herewith the full text of Fischer's characterization and location of his seven regions: "1. *The Northern Tier*, including New England, the upper old northwest, the northern plains and the Pacific northwest, all settled by Yankees but now dominated by other ethnic groups who are Roman Catholic in New England, Lutheran in the middle west. 2. *Greater New York*, small in area but 10 percent of the national population, and a very heavy infusion of middle European and Jewish culture grafted on the old Dutch root. 3. *Midland America*, extending from Pennsylvania west through the Ohio Valley and the middle west to the Rocky Mountains, marked by a diversity of European immigrant groups; the leading religion in many midland counties is Methodist. 4. *The Great Basin*, a predominately Mormon culture in Utah, and parts of Idaho, Nevada, Arizona, Colorado and Wyoming; a mix of New England, midland and highland southern culture. 5. *The Coastal South*, from southern Maryland to Florida and the Texas coast near Houston. Its culture is tempered by large numbers of northern immigrants. 6. *The Southern Highlands*, including Appalachia, the old southwest, the Ozark Plateau, and much of Texas and Oklahoma which are still dominated by the old ethnic groups; the leading religion is Baptist. 7. *Southern California*, a hybrid of highland southern, midland, Hispanic and Jewish culture, spreading into Nevada, Arizona, and New Mexico" (1989, 887–88).

16. "Regional identity was apparent in the colonial period based on the differing behavioral, dress, religious, legal, and so on, codes in place in each colony. Continuity of these transmitted colonial cultural identities is visible today in each region in the patterns of behavior that are acceptable and usual in each region. Some aspect of colonial identities have changed, but the major outlines remain and are evident in the differential rates of the eight conditions presented here" (Sugar 2004, 142).

17. "Regional feeling tends to concentrate more around key cities than vast rural areas—Boston, Philadelphia, Charleston, New Orleans, Denver, and San Francisco, for example. One wonders . . . if we have not moved from town-and-country regionalism to city regionalism since World War II" (Fishwick 1968, 399–400). I would hesitate only at the inclusion of Denver.

18. Some of the cities in question, notably New York, Boston, and Los Angeles, contain distinct subregions, neighborhoods with a degree of cultural autonomy generally recognized by all concerned, if not by the country at large.

19. For an interesting case study of ethnogenesis and fashioning of an updated Hawaiian Culture Area, see Miyares 2008.

20. "In these few pages I have argued for the recognition of Tejano South Texas as a cultural province, one unlike the Mexican American subregions of neighboring borderland states like California, Arizona, and New Mexico" (Arreola 2002, 203). It should be noted that Joel Garreau's (1981) Mexamerica includes much of Southern California as well as other tracts in the standard Southwest.

21. "The unique, almost non-Anglo character of the Southwest, particularly in the less accessible areas, leads to the impression that the Southwest borderlands are not part of the greater United States—except in the convenience of its language, highways, post offices, and monetary and legal system. A 'Third World' groupie can wander and even settle there without need for hassles with immigration authorities. The majority of Anglo-Americans who relocate to the borderlands take on Southwest customs, costumes, and outlook to one degree or another" (P. G. Allen 1997, 345).

22. Moreover, the Hispanic barns of the Southwest are totally dissimilar to those in the remainder of the nation (Vlach 2003, 280–95).

23. And, unlike New England with its *Yankee* or the South with its *Southern Living*, the Southwest has never acquired a commercially successful periodical to extol its regional glories. Although it has gained national attention, *Arizona Highways* is obviously parochial in it coverage.

24. For a concise, informative account of the formation of early American cultural regions, see Mitchell 1978, 66–90.

25. I must single out Joseph Conforti's beautifully written volume for special praise as a superb achievement that comes close to being definitive in its exploration of both the individuality of the region and its evolving self-perception as expressed in literature, political rhetoric, the built landscape, etc.

26. In his discussion of "New England as America," David Waldstreicher (1997, 251–93) deals with the initial, but eventually ineffective, effort to define the United States politically and culturally as New England writ large. Also see Kermes 2008, 15–56.

27. "A 2004 New England poll showed that a whopping 87 percent of those contacted wanted to be identified as New Englanders, compared to the 74 percent of the respondents to a similar poll in the South who wanted to be known as southerners" (Cobb 2005, 328).

28. John Egerton views the process in a dyspeptic spirit. "The thesis of this book is that the Americanization of Dixie and the Southernization of America are homogenizing processes that are full of contradictions and ambiguities and paradox . . . the South and the nation are not exchanging strengths as much as they are exchanging sins" (1974, xx).

29. But, in a later publication, Cobb offers a more nuanced appraisal of a complicated situation. "By undermining some of the more negative traits commonly ascribed to white southerners, improvements in education and economic standing seemed simultaneously to make the more upwardly mobile among them less 'southern' to others but much more aware of being southern themselves. Meanwhile, those

whom economic progress had largely bypassed, the less affluent, less-educated whites, seemed less concerned about losing their regional identity, but more likely to cling to the prejudices and traditionalism that had so long defined that identity" (2005, 221).

30. But Martyn Bone finds something sinister in what appears to be developing. "As local cultures try to formulate some form of resistance to American-dominated globalization, 'the positive substance of what is being defended tends to reduce itself to anthropological tics and oddities.' Literary critic Scott Romine has identified something like this process in the 'conspicuous Southerness' of recent fiction, in which traditional signs of regional identity have become 'radically overdetermined.' Yet even this kind of self-conscious Southern literary regionalism seems to be caught up in that widespread 'collapsing the cultural into the economic' that Jameson identified as the defining characteristic of contemporary globalization. For as Romine observes, 'it is possible—even profitable—to act Southern today in a way that would have been inconceivable a century ago.' The rather eerie result is that conspicuously Southern literature proves its profitability just as larger commercial forces erase the 'positive substance' of the South as an identifiable social reality, and as a distinctive subject for fiction. Indeed, John Smith, a scholar of Southern popular culture, has identified in Southern 'narrative fetishism' an even more disturbing tendency to mimic the dominant cultural-economic logic that ostensibly it resists. Smith observes that 'as the South becomes more 'Americanized'—as identity becomes more and more structured as a lack to be filled by consumption—the paradoxical results may be the increasing commodity-fetishization of southernness itself" (2004, 228; also see Jones and Monteith 2002).

31. "If any generalization is to be ventured at all, it is, surely, that change has brought an even more acute self-consciousness and even greater pluralism than ever before. The South is still a concept active in the everyday lives and exchanges of communities; it is still there as a determining part of their mental maps and speech acts. The difference now is that inventing or imagining—or simply *assuming the existence of*—the South occurs within an environment where the sheer diversity of information available, and the multiplicity of systems supplying that information, make cultural insularity close to impossible. More than ever before (and with more deliberation than ever before), acts of regional self-identification have to be made against the grain" (Gray 2000, 503–4).

32. For a classic account of a reasonably typical Pennsylvania town (Bellefonte, Centre County), see P. F. Lewis 1972.

33. Michael Zuckerman argues forcefully that the Middle Atlantic in general, and the PCA in particular, was especially important in the formation of the larger American identity. "From the first, the people of Pennsylvania, New Jersey, and New York acted under conditions of cultural pluralism that only came to characterize the rest of the country in the nineteenth century" (1982, 5). "Geographers and folklorists . . . found, almost unfailingly, that neither New England nor the South was as influential in the course of American civilization as the colonies of the Middle Atlantic . . . Tracing the dispersion of a remarkable variety of folkways, geographers always found the mark of New England lightest on the land and generally found the impress of Pennsylvania weightiest. Whether they studied architectural design or construction, house types or barn types, naming habits or rural settlement patterns, geographers never found New England influence beyond a narrow northern band

that petered out in the upper Midwest. Though they did sometimes dispute the exact circuits of southern and mid-Atlantic jurisdiction, they usually discovered that the writ of the middle colonies ran furthest" (2003, 324).

34. Writing as a literary critic, Walter Wells offers valuable insights into the development of Los Angeles as the heart of a novel geographic phenomenon, "that there *is* an aesthetically significant Hollywood-Southland regionalism . . . Southland can be seen simultaneously as a literary region with its own identity, and a part of a broader California regionalism. It is a region which begins to emerge in the 1920s, roughly coincident with Los Angeles' transformation from hick town to metropolis and, indeed, with the coming of age of the motion picture industry. Among influences upon its literature, it shares with the rest of California a geophysical immensity and an unparalleled variety of landscape; a social newness and a lack of history save for a relatively recent frontier and agrarian past; and a magnetic appeal for seekers after fortune, fame, or salvation. These shared characteristics are joined, in Hollywood-Southland, by a number of specifically local influences sufficient to justify its claim to separate regionality: a static and languorous subtropical climate; the rapid movement of events and people characteristic of the twentieth-century metropolis; a sprawling stucco and neon landscape set precariously in a land of drought, flood and earthquake, its structures almost as tentative as Hollywood sets, and almost as changeable" (1973, 10). For other observations on Southern California regionalism as glimpsed through the literary lens, see Fine 1995, 2003. The San Francisco literary scene is also noteworthy and distinct from that of the "Southland" (Fine and Skenazy 1995).

35. Findlay goes on with the contention "that, rather than looking mainly within the Pacific Northwest to find some sort of indigenous roots of regional consciousness, we should look more outside the three states. The notion of a Pacific Northwest has been cultivated best by outsiders who have wanted to shape the idea of region for their own purposes, and by inhabitants whose sense of place has depended extensively on their ideas and feelings about locales elsewhere" (1997, 44).

36. Here I am deeply indebted to the masterful studies of the Middle West concept by James Shortridge (1985, 1987, 1989, 1998).

37. But not all commentators reject the existence of a genuine Middle West. In a deplorable travesty of serious scholarship, none of the seven participants in the symposium titled "The Midwest: Myth or Reality?" ever entertains the case for myth. "No one should deny the existence of a geographical Midwest" (McAvoy 1961, v). "The Midwest is real, we have decided. We have agreed to strike out the word 'myth' and the question mark, and leave 'The Midwest: Reality'" (McAvoy 1961, 95).

38. The Middle West, in contrast to the South, New England, and other bona fide cultural regions, suffers from the feebleness of its institutionalization in academe. Thus "Midwestern studies lack the institutional structures so necessary to the flowering of a formal regional literature . . . there is, indeed, no formal organization of Midwestern scholars. Only recently has Indiana University Press created a series devoted to Midwestern studies. You will look in vain for H-net Midwest on the Internet. The Great Lake American Studies Association consists of a group of scholars who happen to live in this region; it is not necessarily an association of people with a particular interest in the history of the region as a place, as a culture, as a way of life" (Cayton 2001, 148–49; also see Cayton and Gray 2001).

39. "What matters most is who people think they are, or more specifically, who they think they are not. Certainly that is the case in the Midwest, the most marginal

and problematic of major American regions. To the extent that it exists at all (about which I have serious doubts), it is only in people's perceptions of themselves and their relationships with other human beings" (Cayton 1998, 64).

40. But, oddly enough, both Hart and Slade and Lee exclude Kansas and Nebraska, two states that, according to various surveys, comprise the most intensely Middle Western pair of any. Incidentally, despite their appeal in terms of physical geography and history, awareness of regionality in the adjacent or overlapping Great Plains has not emerged among either inhabitants or outsiders (J. R. Shortridge 1997).

41. "Contrary to the writings of academicians and journalists, college students from most sections of the country perceive the Middle West to have its core in Nebraska and Kansas . . . Americans view the Middle West overwhelmingly in small town terms . . . Pastoralism apparently has been so much a part of the regional and national identity that people find the idea difficult to abandon. Rather than changing the regional image to fit urban-industrial reality, the public has shifted the regional core westward to the Great Plains where rural society is more dominant" (J. R. Shortridge 1985, 48).

42. The Middle West is " 'standard American'—lacking the presumptions of the East, the traditions of the South, the flamboyance of Texas, the lure of the Golden West" (Mather 1986, 193).

43. "Once this region was enthusiastically depicted as the successful culmination of a national effort, a landscape of created abundance, produced though the heroic labor of human agents over successive generations. Now, however, the image of the Prairie Midwest has shifted once more, acquiring the nostalgic cast of a Grant Wood painting. In the postindustrial U.S. landscape architect Robert L. Thayer Jr. observes 'looking at rural landscapes is therapeutic compensation for the pressures of a technological world.' In this context, people visit the prairie again as tourists, seeking psychic renewal and the assumed simplicity of a past landscape, but not the complications of the modern U.S. farm crisis. Both landscape and nature are sentimentalized. Ironically, the region once proudly extolled as a kind of technological marvel is now construed once again as 'natural,' removed from history and frozen in time, to serve as a place of psychic refuge for beleaguered citizens of a consumer-oriented, post-modern American society" (Raymond 1996, 113–14).

44. But, in a subtle, learned essay, in which he examines the possible affiliation of Alaska and Hawaii with the West, John Whitehead (1997) reaches a generally negative conclusion.

45. Her Western uniformitarianism is explicit in her 1987 and 1998 publications and elsewhere. Limerick's definition of the West is quite curious. "Allowing for a certain shifting of border, the West in this book will generally mean the present-day states of California, Oregon, Washington, Idaho, Utah, Nevada, Arizona, New Mexico, Colorado, Kansas, Nebraska, Oklahoma, Texas, Montana, Wyoming, North Dakota, and South Dakota and, more changeably, Iowa, Missouri, Arkansas, and Louisiana" (1987, 26). Similarly, in his magisterial work on the Great Plains, Walter Prescott Webb (1931) portrays the western half of the nation as being qualitatively different from the eastern.

46. William Wyckoff and Lary Dilsaver continue in the same vein. "Complicating things has been a growing appreciation for the region's geographical and historical diversity. The Willamette Valley and Tucson, the Texas Panhandle and the Wind River mountains—these places have less in common than, say, the Tennessee hills

and the Green Mountains of Vermont. Does it make sense, then, to speak of the 'West' as a region at all?" (1995, 6–7). But they do go on, in their presentation of the mountainous West, to imply that it may be the most quintessentially Western portion of the West. A related quandary is how to deal with the Great Plains in any system of regional cultures—whether as a component of the West or, much more dubiously, as a candidate for classificatory autonomy. Frederick Luebke (1984) and Robert Thacker (1989) deal gingerly with the question but without any recommendations.

47. It is also symptomatic of the situation that, in a chapter on regionalism in the *Columbia Literary History of the United States,* James Cox dismisses the West with the statement "that leaves the West which is not really a region in my context. It is all future and mobility—it is America!" (1988, 784). Then, in a more general view of the arts, Kerwin Lee Klein concludes that "from bi-coastal Asian-American artists to Compton rappers we can imagine an entire sweep of 'westerners' who do not partake of a 'Western' regional consciousness. There is no Western mind" (1996, 213). "For the West, as Carey McWilliams and Wallace Stegner observed, is really many Wests. The broad and bristling land between the ninety-eighth meridian and the Pacific Ocean is a constellation of many ever-changing, ever-shifting regions 'all so different in their history and ethnic compositions, that . . . trying to make a unanimous culture out of them would be a hopeless job. It would be like wrapping five watermelons'" (Steiner and Wrobel 1997, 9).

48. David Hamilton Murdoch offers a suggestive analogy to the Western Myth in the Arthurian Myth so deeply embedded in the British imagination. In any event, "the myth of the West emerged, just as the old century ended, out of a groundswell of nationwide nostalgia. This hankering after the good old days was one response to a present that seemed to have gone very badly wrong and it took the form of an obsessive brooding about the loss of a world where special American values had flourished" (2001, 63; also see Campbell 2002, 21, and Hausladen 2003a, 1).

49. "The term regionalism is of comparatively recent origin and has not yet acquired any accepted precise definition. It was first used in 1874 in the works of Provençal poet de Berluc-Pérussis but did not come into wide currency until the 1890s" (Hintze 1934, 208).

50. It is interesting to note that, in what may have been the earliest extended discussion of regionalism (Hintze 1934), there is only a single dismissive paragraph accorded the United States within an article almost entirely devoted to Europe.

51. Among the feebler stabs at definition we have "regionalism is a more or less explicit form of regional opposition to a dominant central bureaucracy or to another region" (Eysberg 1996, 21). Henry Shapiro's comment also reflects the general fuzziness of our understanding of the concept. "So far as I have been able to ascertain, it was not until the publication of *Webster's Third New International Dictionary of the English Language* in 1961 that our modern regionalist definition of region received formal acknowledgement" (2005, 265). Raymond Williams does cast a bit of light on the obscurity of our reaction to the term. "*Regional* . . . unlike *provincial* or *suburban*, has an alternative positive sense, as in the counter-movement indicated by modern uses of *regionalism*. It carries implications of a valuably distinctive way of life, especially in relation to architecture and cooking" (1985, 266). For general essays on the topic of regionalism, see Hesseltine 1960, Tindall 1993, Zelinsky 2001.

52. I might note parenthetically that the term "regionalism" does enjoy another life of its own recently in government-speak as a way of referring to various consor-

tia of nation-states in the Eastern Hemisphere and Latin America, but that is another story entirely.

53. For general treatments of Regionalism I and, specifically, its career during the New Deal, see Odum and Moore 1938; Dorman 1998; Steiner 1983; and Coats and Farooq 2003. Especially interesting is the southern agrarian Donald Davidson's *The Attack on Leviathan: Regionalism and Nationalism in the United States* (1938), a cranky, verbally adroit rant against cities, modernism, statism, etc.

54. There were, of course, earlier, haphazardly funded crusades to further the cause of literary regionalism, as, for example, the journal *The Midland*, which survived from 1915 to 1933 (Reigelman 1975). Its exchange system "was apparently widespread among all the little magazines of the time, and especially among the regionally oriented ones" (Reigelman 1975, 27). For a sampling of general coverage of the literary blossoming during and around the 1930s, see D. Davidson 1938, 65–101, Spencer 1951, Hönnighausen 1996, Wyile et al. 1997.

55. "The project's development along regional lines mirrored certain other tendencies of the period. The project's regional efforts were paralleled by a quickening interest in TVA and the National Resources Board . . . The findings of the FWP also had an affinity with the resurgence of regional social consciousness expressed in the novels of Faulkner, Steinbeck, Farrell, and Wright and in the paintings of Grant Wood, Charles Burchfield, and Thomas Hart Benton" (Penkower 1977, 242–43).

56. "There is a difference between literary 'realisms': 'provincialism' and 'regionalism.' *Provincialist* writing, I suggest, . . . depicts non-metropolitan experience as charming, trivial, and unsophisticated, and so carries on the long-standing marginalization of local culture, submerging it in a placeless national identity; *regionalism*, by contrast, features the region's difference from a national or imperial culture and directly addresses the difficult and real moments of injustice and oppression in American life based in regional asymmetries" (Watts 2002, 165).

57. Of course, all through the years, the vast majority of authors of fiction, drama, and verse have, wittingly or otherwise, rooted their efforts in familiar territory. But self-consciousness about doing so seems to be a twentieth-century phenomenon. For a glorious essay on the entire topic read Welty 1956.

58. As of "1973, regional organizations in the United States remained anomalies or experiments or both" (Derthick 1974, 4). "There has never been a sustained movement for regional organization that left its impress across the United States. Regionalism (it is not quite accurate to use so concrete a term as 'regional organization') is one of those ideas that grips a few minds or much of an academic discipline, as it gripped sociologists and planners in the 1930s and economists and planners in the 1960s, but then disappears for a while. It has been much subject to intellectual fad and fashion. Perhaps because the fashion has never gripped political scientists, the 'regional idea' has not taken shape as a specific set of proposals for regional organization" (Derthick 1974, 3).

59. For succinct and penetrating discussions of Regionalism II, see C. R. Wilson 1998a, ix–xxiii; Kowalewski 2003; and Hönnighausen 2005b. Wyile et al. offer a brief explanation for its emergence: "In the last twenty years, economic, political, and cultural developments have prompted a renewed focus on regionalism. Decentralization, regional consciousness, and a growing suspicion of institutional nationalism, combined with the development of a global economy and a more eclectic international culture, have undermined the cohesion of the nation-state. The rationalizing effects

of a global market economy have put pressures on local economies and cultures, throwing increasing attention on culture and politics at the regional level, and forcing a redefinition of the notion of community" (1997, xii). Joseph Conforti offers further insights into the genesis of Regionalism II. "The progress of the 'American Century' gave birth to the environmental movement and reinvigorated historic preservation, both of which preached the importance of place. At the same time the suburban, corporate transformation of American life made heritage and historical quaintness a valued commodity. Heritage tourism became a major postindustrial 'industry'" (2001, 314).

60. I might have appended a postmodernist clause to the definition. As C. R. Wilson puts it, "Postmodernism has not developed a regional theory, but one can draw from it means that may help illuminate the emerging shape of contemporary new regionalism . . . Postmodernism represents a sense of limitless cultural possibilities. By 'putting on' identities, one can be anything one pleases. C. Vann Woodward once asked whether the Southern identity would mean much in a homogenized America, anything more than putting on a comfortable old coat. Postmodernists do exactly that, a classic postmodern gesture. One can wear Western boots and be an 'urban cowboy,' prepare blackeyed peas paté and be a Yuppie Southerner when serving it at your party around the swimming pool . . . tour early colonial villages in order to refresh your New England heritage" (1998a, xiv–xv). The geographer Paul Claval writes in the same vein. "Today, the fashion for regionalism leads people to identify with such or such an ensemble because it pleases them, because it offers agreeable landscapes, a clement sky, well-serviced town, or because it was celebrated in literature, poetry, or the cinema" (1998, 159–60).

61. "Touting of regional identity—whether in Salt Lake City or Williamsburg— frequently partakes of the 'heritage' movement: a promotional impulse that often has more to do with kitsch, nostalgia, and economic 'growth coalitions' than with any deep-rooted or stabilizing sense of community" (Kowalewski 2003, 10).

62. "Although it is often contended that areal differentiation is disappearing in our world of 'non-places' (Augé 1995), closer examination reveals a countervailing commercial trend. Far from experiencing a spatial apocalypse, we are witnessing a renewed interest in places as the recent rise of dramatic servicescapes like Niketown, ESPN Zone Chicago, and Bass Outdoor World readily attests" (S. Brown 2003, 1).

63. For general coverage of bioregional thought and practice, as well as eloquent advocacy, see Parsons 1985, Sale 1985, McGinnis 1999, and Kowalewski 2003, 16–17. But perhaps the most thoughtful and persuasive account is Robert Thayer's *LifePlace* (2003).

64. "By the year 2005, there were approximately eighty-three thousand Slow Food members scattered around the world. Italy was first, with thirty-eight thousand members; the United States came in second, with almost fifteen thousand members" (Petrini 2006, 131–32). "You can see it [American creativity] in the thousands of microbreweries, in small local cheese factories, that produce raw-milk cheese using old-world techniques, and its bakeries whose bread is often tastier than that made in Europe" (ibid., 140).

65. Also see maps of microbreweries in 1972, 1982, and 1992 (Flack 1997, 46–48).

66. Although memory can be fallible and I was not especially alert to them at the time, I cannot recall ever seeing any American B&Bs during my American rambles as of the 1950s.

# References

Abbott, Carl (1990). "New West, New South, New Region: The Discovery of the Sunbelt," pp. 7–24 in Mohl 1990.

Aberley, Doug (1999). "Interpreting Bioregionalism: A Story from Many Voices," pp. 13–42 in Michael Vincent McGinnis, ed., *Bioregionalism*. London: Routledge.

Abler, Ronald F. (1973). "Monoculture or Miniculture? The Impact of Communications Media on Culture in Space," pp. 186–95 in David A. Lanegran and Risa Palm, eds., *An Invitation to Geography*. New York: McGraw-Hill.

——— (1975). "Effects of Space-Adjusting Technologies on the Human Geography of the Future," pp. 35–56 in Donald Janelle Abler, Allen Philbrick, and John Sommer, *Human Geography in a Shrinking World*. Scituate, Mass.: Duxbury Press.

Abramson, Rudy, and Jean Haskell, eds. (2006). *Encyclopedia of Appalachia*. Knoxville: University of Tennessee Press.

Ackerman, Marsha E. (2002). *Cool Comfort: America's Romance with Air-conditioning*. Washington, D.C.: Smithsonian Institution Press.

Adams, Robert L. A. (1995). "Golf," pp. 231–69 in Raitz 1995d.

Agnew, John A., and James S. Duncan (1989). "Introduction," pp. 1–8 in Agnew and Duncan, eds., *The Power of Place: Bringing Together Geographical and Sociological Imaginations*. Boston: Unwin Hyman.

Allen, Barbara (1990). "Regional Studies in American Folklore Scholarship," pp. 1–13 in Allen and Thomas J. Schlereth, eds., *Sense of Place; American Regional Cultures*. Lexington: University Press of Kentucky.

Allen, E. John B. (1993). *From Skisport to Skiing: One Hundred Years of an American Sport*. Amherst: University of Massachusetts Press.

Allen, James B. (1966). *The Company Town in the American West*. Norman: University of Oklahoma Press.

Allen, Paula Gunn (1997). "Cuentos de la Tierra Encantada: Magic and Realism in the Southwest Borderlands," pp. 342–65 in Wrobel and Steiner 1997.

Allen, W. F. (1904). *Short History of Standard Time and Its Adoption in North America in 1883*. Philadelphia: Stephen Green Printing Co.

Allwood, John (1977). *The Great Exhibitions*. London: Studio Vista.

Alvey, R. Gerald. (1992). *Kentucky Bluegrass Country.* Jackson: University Press of Mississippi.

Amundson, Michael A. (2002). *Yellowcake Towns: Uranium Mining Communities in the American West.* Boulder: University Press of Colorado.

Anderson, Jay (1984). *Time Machines: The World of Living History.* Nashville: American Association for State and Local History.

Anderson, Kay J. (1987). "The Idea of Chinatown: The Power of Place and Institutional Practice in the Making of a Racial Category," *Annals of the Association of American Geographers* 77: 580–98.

Anderson, Larry (2002). *Benton MacKaye: Conservationist, Planner, and Creator of the Appalachian Trail.* Baltimore: Johns Hopkins University Press.

Anderson, Oscar Edward, Jr. (1972) [1953]. *Refrigeration in America: A History of a New Technology and Its Impact.* Port Washington, N.Y.: Kennikat Press.

Anthony, Carl. (1976). "The Big House and the Slave Quarters. Part II. African Contributions to the New World," *Landscape* 21(1): 9–15.

Appadurai, Arjun (1996). *Modernity at Large: Cultural Dimensions of Globalization.* Minneapolis: University of Minnesota Press.

Applepome, Peter (1996). *Dixie Rising: How the South Is Shaping American Values, Politics, and Culture.* New York: Random House.

Archer, J. Clark, Stephen J. Lavin, Kenneth C. Martis, and Fred M. Shelley (2002). *Atlas of American Politics, 1960–2000.* Washington, D.C.: CQ Press.

——— (2006). *Historical Atlas of U.S. Presidential Elections, 1788–2004.* Washington, D.C.: CQ Press.

Archer, J. Clark, and Fred M. Shelley. 1986. *American Electoral Mosaic.* Washington, D.C.: Association of American Geographers.

Archer, J. Clark, and Peter J. Taylor. 1981. *Section and Party: A Political Geography of American Presidential Elections from Andrew Jackson to Ronald Reagan.* New York: John Wiley & Sons.

Archer, John (2005). *Architecture and Suburbia: From English Villa to American Dream House, 1690–2000.* Minneapolis: University of Minnesota Press.

Arreola, Daniel D. (1984). "Mexican American Exterior Murals," *Geographical Review* 74: 409–24.

——— (2002). *Tejano South Texas: A Mexican American Cultural Province.* Austin: University of Texas Press.

Arsenault, Raymond (1984). "The End of the Long Hot Summer," pp. 176–211 in Mohl 1990.

Ash, Sharon (2006). "The North American Midland as a Dialect Area," pp. 33–56 in Murray and Simon 2006b.

Ashby, LeRoy (2006). *With Amusement for All: A History of American Popular Culture since 1830.* Lexington: University Press of Kentucky.

Asher, Louis E., and Edith Heal (1942). *Send No Money.* Chicago: Argus Books.

Athearn, Robert G. (1986). *The Mythic West in Twentieth-Century America.* Lawrence: University Press of Kansas.

Augé, Marc (1995). *Non-Places: Introduction to an Anthropology of Supermodernity.* London: Verso.

Ayers, Edward L. (1996). "What We Talk about When We Talk about the South," pp. 62–82 in Ayers, Limerick, Nissenbaum, and Onuf 1996.

Ayers, Edward L., and Peter S. Onuf (1996). "Introduction," pp. 1–10 in Ayers, Limerick, Nissenbaum, and Onuf 1996.

Ayers, Edward L., Patricia Nelson Limerick, Stephen Nissenbaum, and Peter S. Onuf (1996). *All Over the Map: Rethinking American Regions.* Baltimore: Johns Hopkins University Press.

Babbitts, Judith (1993). "Household Labor," vol. 2, pp. 1421–32 in Cayton, Gorn, and Williams 1993.

Bachelard, Gaston (1969). *The Poetics of Space.* Boston: Beacon Press.

Badger, Reid (1979). *The Great American Fair: The World's Columbian Exposition and American Culture.* Chicago: Nelson Hall.

Baker, T. Lindsay (1985). *A Field Guide to American Windmills.* Norman: University of Oklahoma Press.

Baldwin, Ian, and Frank Bryan (2007). "The One and Future Republic of Vermont," *Washington Post,* April 1: B1, B5.

Bale, John (1995). "Cricket," pp. 70–96 in Raitz 1995d.

Ball, Donald W., and John W. Loy (1975). *Sport and Social Order: Contributions to the Sociology of Sport.* Reading, Mass.: Addison-Wesley.

Baron, Dennis E. (1990). *The English-Only Question: An Official Language for Americans?* New Haven: Yale University Press.

Barro, Robert J., and Xavier Sala i Martin (1990). *Economic Growth and Convergence across the United States.* Working Paper no. 3419. Cambridge, Mass.: National Bureau of Economic Research.

Bartky, Ian R. (1989). "The Adoption of Standard Time," *Technology and Culture* 30(1): 25–56.

Bassett, Thomas J. (1981). "Reaping on the Margins: A Century of Community Gardening in America," *Landscape* 25(2): 1–8.

Bastian, Robert W. (1975). "Southeastern Pennsylvania and Central Wisconsin Barns: Examples of Independent Parallel Development," *Professional Geographer* 27: 200–205.

Batteau, Allen W. (1990). *The Invention of Appalachia.* Tucson: University of Arizona Press.

Baxandall, Lee (1995). *Lee Baxandall's World Guide to Nude Beaches and Resorts.* Oshkosh, Wisc.: N Editions.

Beardsley, John (1995). *Gardens of Revelation: Environments by Visionary Artists.* New York: Abbeville Press.

Becher, Bernd, and Hilla Becher (2006). *Grain Elevators.* Cambridge: MIT Press.

Beck, Ulrich, Natan Sznaider, and Rainer Winter, eds. (2003). *Global America? The Cultural Consequences of Globalization.* Liverpool: Liverpool University Press.

Becker, Jane S. (1998). *Selling Tradition: Appalachia and the Construction of an American Folk, 1930–1940.* Chapel Hill: University of North Carolina Press.

Becker, Laura L. (1982). "Diversity and Its Significance in an Eighteenth-Century Pennsylvania Town," pp. 196–221 in Michael Zuckerman, ed., *Friends and Neighbors: Group Life in America's First Plural Society.* Philadelphia: Temple University Press.

Belasco, Warren (1979). "Toward a Culinary Common Denominator: The Rise of Howard Johnson's, 1952–1940," *Journal of American Culture* 2: 503–18.

——— (2002). "Food Matters: Perspectives on an Emerging Field," pp. 2–23 in Belasco and Philip Scranton, eds., *Food Nations: Selling Taste in Consumer Societies.* New York: Routledge.

Bell, David, and Gill Valentine (1997). *Consuming Geographies: We Are Where We Eat.* London: Routledge.

Bell, Thomas L. (1996). "Why Seattle? An Examination of an Alternative Rock Culture Hearth," *Journal of Cultural Geography* 18(1): 35–48.

Benedict, Albert, and Robert B. Kent. (2004). "The Cultural Landscape of a Puerto Rican Neighborhood in Cleveland, Ohio," pp. 187–205 in Daniel D. Arreola, ed., *Hispanic Spaces, Latino Places: Community and Cultural Diversity in Contemporary America.* Austin: University of Texas Press.

Benedict, Burton (1983), *The Anthropology of World's Fairs: San Francisco's Panama Pacific International Exposition of 1915.* London: Lowie Museum of Anthropology and Scholar Press.

Bennett, Andy (2000). *Popular Music and Youth Culture: Music, Identity and Place.* Basingstoke: Macmillan.

Berger, Michael L. (1979). *The Devil Wagon in God's Country: The Automobile and Social Change in Rural America, 1893–1929.* Hamden, Conn.: Archon Books.

——— (2001). *The Automobile in American History and Culture: A Reference Guide.* Westport, Conn.: Greenwood Press.

Berger, Peter L., Brigitte Berger, and Hansfried Kellner (1974). *The Homeless Mind: Modernization and Consciousness.* New York: Vintage.

Berland, Jody (1998). "Locating Listening: Technological Space, Popular Music, and Canadian Mediations," pp. 129–50 in Andrew Leyson, David Matless, and George Revill, eds., *The Place of Music.* New York: Guilford.

Berman, Marshall (2006). *On the Town: One Hundred Years of Spectacle in Times Square.* New York: Random House.

Berry, Brian J. L. (1967). *Geography of Market Centers and Retail Distribution.* Englewood Cliffs, N.J.: Prentice-Hall.

——— (1992). *America's Utopian Experiments: Communal Havens from Long-Wave Crises.* Hanover, N.H.: University Press of New England.

Berry, Brian J. L., and William Garrison (1958). "Functional Bases of the Central Place Hierarchy," *Economic Geography* 34: 145–64.

Berry, Brian J. L., and Allen Pred (1965). *Central Place Studies: A Bibliography of Theory and Applications.* Philadelphia: Regional Science Research Institute.

Billig, Michael (1995). *Banal Nationalism.* London: Sage.

Bining, Arthur C. (1938). *Pennsylvania Iron Manufacturing in the Eighteenth Century.* Harrisburg: Pennsylvania Historical and Museum Commission.

Binneweis, Robert O. (2001). *Palisades: 100,000 Acres in 100 Years.* New York: Fordham University Press.

Bishop, Bill (2008). *The Big Sort: Why the Clustering of Like-Minded America Is Tearing Us Apart.* Boston: Houghton Mifflin.

Black, Earl, and Merle Black (2007). *Divided America: The Ferocious Power Struggle in American Politics.* New York: Simon & Schuster.

Blaise, Clark (2000). *Time Lord: Sir Sandford Fleming and the Creation of Standard Time.* New York: Pantheon.

Bloom, Nicholas Dagen (2001). *Suburban Alchemy: 1960s New Towns and the Transformation of the American Dream.* Columbus: Ohio State University Press.

Boal, Dean (1998). *Interlochen: A Home for the Arts.* Ann Arbor: University of Michigan Press.

Boas, Max, and Steve Chain (1976). *Big Mac: The Unauthorized Story of McDonald's.* New York: E. P. Dutton.

Bolton, Kate (1979). "The Great Awakening of the Night: Lighting America's Streets," *Landscape* 23(3): 41–47.

Bonczar, Thomas P. (2003). *Prevalence of Imprisonment in the U.S. Population, 1974– 2001.* Washington, D.C.: Bureau of Justice Statistics.

Bone, Martyn (2004). "The Transnational Turn in the South: Region, Nation, Globalization," pp. 217–35 in Russell Duncan and Clara Juncker, eds., *Transnational America: Contours of Modern US Culture.* Copenhagen: Museum Tusculanum Press.

Bonner, James C. (1945). "Plantation Architecture of the Lower South on the Eve of the Civil War," *Journal of Southern History* 11: 370–88.

Boorstin, Daniel J. (1965). *The Americans: The National Experience.* New York: Random House.

Booth, Dottie (1998). *Nature Calls: The History, Lore, and Charm of Outhouses.* Berkeley: Ten Speed Press.

Borchert, James (1980). *Alley Life in Washington: Family, Community, Religion, and Folklife in the City, 1850–1970.* Urbana: University of Illinois Press.

Borne, Lawrence R. (1990). *Dude Ranching: A Complete History.* Albuquerque: University of New Mexico Press.

Bourdieu, Pierre (1991). *Language and Symbolic Power.* Cambridge: Harvard University Press.

Boydston, Jeanne (1990). *Home and Work: Housework, Wages, and the Ideology of Labor in the Early Republic.* New York: Oxford University Press.

Bradley, Betsy Hunter (1999). *The Works: The Industrial Architecture of the United States.* New York: Oxford University Press.

Bradshaw, Michael (1988). *Regions and Regionalism in the United States.* Jackson: University Press of Mississippi.

Breeze, Carla (2003). *American Art Deco: Architecture and Regionalism.* New York: W. W. Norton.

Brewster, Paul G. (1953). *American Nonsinging Games.* Norman: University of Oklahoma Press.

Brooks, David (2005). "All Cultures Are Not Equal," *New York Times*, August 11: A23.

Brown, Allison (2001). "Counting Farmers Markets," *Geographical Review* 91: 655–74.

——— (2002). "Farmers' Market Research, 1940–2000: An Inventory and Review," *American Journal of Alternative Agriculture* 17(4): 167–76.

Brown, Christopher (2005). *Still Standing: A Century of Urban Train Station Design.* Bloomington: Indiana University Press.

Brown, D. Clayton (1980). *Electricity for Rural America: The Fight for REA.* Westport, Conn.: Greenwood Press.

Brown, Dona (1995). *Inventing New England: Regional Tourism in the Nineteenth Century.* Washington, D.C.: Smithsonian Institution Press.

Brown, Kenneth O. (1992). *Holy Ground: A Study of the American Camp Meeting.* New York: Garland.

Brown, Lawrence A., Tamar E. Mott, and Edward J. Malecki (2007). "Immigrant Profiles of U.S. Urban Areas and Agents of Resettlement," *Professional Geographer* 59: 56–73.

Brown, Linda Keller, and Kay Mussell, eds. (1984). *Ethnic and Regional Foodways in the United States: The Performance of Group Identity.* Knoxville: University of Tennessee Press.

Brown, Richard Maxwell (1983). "The New Regionalism in America, 1970–1981," pp. 37–96 in Robbins, Frank, and Ross 1983.

Brown, Stephen (2003). "No Then There: Of Time, Space, and the Market," pp. 1–16 in Brown and Sherry 2003.

Brown, Stephen, and John F. Sherry Jr., eds. (2003). *Time, Space, and the Market: Retroscapes Rising.* Armonk, N.Y.: M. E. Sharpe.

Brownell, Blaine A. (1990). "Introduction," pp. 1–6 in Mohl 1990.

Brownell, Joseph W. (1960). "The Cultural Midwest," *Journal of Geography* 39: 81–85.

Browning, Clyde E., and Will Gesler (1979). "The Sun Belt–Snow Belt: A Case of Sloppy Regionalizing," *Professional Geographer* 31: 66–74.

Brückner, Martin (2006). *The Geographic Revolution in Early America: Maps, Literacy & National Identity.* Chapel Hill: University of North Carolina Press.

Brunn, Stanley D. (1974). *Geography and Politics in America.* New York: Harper & Row.

Brunvand, Jan Harold (2001). *Encyclopedia of Urban Legends.* Santa Barbara: ABC-CLIO.

Brush, John E. (1953). "The Hierarchy of Central Places in Southwestern Wisconsin," *Geographical Review* 43: 380–402.

Brush, John E., and Howard E. Bracey (1955). "Rural Service Centers in Southwestern Wisconsin and Southern England," *Geographical Review* 45: 559–69.

Bryce, James (1995) [1914]. *The American Commonwealth.* Indianapolis: Liberty Fund.

Buckley, Peter G. (1993). "Popular Entertainment before the Civil War," vol. 3, pp. 1611–25 in Cayton, Gorn, and Williams 1993.

Budra, Paul (2000). "The Cilantro Cannot Hold: Postmodern Cuisine beyond the Golden Arches," pp. 231–44 in Thomas Carmichael and Alison Lee, eds., *Postmodern Times: A Critical Guide to the Contemporary.* DeKalb: Northern Illinois University Press.

Bullard, Loring (2004). *Healing Waters: Missouri's Historic Healing Springs and Spas.* Columbia: University of Missouri Press.

Burg, David F. (1976). *Chicago's White City of 1893.* Lexington: University of Kentucky Press.

Burke, Emily (1850). *Reminiscences of Georgia.* Oberlin, Ohio: Author.

Burnham, Philip (1995). *How the Other Half Lived: A People's Guide to American Historic Sites.* Boston: Faber and Faber.

Campbell, Neil (2000). *The Cultures of the American New West.* Edinburgh: Edinburgh University Press.

Canby, Henry Seidel (1936). *Alma Mater: The Gothic Age of the American College.* New York: Farrar & Rinehart.

Canning, Charlotte M. (2005). *The Most American Thing in America: Circuit Chautauqua as Performance.* Iowa City: University of Iowa Press.

Capitman, Barbara Baer (1988). *Deco Delights: Preserving the Beauty and Joy of Miami Beach Architecture.* New York: E. P. Dutton.

Carlson, Alvar W. (1978). "Designating Historic Rural Areas: A Survey of Northwestern Ohio Barns," *Landscape* 22(3): 29–34.

——— (1990). *The Spanish-American Homeland: Four Centuries in New Mexico's Rio Arriba*. Baltimore: Johns Hopkins University Press.

Carlton, David L. (1995). "How American Is the American South?" pp. 33–56 in Larry J. Griffin and Don H. Doyle, eds., *The South as an American Problem*. Athens: University of Georgia Press.

Carmichael, Barbara A. (1998). "Foxwoods Resort Casino, Connecticut—A Mega-attraction: Who Wants It? Who Benefits? pp. 67–75 in Meyer-Arendt and Hartmann 1998.

Carney, George O. (1974). "Bluegrass Grows All Around: Spatial Dimensions of a Country Music Style," *Journal of Geography* 73(4): 34–55.

——— (1982). "Birthplaces of Recorded Blues Performers, 1890–1920," p. 243 in Rooney, Zelinsky, and Louder 1982.

———, ed. (1994). *The Sound of People & Places: A Geography of American Folk and Popular Music*, 3rd ed. Lanham, Md.: Rowman & Littlefield.

——— (1996). "Western North Carolina: Culture Hearth of Bluegrass Music," *Journal of Cultural Geography* 16(1): 65–85.

Carpenter, Charles (1963). *History of American Schoolbooks*. Philadelphia: University of Pennsylvania Press.

Carringer, Robert (2001). "Hollywood's Los Angeles: Two Paradigms," pp. 247–66 in Charles G. Salas and Michael S. Roth, eds., *Looking for Los Angeles: Architecture, Film, Photography, and the Urban Landscape*. Los Angeles: Getty Publications.

Carver, Craig M. (1987). *American Regional Dialects: A Word Geography*. Ann Arbor: University of Michigan Press.

Carver, Martha (2006). "Get Right with God: Harrison Mayes's Roadside Advertising Campaign for the Lord," pp. 199–211 in Stager and Carver 2006.

Casey, Edward S. (1993). *Getting Back into Place: Toward a Renewed Understanding of the Place-World*. Bloomington: Indiana University Press.

——— (1997). *The Fate of Place: A Philosophical History*. Berkeley: University of California Press.

Cash, W. J. (1941). *The Mind of the South*. New York: Knopf.

Cassidy, Frederic, and Joan Houston Hall, eds. (1985–). *Dictionary of American Regional English*. 5 vols. Cambridge: Harvard University Press.

Caughey, John W. (1951). "The Spanish Southwest: An Example of Subconscious Regionalism," pp. 173–86 in M. Jensen 1951.

Cayton, Andrew (1998). "Commentary," pp. 63–70 in C. R. Wilson 1998b.

——— (2001). "The Anti-region: Place and Identity in the History of the American Midwest," pp. 140–59 in Cayton and Susan E. Gray, eds., *The American Midwest: Essays on Regional History*. Bloomington: Indiana University Press.

Cayton, Andrew, and Susan E. Gray (2001). "The Story of the Midwest: An Introduction," pp. 1–26 in Cayton and Gray, eds., *The American Midwest: Essays on Regional History*. Bloomington: Indiana University Press.

Cayton, Mary Kupiec, Elliott J. Gorn, and Peter W. Williams, eds. (1993). *Encyclopedia of American Social History*. New York: Charles Scribner's Sons.

Cayton, Mary Kupiec, and Peter W. Williams, eds. (2001). *Encyclopedia of American Cultural & Intellectual History*. New York: Charles Scribner's Sons.

Chambers, Thomas A. (2002). *Drinking the Waters: Creating an American Leisure Class at Nineteenth-Century Mineral Springs*. Washington, D.C.: Smithsonian Institution Press.

Chapa, Jorge, Rogelio Saenz, Refugio I. Rochín, and Eileen Diaz McConnell (2004). "Latinos and the Changing Demographic Fabric of the Rural Midwest," pp. 47–73 in Ann V. Millard and Chapa, eds., *Apple Pie & Enchiladas: Latino Newcomers in the Rural Midwest*. Austin: University of Texas Press.

Cherry, Colin (1977). "The Telephone System: Creator of Mobility and Social Change," pp. 112–26 in Ithiel de Sola Pool, ed., *The Social Impact of the Telephone*. Cambridge MIT Press.

Christaller, Walter (1933). *Die Zentralen Orte in Süddeutschland*. Jena: Gustav Fischer.

Chudacoff, Howard P. (2007). *Children at Play: An American History*. New York: New York University Press.

Clark, Christopher (1996). "The Consequences of the Market Revolution in the American North," pp. 23–42 in Melvyn Stokes and Stephen Conway, eds., *The Market Revolution in America: Social, Political, and Religious Expressions, 1800–1880*. Charlottesville: University Press of Virginia.

Claval, Paul (1998). *An Introduction to Regional Geography*. Oxford: Blackwell.

Clay, Grady (1978). *Alleys: A Hidden Resource*. Louisville: Grady Clay.

——— (1994). *Real Places: An Unconventional Guide to American Generic Landscapes*. Chicago: University of Chicago Press.

Cline, Lynn (2007). *Literary Pilgrims: The Santa Fe and Taos Writers' Colonies, 1917–1950*. Albuquerque: University of New Mexico Press.

Coats, Lauren, and Nihad M. Farooq (2003). "Regionalism in the Era of the New Deal," pp. 74–91 in Charles L. Crow, ed., *A Companion to the Regional Literatures of America*. Malden, Mass.: Blackwell.

Cobb, James C. (1982). "From Muskogee to Luckenbach: Country Music and the 'Southernization' of America," *Journal of Popular Culture* 16(3): 81–91.

——— (1992). *The Most Southern Place on Earth: The Mississippi Delta and the Roots of Regional Identity*. New York: Oxford University Press.

——— (2002). "An Epitaph for the North: Reflections on the Politics of Regional and National Identity at the Millennium," *Journal of Southern History* 66: 3–24.

——— (2005). *Away Down South: A History of Southern Identity*. New York: Oxford University Press.

Cockcroft, Eva, John Weber, and Jim Cockcroft (1977). *Toward a People's Art: The Contemporary Mural Movement*. New York: E. P. Dutton.

Cohen, Morris R. (1946). "Baseball as a National Religion," pp. 334–36 in *The Faith of a Liberal*. New York: Henry Holt.

Cohen, Patricia Cline (1982). *A Calculating People: The Spread of Numeracy in Early America*. Chicago: University of Chicago Press.

Cohen-Cruz, Jan (2005). *Local Acts: Community-Based Performance in the United States*. New Brunswick, N.J.: Rutgers University Press.

Coleman, Emily, and Betty Edwards (1977). *Body Liberation*. Los Angeles: J. P. Tacher.

Coleman, Laurence Vail, ed. (1932). *Handbook of American Museums*. Washington, D.C.: American Association of Museums.

Colten, Craig E. (2005). *An Unnatural Metropolis: Wresting New Orleans from Nature*. Baton Rouge: Louisiana State University Press.

Comeaux, Malcolm L. (2005). "What Games Can Say: Two Medieval Games from French Louisiana," *Louisiana History* 46(1): 47–63.

Confederation of American Indians (1986). *Indian Reservations: A State and Federal Handbook*. Jefferson, N.C.: McFarland.

Conforti, Joseph A. (2001). *Imagining New England: Explorations of Regional Identity from the Pilgrims to the Mid-Twentieth Century*. Chapel Hill: University of North Carolina Press.

Connell, John, and Chris Gibson (2003). *Sound Tracks: Popular Music, Identity and Place*. London: Routledge.

Conzen, Michael P. (2001). "American Homelands: A Dissenting View," pp. 238–71 in Nostrand and Estaville 2001.

Coolidge, John (1993). *Mill and Mansion: A Study of Architecture and Society in Lowell, Massachusetts, 1820–1865*, 2nd ed. Amherst: University of Massachusetts Press.

Cooper, Gail (1998). *Air-Conditioning America: Engineers and the Controlled Environment*. Baltimore: Johns Hopkins University Press.

Coopey, Richard, Sean O'Connell, and Dilwyn Porter (2005). *Mail Order Retailing in Britain: A Business and Social History*. Oxford: Oxford University Press.

Corbett, Theodore (2001). *The Making of American Resorts: Saratoga Springs, Ballston Spa, and Lake George*. New Brunswick, N.J.: Rutgers University Press.

Corn, Wanda M. (1983). *Grant Wood: The Regionalist Vision*. New Haven: Yale University Press.

Cott, Nancy F. (1997). *The Bonds of Womanhood: "Woman's Sphere" in New England, 1780–1835*, 2nd ed. New Haven: Yale University Press.

Cowan, Ruth Schwartz (1983). *More Work for Mother: The Ironies of Household Technology from the Open Hearth to the Microwave*. New York: Basic Books.

Cowen, Tyler (2003). *Creative Destruction: How Globalization Is Changing the World's Cultures*. Princeton: Princeton University Press.

Cox, James M. (1988). "Regionalism: A Diminished Thing," pp. 761–84 in Emory Elliott et al., eds., *Columbia Literary History of the United States*. New York: Columbia University Press.

Cox, Thomas R. (1988). *The Park Builders: A History of State Parks in the Pacific Northwest*. Seattle: University of Washington Press.

Craig, Lois (1984). *The Federal Presence: Architecture, Politics, and Symbols in United States Government Buildings*. Cambridge: MIT Press.

Craik, Jennifer (2005). *Uniforms Exposed: From Conformity to Transgression*. Oxford: Berg.

Crawford, James (1992). *Language Loyalties: A Source Book on the Official English Controversy*. Chicago: University of Chicago Press.

Crawford, Margaret (1992). "Earl S. Draper and the Company Town in the American South," pp. 139–72 in Garner 1992b.

——— (1995). *Building the Workingman's Paradise: The Design of American Company Towns*. London: Verso.

Crawford, Mark (1997). *Toxic Waste Sites: An Encyclopedia of Endangered America*. Santa Barbara: ABC-CLIO.

Crawford, Thomas W. (2005). "Stability and Change on the American Religious Landscape: A Centrographic Analysis of Major U.S. Religious Groups." *Journal of Cultural Geography* 22(2): 51–86.

Crawford, William Roy, Sr., Lela Ann Crawford, William Roy Crawford Jr., and J. J. Caddell, eds. (1999). *United States Military Road Atlas*. Falls Church, Va.: Military Living Publications.

Creese, Walter L. (1990). *TVA's Public Planning: The Vision, the Reality.* Knoxville: University of Tennessee Press.

Creswell, Tim (2002). "Introduction: Theorizing Place," pp. 11–31 in Ginette Verstraete and Creswell, eds., *Mobilizing Place, Placing Mobility: The Politics of Representation in a Globalized World.* Amsterdam: Rodopi.

——— (2004). *Place: A Short Introduction.* Malden, Mass.: Blackwell.

Cross, Gary D. (2006). Personal communication. March 30.

Cross, Gary D., and Rick Szostak (2005). *Technology and American Society: A History,* 2nd ed. Upper Saddle River, N.J.: Pearson Prentice Hall.

Cross, Gary D., and John K. Walton (2005). *The Playful Crowd: Pleasure Places in the Twentieth Century.* New York: Columbia University Press.

Crow, Charles L. (2003). "Introduction," pp. 1–14 in Crow, ed., *A Companion to the Regional Literatures of America.* Malden, Mass.: Blackwell.

Cuff, David J., Edward K. Muller, William J. Young, and Wilbur Zelinsky (1989). *The Atlas of Pennsylvania.* Philadelphia: Temple University Press.

Curti, Merle (1968). *The Roots of American Loyalty.* New York: Atheneum.

Curtis, James R. (1980). "Miami's Little Havana: Yard Shrines, Cult Religion and Landscape," pp. 105–19 in Ray Browne, ed., *Rituals and Ceremonies in Popular Culture.* Bowling Green, Ohio: Bowling Green University Popular Press.

——— (1982). "Art Deco Architecture in Miami Beach," *Journal of Cultural Geography* 3(1): 51–63.

Curtis, James R., and Richard F. Rose (1994). "'The Miami Sound': A Contemporary Latin Form of Place-Specific Music," pp. 163–73 in Carney 1994a.

Cutler, Phoebe (1985). *The Public Landscape of the New Deal.* New Haven: Yale University Press.

Czitrom, Daniel J. (1982). *Media and the American Mind: From Morse to McLuhan.* Chapel Hill: University of North Carolina Press.

Danilov, Victor (2005). *Sport Museums and Halls of Fame Worldwide.* Jefferson, N.C.: McFarland.

Datel, Robin Elizabeth (1990). "Southern Regionalism and Historic Preservation in Charleston, South Carolina, 1920–1940, "*Journal of Historical Geography* 16: 197–215.

Davidson, Donald (1938). *The Attack on Leviathan: Regionalism and Nationalism in the United States.* Chapel Hill: University of North Carolina Press.

Davidson, Randall (2006). *9XM Talking: WHA Radio and the Wisconsin Idea.* Madison: University of Wisconsin Press.

Davis, Fred (1979). *Yearning for Yesterday: A Sociology of Nostalgia.* New York: Free Press.

Davis, James A., and Samuel M. Otterstrom (1998). "Growth of Indian Gaming in the United States," pp. 53–66 in Klaus J. Meyer-Arendt and Rudi Hartmann, eds., *Casino Gambling in America: Origins, Trends, and Impacts.* New York: Cognizant.

Davis, Janet M. (2002). *The Circus Age: Culture & Society under the American Big Top.* Chapel Hill: University of North Carolina Press.

Davis, Mike (2000). *Magical Urbanism: Latinos Reinvent the US City.* London: Verso.

Degler, Carl N. (1977). *Place Over Time: The Continuity of Southern Distinctiveness.* Baton Rouge: Louisiana State University Press.

Deitrick, Sabina, Robert A Beauregard, and Cheryl Zarlenga Kerchis (1999). "Riverboat Gambling, Tourism, and Economic Development," pp. 215–44 in Judd and Fainstein 1999.

De León, Arnold (1997). "Region and Ethnicity: Topographical Identities in Texas," pp. 259–74 in Wrobel and Steiner 1997.

DeLony, Eric (1993). *Landmark American Bridges.* New York: American Society of Civil Engineering.

Delyser, Dydia (2003). "'Good, by God, We're Going to Brodie!' Ghost Towns and the American West," pp. 273–95 in Hausladen 2003b.

Dennis, James M. (1986). *Grant Wood: A Study in American Art and Culture.* Columbia: University of Missouri Press.

Derthick, Martha (1974). *Between State and Nation: Regional Organizations of the United States.* Washington, D.C.: Brookings Institution.

—— (2001). *Keeping the Compound Republic: Essays on American Federalism.* Washington, D.C.: Brookings Institution Press.

Detro, Randall A. (1982). "Language and Place Names," pp. 121–48 in Rooney, Zelinsky, and Louder 1982.

Deverell, William (1997). "Privileging the Mission over the Mexican: The Rise of Regional Identity in Southern California," pp. 235–56 in Wrobel and Steiner 1997.

Dewey, John (1920). "Americanism and Localism," *Dial* 68: 684–88.

D'haen, Theo, and Hans Bertens, eds. (1996). *"Writing" Nation and "Writing" Region in America.* Amsterdam: VU University Press.

Dicke, Thomas S. (1992). *Franchising in America: The Development of a Business Method, 1840–1980.* Chapel Hill: University of North Carolina Press.

Dickinson, Bob, and Andy Vladimir (1997). *Selling the Sea: An Inside Look at the Cruise Industry.* New York: John Wiley & Sons.

Dilsaver, Lary M. (2004). *Cumberland Island National Seashore: A History of Conservation Conflict;* Charlottesville: University of Virginia Press.

Dingemans, Dennis J. (1975). "The Urbanization of Suburbia: The Renaissance of the Row House," *Landscape* 20(1): 20–31.

Dixon, John Morris (1974). "Regionalism Lives," *Progressive Architecture* 55(3): 59.

Doan, Edward N. (1947). *The La Follettes and the Wisconsin Idea.* New York: Rinehart.

Doherty, Brian (2004). *This Is Burning Man: The Rise of a New American Underground.* New York: Little, Brown.

Donahue, Thomas S. (2006). "On the Eastern Edge of the Heartland: Two Industrial City Dialects," pp. 105–27 in Murray and Simon 2006b.

Donlon, Jocelyn Hazelwood (2001). *Swinging in Place: Porch Life in Southern Culture.* Chapel Hill: University of North Carolina Press.

Dorman, Robert L. (1998). *Revolt of the Provinces: The Regionalist Movement in America, 1920–1945.* Chapel Hill: University of North Carolina Press.

Doss, Erika Lee (1982). "Borrowing Regionalism: Advertising's Use of American Art in the 1930s and 40s," *Journal of American Culture* 5(4): 10–19.

—— (1984). *Regionalists in Hollywood: Painting, Film, and Patronage.* Ph.D. diss., University of Minnesota, Minneapolis.

Dostrovsky, Nadine, and Richard Harris (2008). "Style for the Zeitgeist: The Stealthy Revival of Historicist Housing since the Late 1960s," *Professional Geographer* 60: 314–32.

Douglas, Jack D., Paul K. Rasmussen, and Carol Ann Flanagan (1977). *The Nude Beach.* Beverly Hills, Calif.: Sage.

Douglas, Susan J. (2004). *Listening: Radio and the American Imagination*. Minneapolis: University of Minnesota Press.

Dow, Maynard Weston (1978). "The Impact of Communications Media upon Red Sox Fandom," *Proceedings of the New England–St. Lawrence Valley Geographical Society* 8: 11–22.

Dowd, Timothy, Kathleen Liddle, and Jenna Nelson (2004). "Music Festivals as Scenes: Examples from Serious Music, Womyn's Music, and SkatePunk," pp. 149–67 in Andy Bennett and Richard A. Peterson, eds., *Music Scenes: Local, Translocal, and Virtual*. Nashville: Vanderbilt University Press.

Downing, Andrew Jackson (1842). *Cottage Residences*. New York: Wiley & Putnam.

——— (1861). *The Architecture of Country Houses*. New York: D. Appleton.

Drescher, Timothy W. (1994). *San Francisco Murals: Community Creates Its Muse, 1919–1994*. Saint Paul: Pogo Press.

Dubinsky, Karen (1999). *The Second Greatest Disappointment: Honeymooning and Tourism at Niagara Falls*. New Brunswick, N.J.: Rutgers University Press.

Dunbar, Gary S. (1961). "The Popular Regions of Virginia," *University of Virginia Newsletter* 38(3): 10–12.

Duncan, Russell (2004). "Crossing Borders: Hispanic Atlanta, 1990–2004," pp. 237–55 in Duncan and Clara Juncker, eds., *Transnational America: Contours of Modern US Culture*. Copenhagen: Museum Tusculanum Press.

Durand, Jorge, Douglas S. Massey, and Chiara Capoferro (2005). "The New Geography of Mexican Immigration," pp. 1–20 in Victor Zuñiga and Rubén Hernández-Leon, eds., *New Destinations: Mexican Immigration in the United States*. New York: Russell Sage Foundation.

Durand, Loyal (1943). "Dairy Barns of Southeastern Wisconsin," *Economic Geography* 19: 37–44.

——— (1956). "Mountain Moonshining in East Tennessee," *Geographical Review* 46: 168–81.

Durlach, Hansi (1980). *The Short Season of Sharon Springs: Portrait of Another New York*. Ithaca: Cornell University Press.

Eadington, William R. (1998). "Casino Gaming – Origins, Trends, and Impacts," pp. 3–15 in Klaus J. Meyer-Arendt and Rudi Hartmann, eds., *Casino Gambling in America: Origins, Trends, and Impacts*. New York: Cognizant.

Easterlin, Richard A (1960). "Interregional Differences in Per Capita Income, Population, and Total Income, 1840–1950," pp. 73–140 in *Trends in the American Economy in the Nineteenth Century: A Report of the National Bureau of Economic Research, New York*. Princeton: Princeton University Press.

Eberhard, Wolfram (1965). *Conquerors and Rulers*. Leiden: Brill.

Edensor, Tim (2002). *National Identity, Popular Culture, and Everyday Life*. London: Berg.

Edwards, Brian (2005). *The Modern Airport Terminal: New Approaches to Airport Architecture*, 2nd ed. London: Spon Press.

Eells, Eleanor (1986). *Eleanor Eells' History of Organized Camping: The First 100 Years*. Martinsville, Ind.: American Camping Association.

Egerton, John (1974). *The Americanization of Dixie: The Southernization of America*. New York: Harper's Magazine Press.

Ehrich, Paul W., and Gerald M. Henderson (1968). "Culture Area," pp. 563–68 in David L. Sills, ed., *International Encyclopedia of the Social Sciences*, vol. 3. New York: Macmillan.

Elazar, Daniel J. (1966). *American Federalism: A View from the States*. New York: Harper & Row.

——— (1994). *The American Mosaic: The Impact of Space, Time and Culture on American Politics*. Boulder, Colo.: Westview Press.

Eldridge, Hope T., and Dorothy Swaine Thomas (1964). *Population Redistribution and Economic Growth, United States, 1870–1950. III. Demographic Analysis and Interrelations*. Philadelphia: American Philosophical Society.

Elias, Amy J. (2002). "Postmodern Southern Vacation: Vacation Advertising, Globalization, and Southern Regionalism," pp. 253–82 in Jones and Monteith 2002.

Elson, Ruth Miller (1964). *Guardians of Tradition: American Schoolbooks of the Nineteenth Century*. Lincoln: University of Nebraska Press.

Elting, John R. (1974). *Military Uniforms in America: The Era of the American Revolution*. San Rafael, Calif.: Presidio Press.

Elting, John R., and Michael J. McAfee (1982). *Military Uniforms in America*, vol 3: *Long Endure: The Civil War Period, 1852–1867*. Novato, Calif.: Presidio Press.

Emerson, William K. (1996). *Encyclopedia of United States Army Insignia and Uniforms*. Norman: University of Oklahoma Press.

Emmet, Boris, and John E. Jeuck (1950). *Catalogues and Counters: A History of Sears, Roebuck and Company*. Chicago: University of Chicago Press.

Engler, Mira (2004). *Designing America's Waste Landscapes*. Baltimore: Johns Hopkins University Press.

Enriquez, Juan (2005). *The Untied States of America: Polarization, Fracturing, and Our Future*. New York: Crown.

Ensminger, Robert F. (1992). *The Pennsylvania Barn: Its Origin, Evolution, and Distribution in North America*. Baltimore: Johns Hopkins University Press.

Entrikin, J. Nicholas (1996). "Place and Region 2," *Progress in Human Geography* 20: 215–21.

Epstein, Rachel (1996). *Mailbox U.S.A.: Stories of Mailbox Owners and Makers: A Celebration of Mailbox Art in America*. Salt Lake City: Gibbs Smith.

Estaville, Lawrence E. (2001). "*Nouvelle Acadie*: The Cajun Homeland," pp. 83–100 in Nostrand and Estaville 2001.

Everett, Holly J. (2002). *Roadside Crosses in Contemporary Memorial Culture*. Denison: University of North Texas Press.

Evers, Alf, Elizabeth Cromley, Betsy Blackman, and Neil Harris (1979). *Resorts of the Catskills*. New York: St. Martin's Press.

Evinger, William R. (1998). *Directory of U.S. Military Bases Worldwide*, 3rd ed. Phoenix: Oryx Press.

Ewen, Stuart (2001). *Captains of Consciousness: Advertising and the Social Roots of the Consumer Culture*. New York: Basic Books.

Eysberg, E. D. (1996). "Regionalism in North America," pp. 21–34 in D'haen and Bertens 1996.

Fairfax, Geoffery W. (1971). *The Architecture of Honolulu*. Sydney: Island Heritage Ltd.

Faust, Drew Gilpin (1988). *The Creation of Confederate Nationalism: Ideology and Identity in the Civil War South*. Baton Rouge: Louisiana State University Press.

Feffer, John (2008). "Global Tastes," pp. 186–96 in John Knechtel, ed., *Food*. Cambridge: MIT Press.

Fernald, Anya, Serena Milano, and Piero Sarelo (2004). *A World of Presidia: Food, Culture & Community*. Bra, Italy: Slow Food Editore.

Ferris, William R. (1979). *Blues from the Delta: An Illustrated Documentary on the Music and Musicians of the Mississippi Delta*. New York: Anchor Books.

—— (1982). *Local Color: A Sense of Place in Folk Art*. New York: McGraw-Hill.

Findlay, John M. (1992). *Magic Lands: Western Cityscapes and American Culture after 1940*. Berkeley: University of California Press.

—— (1997). "A Fishy Proposition: Regional Identity in the Pacific Northwest," pp. 37–70 in Wrobel and Steiner 1997.

Fine, David (1995). "Introduction," pp. 1–26 in Fine, ed., *Los Angeles in Fiction*, rev. ed. Albuquerque: University of New Mexico Press.

—— (2003). "Los Angeles as a Literary Region," pp. 397–411 in Charles L. Crow, ed., *A Companion to the Regional Literatures of America*. Malden, Mass.: Blackwell.

Fine, David, and Paul Skenazy, eds. (1995). *San Francisco in Fiction: Essays in a Regional Literature*. Albuquerque: University of New Mexico Press.

Finley, Robert, and E. M. Scott (1940). "A Great Lakes-to-Gulf Profile of Dispersed Dwelling Types," *Geographical Review* 30: 412–19.

Fiorina, Morris P. (2006). *Culture War? The Myth of a Polarized America*. New York: Pearson.

Fischer, Claude S. (1992). *America Calling: A Social History of the Telephone to 1940*. Berkeley: University of California Press.

Fischer, Claude S., and C. Ann Stueve (1977). "'Authentic Community': The Role of Place in Modern Life," pp. 163–86 in Fischer, ed., *Networks and Places: Social Relations in the Urban Setting*. New York: Free Press.

Fischer, David Hackett (1989). *Albion's Seed: Four British Folkways in America*. New York: Oxford University Press.

Fischer, Louis A. (1925). *History of the Standard Weights and Measures of the United States*. Miscellaneous Publication, Bureau of Standards, no. 64. Washington, D.C.: GPO.

Fisher, Peter (2004). "Experiencing Climate: Architecture and Environmental Diversity," pp. 217–31 in Koen Steemers and Mary Ann Steane, eds., *Environmental Diversity in Architecture*. New York: Spon Press.

Fishwick, Marshall (1968). "What Ever Happened to Regionalism?" *Southern Humanities Review* 2: 393–401.

—— (1978). *The World of Ronald McDonald*. Bowling Green, Ohio: Bowling Green University Popular Press.

Fite, Gilbert C. (1952). *Mount Rushmore*. Norman: University of Oklahoma Press.

FitzGerald, Frances (1979). *America Revised: History Schoolbooks in the Twentieth Century*. Boston: Little, Brown.

—— (1986). *Cities on a Hill: A Journey through Contemporary American Cultures*. New York: Simon & Schuster.

Flack, Wes (1997). "American Microbreweries and Neolocalism: 'Ale-ing' for a Sense of Place," *Journal of Cultural Geography* 16(2): 37–54.

Flanagan, Hallie (1940). *Arena: The History of the Federal Theatre*. New York: Benjamin Blom.

Florida, Richard (2002). "The Economic Geography of Talent," *Annals of the Association of American Geographers* 92: 743–55.

—— (2005). *Cities and the Creative Class*. New York: Routledge.

—— (2008). *Who's Your City? How the Creative Economy Is Making Where You Live the Most Important Decision of Your Life*. New York: Basic Books.

Florin, Lambert (1971). *Ghost Towns of the West*. New York: Promontory Press.

Fogarty, Robert S. (1990). *All Things New: American Communes and Utopian Movements, 1860–1914*. Chicago: University of Chicago Press.

Foglesong, Richard (1999). "Walt Disney World and Orlando: Deregulation as a Strategy for Tourism," pp. 89–116 in Judd and Fainstein 1999.

Ford, Larry (1971). "Geographic Factors in the Origin, Evolution, and Diffusion of Rock and Roll Music," *Journal of Geography* 70: 455–64.

Forman, Murray (2002). *The "Hood" Comes First: Race, Space, and Place in Rap and Hip-hop*. Middletown, Conn.: Wesleyan University Press.

Francaviglia, Richard V. (1971). "The Cemetery as an Evolving Cultural Landscape," *Annals of the Association of American Geographers* 61: 501–9.

—— (1972). "Western American Barns: Architectural Form and Climatic Considerations," *Yearbook of the Association of Pacific Coast Geographers* 32: 153–60.

—— (1978). *The Mormon Landscape: Existence, Creation, and Perception of a Unique Image in the American West*. New York: AMS.

—— (1991). *Hard Places: Reading the Landscape of America's Historic Mining Districts*. Iowa City: University of Iowa Press.

—— (1996). *Main Street Revisited: Time, Space, and Image Building in Small-Town America*. Iowa City: University of Iowa Press.

—— (2000). "Selling Heritage Landscapes," pp. 44–69 in Arnold R. Alanen and Robert Z. Melnick, eds., *Preserving Cultural Landscapes in American*. Baltimore: Johns Hopkins University Press.

Franklin, Wayne (2007). *James Fenimore Cooper: The Early Years*. New Haven: Yale University Press.

Frantz, Douglas, and Catherine Collins (1999). *Celebration, U.S.A.: Living in Disney's Brave New Town*. New York: Henry Holt.

Frantz, Klaus (1999). *Indian Reservations in the United States: Territory, Sovereignty, and Socioeconomic Change*. Chicago: University of Chicago Press.

Frazer, Timothy (2006), "Midland(s) Dialect Geography: Social and Demographic Variables," pp. 199–207 in Murray and Simon 2006b.

Fredericksson, Kristine (1985). *American Rodeo: From Buffalo Bill to Big Business*. College Station: Texas A&M University Press.

Frenkel, Stephen, and Judy Walton (2000). "Bavarian Leavenworth and the Symbolic Economy of a Theme Town," *Geographical Review* 90: 559–84.

Frey, William H., and Kao-Lee Liaw (1999). "Internal Migration of Foreign-born Latinos and Asians: Are They Assimilating Geographically?" pp. 212–30 in Kavita Pandit and Suzanne Davies Withers, eds., *Migrations and Restructuring in the United States: A Geographic Perspective*. Lanham, Md.: Rowman & Littlefield.

Friedlander, Amy (1996). *"In God We Trust"; All Others Pay Cash: Banking as an American Infrastructure, 1800–1935*. Reston, Va.: Corporation for National Research Initiatives.

Friedmann, John, and Clyde Weaver (1979). *Territory and Function: The Evolution of Regional Planning*. London: Edward Arnold.

Fuller, Katherine (2006). "Myrtle Beach: Music and Motels," pp. 153–65 in Claudette Stager and Martha Carver, eds., *Looking beyond the Highway: Dixie Roads and Culture*. Knoxville: University of Tennessee Press.

Fuller, Wayne E. (1964). *RFD: The Changing Face of Rural America*. Bloomington: Indian University Press.

——— (1972). *The American Mail: Enlarger of the Common Life*. Chicago: University of Chicago Press.

Funnell, Charles (1975). *By the Beautiful Sea: The Rise and High Times of That Great American Resort, Atlantic City*. New York: Knopf.

Fussell, Paul (2002). *Uniforms: Why We Are What We Wear*. Boston: Houghton Mifflin.

Gaines, Donna (1994). "The Local Economy of Suburban Scenes," pp. 47–65 in Jonathon S. Epstein, ed., *Adolescents and Their Music: If It's Too Loud, You're Too Old*. New York: Garland.

Gard, Robert (1955). *Grassroots Theater: A Search for Regional Arts in America*. Madison: University of Wisconsin Press.

Gardner, Charles (1982). "Anglo-French-American Fiddling Styles," p. 239 in Rooney, Zelinsky, and Louder 1982.

Garland, Hamlin (1960) [1894]. *Crumbling Idols*. Cambridge: Harvard University Press.

Garner, John S. (1992a). "Introduction." pp. 3–14 in Garner 1992b.

———, ed. (1992b). *The Company Town: Architecture and Society in the Early Industrial Age*. New York: Oxford University Press.

Garreau, Joel (1981). *The Nine Nations of North America*. Boston: Houghton Mifflin.

Garwood, Alfred N. (1988). *Regional Differences in America: A Statistical Sourcebook*. Seattle: Numbers & Concepts.

Gary, Don L. (1973). *A Geographic Systems Analysis of the Commercial Crawfish Industry in South Louisiana*. Ph.D diss., Oregon State University.

Gastil, Raymond D. (1971). "Homicide and a Regional Culture of Violence," *American Sociological Review* 36: 412–27.

——— (1974). "The Pacific Northwest as a Cultural Region," *Pacific Northwest Quarterly* 64: 147–56.

——— (1975). *Cultural Regions of the United States*. Seattle: University of Washington Press.

Gaustad, Edwin Scott, and Philip L. Barlow (2001). *New Historical Atlas of Religion in America*. New York: Oxford University Press.

Gebhard, David (1990). "The Myth and Power of Place: Hispanic Revivalism in the American Southwest," pp. 143–58 in Markovich, Preiser, and Sturm 1990.

Geffen, Alice M., and Carole Berglie (1986). *Food Festival: The Ultimate Guidebook to America's Best Regional Food Celebrations*. New York: Pantheon.

Gellner, Arrol, and Douglas Keister (2002). *Ready to Roll: A Celebration of the Classic American Travel Trailer*. New York: Penguin.

George-Warren, Holly, and Michelle Freedman (2001). *How the West Was Worn*. New York: Harry N. Abrams.

Gerbasi, Gina T. (2006). "Athens' Farmers' Market: Evolving Dynamics and Hidden Benefits to a Southeast Ohio Rural Community," *Focus* 49(2): 1–6.

Gerlach, Jerry, and James Janke (2001). "The Mall of America as a Tourist Attraction," *Focus* 46(3): 32–36.

Gerson, Kathleen, C. Ann Stueve, and Claude S. Fischer (1977). "Attachment to Place," pp. 139–61 in Fischer, ed., *Networks and Places: Social Relations in the Urban Setting*. New York: Free Press.

Getis, Arthur (2007). Personal communication. December 7.

Gilbert, Anne (1988). "The New Regional Geography in English and French-Speaking Countries," *Progress in Human Geography* 12: 208–28.

Gill, Brendan (1990). *Money Matters: A Critical Look at Bank Architecture*, pp. 1–6. New York: McGraw-Hill.

Gilmore, Lee, and Mark Van Proyen, eds. (2005). *AfterBurn: Reflections on Burning Man*. Albuquerque: University of New Mexico Press.

Gilmore, Ruth Wilson (2007). *Golden Gulag: Prisons, Surplus, Crisis and Opposition in Globalizing California*. Berkeley: University of California Press.

Gilmore-Lehne, William J. (1993). "Literacy," vol. 3, pp. 2413–26 in Cayton, Gorn, and Williams 1993.

Glasmeier, Amy (2003). *An Atlas of Poverty in America: One Nation Pulling Apart*. New York: Routledge.

Glass, Joseph W. (1986). *The Pennsylvania Culture Region: A View from the Barn*. Ann Arbor: UMI Research Press.

Glassie, Henry (1968). *Pattern in the Material Culture of the Eastern United States*. Philadelphia: University of Pennsylvania Press.

Glenn, Norval D. (1967). "Massification versus Differentiation: Some Trend Data from National Surveys," *Social Forces* 46: 172–80.

Glenn, Norval D., and J. L. Simmons (1967). "Are Regional Cultural Differences Diminishing?" *Public Opinion Quarterly* 31(2): 176–93.

Goff, Leslie (1993). *On Cloud Nine: Writers' Colonies, Retreats, Ranches, Residences, and Sanctuaries*. New York: Poets & Writers, Inc.

Gohlke, Frank (1992). *Measures of Emptiness: Grain Elevators in the American Landscape*. Baltimore: Johns Hopkins University Press.

Goldberg, Michelle (2006). *Kingdom Coming: The Rise of Christian Nationalism*. New York: W. W. Norton.

Goldberger, Paul. (1981). *The Skyscraper*. New York: Knopf.

Golden, Jane, Robin Rice, and Monica Yant Kinney (2002). *Philadelphia Murals and the Stories They Tell*. Philadelphia: Temple University Press.

Goodacre, Beth, and Gavin Baldwin (2002). *Living the Past: Reconstruction, Recreation, Re-enactment and Education at Museums and Historical Sites*. London: Middlesex University Press.

Goodall, Brian (1987). *The Penguin Dictionary of Human Geography*. New York: Viking Penguin.

Goodman, Douglas J. (2007). "Globalization and Consumer Culture," pp. 330–51 in George Ritzer, ed., *The Blackwell Companion to Globalization*. Malden, Mass.: Blackwell.

Goodsell, Charles T. (2001). *The American Statehouse: Interpreting Democracy's Temples*. Lawrence: University Press of Kansas.

Goodstein, Elizabeth S. (2005). *Experience without Qualities: Boredom and Modernity*. Stanford: Stanford University Press.

Goodstein, Ethel S. (1990). "Georgia O'Keeffe's New Mexico: The Artist's Vision of the Land and Its Architecture," pp. 225–36 in Markovich, Preiser, and Sturm 1990.

Gordon, Alastair (2004). *Naked Airport: A Cultural History of the World's Most Revolutionary Structure*. New York: Henry Holt.

Goss, Jon (1999). "Once-Upon-a-Time in the Commodity World: An Unofficial Guide to Mall of America," *Annals of the Association of American Geographers* 89: 45–75.

Gottdiener, Mark (2001). *The Theming of America: American Dreams, Media Fantasies, and Themed Environments*, 2nd ed. Boulder, Colo.: Westview Press.

Gottdiener, Mark, Claudia C. Collins, and David R. Dickens (1999). *Las Vegas: The Social Production of an All-American City*. Malden, Mass.: Blackwell.

Gowans, Alan (1986). *The Comfortable House: North American Suburban Architecture, 1890–1930*. Cambridge: MIT Press.

Goździak, Elżbieta, and Susan F. Martin, eds. (2005). *Beyond the Gateway: Immigrants in a Changing America*. Lanham, Md.: Lexington Books.

*Grain Elevators of North America*, 5th ed. (1942). Chicago: Grain & Feed Journals.

Grant, John, and Ray Jones (1998). *Legendary Lighthouses*. Old Saybrook, Conn.: Globe Pequot Press.

Grantham, Dewey W. (1994). *The South in Modern America: A Region at Odds*. New York: HarperCollins.

Gray, Richard (1986). *Writing the South: Ideas of an American Region*. Cambridge: Cambridge University Press.

——— (2000). *Southern Aberrations: Writers of the American South and the Problems of Regionalism*. Baton Rouge: Louisiana State University Press.

Greenfield, Beth (2006). "Gay Getaways: The New Wave," *New York Times*, July 14: D1, D12.

Grella, George (2003). "The Hall of Fame and the American Mythology," pp. 151–60 in Edward J. Reilly, ed., *Baseball and American Culture*. New York: Haworth Press.

Griebel, Helen Bradley (1995). "The West African Origin of the African-American Headwrap," pp. 207–26 in Joanne B. Eicher, ed., *Dress and Ethnicity: Change across Space and Time*. Oxford: Berg.

Griffin, Larry J., and Ashley B. Thompson (2003). "Enough about the Disappearing South. What about the Disappearing Southerner?" *Southern Cultures* 9: 51–65.

Griswold, Wendy (2008). *Regionalism and the Reading Class*. Chicago: University of Chicago Press.

Grob, Gerald N. (1973). *Mental Institutions in America: Social Policy to 1875*. New York: Free Press.

Gudis, Catherine (2004). *Buyways: Billboards, Automobiles, and the American Landscape*. New York: Routledge.

Guedon, Mary Scholz (1987). *Regionalist Art: Thomas Hart Benton, John Steuart Curry, and Grant Wood: A Guide to the Literature*. Metuchen, N.J.: Scarecrow Press.

Gumprecht, Blake (1998). "Lubbock on Everything: The Evocation of Place in Popular Music." *Journal of Popular Culture* 18(1): 61–82.

——— (2003a). "The American College Town," *Geographical Review* 93: 51–80.

——— (2003b). "Stadium Culture: College Athletics and the Making of Place in the American College Town," *Southeastern Geographer* 43(1): 28–53.

——— (2006). "Fraternity Row, the Student Ghetto, and the Faculty Enclave: Characteristic Residential Districts in the American College Town," *Journal of Urban History* 32(2): 231–73.

——— (2008). *The American College Town*. Amherst: University of Massachusetts Press.

Gustafson, Per (2006). "Place Attachment and Mobility," pp. 17–31 in McIntyre, Williams, and McHugh 2006.

Gutman, Richard J. S. (2000). *American Diner, Then and Now*. Baltimore: Johns Hopkins University Press.

Haas, Irvin (1974). *America's Historic Villages and Restorations.* New York: Arco.
———(1976). *Historic Homes of American Presidents.* New York: David McKay.
——— (1979). *Citadels, Ramparts, and Stockades: America's Historic Forts.* New York: Everest House.
Hackney, Sheldon (1969). "Southern Violence," pp. 505–27 in Hugh Davis Graham and Ted Robert Gurr, eds., *The History of Violence in America.* New York: Bantam.
Haehnle, Brigitte (2005). "Cascadia: A 'Region' in the Pacific Northwest," pp. 225–36 in Hönnighausen, Ortlepp, Peacock, and Steiner 2005.
Haines, Michael R. (2002). *Ethnic Differences in Demographic Behavior in the United States: Has There Been Convergence?* Working Paper 9042. Cambridge: National Bureau of Economic Research.
Hale, Ruth Feser (1971). *A Map of Vernacular Regions in America.* Ph.D. diss., University of Minnesota, Minneapolis.
——— (1984). "Vernacular Regions of America," *Journal of Cultural Geography* 5(1): 131–40.
Halttunen, Karen (2006). "Groundwork: American Studies in Place," *American Quarterly* 58(1): 1–15.
*The Handbook of Private Schools,* 86th ed. (2005). Boston: Porter Sargent Publishers.
Harker, Michael P. (2008). *Harker's One-Room Schoolhouses: Visions of an Iowa Icon.* Iowa City: University of Iowa Press.
Harmon, John E. (1985). "Bowling Regions of North America," *Journal of Cultural Geography* 6(1): 109–24.
Harper, Glenn A., and Steve Gordon (1995). "The Modern Midwestern Barn, 1900–Present," pp. 213–36 in Allen G. Noble and Hubert G. H. Wilhelm, eds., *Barns of the Midwest.* Athens: Ohio University Press.
Harris, Neil (1983). "John Philip Sousa and the Culture of Reassurance," pp. 11–40 in John Newsome, ed., *Perspectives on John Philip Sousa.* Washington, D.C.: Library of Congress.
Harrison, Blake (2006). *The View from Vermont: Tourism and the Making of an American Rural Landscape.* Burlington: University of Vermont Press.
Hart, J. Fraser (1968). "Field Patterns in Indiana," *Geographical Review* 58: 450–71.
——— (1972). "The Middle West," pp. 258–82 in Hart, ed., *Regions of the United States.* New York: Harper & Row.
Hart, J. Fraser, and E. C. Mather (1961). "The Character of Tobacco Barns and Their Role in the Tobacco Economy of the United States," *Annals of the Association of American Geographers* 51: 274–93.
Hart, J. Fraser, Michelle J. Rhodes, and John T. Morgan (2002). *The Unknown World of The Mobile Home.* Baltimore: Johns Hopkins University Press.
Hart, Susannah, and John Murphy, eds. (1998). *Brands: The New Wealth Creators.* New York: New York University Press.
Harvey, David (1996). *Justice, Nature, and the Geography of Difference.* Cambridge, Mass.: Blackwell.
Harvey, Thomas W. (1981). "Mail-Order Architecture in the Twenties," *Landscape* 25(3): 1–9.
——— (1982). *The Making of Railroad Towns in Minnesota's Red River Valley.* M.A. thesis, Pennsylvania State University.
——— (1983). "Railroad Towns: Urban Forms on the Prairie," *Landscape* 27(3): 26–34.

Hausladen, Gary J. (2003a). "Introduction," pp. 1–18 in Hausladen 2003b.

———, ed. (2003b). *Western Places, American Myths: How We Think about the West.* Reno: University of Nevada Press.

Haverluk, Terrence W. (2003). "Mex-America: From Margin to Mainstream," pp. 166–83 in Hausladen 2003b.

——— (2004). "Hispanization of Hereford, Texas," pp. 277–91 in Daniel D. Arreola, ed., *Hispanic Spaces, Latino Places: Community and Cultural Diversity in Contemporary America.* Austin: University of Texas Press.

Hazlehurst, J. N. (1901). *Towers and Tanks for Waterworks: The Theory and Practice of Their Design and Construction.* New York: John Wiley & Sons.

Heatwole, Charles A. (1978). "The Bible Belt: A Problem in Regional Definition," *Journal of Geography* 77: 50–56.

Hecht, Melvin E. (1975). "The Decline of the Grass Lawn Tradition in Tucson," *Landscape* 19(3): 3–10.

Henretta, James A. (1991). *The Origins of American Capitalism: Collected Essays.* Boston: Northeastern University Press.

Herbst, John A. (1989). "Historic Houses," pp. 98–114 in Leon and Rosenzweig 1989.

Hershberg, Theodore, Alan N. Burstein, Eugene P. Erickson, Stephanie W. Greenberg, and William L. Yancey (1981). "A Tale of Three Cities: Blacks, Immigrants, and Opportunity in Philadelphia, 1850–1880, 1930, 1970," pp. 460–91 in Hershberg, ed., *Philadelphia: Work, Space, Family, and Group Experience in the Nineteenth Century.* New York: Oxford University Press.

Hesseltine, William B. (1960). "Sectionalism and Regionalism in American History," *Journal of Southern History* 26: 25–34.

Hill, Samuel S. (1985). "Religion and Region in America," *Annals of the American Academy of Political and Social Science* 480: 132–41.

Hilliard, Robert L., and Michael C. Keith (2005). *The Quieted Voice: The Rise and Demise of Localism in American Radio.* Carbondale: Southern Illinois University Press.

Hilliard, Sam Bowers (1972). *Hog Meat and Hoecake: Food Supply in the Old South.* Carbondale: Southern Illinois University Press.

Hilton, George W., and John F. Due (1960). *The Electric Interurban Railways in America.* Stanford: Stanford University Press.

Hintze, Hedwig (1934). "Regionalism," *Encyclopedia of the Social Science,* vol. 13, 208–18. New York: Macmillan.

Hirsch, Paul M. (1978). "Television as a National Medium," pp. 389–427 in David Street and Associates, *Handbook of Contemporary Urban Life.* San Francisco: Jossey-Bass.

Hirshorn, Paul, and Steven Izenour (1979). *White Towers.* Cambridge: MIT Press.

Hoelscher, Steven D. (1998). *Heritage on Stage: The Invention of Ethnic Place in America's Little Switzerland.* Madison: University of Wisconsin Press.

——— (2005). "Memory, Heritage, and Tradition in the Construction of Regional Identity: A View from Geography," pp. 27–45 in Hönnighausen, Frey, Peacock, and Steiner 2005.

Holland, Francis Ross, Jr. (1981). *America's Lighthouses: An Illustrated History.* Brattleboro, Vt.: Stephen Greene Press.

Holman, David Marion (1995). *A Certain Slant of Light: Regionalism and the Form of Southern and Midwestern Fiction.* Baton Rouge: Louisiana State University Press.

Holt, Dean W. (1992). *American Military Cemeteries: A Comprehensive Illustrated Guide to the Hallowed Grounds of the United States, including Cemeteries Overseas.* Jefferson, N.C.: McFarland.

Hönnighausen, Lothar (1996). "The Old and the New Regionalism," pp. 3–20 in D'haen and Bertens 1996.

——— (2005a). "Introduction: Concepts of Regionalism," pp. xiii–xvii in Hönnighausen, Frey, Peacock, and Steiner 2005.

——— (2005b). "Defining Regionalism in North American Studies," pp. 159–84 in Hönnighausen, Frey, Peacock, and Steiner 2005.

Hönnighausen, Lothar, Marc Frey, James Peacock, and Niklaus Steiner, eds. (2005). *Concepts of Regionalism,* vol. 1 of *Regionalism in the Age of Globalism.* Madison, Wisc.: Center for the Study of Upper Midwestern Cultures.

Hönnighausen, Lothar, Anke Ortlepp, James Peacock, and Niklaus Steiner, eds. (2005). *Forms of Regionalism,* vol. 2 of *Regionalism in the Age of Globalism.* Madison, Wisc.: Center for the Study of Upper Midwestern Cultures.

Hopkins, Jerry, Baron Wolman, and Jim Marshall (1970). *Festival! The Book of American Music Celebrations.* New York: Macmillan.

Horwitz, Tony (1998). *Confederates in the Attic: Dispatches from the Unfinished Civil War.* New York: Pantheon.

Hoyt, Charles King (1980). *Public, Municipal, and Community Buildings.* New York: McGraw-Hill.

Hubka, Thomas C. (2004). *Big House, Little House, Back House, Barn: The Connected Farm Buildings of New England.* Hanover, N.H.: University Press of New England.

Hudson, John C. (1984). "Cultural Geography and the Upper Great Lakes Region," *Journal of Cultural Geography* 5: 19–32.

——— (1985). *Plains Country Towns.* Minneapolis: University of Minnesota Press.

Huebner, Jeff (2001). *Murals: The Great Walls of Joliet.* Urbana: University of Illinois Press.

Hufbauer, Benjamin (2005). *Presidential Temples: How Memorials and Libraries Shape Public Memory.* Lawrence: University Press of Kansas.

Hufford, Mary (2005). "Ramp Suppers, Biodiversity, and the Integrity of the Mountains," pp. 108–16 in Ronni Lundy, ed., *Cornbread Nation 3: Foods of the Mountain South.* Chapel Hill: University of North Carolina Press.

Hugill, Peter J. (1999). *Global Communication since 1844: Geopolitics and Technology.* Baltimore: Johns Hopkins University Press.

Hummon, David M. (1992). "Community Attachment: Local Sentiment and Sense of Place," pp. 253–78 in Irwin Altman and Setha M. Low, eds., *Place Attachment.* New York: Plenum Press.

Hunner, Jon (2004). *Inventing Los Alamos: The Growth of an Atomic Community.* Norman: University of Okalahoma Press.

Huxtable, Ada Louise (1984). *The Tall Building Artistically Reconsidered: The Search for a Skyscraper Style.* New York: Pantheon.

Hynes, H. Patricia (1996). *A Patch of Eden: America's Inner-City Gardens.* White River Junction, Vt.: Chelsea Green.

Igo, Sarah E. (2007). *The Averaged American: Surveys, Citizens, and the Making of a Mass Public.* Cambridge: Harvard University Press.

Ilfeld, Fred, Jr., and Roger Lauer (1964). *Social Nudism in America.* New Haven: College and University Press.

Inglehart, Ronald, and Christian Welzel (2005). *Modernization, Cultural Change, and Democracy.* Cambridge: Cambridge University Press.

Ingram, E. W., Sr. (1964). *All This from a 5-Cent Hamburger! The Story of the White Castle System.* New York: Newcomen Society.

Irvine, Chippy (1990). *Second Homes.* New York: Bantam.

Iyer, Pico (2000). *The Global Soul: Jet Lag, Shopping Malls, and the Search for Home.* New York: Knopf:

Jackson, Donald C. (1988). *Great American Bridges and Dams.* Washington, D.C.: Preservation Press.

Jackson, John Brinckerhoff (1972). *American Space: The Centennial Years, 1865–1876.* New York: W. W. Norton.

—— (1979). "The Order of a Landscape: Reason and Religion in Newtonian America," pp. 153–63 in D. W. Meinig, ed., *The Interpretation of Ordinary Landscapes: Geographical Essays.* New York: Oxford University Press.

Jackson, Kenneth T., and Camilo José Vergara (1990). *Silent Cities: The Evolution of the American Cemetery.* Princeton: Princeton Architectural Press.

Jackson, Richard H. (1978). "Religion and Landscape in the Mormon Cultural Region," pp. 100–127 in Karl W. Butzer, ed., *Dimensions of Human Geography.* Research Paper 186. Chicago: University of Chicago, Department of Geography.

—— (2003). "Mormon Wests: The Creation and Evolution of an American Region," pp. 135–65 in Hausladen 2003b.

Jackson, Richard H., and Lloyd Hudman (1987). "Border Towns, Gambling and the Mormon Culture Region," *Journal of Cultural Geography* 8(1): 35–48.

Jackson, Richard H., and Robert L. Layton (1976). "The Mormon Village: Analysis of a Settlement Type," *Professional Geographer* 28: 136–41.

Jacobs, Michael (1985). *The Good and Simple Life: Artist Colonies in Europe and America.* Oxford: Phaidon.

Jacobs, Norman (1992) [1959]. *Mass Media in Modern Society.* New Brunswick, N.J.: Transaction.

Jacobson, Joanne (1991). "The Idea of the Midwest," *Revue Française d'Études Americaines* 48–49: 235–45.

Jakle, John A. (2001). *City Lights: Illuminating the American Night.* Baltimore: Johns Hopkins University Press.

—— (2004). *Signs in America's Auto Age: Signatures of Landscape and Place.* Iowa City: University of Iowa Press.

Jakle, John A., and Keith A. Sculle (1999). *Fast Food: Roadside Restaurants in the Automobile Age.* Baltimore: Johns Hopkins University Press.

Jakle, John A., Keith A. Sculle, and Jefferson S. Rogers (1996). *The Motel in America.* Baltimore: Johns Hopkins University Press.

Janiskee, Robert L. (1994). "Some Macroscale Growth Trends in America's Community Festival Industry," *Festival Management & Event Tourism* 1: 1–5.

—— (1996a). "The Temporal Distribution of America's Community Festivals," *Festival Management & Event Tourism* 3: 129–37.

—— (1996b). "Oktoberfest, American Style," *Festival Management & Event Tourism* 3: 197–99.

Janke, James, and Jerry Gerlach (2002). "Native American Casino Gambling in Wisconsin and Minnesota," *Focus* 47(2): 14–20.

Jeane, Donald G. (1969). "The Traditional Upland South Cemetery," *Landscape* 18(2): 39–41.

———(1989). "The Upland South Folk Cemetery Complex," pp. 107–36 in Richard E. Meyer, ed., *Cemeteries & Gravemarkers: Voices of American Culture.* Ann Arbor: UMI Research Press.

Jenkins, Virginia Scott (1994). *The Lawn: A History of an American Obsession.* Washington, D.C.: Smithsonian Institution Press.

Jensen, Joli (1998). *The Nashville Sound: Authenticity, Commercialization, and Country Music.* Nashville: Vanderbilt University Press.

Jensen, Merrill, ed. (1951). *Regionalism in America.* Madison: University of Wisconsin Press.

John, Richard R. (1995). *Spreading the News: The American Postal System from Franklin to Morse.* Cambridge: Harvard University Press.

Johnson, Charles A. (1955). *The Frontier Camp Meeting: Religion's Harvest Time.* Dallas: Southern Methodist University Press.

———(1976). "Political Culture in American States: Elazar's Formulation Examined," *American Journal of Political Science* 20: 491–509.

Johnson, Hildegard Binder (1975). "The United States Land Survey as a Principle of Order," pp. 114–30 in Ralph E. Ehrenberg, ed., *Pattern and Process: Research in Historical Geography.* Washington, D.C.: Howard University Press.

———(1976). *Order upon the Land: The U.S. Rectangular Survey and the Upper Mississippi Country.* New York: Oxford University Press.

Jolley, Harley E. (1969). *The Blue Ridge Parkway.* Knoxville: University of Tennessee Press.

Jones, Suzanne W., and Sharon Monteith, eds. (2002). *South to a New Place: Region, Literature, Culture.* Baton Rouge: Louisiana State University Press.

Jones, Thomas C. (1977). *The Halls of Fame: Featuring Specialized Museums of Sports, Agronomy, Entertainment, and the Humanities.* Chicago: J. G. Ferguson.

Jordan, Terry G. (1974). "Antecedents of the Long Lot in Texas," *Annals of the Association of American Geographers* 64: 70–86.

———(1978a). *Texas Log Buildings: A Folk Architecture.* Austin: University of Texas Press.

———(1978b). "Perceptual Regions in Texas," *Geographical Review* 68: 293–307.

———(1980). "'The Roses So Red and the Lilies So Fair': Southern Folk Cemeteries in Texas," *Southwestern Historical Quarterly* 83: 227–58.

———(1982). *Texas Graveyards: A Cultural Legacy.* Austin: University of Texas Press.

———(1985). *American Log Buildings: An Old World Heritage.* Chapel Hill: University of North Carolina Press.

Jordan-Bychkov, Terry G. (2003). *The Upland South: The Making of an American Folk Region and Landscape.* Santa Fe: Center for American Places.

Jordan-Bychkov, Terry G., and Mona Domosh (1999). *The Human Mosaic: A Thematic Introduction to Cultural Geography,* 8th ed. New York: Longman.

Joseph, Nathan (1986). *Uniforms and Nonuniforms: Communication through Clothing.* Westport, Conn.: Greenwood Press.

Judd, Dennis R. (1999). "Constructing the Tourist Bubble," pp. 35–53 in Judd and Fainstein 1999.

Judd, Dennis R., and Susan S. Fainstein, eds. (1999). *The Tourist City.* New Haven: Yale University Press.

Kandel, William, and Emilio A. Parrado (2004). "Hispanics in the American South and the Transformation of the Poultry Industry," pp. 255–76 in Daniel D. Arreola, ed., *Hispanic Spaces, Latino Places: Community and Cultural Diversity in Contemporary America*. Austin: University of Texas Press.

Kanfer, Stefan (1989). *A Summer World: The Attempt to Build a Jewish Eden in the Catskills, from the Days of the Ghetto to the Rise and Decline of the Borscht Belt*. New York: Farrar, Straus & Giroux.

Kaplan, Fred (2009). *1959: The Year Everything Changed*. New York: John Wiley & Sons.

Kasson, Joy S. (2000). *Buffalo Bill's Wild West: Celebrity, Memory and Popular History*. New York: Hill & Wang.

Kaszynski, William (2000). *The American Highway: The History and Culture of Roads in the United States*. Jefferson, N.C.: McFarland.

Katz, James E. (1999). *Connections: Social and Cultural Studies of the Telephone in American Life*. New Brunswick, N.J.: Transaction.

Kazin, Alfred (1942). *On Native Grounds: An Interpretation of Modern American Prose Literature*. New York: Reynal & Hitchcock.

Keister, Douglas (2004). *Silver Palaces*. Salt Lake City: Gibbs Smith.

Kelbaugh, Douglas (1997). *Common Place: Toward Neighborhood and Regional Design*. Seattle: University of Washington Press.

Kemp, Jim (1987). *American Vernacular: Regional Influences in Architecture and Interior Design*. New York: Viking.

Kenney, William Howland (1999). *Recorded Music in American Life: The Phonograph and Popular Memory, 1890–1945*. New York: Oxford University Press.

Kermes, Stephanie (2008). *Creating an American Identity: New England, 1789–1825*. New York: Palgrave Macmillan.

Keve, Paul W. (1991). *Prisons and the American Conscience: A History of U.S. Federal Corrections*. Carbondale: Southern Illinois University Press.

Kielbowicz, Richard B. (1989). *News in the Mail: The Press, Post Office, and Public Information*. Westport, Conn.: Greenwood Press.

Kim, Sukkoo (1997). *Economic Integration and Convergence: U.S. Regions, 1840–1987*. Working Paper 6335. Cambridge: National Bureau of Economic Research.

Kines, Pat Decker (1979). "The Vanishing Lookout Tower," *Landscape* 23(1): 23–27.

King, Anthony (1995). *The Bungalow: The Production of a Global Culture*, 2nd ed. New York: Oxford University Press.

Kirby, Jack Temple (1986). *Media-Made Dixie: The South in the American Imagination*, rev. ed. Athens: University of Georgia Press.

Klein, Kerwin Lee (1996). "Reclaiming the 'F' Word, or Being and Becoming Postwestern," *Pacific Historical Review* 65: 179–215.

Knepper, Cathy D. (2001). *Greenbelt, Maryland: A Living Legacy of the New Deal*. Baltimore: Johns Hopkins University Press.

Kniffen, Fred B. (1936). "Louisiana House Types," *Annals of the Association of American Geographers* 26: 176–93.

——— (1951). "The American Covered Bridge," *Geographical Review* 41: 114–23.

——— (1965). "Folk Housing: Key to Diffusion," *Annals of the Association of American Geographers* 55: 549–77.

——— (1968). *Louisiana: Its Land and People*. Baton Rouge: Louisiana State University Press.

Kniffen, Fred B., and Henry Glassie (1966). "Building in Wood in the Eastern United States: A Time-Place Perspective," *Geographical Review* 56: 40–66.

Kotkin, Joel (2000). *The New Geography: How the Digital Revolution Is Reshaping the American Landscape.* New York: Random House.

Kovacik, Charles F., and John Winberry (1987). *South Carolina: A Geography.* Boulder, Colo.: Westview Press.

Kowalewski, Michael (2003). "Contemporary Regionalism," pp. 7–24 in Charles L. Crow, ed., *A Companion to the Regional Literatures of America.* Malden, Mass.: Blackwell.

Kozinets, Robert V. (2003). "The Moment of Infinite Fire," pp. 199–216 in Brown and Sherry 2003.

Kraidy, Marwan M. (2005). *Hybridity, or the Cultural Logic of Globalization.* Philadelphia: Temple University Press.

Kramer, Michael P. (1992). *Imagining Language in America: From the Revolution to the Civil War.* Princeton: Princeton University Press.

Kraybill, Donald G., and Carl F. Bowman (2001). *On the Backroad to Heaven: Old Order Hutterites, Mennonites, Amish, and Brethren.* Baltimore: Johns Hopkins University Press.

Krell, Alan (2002). *The Devil's Rope: A Cultural History of Barbed Wire.* London: Reaktion Books.

Kretzschmar, William A., Jr. (2003). "Linguistic Atlases of the United States and Canada," pp. 25–56 in Dennis R. Preston, ed., *Needed Research in American Dialects.* Publication of the American Dialect Society no. 88. Durham, N.C.: Duke University Press.

Kreyling, Michael (1998). *Inventing Southern Literature.* Jackson: University Press of Mississippi.

Kritz, Mary M., and Douglas T. Gurak (2006). "Non-Traditional Immigrant Destinations: Who Goes Where and Why?" Paper presented at Gordon DeJong Symposium on Social Demography, Pennsylvania State University, September.

Kuhlken, Robert, and Rocky Sexton (1994). "The Geography of Zydeco Music," pp. 63–76 in Carney 1994a.

Kumar, Martha Joynt (1983). "Presidential Libraries: Gold Mine, Booby Trap, or Both?" pp. 199–224 in George C. Edwards III and Stephen J. Wayne, eds., *Studying the Presidency.* Knoxville: University of Tennessee Press.

Kummer, Corby (2002). *The Pleasures of Slow Food.* San Francisco: Chronicle Books.

Kunstler, James Howard (1993). *The Geography of Nowhere: The Rise and Decline of America's Man-Made Landscape.* New York: Simon & Schuster.

Kupferberg, Herbert (1976). *Tanglewood.* New York: McGraw-Hill.

Kurath, Hans (1939–43). *Linguistic Atlas of New England.* Providence: Brown University.

——— (1949). *A Word Geography of the Eastern United States:* Ann Arbor: University of Michigan Press.

Kuznets, Simon, Ann Ratner Miller, and Richard A. Easterlin (1960). *Population Redistribution and Economic Growth. United States, 1870–1950. II. Analyses of Economic Change.* Philadelphia: American Philosophical Society.

Labov, William, Sharon Ash, and Charles Boberg (2005). *The Atlas of American English: Phonetics, Phonology and Sound Change.* Berlin: Mouton de Gruyter.

Labovitz, Sanford (1965). "Territorial Differentiation and Societal Change," *Pacific Sociological Review* 8(2): 70–75.

Labovitz, Sanford, and Ross Purdy (1970). "Territorial Differentiation and Societal Change in the United States and Canada," *American Journal of Economics and Sociology* 29: 127–47.

Ladd, Barbara (2002). "Dismantling the Monolith: Southern Places—Past, Present, and Future," pp. 44–57 in Jones and Monteith 2002.

Lamme, Ary J. III (2001). "Old Order Amish Homelands," pp. 44–52 in Nostrand and Estaville 2001.

Lancaster, Clay (1986) [1958]. "The American Bungalow," pp. 79–106 in Upton and Vlach 1986.

Landy, Elliott (1994). *Woodstock Vision: The Spirit of a Generation.* New York: Continuum.

Lane, Mervin, ed. (1990). *Black Mountain College Sprouted Seeds: An Anthology of Personal Accounts.* Knoxville: University of Tennessee Press.

Lang, William L. (2001). "Series Editor's Preface," pp. v–vii in William G. Robbins, ed., *The Great Northwest: The Search for Regional Identity.* Corvallis: Oregon State University Press.

Langdon, Philip (1986). *Orange Roofs, Golden Arches: The Architecture of American Chain Restaurants.* New York: Knopf.

Latham, Frank B. (1972). *1872–1972: A Century of Serving Consumers: The Story of Montgomery Ward.* Chicago: Montgomery Ward & Co.

Lauria, Mickey, and Lawrence Knopp (1985). "Toward an Analysis of the Role of Gay Communities in the Urban Renaissance," *Urban Geography* 6: 152–69.

Laventhol and Horwath (1987). *The Conference Center Industry: 8th Annual Statistical and Financial Profile.* Philadelphia: Laventhol and Horwath.

——— (1989). *The Conference Center Industry: 10th Annual Statistical and Financial Profile.* Philadelphia: Laventhol and Horwath.

Lawlor, Mary (2006). *Public Native America: Tribal Self-Representations in Casinos, Museums, and Powwows.* New Brunswick, N.J.: Rutgers University Press.

Lawrence, Henry W. (1983). "Southern Spas: Source of the American Resort Tradition," *Landscape* 27(2): 1–12.

Lawrence, Vera Brodsky (1975). *Music for Patriots, Politicians, and Presidents: Harmonies and Discords of the First Hundred Years.* New York: Macmillan.

Lawson, Laura J. (2005). *City Bountiful: A Century of Community Gardening in America.* Berkeley: University of California Press.

Lazo, Alejandro (2007). "A Shorter Link between the Farm and Dinner Plate," *Washington Post,* July 29: A-1, A-19.

Lea, Diane (2003). "America's Preservation Ethos: A Tribute to Enduring Ideals," pp. 1–20 in Robert E. Stripe, ed., *A Richer Heritage: Historical Preservation in the Twenty-first Century.* Chapel Hill: University of North Carolina Press.

Leach, Sara Amy (2006). "The Daughters of the American Revolution, Roane F. Byrnes, and the Birth of the Natchez Trace," pp. 99–114 in Stager and Carver 2006.

Leach, William (1999). *Country of Exiles: The Destruction of Place in American Life.* New York: Pantheon.

Lebhar, Godfrey M. (1952). *Chain Stores in America, 1859–1950.* New York: Chain Store Publishing.

Lebovich, William L. (1984). *America's City Halls.* Washington, D.C.: Preservation Press.

Lefaivre, Liane (2003). "Critical Regionalism: A Facet of Modern Architecture since 1945," pp. 22–55 in Lefaivre and Alexander Tzonis, *Critical Regionalism: Architecture and Identity in a Globalized World.* Munich: Prestel.

Lefebvre, Henri (1991). *The Production of Space.* Oxford: Blackwell.

Leighninger, Robert D., Jr. (2007). *Long-Range Public Investment: The Forgotten Legacy of the New Deal.* Columbia: University of South Carolina Press.

Lemon, James T. (1972). *The Best Poor Man's Country: A Geographical Study of Southeastern Pennsylvania.* Baltimore: Johns Hopkins University Press.

Lenthall, Bruce (2007). *Radio's America: The Great Depression and the Rise of Modern Mass Culture.* Chicago: University of Chicago Press.

Leon, Warren, and Margaret Piatt (1989). "Living-History Museums," pp. 64–97 in Leon and Rosenzweig 1989.

Leon, Warren, and Roy Rosenzweig, eds. (1989). *History Museums in the United States.* Urbana: University Illinois Press.

Leonard, Thomas C. (1995). *News for All: America's Coming-of-Age with the Press.* New York: Oxford University Press.

Lerner, Max (1957). *America as a Civilization.* New York: Simon & Schuster.

Levi, Vicki Gold, and Steven Heller (2004). *Times Square Style: Graphics from the Great White Way.* New York: Princeton Architectural Press.

Levy, Alan H. (1998). *Edward MacDowell: An American Master.* Lanham, Md.: Scarecrow Press.

Lewis, Peirce F. (1972). "Small Town in Pennsylvania," *Annals of the Association of American Geographers* 62: 323–51.

——— (1975). "Common Houses, Common Spoor," *Landscape* 10(2): 1–22.

——— (1983). "The Galactic Metropolis," pp. 23–49 in Rutherford J. Platt and George Macinko, eds., *Land Use Issues of Nonmetropolitan America.* Minneapolis: University of Minnesota Press.

——— (1993). "The Making of Vernacular Taste: The Case of *Sunset* and *Southern Living*," pp. 107–18 in John Dixon Hunt and Joachim Wolschke-Bulmahn, eds., *Dumbarton Oaks Colloquium on the History of Landscape Architecture: XIV.* Washington, D.C.: Dumbarton Oaks.

——— (2003). *New Orleans: The Making of an Urban Landscape,* 2nd ed. Santa Fe: Center for American Places.

Lewis, Robert M., ed. (2003). *From Traveling Show to Vaudeville: Theatrical Spectacle in America.* Baltimore: Johns Hopkins University Press.

Lewis, Tom (1997). *Divided Highways: Building the Interstate Highways, Transforming American Life.* New York: Viking.

Lichter, Daniel T., and Kenneth M. Johnson (2006). "Emerging Rural Settlement Patterns and the Geographic Redistribution of America's New Immigrants," *Rural Sociology* 71(1): 109–31.

Liebs, Chester H. (1985). *Main Street to Miracle Mile: American Roadside Architecture.* Boston: Little, Brown.

Limerick, Patricia Nelson (1987). *The Legacy of Conquest: The Unbroken Past of the American West.* New York: W. W. Norton.

——— (1996). "Region and Reason," pp. 83–104 in Ayers, Limerick, Nissenbaum, and Onuf 1996.

—— (1998). "The Realization of the American West," pp. 71–98 in C. R. Wilson 1998b.

Linklater, Andro (2002). *Measuring America: How the United States Was Shaped by the Greatest Land Sale in History.* London: Harper Collins.

Linden, Blanche M. G. (2007). *Silent City on a Hill: Picturesque Landscapes of Memory and Boston's Mount Auburn Cemetery.* Amherst: University of Massachusetts Press in association with Library of American Landscape History.

Lippard, Lucy R. (1997). *The Lure of the Local: Senses of Place in a Multicentered Society.* New York: New Press.

Lipset, Seymour Martin (1990). *Continental Divide: The Values and Institutions of the United States and Canada.* New York: Routledge.

—— (1996). *American Exceptionalism: A Double-Edged Sword.* New York: W. W. Norton.

Lipsitz, George (1994). *Dangerous Crossroads: Popular Music, Postmodernism, and the Poetics of Place.* London: Verso.

Littlefield, Bruce (2007). *Garage Sale America.* New York: Collins Design.

Lloyd, Timothy Charles (1981). "The Cincinnati Chili Culinary Complex," *Western Folklore* 40: 28–40.

Lockwood, Yvonne, and William G. Lockwood (1991). "Pasties in Michigan's Upper Peninsula: Foodways, Interethnic Relations, and Regionalism," pp. 3–20 in Stephen Stern and John Allan Cicala, eds., *Creative Ethnicity: Symbols and Strategies of Contemporary Ethnic Life.* Logan: Utah State University Press.

Loftin, Colin, and Robert H. Hill (1974). "Regional Subculture and Homicide: An Examination of the Gastil-Hackney Thesis," *American Sociological Review* 39: 714–25.

Lohof, Bruce A. (1974). "The Service Station in America: The Evolution of a Vernacular Form," *Industrial Archaeology* 11(1): 1–13.

Lomax, Alan (1960). *Folk Songs of North America.* Garden City, N.Y.: Doubleday.

Longstreth, Richard (1986). "Compositional Types in American Commercial Architecture," pp. 12–23 in Camille Wells, ed., *Perspective in Vernacular Architecture, II.* Columbia: University of Missouri Press.

Lösch, August (1954). *The Economics of Location.* New Haven: Yale University Press.

Low, Setha (2003). *Behind the Gates: Life, Security, and the Pursuit of Happiness in Fortress America.* New York: Routledge.

Lowenthal, David (1985). *The Past Is a Foreign Country.* Cambridge: Harvard University Press.

—— (1996). *Possessed by the Past: The Heritage and the Spoils of History.* New York: Free Press.

Luccarelli, Mark (1995). *Lewis Mumford and the Ecological Region: The Politics of Planning.* New York: Guilford.

Ludwig, Allen I. (1966). *Graven Images: New England Stonecarving and Its Symbols.* Middletown, Conn.: Wesleyan University Press.

Luebke, Frederick C. (1984). "Regionalism and the Great Plains: Problems of Concept and Method," *Western Historical Quarterly* 15: 19–38.

Luger, Michael I., and Harvey A. Goldstein (1991). *Technology in the Garden: Research Parks and Regional Economic Development.* Chapel Hill: University of North Carolina Press.

Lury, Celia (2004). *Brands: The Logos of the Global Economy.* London: Routledge.

Lutwack, Leonard (1984). *The Role of Place in Literature.* Syracuse: Syracuse University Press.

Lynn, Robert Wood (1973). "Civil Catechetics in Mid-Victorian America: Some Notes about the American Civil Religion, Past and Present," *Religious Education* 68: 5–27.

Lyson, T. A., G. W. Gillespie Jr., and D. Hilchey (1995). "Farmers' Markets and the Local Community: Bridging the Formal and Informal Economy," *American Journal of Alternative Agriculture* 10(3): 108–13.

Macdonald, Kent (1985). "The Commercial Strip: From Main Street to Television Road," *Landscape* 28(2): 12–19.

——— (1994). "Reston Revisited," *Landscape* 32(2): 28–33.

Madsen, Deborah L. (1998). *American Exceptionalism.* Jackson: University Press of Mississippi.

Maha-Keplinger, Lisa (1993). *Grain Elevators.* New York: Princeton Architectural Press.

Maisel, Robert (1974). "The Flea Market as an Action Scene," *Urban Life* 2(4): 488–505.

Marchand, Roland (1985). *Advertising the American Dream: Making Way for Modernity, 1920–1940.* Berkeley: University of California Press.

Margolin, Victor, Ira Brichta, and Vivian Brichta (1979). *The Promise and the Product: 200 Years of American Advertising Posters.* New York: Macmillan.

Markey, Douglas C. (1986). *On the Edge of Empire: Foodways in Western Australia, 1829–1979.* Ph.D. diss., Pennsylvania State University.

Markovich, Nicholas C. (1990). "Santa Fe Renaissance: City Planning and Stylistic Preservation, 1912," pp. 197–212 in Markovich, Preiser, and Sturm 1990.

Markovich, Nicholas C., Wolfgang F. E. Preiser, and Fred G. Sturm, eds. (1990). *Pueblo Style and Regional Architecture.* New York: Van Nostrand Reinhold.

Markusen, Ann, Scott Campbell, Peter Hall, and Sabina Deitrick (1991). *The Rise of the Gunbelt: The Military Remapping of Industrial America.* New York: Oxford University Press.

Marling, Karal Ann (1982). *Wall-to-Wall America: A Cultural History of Post Office Murals in the Great Depression.* Minneapolis: University of Minnesota Press.

——— (1984). *The Colossus of Roads: Myths and Symbol along the American Highway.* Minneapolis: University of Minnesota Press.

Marsh, Ben (1987). "Continuity and Decline in the Anthracite Towns of Pennsylvania," *Annals of the Association of American Geographers* 77: 337–52.

Martin, Lowell A. (1998). *Enrichment: A History of the Public Library in the United States in the Twentieth Century.* Lanham, Md.: Scarecrow Press.

Martinez, J. Michael, and Robert M. Harris (2000a). "Graves, Worms, and Epitaphs: Confederate Monuments in the Southern Landscape," pp. 130–92 in Martinez, William D. Richardson, and Ron McNich-Su, eds., *Confederate Symbols in the Contemporary South.* Gainesville: University Press of Florida.

Martinez and Richardson 2000b. "Introduction," pp. 1–22 in Martinez, William D. Richardson, and Ron McNinch-Su, eds., *Confederate Symbols in the Contemporary South.* Gainesville: University Press of Florida.

Martinez, J. Michael, William D. Richardson, and Ron McNinch-Su, eds. (2000). *Confederate Symbols in the Contemporary South.* Gainesville: University Press of Florida.

Martis, Kenneth C. (1989). *The Historical Atlas of Political Parties in the United States.* New York: Macmillan.

———(1993). *The Historical Atlas of State Power in Congress, 1790–1990.* Washington, D.C.: Congressional Quarterly.

Marvin, Carolyn, and David W. Ingle (1999). *Blood Sacrifice and the Nation: Totem Rituals and the American Flag.* Cambridge: Cambridge University Press.

Massey, Doreen (1995). "The Conceptualization of Place," pp. 46–85 in Massey and Jess 1995b.

Massey, Doreen, and Pat Jess (1995a). "Places and Cultures in an Uneven World," pp. 215–39 in Massey and Jess 1995b.

———, eds. (1995b). *A Place in the World? Places, Cultures and Globalization.* Oxford: Open University.

Mather, Cotton (1986). "The Midwest: Image and Reality," *Journal of Geography* 85: 190–94.

Mather, Cotton, and John Fraser Hart (1954). "Fences and Farms," *Geographical Review* 44: 201–23.

Matthews, Glenna (1987). *"Just a Housewife": The Rise and Fall of Domesticity in America.* New York: Oxford University Press.

McAlester, Virginia, and Les McAlester (1984). *A Field Guide to American Houses.* New York: Knopf.

McAvoy, Thomas T., ed. (1961). *The Midwest: Myth or Reality?* Notre Dame: University of Notre Dame Press.

McCormack, Mary (1985). *The Generation Gap: The View from Both Sides.* London: Constable.

McCrank, Lawrence J. (1997). "Religious Orders and Monastic Communalism in America," pp. 204–52 in Donald E. Pitzer, ed., *America's Communal Utopias.* Chapel Hill: University of North Carolina Press.

McDavid, Raven L., Jr. (1958). "The Dialects of American English," pp. 480–543 in W. N. Francis, ed., *The Structure of American English.* New York: Ronald Press.

McDonald, James R. (1972). *A Geography of Regions.* Dubuque: Wm. C. Brown.

McGinnis, Michael Vincent, ed. (1999). *Bioregionalism.* London: Routledge.

McGrath, Mary Ann, John F. Sherry Jr., and Deborah D. Heisley (1993). "An Ethnographic Study of an Urban Periodic Marketplace: Lessons from the Midville Farmers' Market," *Journal of Retailing* 69: 280–319.

McGreevy, Patrick (1994). *Imagining Niagara: The Making and Meaning of Niagara Falls.* Amherst: University of Massachusetts Press.

McHenry, Stewart G. (1986) [1978]. "Eighteenth-Century Field Patterns as Vernacular Art," pp. 107–23 in Upton and Vlach 1986.

McHugh, Kevin E. (2006). "Citadels in the Sun," pp. 262–77 in McIntyre, Williams, and McHugh 2006.

McIntyre, Norman, Daniel R. Williams, and Kevin E. McHugh, eds. (2006). *Multiple Dwelling and Tourism: Negotiating Place, Home, and Identity.* Wallingford, U.K.: CABI.

McKee, Brian J. (1997). *Historic American Covered Bridges.* New York: ASCE Press.

McKinney, John C., and Linda Brookover Bourque (1971). "The Changing South: National Incorporation of a Region," *American Sociological Review* 36: 399–417.

McKinzie, Richard D. (1973). *A New Deal for Artists.* Princeton: Princeton University Press.

McManis, Douglas R. (1975). *Colonial New England: A Historical Geography*. New York: Oxford University Press.

McMillan, Elizabeth (1994). *Beach Houses: From Malibu to Laguna*. New York: Rizzoli.

McPherson, Tara (2003). *Reconstructing Dixie: Race, Gender, and Nostalgia in the Imagined South*. Durham, N.C.: Duke University Press.

McWhiney, Grady (1987). *Cracker Culture in the Old South*. Tuscaloosa: University of Alabama Press.

McWilliams, Carey (1930). *The New Regionalism in American Literature*. Seattle: University of Washington Book Store.

Meeks, Carroll L. V. (1956). *The Railroad Station: An Architectural History*. New Haven: Yale University Press.

Meinig, Donald W. (1965). "The Mormon Culture Region: Strategies and Patterns in the Geographies of the American West, 1847–1964," *Annals of the Association of American Geographers* 55: 191–220.

——— (1968). *Imperial Texas: An Interpretive Essay in Cultural Geography*. Austin: University of Texas Press.

——— (1971). *Southwest: Three Peoples in Geographical Change, 1600–1970*. New York: Oxford University Press.

——— (1972). "American Wests: Preface to a Geographical Interpretation," pp. 159–84 in John Fraser Hart, ed., *Regions of the United States*. New York: Harper & Row.

——— (1986–2004). *The Shaping of America: A Geographical Perspective on 500 Years of History*. 4 vols. New Haven: Yale University Press.

——— (1996). "The Mormon Nation and American Empire," *Journal of Mormon History* 22(1); 33–51.

Mellow, Nicole (2008). *The State of Disunion: Regional Sources of Modern American Partisanship*. Baltimore: Johns Hopkins University Press.

Menendez, Albert J. (2005). *The Geography of Presidential Elections in the United States, 1868–2004*. Jefferson, N.C.: McFarland.

Merrill, Michael (1977). "Cash Is Good to Eat: Self-Sufficiency and Exchange in the Rural Economy of the United States," *Radical History Review* 4(1): 42–71.

Merrill, Perry H. (1981). *Roosevelt's Forest Army: A History of the Civilian Conservation Corps, 1933–1942*. Montpelier, Vt.: Author.

Metcalf, Allan (2000). *How We Talk: American Regional English Today*. Boston: Houghton Mifflin.

Meyer, Jeffrey F. (2001). *Myths in Stone: Religious Dimensions of Washington, D.C.* Berkeley: University of California Press.

Meyer, Richard E., ed. (1989). *Cemeteries & Gravemarkers: Voices of American Culture*. Ann Arbor: UMI Research Press.

Meyer, Roy W. (1991). *Everyone's Country Estate: A History of Minnesota State Parks*. St. Paul: Minnesota Historical Society Press.

Meyer-Arendt, Klaus (1998). "From the River to the Sea: Casino Gambling in Mississippi," pp. 151–67 in Meyer-Arendt and Hartmann 1998.

Meyer-Arendt, Klaus J., and Rudi Hartmann, eds. (1998). *Casino Gambling in America: Origin, Trends, and Impacts*. New York: Cognizant.

Meyrowitz, Joshua (1985). *No Sense of Place: The Impact of Electronic Media on Social Behavior*. New York: Oxford University Press.

Miele, Mara, and Jonathan Murdoch (2002). "Slow Food," pp. 250–54 in George Ritzer, ed., *McDonaldization: The Reader*. Thousand Oaks, Calif.: Pine Forge Press.

Mihm, Stephen (2007). *A Nation of Counterfeiters: Capitalists, Con Men, and the Making of the United States*. Cambridge: Harvard University Press.

Military Living Publications (2002). *United States Military Road Atlas*. Falls Church, Va.: MLP.

Millard, Ann V., Maríaelena D. Jefferds, Ken R. Crane, and Isidore Flores (2004). "Research Overview: The Rural Midwestern Context and Qualitative Methods," pp. 75–98 in Millard and Jorge Chapa, *Apple Pie & Enchiladas: Latino Newcomers in the Rural Midwest*. Austin: University of Texas Press.

Miller, David E. (2005). *Toward a New Regionalism: Environmental Architecture in the Pacific Northwest*. Seattle: University of Washington Press.

Miller, E. Joan Wilson (1968). "The Ozark Culture Region as Revealed by Traditional Materials," *Annals of the Association of American Geographers* 58: 51–77.

Miller, Timothy (1998). *The Quest for Utopia in Twentieth-Century America*, vol. 1: *1900–1960*. Syracuse: Syracuse University Press.

——— (1999). *The 60s Communes: Hippies and Beyond*. Syracuse: Syracuse University Press.

Mings, Robert C., and Kevin E. McHugh (1989). "The RV Resort Landscape," *Journal of Cultural Geography* 10(1); 35–49.

Minnich, Harvey C. (1936). *William Holmes McGuffey and His Readers*. New York: American Book Co.

Minshull, Roger (1967). *Regional Geography: Theory and Practice*. London: Hutchinson University Library.

Mintz, Sidney (2002). "Eating American," pp. 23–33 in Carole M. Counihand, ed., *Food in the USA: A Reader*. New York: Routledge.

Mitchell, Robert D. (1978). "The Formation of Early American Cultural Regions," pp. 66–90 in J. R. Gibson, ed., *European Settlement and Development in North America*. Toronto: University of Toronto Press.

Miyares, Ines M. (2008). "Expressing 'Local Culture' in Hawaii," *Geographical Review* 98: 513–31.

Mohl, Raymond A., ed. (1990). *Searching for the Sunbelt: Historical Perspectives on a Region*. Knoxville: University of Tennessee Press.

Mondra, Ronald C., and M. B. Roberts (1998). *Garish Gardens: Outlandish Lawns*. Minocqua, Wisc.: Willow Creek Press.

Moline, Norman T. (1971). *Mobility and the Small Town, 1900–1930*. Department of Geography Research Paper no. 132. Chicago: University of Chicago.

Monaghan, E. Jennifer (1982). *A Common Heritage: Noah Webster's Blue-Black Speller*. Hamden, Conn.: Archon Books.

Mondale, Clarence (1989). "Concepts and Trends in Regional Studies," *American Studies International* 27(1): 13–37.

Montgomery, Michael (2003). "The History of American English," pp. 1–23 in Dennis R. Preston, ed., *Needed Research in American Dialects*. Publication of the American Dialect Society no. 88. Durham, N.C.: Duke University Press.

Mood, Fulmer (1951). "The Origin, Evolution, and Application of the Sectional Concept, 1750–1900," pp. 5–98 in M. Jensen 1951.

Moon, Ben L. (1970). "City Magazines, Past and Present," *Journalism Quarterly* 47(4): 711–18.

*Moonshine: The Poison Business* (1971). New York: Licensed Beverage Industries. Inc.

Moore, Frank (1846). *Songs and Ballads of the American Revolution*. New York: Appleton.

Morain, Thomas (1979). "In the American Grain: The Popularity of Living History Farms," *Journal of American Culture* 2(3): 550–57.

Moran, Joe (2005). *Reading the Everyday*. London: Routledge.

Moreau, Joseph (2003). *Schoolbook Nation: Conflicts over American History Textbooks from the Civil War to the Present*. Ann Arbor: University of Michigan Press.

Morgan, Michael (1986). "Television and the Erosion of Regional Diversity," *Journal of Broadcasting & Electronic Media* 30 (2): 123–39.

Morrill, Richard, Larry Knopp, and Michael Brown (2007). "How Real Are Red America and Blue America?" *Focus* 50(1): 22–29.

Morrison, Terri, and Wayne A. Conaway (2006). *Kiss, Bow, or Shake Hands: The Best-selling Guide to Doing Business in More than 60 Countries*, 2nd ed. Avon, Mass.: Adams Media.

Morrissey, Katherine G. (1997). *Mental Territories: Mapping the Inland Empire*. Ithaca: Cornell University Press.

Morse, Edward A., and Ernest P. Goss (2007). *Governing Fortune: Casino Gambling in America*. Ann Arbor: University of Michigan Press.

Mosher, Anne E. (2004). *Capital's Utopia: Vandergrift, Pennsylvania, 1855–1916*. Baltimore: Johns Hopkins University Press.

Muilenburg, Grace, and Ada Swineford (1975). *Land of the Post Rock: Its Origins, History, and People*. Lawrence: University Press of Kansas.

Mumford, Lewis (1928–29). "The Theory and Practice of Regionalism," *Sociological Review* 20 ( January 1928): 18–33; (April 1929): 131–40.

Murauskas, G. Tomas, J. Clark Archer, and Fred M. Shelley (1988). "Metropolitan, Nonmetropolitan, and Sectional Variations in Voting Behavior in Recent Presidential Elections," *Western Political Quarterly* 41(1): 64–84.

Murdoch, David Hamilton (2001). *The American West: The Invention of a Myth*. Reno: University of Nevada Press.

Murphy, Alexander B. (1991). "Regions as Social Constructs: The Gap between Theory and Practice," *Progress in Human Geography* 15(1): 22–35.

Murphy, David (1989). "Building in Clay on the Central Plains," pp. 74–85 in Thomas Carter and Bernard L. Herman, eds., *Perspectives in Vernacular Architecture, III*. Columbia: University of Missouri Press.

Murray, Thomas E., and Beth Lee Simon (2006a). "What Is Dialect? Revisiting the Midland," pp. 1–30 in Murray and Simon 2006b.

———, eds. (2006b). *Language Variation and Change in the American Midland: A New Look at "Heartland" English*. Amsterdam: John Benjamins.

Murray-Wooley, Carolyn, and Karl Raitz (1992). *Rock Fences of the Bluegrass*. Lexington: University Press of Kentucky.

Murtagh, William J. (2006). *Keeping Time: The History and Theory of Preservation in America*, 3rd ed. New York: John Wiley & Sons.

Myers, Kenneth (1987). *The Catskills: Painters, Writers, and Tourists in the Mountains, 1820–1895*. Yonkers: Hudson River Museum of Westchester.

Myers, Kenneth A. (2001). "The Homogenization of Culture," pp. 102–14 in Don Eberly, ed., *Building a Healthy Culture: Strategies for an American Renaissance*. Grand Rapids, Mich.: William B. Eerdmans.

Nairn, Ian (1965). *The American Landscape: A Critical View*. New York: Random House.

Nakagawa, Tadashi (1987). *The Cemetery as a Cultural Manifestation: Louisiana Necrogeography*. Ph.D. diss., Louisiana State University.

Napton, Darrell E., and Christopher R. Laingen (2008). "Expansion of Golf Courses in the United States," *Geographical Review* 98: 24–41.

Nash, Roderick (1970). "The American Invention of National Parks," *American Quarterly* 22: 726–35.

National Park Service (1994). *National Register of Historic Places, 1966 to 1994.* Washington, D.C.: Preservation Press and National Conference of State Historic Preservation Officers.

Neilson, Brian J. (1995). "Baseball," pp. 30–69 in Raitz 1995d.

Newcomb, Rexford (1937). *Spanish-Colonial Architecture in the United States.* New York: J. J. Auguston.

Newman, William M., and Peter L. Halvorson (1984). "Religion and Regional Culture: Patterns of Concentration and Change among Religious Denominations," *Journal for the Scientific Study of Religion* 23: 304–15.

Newton, Esther (1993). *Cherry Grove, Fire Island: Sixty Years in America's First Gay and Lesbian Town.* New York: Beacon Press.

Newton, Milton B., Jr. (1977). "Sliced Tomatoes for Breakfast," *Pioneer America* 9(1): 11.

Nietz, John A. (1961). *Old Textbooks.* Pittsburgh: University of Pittsburgh Press.

Nisbet, Robert (1975). *Twilight of Authority.* New York: Oxford University Press.

——— (1990). "Men and Money: Reflections by a Sociologist," pp. 7–13 in *Money Matters: A Critical Look at Bank Architecture.* New York: McGraw-Hill.

Nisbett, Richard E., Gregory Polly, and Sylvia Lang (1995). "Homicide and U.S. Regional Culture," pp. 135–51 in R. Barry Ruback and Neil Alan Weiner, eds., *Interpersonal Violent Behaviors: Social and Cultural Aspects.* New York: Springer.

Nissenbaum, Stephen (1996). "New England as Region and Nation," pp. 38–61 in Ayers, Limerick, Nissenbaum, and Onuf 1996.

——— (1998). "Inventing New England," pp. 105–26 in C. R. Wilson 1998b.

Noah, Harold J., Carl E. Prince, and C. Russell Riggs (1962). "History in High School Texts: A Note," *School Review* 70: 415–36.

Noble, Allen G. (1981). "The Diffusion of Silos," *Landscape* 25(1): 11–14.

——— (1984a). *Wood, Brick, and Stone: The North American Settlement Landscape,* vol. 1: *Houses.* Amherst: University of Massachusetts Press.

——— (1984b). *Wood, Brick, and Stone. The North American Settlement Landscape,* vol. 2: *Barns and Farm Structures.* Amherst: University of Massachusetts Press.

Noble, Allen G., and Richard K. Cleek (1995). *The Old Barn Book: A Field Guide to North American Barns and Other Farm Structures.* New Brunswick, N.J.: Rutgers University Press.

Noble, Allen G., and Hubert G. H. Wilhelm (1995). "The Farm Barns of the American Midwest," pp. 1–23 in Noble and Wilhelm, eds., *Barns of the Midwest.* Athens: Ohio University Press.

Noble, Dennis L. (1997). *Lighthouses & Keepers: The U.S. Lighthouse Service and Its Legacy.* Annapolis, Md.: Naval Institute Press.

Norberg-Hodge, Helena, Todd Merrifield, and Steven Gorelick (2002). *Bringing the Food Economy Home: Local Alternatives to Global Agribusiness.* London: Zed.

Nostrand, Richard L. (1970). "The Hispanic-American Borderland: Delimitation of an American Culture Region," *Annals of the Association of American Geographers* 60: 638–61.

——— (1992). *The Hispano Homeland.* Norman: University of Oklahoma Press.

Nostrand, Richard L., and Lawrence E. Estaville, eds. (2001). *Homelands: A Geography of Culture and Place across America*. Baltimore: Johns Hopkins University Press.

Nottage, James H. (2001). "Fashioning the West: The Pre-Twentieth-Century Origins of Western Wear," pp. 10–39 in Holly George-Warren and Michelle Freedman, *How the West Was Worn*. New York: Harry N. Abrams.

Oakley, J. Ronald (1986). *God's Country: America in the Fifties*. New York: Dembner Books.

O'Brien, Michael (1979). *The Idea of the American South, 1920–1941*. Baltimore: Johns Hopkins University Press.

O'Connell, Nicholas (2003). *On Sacred Ground: The Spirit of Place in Pacific Northwest Literature*. Seattle: University of Washington Press.

Odum, Howard P. (1936). *Southern Regions of the United States*. Chapel Hill: University of North Carolina Press.

Odum, Howard P., and Harry Estill Moore (1938). *American Regionalism: A Cultural Historical Approach to National Integration*. New York: Henry Holt.

Ogden, Annegret (1986). *The Great American Housewife*. Westport, Conn.: Greenwood Press.

Okrant, Mark J., and Paul F. Starrs (1995). "Rodeo," pp. 296–320 in Raitz 1995d.

O'Malley, Michael (1990). *Keeping Watch: A History of American Time*. New York: Viking.

O'Malley, Therese (1999). "The Lawn in Early American Landscape and Garden Design," pp. 65–87 in Georges Teyssot, ed., *The American Lawn*. New York: Princeton Architectural Press.

Opie, Iona, and Peter Opie (1969). *Children's Games in Street and Playground*. London: Oxford University Press.

Osborne, Richard E. (1996). *World War II Sites in the United States: A Tour Guide & Directory*. Indianapolis: Riebel-Roque Publishing.

Ostergren, Robert (2005). "Concepts of Region: A Geographical Perspective," pp. 1–14 in Hönnighausen, Frey, Peacock, and Steiner 2005.

Ownby, Ted (2007). "Introduction," pp. vii–xiv in Ownby, ed., *Manners and Southern History*. Jackson: University Press of Mississippi.

Paasi, Anssi (1986). "The Institutionalization of Regions: A Theoretical Framework for Understanding the Emergence of Regions and the Constitution of Regional Identity," *Fennia* 164(1): 105–46.

——— (2002a). "Bounded Space in the Mobile World: Deconstructing 'Regional Identity,'" *Tijdschrift voor Economische en Sociale Geografie* 93(1): 137–48.

——— (2002b). "Place and Region: Regional Worlds and Words," *Progress in Human Geography* 26: 802–11.

——— (2003). "Region and Place: Regional Identity in Question," *Progress in Human Geography* 27: 475–85.

Paddleford, Clementine (1960). *How America Eats*. New York: Charles Scribner's Sons.

Park, Marlene, and Gerald E. Markowitz (1984). *Democratic Vistas: Post Offices and Public Art in the New Deal*. Philadelphia: Temple University Press.

Parkins, Almon E. (1949). *The South: Its Economic-Geographic Development*. New York: John Wiley & Sons.

Parr, Martin (1999). *Boring Postcards*. London: Phaidon.

Parsons, James J. (1985). "On 'Bioregionalism' and Watershed Consciousness," *Professional Geographer* 37: 1–6.

——— (1988). "Hillside Letters in the Western Landscape," *Landscape* 30(1): 15–23.

Parsons, Patrick R., and Robert M. Frieden (1998). *The Cable and Satellite Television Industries*. Boston: Allyn & Bacon.

Patterson, John S. (1989). "From Battle Ground to Pleasure Ground: Gettysburg as a Historic Site," pp. 128–57 in Leon and Rosenzweig 1989.

Pattison, William D. (1957). *Beginnings of the American Rectangular Survey System, 1784–1800*. Department of Geography Research Paper no. 50. Chicago: University of Chicago.

Paullin, Charles O., and John K. Wright (1932). *Atlas of the Historical Geography of the United States*. Washington, D.C.: Carnegie Institution of Washington; New York: American Geographical Society.

Paxson, Heather (2006). "Artisanal Cheese and Economies of Sentiment in New England," pp. 201–17 in Richard Wilk, ed., *Fast Food / Slow Food: The Cultural Economy of the Global Food System*. Lanham, Md.: Altamira Press.

Pearcy, G. Etzel (1973). *A Thirty-Eight State U.S.A.* Plycon Monograph Series no. 2. Fullerton, Calif.: Plycon Press.

Pearson, Nathan W., Jr. (1987). *Goin' to Kansas City*. Urbana: University of Illinois Press.

Penkower, Monty Noam (1977). *The Federal Writers' Project: A Study in Government Patronage of the Arts*. Urbana: University of Illinois Press.

Pennsylvania, Office of Mental Health (1963). *State and Private Mental Health Institutions and Facilities Serving Emotionally Disturbed Children and the Mentally Retarded in Pennsylvania*. Harrisburg.

Perkin, Judy, and Stephanie F. McCann (1984). "Food for Ethnic Americans: Is the Government Trying to Turn the Melting Pot into a One-Dish Dinner?" pp. 238–58 in Linda Keller Brown and Kay Mussell, eds., *Ethnic and Regional Foodways in the United States: The Performance of Group Identity*. Knoxville: University of Tennessee Press.

Perkins, Edwin J. (1988). *The Economy of Colonial America*, 2nd ed. New York: Columbia University Press.

Peterson, Elizabeth (1996). *The Changing Faces of Tradition: A Report on the Folk and Traditional Arts in the United States*. Research Division Report no. 38. Washington, D.C.: National Endowment for the Arts.

Peterson, Fred W. (2000). "Anglo-American Wooden Frame Farmhouses in the Midwest, 1830–1900: Origins of Balloon Frame Construction," pp. 3–16 in Sally McMurry and Annmarie Adams, eds., *People, Power, Places: Perspectives in American Vernacular Architecture, VIII*. Knoxville: University of Tennessee Press.

Peterson, Richard A., and Andy Bennett (2004). "Introducing Music Scenes," pp. 1–15 in Bennett and Peterson, eds., *Music Scenes: Local, Translocal, and Virtual*. Nashville: Vanderbilt University Press.

Peterson, Richard A., and Paul Di Maggio (1975). "From Region to Class, the Changing Locus of Country Music: A Test of the Massification Hypothesis," *Social Forces* 53: 497–506.

Petrini, Carlo (2002). *Slow Food: The Case for Taste*. New York: Columbia University Press.

——— (2006). *Slow Food Revolution: A New Culture for Eating and Living*. New York: Rizzoli.

Pickle, Linda, Michael Mungiole, Gretchen K. Jones, and Andrew A. White (1996). *Atlas of United States Mortality.* Hyattsville, Md.: National Center for Health Statistics.

Pierce, Bessie Louise (1930). *Civic Attitudes in American School Textbooks.* Chicago: University of Chicago Press.

Pierson, George (1955). "The Obstinate Concept of New England: A Study in Denudation," *New England Quarterly* 28: 3–17.

——— (1973). *The Moving American.* New York: Knopf.

Pieterse, Jan Nederveen (1995). "Globalization as Hybridization," pp. 45–68 in Mike Featherstone, Scott Lash, and Roland Robertson, eds., *Global Modernities.* London: Sage.

Pildas, Ave (1980). *Movie Palaces.* New York: Clarkson N. Potter.

Pillsbury, Richard (1968). *The Urban Street Patterns of Pennsylvania before 1815: A Study in Cultural Geography.* Ph.D. diss., Pennsylvania State University.

——— (1995a). "Carolina Thunder: A Geography of Southern Stock Car Racing," pp. 229–38 in George O. Carney, ed., *Fast Food, Stock Cars, and Rock 'n' Roll: Place and Space in American Pop Culture.* Lanham, Md.: Rowman & Littlefield.

——— (1995b). "Stock Car Racing," pp. 270–95 in Raitz 1995d.

——— (2006). "Landscape, Cultural," pp. 1–34 in Pillsbury, ed., *The New Encyclopedia of Southern Culture*, vol. 2: *Geography.* Chapel Hill: University of North Carolina Press.

Pitzer, Donald E. (1997). *America's Communal Utopias.* Chapel Hill: University of North Carolina Press.

Plowden, David (1984). *Bridges: The Spans of North America.* New York: W. W. Norton.

——— (2003). *The American Barn.* New York: W. W. Norton.

Polanyi, Karl (1944). *The Great Transformation.* New York: Holt, Rinehart & Winston.

Pomada, Elizabeth, and Michael Larsen (1978). *Painted Ladies: San Francisco's Resplendent Victorians.* New York: E. P. Dutton.

Poole, W. Scott (2005). "Lincoln in Hell: Class and Confederate Symbols in the American South," pp. 121–48 in Michael E. Geisler, ed., *National Symbols, Fractured Identities: Contesting the National Narrative.* Middlebury, Vt.: Middlebury College Press.

Porter, Philip W., and Fred E. Lukermann (1976). "The Geography of Utopia," pp. 197–223 in David Lowenthal and Martyn J. Bowden, eds., *Geographies of the Mind: Essays in Historical Geography in Honor of John Kirtland Wright.* New York: Oxford University Press.

Postman, Neil (1985). *Amusing Ourselves to Death: Public Discourse in the Age of Show Business.* New York: Viking.

Potok, Mark (2000). "Red Hot 'Patriot' Movement Cools Down," *Intelligence Report* [Southern Poverty Law Center] 98: 16–24.

Preston, Dennis R., ed. (2003). *Needed Research in American Dialects.* Publications of the American Dialect Society no. 88. Durham, N.C.: Duke University Press.

Preston, Howard Lawrence (1991a). *Dirt Roads to Dixie: Accessibility and Modernization in the South, 1885–1935.* Knoxville: University of Tennessee Press.

——— (1991b). "Will Dixie Disappear? Cultural Contours of a Region in Transition," pp. 188–216 in Joe P. Dunn and Preston, eds., *The Future South: A Historical Perspective for the Twenty-first Century.* Urbana: University of Illinois Press.

Price, Edward T. (1968). "The Central Courthouse Square in the American County Seat," *Geographical Review* 58: 29–60.

———(1995). *Dividing the Land: Early American Beginnings of Our Present Private Property Mosaic.* Geography Research Paper no. 238. Chicago: University of Chicago.

Pudup, Mary Beth (1988). "Arguments within Regional Geography," *Progress in Human Geography* 12: 369–90.

Puljak, Karl (2006). "Buy One, Get Two Free: Fireworks," pp. 213–27 in Stager and Carver 2006.

Putnam, Robert D. (2000). *Bowling Alone: The Collapse and Revival of American Community.* New York: Simon & Schuster.

Pyle, Jane (1971). Farmers' Markets in the United States," *Geographical Review* 61: 167–97.

Rabin, Carol Price (1983). *Music Festivals in America,* rev. ed. Stockbridge, Mass.: Berkshire Traveller Press.

Radford, John P. (1976). "Race, Residence, and Ideology: Charleston, South Carolina in the Mid-Nineteenth Century," *Journal of Historical Geography* 2(4): 329–46.

Rae, John B. (1971). *The Road and the Car in American Life.* Cambridge: MIT Press.

Raento, Paulina (2003). "The Return of the One-Armed Bandit: Gambling and the West," pp. 225–52 in Hausladen 2003b.

Raitz, Karl B. (1975). "The Wisconsin Tobacco Shed: A Key to Ethnic Settlement and Diffusion," *Landscape* 20(1): 32–37.

———(1978). "The Barns of Barren County," *Landscape* 22(2): 19–26.

———(1980). *The Kentucky Bluegrass: A Regional Profile and Guide.* Studies in Geography no. 14. Chapel Hill: University of North Carolina Press.

———(1995a). "The Theater of Sport: A Landscape Perspective," pp. 1–29 in Raitz 1995d.

———(1995b). "Thoroughbred Racing," pp. 321–56 in Raitz 1995d.

———(1995c). "Fox Hunting," pp. 357–81 in Raitz 1995d.

———, ed. (1995d). *The Theater of Sport.* Baltimore: Johns Hopkins University Press.

———(1998). "American Foxhunting: Landscape Ensemble and Gratification," pp. 157–71 in George O. Carney, ed., *Baseball, Barns, and Bluegrass: A Geography of American Folklife.* Lanham, Md.: Rowman & Littlefield.

*Rand McNally Commercial Atlas & Marketing Guide*, vol. 1: *Guide*, 135th ed. (2004). Chicago.

Rangaswamy, Padma (2006). "Asian Indians in Chicago," pp. 128–40 in John P. Koval, Barry Bennette, Michael I. J. Bennette, Fassil Demissie, Roberta Garner, and Kiljoon Kim, eds., *The New Chicago: A Social and Cultural Analysis.* Philadelphia: Temple University Press.

Ray, Angela G. (2005). *The Lyceum and Public Culture in the Nineteenth-Century United States.* East Lansing: Michigan State University Press.

Ray, Celeste (2005). "Dynamism and Gatekeeping in the Study of Regions: An Anthropological Approach," pp. 77–85 in Hönnighausen, Frey, Peacock, and Steiner 2005.

Raymond, C. Elizabeth (1996). "Middle Ground: Evolving Regional Images in the American Middle West," pp. 95–116 in D'haen and Bertens 1996.

Reddin, Paul (1999). *Wild West Shows.* Urbana: University of Illinois Press.

Reed, John Shelton (1976). "The Heart of Dixie: An Essay in Folk Geography," *Social Forces* 54: 925–39.

—— (1982). *One South: An Ethnic Approach to Regional Culture*. Baton Rouge: Louisiana State University Press.

—— (1983). *Southerners: The Social Psychology of Sectionalism*. Chapel Hill: University of North Carolina Press.

—— (1990). *Whistling Dixie: Dispatches from the South*. Columbia: University of Missouri Press.

—— (2005). "The South's Midlife Crisis," pp. 254–64 in John Lowe, ed., *Bridging Southern Cultures: An Interdisciplinary Approach*. Baton Rouge: Louisiana State University Press.

Reiff, Daniel D. (2000). *Houses from Books: Treatises, Pattern Books, and Catalogs in American Architecture, 1783–1950: A History and Guide*. University Park: Pennsylvania State University Press.

Reigelman, Milton M. (1975). *The Midland: A Venture in Literary Regionalism*. Iowa City: University of Iowa Press.

Relph, Edward (1976). *Place and Placelessness*. London: Pion.

—— (1981). *Rational Landscapes and Humanistic Geography*. London: Croom Helm.

—— (1987). *The Modern Urban Landscape*. Baltimore: Johns Hopkins University Press.

Reps, John W. (1965). *The Making of Urban America*. Princeton: Princeton University Press.

—— (1981). *The Forgotten Frontier: Urban Planning in the American West before 1890*. Columbia: University of Missouri Press.

Rhyne, David W. (1979). *The Army Post in American Culture: A Historical Geography of Army Posts in the United States*. M.S. thesis, Pennsylvania State University.

Rice, Bradley R. (1990). "Searching for the Sunbelt," pp. 212–23 in Mohl 1990.

Richardon, E. P. (1951). "Regionalism in American Painting," pp. 261–72 in M. Jensen 1951.

Rickert, John E. (1967). "House Facades of the Northeastern United States: A Tool of Geographic Analysis," *Annals of the Association of American Geographers* 57: 211–38.

Rieser, Andrew Chamberlin (2001). "Lyceums, Chautauquas, and Institutes for Useful Knowledge," vol. 3, pp. 351–62 in Cayton and Williams 2001.

Rifkind, Carole (1977). *Main Street: The Face of Urban America*. New York: Harper & Row.

Riley, Robert B. (1980). "Speculations on the New American Landscape," *Landscape* 24(3): 1–9.

Riley, Sam G., and Gary W. Selnow (1989). *Index to City and Regional Magazines of the United States*. New York: Greenwood Press.

—— (1991). *Regional Interest Magazines of the United States*. New York: Greenwood Press.

Rinschede, Gisbert (1990). "Catholic Pilgrimage Places in the United States," pp. 63–135 in Rinschede and S. M. Bhardwaj, eds., *Pilgrimage in the United States*. Berlin: Dietrich Reimer Verlag.

—— (1999). *Religionsgeographie*. Braunschweig: Westermann.

Ritzer, George (1993). *The McDonaldization of Society: An Investigation into the Changing Character of Contemporary Social Life*. Newbury Park, Calif.: Pine Forge Press.

Robbins, William G. (1983). "Introduction," pp. 1–9 in Robbins, Frank, and Ross 1983.

Robbins, William G., Robert J. Frank, and Richard E. Ross, eds. (1983). *Regionalism and the Pacific Northwest.* Corvallis: Oregon State University Press.

Roberts, Diane (2002). "The South of the Mind," pp. 363–73 in Jones and Monteith 2002.

Roberts, John W. (2006). *The History of the Federal Penitentiary at Lewisburg.* Lewisburg, Pa.: Union County Historical Society.

Roberts, Warren E. (1984). *Log Buildings of Southern Indiana.* Bloomington: Trickster Press.

Robertson, David (2006). *Hard as the Rock Itself: Place and Identity in the American Mining Town.* Boulder: University Press of Colorado.

Robertson, Roland (1995). "Globalization: Time-Space and Homogeneity-Heterogeneity," pp. 25–44 in Mike Featherstone, Scott Lash, and Robertson, eds., *Global Modernities.* London: Sage.

Robinson, John, and Alfred Calais (1966). *California State Parks.* Menlo Park, Calif.: Lane Books.

Rohe, Randall (1984). "The Geography and Material Culture of the Western Mining Town," *Material Culture* 16: 99–120.

——— (1985). "Settlement Patterns of Logging Camps in the Great Lakes Region," *Journal of Cultural Geography* 6(1): 79–107.

Rollins, Richard M. (1980). *The Long Journey of Noah Webster.* Philadelphia: University of Pennsylvania Press.

Rooney, John F., Jr. (1974). *A Geography of American Sport from Cabin Creek to Anaheim.* Reading, Mass.: Addison-Wesley.

Rooney, John F., Jr., and Paul L. Butt (1978). "Beer, Bourbon and Boone's Farm: A Geographical Examination of Alcoholic Drink in the United States," *Journal of Popular Culture* 11(4): 832–56.

Rooney, John F., Jr., and Richard Pillsbury (1992). *Atlas of American Sport.* New York: Macmillan.

Rooney, John F., Jr., Wilbur Zelinsky, and Dean R. Louder, eds. (1982). *This Remarkable Continent: An Atlas of the United States and Canadian Society and Cultures.* College Station: Texas A&M University Press.

Rose, Gillian (1995). "Place and Identity: A Sense of Place," pp. 87–132 in Massey and Jess 1995b.

Rosenberry, Lois (Kimball) Mathews (1909). *The Expansion of New England: The Spread of New England Settlement and Institutions to the Mississippi River, 1620–1865.* Boston: Houghton Mifflin.

Ross, Alex (2007). *The Rest Is Noise: Listening to the Twentieth Century.* New York: Farrar, Straus & Giroux.

Rossi, John P. (2000). *The National Game: Baseball and American Culture.* Chicago: Ivan R. Dee.

Roszak, Theodore (1972). *Where the Wasteland Ends: Politics and Transcendence in Postindustrial Society.* New York: Doubleday.

Roth, Leland M. (1992). "Company Towns in the Western United States," pp. 173–205 in Garner 1992b.

Rothman, Hal (2002). *Neon Metropolis: How Las Vegas Started the Twenty-first Century.* New York: Routledge.

Rowsome, Frank (1961). *The Verse by the Side of the Road: The Story of the Burma Shave Signs and Jingles*. New York: E. P. Dutton.

Royce, Josiah (1908). *Race Questions, Provincialism, and Other American Problems*. New York: Macmillan.

Rubin, Louis D., Jr. (1988). "Changing, Enduring, Forever Still the South," pp. 222–29 in Dudley Clendinen, ed., *The Prevailing South: Life & Politics in a Changing Culture*. Atlanta: Longstreet Press.

Rubinstein, Ruth P. (1995). *Dress Codes: Meanings and Messages in American Culture*. Boulder, Colo.: Westview Press.

Runte, Alfred (1997). *National Parks: The American Experience*, 3rd ed. Lincoln: University of Nebraska Press.

Russell, George L. (2001). *Native American Reservations* [Map]. Author.

Ryan, Bruce (1995). "Tennis," pp. 141–67 in Raitz 1995d.

Rycroft, Simon (1998). "Global Undergrounds: The Cultural Politics of Sound and Light in Los Angeles, 1965–1975," pp. 222–48 in Andrew Leyshon, David Matless, and George Revill, eds., *The Place of Music*. New York: Guilford.

Rydell, Robert William, II (1980). *All The World's a Fair: America's International Expositions, 1876–1916*. Ph.D. diss., University of California, Berkeley.

Ryden, Kent C. (1993). *Mapping the Invisible Landscape: Folklore, Writing, and the Sense of Place*. Iowa City: University of Iowa Press.

Sack, Robert David (1986). *Human Territoriality: Its Theory and History*. Cambridge: Cambridge University Press.

———(1997). *Homo Geographicus: A Framework for Action, Awareness, and Moral Concern*. Baltimore: Johns Hopkins University Press.

Sale, Kirkpatrick (1975). *Power Shift: The Rise of the Southern Rim and Its Challenge to the Eastern Establishment*. New York: Random House.

———(1985). *Dwellers in the Land: The Bioregional Vision*. San Francisco: Sierra Club Books.

Sales, Amy L., and Leonard Saxe (2004). *"How Goodly Are Thy Tents": Summer Camps as Jewish Socializing Experiences*. Hanover, N.H.: University Press of New England.

Samuel, Lawrence R. (2001). *Brought to You By: Postwar Television Advertising and the American Dream*. Austin: University of Texas Press.

Sandler, Rob (1993). *Architecture in Hawai'i: A Chronological Survey*. Honolulu: Mutual Publishing.

Sarasohn, David (1983). "Regionalism Tending toward Sectionalism," pp. 223–36 in Robbins, Frank, and Ross 1983.

Saulny, Susan (2008). "Cutting Out the Middlemen, Shoppers Buy Slices of Farms," *New York Times*, July 10: A1, A16.

Sayer, Andrew (1989). "The 'New' Regional Geography and Problems of Narrative," *Environment and Planning D: Society and Space* 7: 253–76.

Schivelbusch, Wolfgang (1986). *The Railway Journey: The Industrialization of Time and Space in the 19th Century*. Berkeley: University of California Press.

Schlereth, Thomas J. (1989a). "Country Stores, County Fairs, and Mail-Order Catalogues: Consumption in Rural America," pp. 339–75 in Simon J. Bronner, ed., *Consuming Visions: Accumulation and Display of Goods in America, 1880–1920*. New York: W. W. Norton.

——— (1989b). "Chautauqua: A Middle Landscape of the Middle Class," pp. 219–34 in Schlereth, *Cultural History and Material Culture: Everyday Life, Landscapes, Museums*. Ann Arbor: UMI Research Press.

Schmidt, Leigh Eric (1989). *Holy Fairs: Scottish Communions and American Revivals in the Early Modern Period*. Princeton: Princeton University Press.

Schneider, Alan (1973). "Foreword," pp. vii–xi in Joseph Wesley Zeigler, *Regional Theater: The Revolutionary Stage*. Minneapolis: University of Minnesota Press.

Schnell, Steven M. (2003). "Creating Narratives of Place and Identity in 'Little Sweden, U.S.A.,'" *Geographical Review* 93: 1–29.

——— (2007). "Food with a Farmer's Face: Community-Supported Agriculture in the United States," *Geographical Review* 97: 550–64.

Schnell, Steven M., and Joseph F. Reese (2005). "Microbreweries as Tools of Local Identity," *Journal of Cultural Geography* 21(1): 45–69.

Sciorra, Joseph (1989). "Yard Shrines and Sidewalk Altars of New York's Italian-Americans," pp. 185–98 in Thomas Carter and Bernard L. Herman, eds., *Perspectives in Vernacular Architecture, III*. Columbia: University of Missouri Press.

Scofield, Edna (1936). "The Evolution and Development of Tennessee Houses," *Journal of the Tennessee Academy of Sciences* 2: 229–40.

Seabrook, John (2007). "Sowing for Apocalypse: The Quest for a Global Seed Bank," *New Yorker* 83(25) (April 27): 60–71.

Seale, William (2006). "American Vernacular: The Courthouse as a Building Type," pp. 35–62 in Steven Flanders, ed., *Celebrating the Courthouse: A Guide for Architects, Their Clients, and the Public*. New York: W. W. Norton.

Sears, John F. (1985). "Doing Niagara Falls in the Nineteenth Century," pp. 103–15 in Jeremy Elwell Adamson, ed., *Niagara: Two Centuries of Changing Attitudes, 1697–1901*. Washington, D.C.: Corcoran Gallery of Art.

——— (1989). *Sacred Places: American Tourist Attractions in the Nineteenth Century*. New York: Oxford University Press.

Sechrist, Dale K. (1992). "Locating Prisons: Open versus Closed Approaches to Siting," *Crime and Delinquency* 38(1): 88–104.

Sellers, Charles (1991). *The Market Revolution: Jacksonian America, 1815–1846*. New York: Oxford University Press.

Selth, Jefferson P. (1985). *Alternative Lifestyles: A Guide to Research Collections on Intentional Communities, Nudism, and Sexual Freedom*. Bibliographies and Indexes in Sociology no. 6. Westport, Conn.: Greenwood Press.

Severson, Kim (2006). "Why Roots Matter More: Health Scares and Mass-produced Food Strengthen Demand for Local Grown," *New York Times*, November 15: E1, E6.

Sexton, R. W., ed. (1931). *American Public Buildings Today*. New York: Architectural Book Publishing Co.

Sexton, Richard (1995). *Parallel Utopias: The Quest for Community*. San Francisco: Chronicle Books.

Shafer, Byron E., ed. (1991). *Is America Different? A New Look at American Exceptionalism*. Oxford: Oxford University Press.

Shafer, Byron E., and Richard Johnston (2006). *The End of Southern Exceptionalism: Class, Race, and Partisan Change in the Postwar South*. Cambridge: Harvard University Press.

Shapiro, Henry D. (1978). *Appalachia on Our Mind: The Southern Mountains and Mountaineers in the American Consciousness, 1870–1920.* Chapel Hill: University of North Carolina Press.

——— (2005). "How Region Changed Its Meaning and Appalachia Changed Its Standing in the Twentieth Century," pp. 265–87 in John Lowe, ed., *Bridging Southern Cultures: An Interdisciplinary Approach.* Baton Rouge: Louisiana State University Press.

Sharkansky, Ira (1969). *Regionalism in American Politics.* Indianapolis: Bobbs-Merrill.

Shellito, Bradley A. (2006). "Second-Home Distributions in the USA's Upper Great Lakes States: Analysis and Implications," pp. 194–206 in McIntyre, Williams, and McHugh 2006.

Sheppard, Carl D., and Stephen D. Schreiber (1990). "Escape from the Southwest: The Pueblo Style in Minnesota and Florida," pp. 167–74 in Markovich, Preiser, and Sturm 1990.

Shils, Edward (1975). *Center and Periphery: Essays in Macrosociology.* Chicago: University of Chicago Press.

Shipp, Steve (1996). *American Art Colonies, 1850–1930: A Historical Guide to America's Original Art Colonies and Their Artists.* Westport, Conn.: Greenwood Press.

Shoemaker, Ervin C. (1966). *Noah Webster: Pioneer of Learning.* New York: AMS Press.

Short, C. W., and R. Stanley-Brown (1939). *Public Buildings: A Survey of Architecture of Projects Constructed by Federal and Other Governmental Bodies between the Years 1933 and 1939 with the Assistance of the Public Works Administration.* Washington, D.C.: GPO.

Shortridge, Barbara Gimla (1987). *Atlas of American Women.* New York: Macmillan.

——— (2003). "A Food Geography of the Great Plains," *Geographical Review* 93: 507–29.

Shortridge, Barbara Gimla, and James R. Shortridge (1998). *The Taste of American Place: A Reader on Regional and Ethnic Foods.* Lanham, Md.: Rowman & Littlefield.

Shortridge, James R. (1976). "Patterns of Religion in the United States," *Geographical Review* 66: 420–34.

——— (1977). "A New Regionalization of American Religion," *Journal for the Scientific Study of Religion* 16: 143–53.

——— (1985). "The Vernacular Middle West," *Annals of the Association of American Geographers* 75: 48–57.

——— (1987). "Changing Usage of Four American Regional Labels," *Annals of the Association of American Geographers* 77: 325–36.

——— (1989). *The Middle West: Its Meaning in American Culture.* Lawrence: University Press of Kansas.

——— (1997). "The Expectations of Others: Struggles toward a Sense of Place in the Northern Plains," pp. 114–35 in Wrobel and Steiner 1997.

——— (1998). "The Persistence of Regional Labels in the United States: Reflections from a Midwestern Perspective," pp. 45–63 in C. R. Wilson 1998b.

Shove, Elizabeth (2004). "Social, Architectural and Environmental Convergence," pp. 19–29 in Koen Steemers and Mary Ann Steane, eds., *Environmental Diversity in Architecture.* London: Spon Press.

Shryock, Richard H. (1964). "The Middle Atlantic Area in American History," *Proceedings of the American Philosophical Society* 108: 147–55.

Shurtleff, Harold R. (1939). *The Log Cabin Myth*. Cambridge: Harvard University Press.

Simon, Carola (2005). "Commodification of Regional Identities: The 'Selling' of Waterland," pp. 31–45 in G. J. Ashworth and Brian Graham, eds., *Senses of Place: Senses of Time*. Burlington, Vt.: Ashgate.

Simpson, David (1986). *The Politics of American English, 1776–1850*. New York: Oxford University Press.

Sirefman, Susanna (2004). *Whereabouts: New Architecture with Local Identities*. New York: Monacelli Press.

Slade, Joseph W., and Judith Yaros Lee, eds. (2004). *The Midwest*. The Greenwood Encyclopedia of American Regional Cultures. Westport, Conn.: Greenwood Press.

Sloane, David C. (1991). *The Last Great Necessity: Cemeteries in American History*. Baltimore: Johns Hopkins University Press.

Sloane, Eric (1954). *American Barns and Covered Bridges*. New York: W. Funk.

———(1985). *An Age of Barns*. New York: Dodd Mead.

Smith, Carl S. (1984). *Chicago and the American Literary Imagination, 1880–1920*. Chicago: University of Chicago Press.

Smith, Jonathan M. (2007). "The Texas Aggie Bonfire: A Conservative Reading of Regional Narratives, Traditional Practices, and a Paradoxical Place," *Annals of the Association of American Geographers* 97: 182–201.

Smulyan, Susan (2001). "Advertising," vol. 3, pp. 527–36 in Cayton and Williams 2001.

Snell, Tricia, ed. (2000). *Artists' Communities: A Directory of Residences in the United States That Offer Time and Space for Creativity*, 2nd ed. New York: Allworth Press.

Soderberg, Paul, and Helen Washington (1977). *The Big Book of Halls of Fame in the United States and Canada*. New York: R. R. Bowker.

Sokolov, Raymond (1981). *Fading Feast: A Compendium of Disappearing American Regional Foods*. New York: Farrar, Straus & Giroux.

Sola Pool, Ithiel de (1977). "Introduction," pp. 1–9 in Sola Pool, ed., *The Social Impact of the Telephone*. Cambridge: MIT Press.

Soleri, Paolo (1987). *Arcosanti: An Urban Laboratory?* Santa Monica, Calif.: VTI Press.

Sommer, Robert (1980). *Farmers Markets of America: A Renaissance*. Santa Barbara, Calif.: Capra Press.

Sosnik, Douglas B., Matthew J. Dowd, and Ron Fournier (2006). *Applebee's America: How Successful Political, Business, and Religious Leaders Connect with the New American Community*. New York: Simon & Schuster.

Speck, Lawrence W., and Wayne Attoe, eds. (1987). "New Regionalism," special issue of *Center: A Journal for Architecture in America*, vol. 3. New York: Rizzoli.

Spencer, Benjamin T. (1951). "Regionalism in American Literature," pp. 220–60 in M. Jensen 1951.

Sper, Felix (1948). *From Native Roots: A Panorama of Our Regional Drama*. Caldwell, Idaho: Caxton Printers.

Squeri, Lawrence (2003). *Better in the Poconos: The Story of Pennsylvania's Vacationland*. University Park: Pennsylvania State University Press.

Stager, Claudette, and Margaret Carver, eds. (2006). *Looking beyond the Highway: Dixie Roads and Culture*. Knoxville: University of Tennessee Press.

Stansfield, Charles A., Jr. (1990). "Cape May: Selling History by the Sea," *Journal of Cultural Geography* 11(1): 25–37.

Starbuck, James C. (1976). *Theme Parks: A Partially Annotated Bibliography of Articles about Modern Amusement Parks.* Council of Planning Librarians Exchange, Bibliography 953. Monticello, Ill.: Council of Planning Librarians Exchange.

Starrett, W. A. (1928). *Skyscrapers and the Men Who Build Them.* New York: Charles Scribner's Sons.

Starrs, Paul F. (1994). "The Importance of Places, or a Sense of Where You Are," *Spectrum* 67(3): 5–17.

Starrs, Paul F., and John B. Wright (2005). "Utopia, Dystopia, and Sublime Apocalypse in Montana's Church Universal and Triumphant," *Geographical Review* 95: 97–121.

Steere, Edward (1953–54). "Expansion of the National Cemetery System, 1880–1900," *Quartermaster Review* 33(2): 20–21, 131–37.

Stegner, Wallace (1992). *Where the Bluebird Sings to the Lemonade Springs: Living and Writing in the West.* New York: Random House.

Steinberg, Ted (2006). *American Green: The Obsessive Quest for the Perfect Lawn.* New York: W. W. Norton.

Steiner, Michael C. (1983). "Regionalism in the Great Depression," *Geographical Review* 73: 430–46.

Steiner, Michael C., and Clarence Mondale (1988). *Region and Regionalism in the United States: A Sourcebook for the Humanities and Social Sciences.* New York: Garland.

Steiner, Michael C., and David M. Wrobel (1997). "Many Wests: Discovering a Dynamic Western Regionalism," pp. 1–30 in Wrobel and Steiner 1997.

Steinhiber, Berthold (2003). *Ghost Towns of the American West.* New York: Harry N. Abrams.

Sterngass, Jon (2001). *First Resorts: Pursuing Pleasure at Saratoga Springs, Newport & Coney Island.* Baltimore: Johns Hopkins University Press.

Stewart, George R. (1954). *American Ways of Life.* Garden City: Doubleday.

Stewart, Janet Ann (1974). *Arizona Ranch Houses: Southern Territorial Style, 1867–1900.* Tucson: Arizona Historical Society.

Stilgoe, John R. (1982). *Common Landscape of America, 1580–1845.* New Haven: Yale University Press.

——— (1983). *Metropolitan Corridor: Railroads and the American Scene.* New Haven: Yale University Press.

Stipe, Robert E., ed. (2003). *A Richer Heritage: Historic Preservation in the Twenty-first Century.* Chapel Hill: University of North Carolina Press.

Stokes, Melvyn (1996). "Introduction," pp. 1–20 in Stokes and Stephen Conway, eds., *The Market Revolution in America: Social, Political and Religious Expressions, 1800–1880.* Charlottesville: University Press of Virginia.

Stone, James (1941). "War Music and War Psychology in the Civil War," *Journal of Abnormal and Social Psychology* 36: 543–60.

Strasser, Susan (1989). *Satisfaction Guaranteed: The Making of the American Mass Market.* New York: Pantheon.

Strombeck, Janet, and Richard Strombeck (1980). *The Classic Outhouse Book.* Delafield, Wisc.: Sun Designs Rexstrom.

Stroud, Hubert B. (1995). *The Promise of Paradise: Recreational and Retirement Communities in the United States since 1950.* Baltimore: Johns Hopkins University Press.

Stump, Roger (1984). "Regional Divergence in Religious Affiliation in the United States," *Sociological Analysis* 45(4): 283–99.

Suchan, Trudy A., Marc J. Perry, and James D. Fitzsimmons (2007). *Census Atlas of the United States*. Series CENS R-29. Washington, D.C.: U.S. Census Bureau.

Suckow, Ruth (1930). "The Folk Idea in American Life," *Scribner's Magazine* 88 (September): 245–55.

Sugar, Max (2004). *Regional Identity and Behavior*. New York: Kluwer Academic/Plenum.

Suttles, Gerald D. (1984). "The Cumulative Texture of Local Urban Culture," *American Journal of Sociology* 90: 283–302.

—— (1990). *The Man-Made City: The Land-Use Confidence Game in Chicago*. Chicago: University of Chicago Press.

Sutton, Robert P. (2003). *Communal Utopias and the American Experience: Religious Communities, 1732–2000*. Westport, Conn.: Praeger.

Sutton-Smith, B., and B. C. Rosenberg (1961). "Sixty Years of Historical Change in the Game Preferences of American Children," *Journal of American Folklore* 74: 17–46.

Swanton, John R. (1979). *The Indians of the Southeastern United States*. Washington, D.C.: Smithsonian Institution Press.

Tawa, Nicholas (1984). *A Music for the Millions: Antebellum Democratic Attitudes and the Birth of American Popular Music*. New York: Pendragon Press.

Taylor, Charles (2007). *A Secular Age*. Cambridge: Harvard University Press.

Taylor, Joe Gray (1982). *Eating, Drinking, and Visiting in the South: An Informal History*. Baton Rouge: Louisiana State University Press.

Tedlow, Richard S. (1993). "The Fourth Phase of Marketing: Marketing History and the Business World Today," pp. 8–35 in Tedlow and Geoffrey Jones, eds., *The Rise and Fall of Mass Marketing*. London: Routledge.

Teyssot, Georges (1999). "The American Lawn: Surface of Everyday Life," pp. 1–39 in Teyssot, ed., *The American Lawn*. New York: Princeton Architectural Press.

Thacker, Robert (1989). *The Great Prairie Fact and Literary Imagination*. Albuquerque: University of New Mexico Press.

Thayer, Robert L., Jr. (1990). "Pragmatism in Paradise: Technology and the American Landscape," *Landscape* 30(3): 1–11.

—— (2003). *Lifeplace: Bioregional Thought and Practice*. Berkeley: University of California Press.

Thayer, Stuart (1997). *Traveling Showmen: The American Circus before the Civil War*. Detroit: Astley & Ricketts.

Thernstrom, Stephan (1973). *The Other Bostonians: Poverty and Progress in the American Metropolis, 1880–1970*. Cambridge: Harvard University Press.

Thomas, Bernice L. (1997). *America's 5 & 10 Cent Store: The Kress Legacy*. New York: John Wiley & Sons.

Thomas, John L. (1990). "Lewis Mumford, Benton Mackaye, and the Regional Vision," pp. 66–99 in Thomas P. Hughes and Agatha C. Hughes, eds., *Lewis Mumford: Public Intellectual*. New York: Oxford University Press.

Thompson, Robert Luther (1974). *Wiring a Continent: The History of the Telegraph Industry in the United States, 1832–1866*. Princeton: Princeton University Press.

Thompson, Robert S. (2007). "The Air Conditioning Capital of the World: Houston and Climate Control," pp. 88–107 in Martin V. Melosi and Joseph A. Pratt, eds., *Energy Metropolis: An Environmental History of Houston and the Gulf Coast*. Pittsburgh: University of Pittsburgh Press.

Till, Karen (1993). "Neotraditional Towns and Urban Villages: The Cultural Production of a Geography of 'Otherness,'" *Environment and Planning D: Society and Space* 11: 709–32.

Tindall, George B. (1993). "Regionalism," vol. 1, pp. 531–41 in Cayton, Gorn, and Williams 1993.

Tishler, William H. (1979). "Stovewood Architecture," *Landscape* 23(3): 28–31.

Tocqueville, Alexis de (1945) [1835]. *Democracy in America.* New York: Vintage Books.

Toffler, Alvin (1970). *Future Shock.* New York: Bantam.

Tomlinson, John (1999). *Globalization and Culture.* Chicago: University of Chicago Press.

Torrey, Volta (1976). *Wind-Catchers: American Windmills of Yesterday and Tomorrow.* Brattleboro, Vt.: Stephen Greene Press.

Trachtenberg, Alan (1965). *Brooklyn Bridge: Fact and Symbol.* New York: Oxford University Press.

Trant, Kate, ed. (2005). *Home Away from Home: The World of Camper Vans and Motorhomes.* London: Black Dog Publishing.

Travis, Kevin M., and Francis J. Sheridan (1983). "Community Involvement in Prison Siting," *Corrections Today* 45: 14.

Trépanier, Cécyle (1989). *French Louisiana at the Threshold of the 21st Century.* Projet Louisiane, Monographie, no. 3. Quebec: Université Laval, Département de Géographie.

Trewartha, Glenn T. (1946). "Types of Rural Settlement in Colonial America," *Geographical Review* 36: 568–96.

——— (1948). "Some Regional Characteristics of American Farmsteads," *Annals of the Association of American Geographers* 38: 169–225.

Troester, Maura (2003). "Roadside Retroscape: History and the Marketing of Tourism in the Middle of Nowhere," pp. 115–40 in Brown and Sherry 2003.

Tuan, Yi-Fu (1974). "Space and Place: Humanistic Perspective," *Progress in Human Geography* 6: 223–46.

——— (1977). *Space and Place: The Perspective of Experience.* Minneapolis: University of Minnesota Press.

——— (1978). "Sacred Space: Exploration of an Idea," pp. 84–99 in Karl W. Butzer, ed., *Dimensions of Human Geography.* Research Paper 186. Chicago: University of Chicago, Department of Geography.

——— (1980). "Rootedness versus Sense of Place." *Landscape* 24(1): 3–8.

Tunnard, Christopher, and Boris Pushkarev (1963). *Man-Made America: Chaos or Control?* New Haven: Yale University Press.

Tunnard, Christopher, and Henry Hope Reed (1956). *American Skyline.* New York: New American Library.

Turner, Frederick Jackson (1914). "Geographical Influences in American Political History," *Bulletin of the American Geographical Society* 46: 591–95.

——— (1932). *The Significance of Sections in American History.* New York: Henry Holt.

Turow, Joseph (1997). *Breaking Up America: Advertisers and the New Media World.* Chicago: University of Chicago Press.

Ulrich, Laurel Thatcher (1983). *Good Wives: Image and Reality in the Lives of Women in Northern New England, 1650–1750.* New York: Oxford University Press.

U.S. Customs Service (1997). *Official Uniform Program Catalog.* Nashville: R&R Uniforms, Inc.

U.S. Geological Survey (1970). *The National Atlas of the United States of America.* Washington, D.C.: U.S. Deparrtment of the Interior.

U.S. Rural Electrification Administration, Department of Agriculture (1974). *Rural Telephone Service: Twenty-five Years of Progress.* Washington, D.C.: U.S. Deparrtment of Agriculture.

U.S. Rural Electrification Administration (1986). *A Brief History of the Rural Electric and Telephone Programs.* Washington, D.C.: U.S. Department of Agriculture.

Upton, Dell (1996). "Ethnicity, Authenticity, and Invented Tradition," *Historical Archaeology* 30: 1–7.

Upton, Dell, and John Michael Vlach, eds. (1986). *Common Places: Readings in American Vernacular Architecture.* Athens: University of Georgia Press.

Valenza, Janet Mace (2000). *Taking the Waters in Texas: Springs, Spas, and Fountains of Youth.* Austin: University of Texas Press.

Valerio, Christy (1997). *Elderly Americans: Where They Choose to Retire.* New York: Garland.

Van Slyck, Abigail A. (1995). *Free to All: Carnegie Libraries & American Culture, 1890–1920.* Chicago: University of Chicago Press.

——— (2006). *A Manufactured Wilderness: Summer Camps and the Shaping of American Youth, 1890–1960.* Minneapolis: University of Minnesota Press.

Vance, James B., Jr. (1970). *The Merchant's World: The Geography of Wholesaling.* Englewood Cliffs, N.J.: Prentice-Hall.

——— (1986). *Capturing the Horizon: The Historical Geography of Transportation since the Transportation Revolution of the Sixteenth Century.* New York: Harper & Row.

Vance, Rupert B. (1935). *Human Geography of the South: A Study in Regional Resources and Human Adequacy,* 2nd ed. Chapel Hill: University of North Carolina Press.

——— (1968). "Region," vol. 13, pp. 377–82 in David L. Sills, ed., *International Encyclopedia of the Social Sciences.* New York: Crowell and Macmillan.

——— (1982) [1960]. "The Sociological Implications of Southern Regionalism," pp. 208–19 in John Shelton Reed and Daniel Joseph Singal, eds., *Regionalism and the South: Selected Papers of Rupert Vance.* Chapel Hill: University of North Carolina Press.

Venturi, Robert (1972). *Learning from Las Vegas.* Cambridge: MIT Press.

Veysey, Laurence R. (1960). "Myth and Reality in Approaching American Regionalism," *American Quarterly* 12(1): 31–43.

——— (1973). *The Communal Experience: Anarchist and Mystical Communities in Twentieth Century America.* Chicago: University of Chicago Press.

Vieyra, Daniel I. (1979). *"Fill 'er Up": An Architectural History of America's Gas Stations.* New York: Collier Books.

Vlach, John Michael (1977). "Graveyards and Afro-American Art," pp. 161–65 in *Long Journey Home: Folklife in the South.* Chapel Hill: Southern Exposure.

——— (1986) [1976]. "The Shotgun House: An African Architectural Legacy," pp. 58–78 in Upton and Vlach 1986.

——— (2003). *Barns.* New York: W. W. Norton; Washington, D.C.: Library of Congress.

Voigt, David Q. (1976). *America through Baseball.* Chicago: Nelson-Hall.

Von Glahn, Denise (2003). *The Sounds of Places: Music and the American Cultural Landscape.* Boston: Northeastern University Press.

Waite, Marjorie Peabody (1933). *Yaddo Yesterday and Today.* Saratoga Springs, N.Y.: Author.

Waldstreicher, David (1997). *In the Midst of Perpetual Fetes: The Making of American Nationalism, 1776–1820.* Chapel Hill: University of North Carolina Press.

Wallis, Allan D. (1991). *Wheel Estate: The Rise and Decline of Mobile Homes.* New York: Oxford University Press.

Walter, Eugene Victor (1988). *Placeways: A Theory of the Human Environment.* Chapel Hill: University of North Carolina Press.

Warfel, Harry R. (1936). *Noah Webster, Schoolmaster to America.* New York: Macmillan.

Warner, Sam Bass, Jr. (1968). *The Private City: Philadelphia in Three Periods of Its Growth.* Philadelphia: University of Pennsylvania Press.

Warren, Louis S. (2005). *Buffalo Bill's America: William Cody and the Wild West Show.* New York: Knopf.

Wartella, Ellen, and Sharon Mazzarella (1990). "An Historical Comparison of Children's Use of Time with Media: 1920s to 1980s," pp. 173–94 in R. Butsch, ed., *For Fun and Profit.* Philadelphia: Temple University Press.

Watts, Edward (2002). *An American Colony: Regionalism and the Roots of Midwestern Culture.* Athens: Ohio University Press.

Webb, Walter Prescott (1931). *The Great Plains.* Lincoln: University of Nebraska Press.

Webber, Melvin M (1964a). "Culture, Territoriality, and the Elastic Mile," *Papers of the Regional Science Association* 13: 283–304.

——— (1964b). "The Urban Place and the Nonplace Urban Realm," pp. 79–153 in Webber et al., *Explorations into Urban Structure.* Philadelphia: University of Pennsylvania Press.

——— (1970). "Order in Diversity: Community without Propinquity," pp. 533–49 in Harold M. Proshansky, ed., *Environmental Psychology.* New York: Holt, Rinehart & Winston.

Weber, Eugen (1976). *Peasants into Frenchmen: The Modernization of Rural France, 1870–1914.* Stanford: Stanford University Press.

Weeks, Jim (2003). *Gettysburg: Memory, Market, and an American Shrine.* Princeton: Princeton University Press.

Weightman, Barbara A. (1980). "Gay Bars as Private Places," *Landscape* 24(1): 9–16.

Weinstein, Stephen Frederick (1984). *The Nickel Empire: Coney Island and the Creation of Urban Seaside Resorts in the United States.* Ph.D. diss., Columbia University.

Weiss, Ellen (1987). *City in the Woods: The Life and Design of an American Camp Meeting on Martha's Vineyard.* New York: Oxford University Press.

Weiss, Michael J. (1988). *The Clustering of America.* New York: Harper & Row.

——— (1994). *Latitudes & Attitudes: An Atlas of American Tastes, Trends, Politics, and Passions from Abilene, Texas to Zanesville, Ohio.* Boston: Little, Brown.

——— (2000). *The Clustered World: How We Live, What We Buy, and What It All Means about Who We Are.* Boston: Little, Brown.

Wells, Rosalie (1931). *Covered Bridges in America.* New York: William Edwin Rudge.

Wells, Walter (1973). *Tycoons and Locusts: A Regional Look at Hollywood Fiction of the 1930s.* Carbondale: Southern Illinois University Press.

Welsch, Roger L. (1968). *Sod Walls: The Story of the Nebraska Sod House.* Broken Bow, Neb.: Purcells, Inc.

Welty, Eudora (1956). "Place in Fiction," *South Atlantic Quarterly* 55: 57–72.

West, Elliott (1996). *Growing Up in Twentieth-Century America: A History and Reference Guide.* Westport, Conn.: Greenwood Press.

West, Patricia (1999). *Domesticating History: The Political Origins of America's House Museums.* Washington, D.C.: Smithsonian Institution Press.

Wheeler, Mary Bray, ed. (1990). *Directory of Historical Organizations in the United States and Canada,* 14th ed. Nashville: AASCH Press.

Whisnant, David E. (1983). *All That Is Native & Fine: The Politics of Culture in an American Region.* Chapel Hill: University of North Carolina Press.

White, C. Albert (1982). *A History of the Rectangular Survey System.* Washington, D.C.: GPO.

White, Horace (1914). *Money and Banking Illustrated by American History,* 5th ed. Boston: Ginn.

Whitehead, John S. (1997). "Noncontiguous Wests: Alaska and Hawai'i," pp. 315–41 in Wrobel and Steiner 1997.

Whittlesey, Derwent (1954). "The Regional Concept and the Regional Method," pp. 19–68 in Preston E. James and Clarence F. Jones, eds., *American Geography: Inventory & Prospect.* Syracuse: Syracuse University Press.

Wiebe, Robert H. (1967). *The Search for Order, 1877–1920.* New York: Hill & Wang.

Wiegand, Wayne A. (1989). *"An Active Instrument for Propaganda": The American Public Library during World War I.* New York: Greenwood Press.

Wilentz, Sean (1997). "Society, Politics, and the Market Revolution, 1815–1849," pp. 51–84 in Eric Foner, ed., *The New American History.* Philadelphia: Temple University Press.

Wilkinson, Sylvia (1980). "Red-necks on Wheels: The Stock Car Culture," pp. 129–39 in Louis D. Rubin Jr., ed., *The American South: Portrait of a Culture.* Baton Rouge: Louisiana State University Press.

Williams, Daniel R., and B. P. Kaltenborn (1999). "Leisure Places and Modernity: The Use and Meaning of Recreational Cottages in Norway and the USA," pp. 214–30 in D. Crouch, ed., *Leisure/Tourism Geographies: Practices and Geographical Knowledge.* London: Routledge.

Williams, John Alexander (2002). *Appalachia: A History.* Chapel Hill: University of North Carolina Press.

Williams, Patrick (1988). *The American Public Library and the Problem of Purpose.* New York: Greenwood Press.

Williams, Raymond (1985). *Keywords: A Vocabulary of Culture and Society,* rev. ed. New York: Oxford University Press.

Wilson, Charles Reagan (1997). "American Regionalism in a Postmodern World," *Amerikastudien/American Studies* 42: 142–58.

——— (1998a). "Introduction," pp. ix–xxiii in C. R. Wilson 1998b.

———, ed. (1998b). *The New Regionalism.* Jackson: University Press of Mississippi.

Wilson, Chris (1990). "New Mexico in the Tradition of Romantic Reaction," pp. 175–94 in Markovich, Preiser, and Sturm 1990.

——— (1997). *The Myth of Santa Fe: Creating a Modern Regional Tradition.* Albuquerque: University of New Mexico Press.

Wilson, Janelle L. (2005). *Nostalgia: Sanctuary of Meaning.* Lewisburg: Bucknell University Press.

Wilson, Joe (1996). "Blues and Bluegrass: Tough Arts of the Underclass," pp. 82–89 in Elizabeth Peterson, *The Changing Faces of Tradition: A Report on the Folk and Traditional Arts in the United States.* Research Division Report no. 38. Washington, D.C.: National Endowment for the Arts.

Windrow, Martin C., and Gerry Embleton (1970). *Military Dress of North America, 1665–1970.* New York: Scribner's.

Winkler, John K. (1970) [1940]. *Five and Ten: The Fabulous Life of F. W. Woolworth.* Freeport, N.Y.: Books for Libraries Press.

Winter, Robert (1980). *The California Bungalow.* Los Angeles: Hennessey & Ingalls.

Wiseman, Carter, ed. (2007). *A Place for the Arts: The MacDowell Colony, 1907–2007.* Hanover, N.H.: University Press of New England.

Wolfram, Walt, and Natalie Schilling-Estes (1998). *American English: Dialects and Variation.* Malden, Mass.: Blackwell.

Wood, Denis (2006). Personal communication. October 24.

Wood, Joseph S. (1997a). *The New England Village.* Baltimore: Johns Hopkins University Press.

——— (1997b). "Vietnamese American Place Making in Northern Virginia," *Geographical Review* 87: 58–72.

Wood, Robert E. (1948). *Mail Order Retailing Pioneered in Chicago.* New York: Newcomen Society of England, American Branch.

Woodbridge, Sally (1974). "The Great Northwest Revival," *Progressive Architecture* 55(8): 46–63.

Workman, R. Bryce (1991). *National Park Service Uniforms: Badges and Insignia, 1894–1991.* Harpers Ferry, W.Va.: National Park Service History Collection.

Wright, John K., ed. (1933). *New England's Prospect: 1933.* New York: American Geographical Society.

Wrobel, David M. (1996). "Beyond the Frontier-Region Dichotomy," *Pacific Historical Review* 65: 401–29.

Wrobel, David M., and Michael C. Steiner, eds. (1997). *Many Wests: Place, Culture & Regional Identity.* Lawrence: University Press of Kansas.

Wyckoff, William, and Lary M. Dilsaver (1995). "Defining the Mountainous West," pp. 1–59 in Wyckoff and Dilsaver, eds., *The Mountainous West: Explorations in Historical Geography.* Lincoln: University of Nebraska Press.

Wyile, Herb, Christian Riegel, Karen Overbye, and Don Perkins (1997). "Introduction: Regionalism Revisited," pp. ix–xiv in Riegel, Wyile, Overbye, and Perkins, eds., *A Sense of Place: Re-Evaluating Regionalism in Canadian and American Writing.* Edmonton: University of Alberta Press.

Yanni, Carla (2007). *The Architecture of Madness: Insane Asylums in the United States.* Minneapolis: University of Minnesota Press.

Yorgason, Ethan R. (2003). *Transformation of the Mormon Culture Region.* Urbana: University of Illinois Press.

Zeigler, Joseph Wesley (1973). *Regional Theatre: The Revolutionary Stage.* Minneapolis: University of Minnesota Press.

Zelinsky, Wilbur (1953). *The Settlement Patterns of Georgia.* Ph.D. diss., University of California, Berkeley.

——— (1954). "The Greek Revival House in Georgia," *Journal of the Society of Architectural Historians* 13: 9–12.

——— (1955). "Some Problems in the Distribution of Generic Terms in the Place-Names of the Northeastern United States," *Annals of the Association of American Geographers* 45: 1–26.

——— (1958). "The New England Connecting Barn," *Geographical Review* 48: 540–53.

——— (1959). "Walls and Fences," *Landscape* 8(3): 14–20.

——— (1961). "An Approach to the Religious Geography of the United States: Patterns of Church Membership in 1952," *Annals of the Association of American Geographers* 51: 139–93.

——— (1967). "Classical Town Names in the United States," *Geographical Review* 57: 463–95.

——— (1970). "Cultural Variation in Personal Name Patterns in the Eastern United States," *Annals of the Association of American Geographers* 60: 743–69.

——— (1974). "Selfward-Bound? Personal Preference Patterns and the Changing Map of American Society," *Economic Geography* 50: 144–79.

——— (1977). "The Pennsylvania Town: An Overdue Geographical Account," *Geographical Review* 67: 127–47.

——— (1980). "North America's Vernacular Regions," *Annals of the Association of American Geographers* 70: 1–16.

——— (1982). "General Cultural and Popular Regions," pp. 3–24 in Rooney, Zelinsky, and Louder 1982.

——— (1983). "Nationalism in the American Place-Name Cover," *Names* 30: 1–28.

——— (1985). "The Roving Palate: North America's Ethnic Restaurant Cuisines," *Geoforum* 16(1): 51–72.

——— (1988a). *Nation into State: The Shifting Symbolic Foundations of American Nationalism.* Chapel Hill: University of North Carolina Press.

——— (1988b). "Where Every Town Is Above Average: Welcoming Signs along America's Highways," *Landscape* 30(1): 1–10.

——— (1992a). *The Cultural Geography of the United States,* rev. ed. Englewood Cliffs, N.J.: Prentice-Hall.

——— (1992b). "The Changing Character of North American Culture Areas," pp. 113–35 in Glenn E. Lich, ed., *Regional Studies: The Interplay of Land and People.* College Station: Texas A&M University Press.

——— (1992c). "On the Superabundance of Signs in Our Landscape: Selections from a Slide Lecture," *Landscape* 31(3): 30–38.

——— (1994a). "Gathering Places for America's Dead: How Many, Where, and Why?" *Professional Geographer* 46(1): 29–38.

——— (1994b). *Exploring the Beloved Country: Geographic Forays into American Society and Culture.* Iowa City: University of Iowa Press.

——— (1994c). "The Historical Geography of Season of Marriage: North America, 1844–1974," pp. 132–55 in Zelinsky 1994b.

——— (2001). "Regionalism," vol. 2, pp. 463–72 in Cayton and Williams 2001.

——— (2004). "Globalization Reconsidered: The Historical Geography of Modern Western Male Attire," *Journal of Cultural Geography* 22(1): 83–134.

——— (2007). "The Gravestone Index: Tracking Personal Religiosity across Nations, Regions, and Periods," *Geographical Review* 97: 441–66.

Zerner, Charles J. (1977). "The Street Hearth of Play: Children in the City," *Landscape* 22(1): 19–30.

Zielinski, John M. (1989). *Amish Barns across America*. Iowa City: Amish Heritage Association.

Zola, Gary P. (2006). "Jewish Camping and Its Relationship to the Organized Camping Movement in America," pp. 1–26 in Michael M. Lorge and Zola, eds., *A Place of Our Own: The Rise of Reform Jewish Camping*. Tuscaloosa: University of Alabama Press.

Zook, Nicholas (1971). *Museum Villages USA*. Barre, Mass.: Barre Publishers.

Zuckerman, Michael (1982). "Introduction: Puritans, Cavaliers, and the Motley Middle," pp. 3–25 in Zuckerman, ed., *Friends and Neighbors: Group Life in American's First Plural Society*. Philadelphia: Temple University Press.

——— (2003). "Regionalism," pp. 311–33 in Daniel Vickers, ed., *A Companion to Colonial America*. Malden, Mass.: Blackwell.

——— (2008). Personal communication. August 3.

Zukin, Sharon (2004). *Point of Purchase: How Shopping Changed American Culture*. New York: Routledge.

Zurier, Rebecca (1991). *The Firehouse: An Architectural and Cultural History*. New York: Artabras.

# Index

351